EVERYDAY SOCIOLOGY:
Culture, Power, and the Social World
First Edition

L. SUSAN WILLIAMS

cognella® | ACADEMIC PUBLISHING

Bassim Hamadeh, CEO and Publisher
Kassie Graves, Director of Acquisitions and Sales
Jamie Giganti, Senior Managing Editor
Miguel Macias, Senior Graphic Designer
Angela Schultz, Acquisitions Editor
Michelle Piehl, Project Editor
Trey Soto, Licensing Coordinator
Berenice Quirino, Associate Production Editor
Sue Murray, Interior Designer

Cover image copyright © 2016 iStockphoto LP/Steve Debenport.

Printed in the United States of America

ISBN: 978-1-5165-1039-9 (pbk) / 978-1-5165-1040-5 (br)

Contents

SECTION II: A CULTURE OF SOCIAL CONTROL

SECTION III: FACES OF POWER

SECTION IV: SOCIAL INEQUALITY, POWER, AND PROGRESS

SECTION V: AND FINALLY . . .

Introduction

This is a book about the everyday

On the surface, everyday happenings pretend to be ordinary, while standout events—such as floods or the Great Chicago Fire or industrialization—are seen as spectacular but episodic. Yet secretly obscured in the everyday minutia of life lies a shadow structure of practices, patterns, and power mechanisms that, once bared, reveal mysteries of humankind. What could be more intriguing? This project guides you through a few of these revelations, rendering a revolution of everyday life—one in which you see the world and your place in it as both remarkable and, at first, odd.

"How?" is probably your first inquiry into such a journey—a simple question with profound implications. Much like the magician's sleight of hand, dealing with the invisible requires close attention but also certain insider intelligence and considerable rehearsal. In sociology, we reach far beyond "observations of the obvious," and engage an amalgamation of social facts, scientific methods of inquiry, and critical thinking to assemble a toolbox of the trade. Part of our arsenal includes social theory—a system of statements about how particular social facts are related—and scientific methods, which consist of various approaches to gathering evidence and analyzing data. Together, this scientific enterprise constitutes epistemology, or simply, a way of knowing.

The essence of sociology includes not just individuals, but ways in which we fit together as a society. The analogy of trees and forest illustrates this principle. While trees (and individuals) are intuitively interesting and fun to observe up close, the forest (and society) is infinitely more complex, providing perpetual possibilities of attributes (is it tropical or boreal?), configurations (what are the interior and peripheral habitats?), and peculiarities (e.g., the suppression of naturally occurring blazes may exert unintended consequences). Similarly, while individuals make up units of society, the sociological enterprise focuses on both agency and structure. Agency represents capacity and purposive action by individuals; structure constitutes patterns of behavior with some scope and permanence, typically forming constraints to agency. It's push and pull. Ultimately, we are interested in interactions between the two, or what C. Wright Mills (1959) defines as the sociological imagination: a quality of mind that allows one to grasp "history and biography and the relations between the two within society" (p. 3). In other words, we constitute a conglomerate of our biological selves and our social selves; only in understanding that interaction can we begin to decipher our sociocultural system.

Why is a sociological lens important?

As a science, the purpose of sociology is to explain social phenomena, and to do so with a considerable degree of intellectual integrity. The inevitability of any ecological system is change, and the primary challenge of our social world is to adapt. Description, insight, and prediction, then, become critical parts of the process in understanding change. The individual and his or her society form a dialectic; it incorporates opposing forces, both gradual change and pressing crises, and turning (or tipping) points that resolve (temporarily) its internal contradictions. As one example, industrialization required The Family (as a social entity) to convert from a unit of production to a unit of consumption, with reverberating changes from child labor to household division of labor to fertility patterns (Ross 1977). In turn, contemporary family structures make demands on industry and government in terms of childcare, parental leave, and flex-work. More currently, the techno revolution has brought dramatic leaps in communication channels, social activism, and energy systems, demonstrating remarkable malleability of human minds and bodies. As one example of this nature/nurture interaction, brain structures respond accordingly; with the advent of increasingly eclipsed communication (think Twitter, Instagram, Vine) and habitual gaming, attention span has shortened from twelve seconds in 2000 (about the time the mobile revolution began), to eight seconds today. At nine seconds, even goldfish have longer attention spans! (Watson 2015).

Whether these changes are positive or negative is up for debate, but the fact remains—our minds (and bodies) reprogram according to our environment. That becomes profoundly relevant to an understanding of our everyday performances. At an elementary level, we might tell ourselves that, oh well, we will just multitask more efficiently. Not true, says a long line of research. First, we don't really perform two things at once; we rapidly switch back and forth, often making the process more mentally taxing, less accurate, and ineffective (Hamilton 2008). Regardless, we all swim in the same waters, where we are a conglomerate between our biological selves and our social selves. It's not one or the other.

Where from here?

One of the ways sociologists—both novices and professionals—investigate the social world is through reflexivity. By reflexivity, we refer to separate but related processes. First, a reflexive relationship is bidirectional; like a two-headed arrow, it suggests both cause and effect as mutually reinforcing, each bending back upon the other (Merton 1948). We've already intimated this kind of relationship in a few ways: with dialectic tensions, through intersections of biography and history, and the often antagonistic relationship between agency and structure. Second, reflexivity refers to the idea that observations are not independent of the observer. That is, scientific inquiry (even in the so-called "hard" sciences) is not objective. We must take into account the fallibility of humans, and thus that of constructed knowledge itself (which actually is all knowledge). The observer must take into account one's own biases, assumptions, and foibles, which is akin to trying to turn around to see the back of one's head; it can't be done with precision. But much as we would position a mirror to see a likeness of our head, we can utilize tools of inquiry to optimize our powers of observation. Adhering to scientific methods keeps us accountable. Reflexivity, then, includes both the overt study of social behavior and idiosyncratic awareness to our subject matter. A related and oft-repeated sociological principle of the subjective nature of inquiry was first articulated by W. I. and Dorothy Thomas (1928), known as the Thomas Theorem: "If men [sic] define situations as real, they are real in their consequences" (p. 572). We will return to this principle later.

In science, we rely on theoretical road maps, especially those that have proven to be instructive guideposts in past experiences. Throughout units of this book, you will find reference to various theories. But rather than a headline chapter titled "Capital-T Theory," you will note various perspectives embedded in different readings. Rather than enumerate the dozens (if not more) of individual theories that sociologists refer to in scientific papers, it's more useful *at this point* to understand and recognize three "umbrella" perspectives of social thought—that is, clusters of theories that have basic premises in common. First, consensus-based theories (also referred to as functionalism) assume that a society is based largely on agreement about good/bad, right/wrong, and boundary maintenance; the goal is to keep everyone in line with agreed-upon norms, values, and regulations (conformity) while preserving the status quo. Emile Durkheim, Robert Merton, and Talcott Parsons are well-known functionalist theorists. Second, and in sharp contrast with consensus, conflict theories claim certain individuals and groups hold an inordinate amount of resources and power, which they use to exploit groups with lesser power; the goal is to raise class consciousness (awareness of one's relative place in the system) and understand that significant change occurs only through conflict. Major contributors to conflict theory include Karl Marx, Antonio Gramsci, and C. Wright Mills. Third, interactionist-based theories focus on processes (interactions) between people and the interplay between individuals and institutions. The goal of interactionist-based theory is to understand communication channels, power/control dynamics, the social construction of situations, and the interpretation of realities; change is relative and embedded in process. George Herbert Mead, Max Weber, and Herbert Blumer are major contributors to interactionist-based theory.

Within the interactionist perspective, this book significantly relies on social constructionism or the social construction of reality. First introduced by Peter Berger and Thomas Luckmann (1966), its central premise is that interactions, over time, become lasting patterns of behavior, values, and beliefs, eventually becoming ritualized or institutionalized. Everyday reality is manufactured through ongoing human productions, which, in turn, become social habits, lasting and largely unquestioned. One way sociologists attempt to reveal mechanisms of social construction is by upending everyday taken-for-granted minutia. For example, what if, suddenly, the taxi driver becomes a window dresser (and vice versa)? The construction worker and the runway model switch places? Our so-called "objective" assumptions attached to these statuses are bared and the "natural" order of the world as we know it brought to question. With what confidence do we give our destination address to the window dresser, and do we tip her or him? What assumptions surface about gender and body shape of the construction worker and the model? As we react to these scenarios, our role as The Audience becomes more transparent, thereby changing reality before our eyes. Thomas's adage about perception becomes even clearer: situations perceived to be real are real in their consequences.

Ferrell, Hayward, and Young (2008) briefly describe a "constellation" of perspectives that fall under the interactionist umbrella; these theories help expose underpinnings of everyday events that, while seeming casual and trivial, nevertheless stitch together consequential workings of the social order. The first perspective is symbolic interactionism (attributed to Mead 1934 and Blumer 1969), which projects the role of people actively shaping their everyday existence, underscoring the constructed, shared meaning (i.e., symbolic) of "things." Second, phenomenology (Alfred Schutz [1944] inspired the work of Berger and Luckmann) focuses on subjective style of everyday experiences of consciousness, or "the way things appear." Third, ethnomethodology (Garfinkel 1954) is the study of methods or techniques that people use to understand and construct the social order; one perspective, dramaturgy, posits that individuals maintain "two-sided" identities, performed in backstage and front-stage roles. Erving Goffman's (1959) influential *The Presentation of Self in Everyday Life* exemplifies this framing of particular social life elements.

Undergirding these interactionist perspectives, cultural criminology (originated by Ferrell and Sanders 1995), incorporates cultural forces, those "threads of collective meaning that wind in and around the everyday troubles of social actors, animating the situations and circumstances in which their troubles play out" (2008, 3); and power inherent in mechanisms of rule-making and rule-breaking, and the everyday movements of resistance, large and small. Together, cultural criminology constitutes a "'loose federation of outlaw intellectual critiques' (Ferrell 2007, 99) organized around issues of meaning, representation, and power" (Ferrell, Hayward, and Young 2008, 210).

The homeless professor

A thought-provoking project by English artist Maxwell Ruston (2016), titled "Left Out," exemplifies a visual representation of symbolic interactionism. Emanating from personal experience, the artist produced a realistic-like sculpture representing a human figure, doubled over, fully encased in a black garbage bag. The project was displayed on the streets of London; roughly one-half of passersby ignored it while others stopped in startling curiosity or alarm. As one onlooker rationalized, "There's a message in there about certain kinds of people being disposable."

It is not unusual for art to draw out peculiarities and nitty-gritty samples of life's meanings; some of the most recognizable address the seemingly trivial yet compelling everyday moments that betray underlying social tribulation and misery, and, occasionally, redemption. Consider Rodin's *The Thinker* or the armless *Venus de Milo*, both standing immemorial as testament to simple beauty and intellect. Think of Eisenstaedt's photo of an American sailor kissing the nurse in Times Square at the end of World War II, or Filo's Pulitzer-winning image after National Guardsmen fired upon unarmed students at Kent State; they immediately evoke emotion but also bear the magnitude of weighty cultural markings. As artist Leonardo Drew voiced, "There is the artwork that you physically make but there's also the journey that happens on the inside" (Brooks 2014). The garbage bag-inspired "Left Out" is one of those for me; it touches me.

This brings me to a story I'll call "The Homeless Professor." You see, for twenty years I have asked my students to take their project to the streets, literally; that is, I require that they become "homeless" for a day. I realize this assignment is not necessarily original or innovative. Quite frankly, I had grown a little weary of the assignment myself; I've read around five thousand papers on this street experience over the years. Still, students continue to write me—sometimes years later—relating how one simple exercise exposed the "othering" process that constructs an "us versus them" way of thinking about the world; inevitably, they report that this simple acknowledgement changed their own worldview. Sometimes, it's as simple as that—once we see, we cannot un-see that social fact.

So, how did I become homeless? Before the concept of "homeless" becomes meaningful, we first need a sense of "home." (This process is what we in sociology call "unpacking" a concept.) We could look to the dictionary or the more contemporary version of common knowledge, Wikipedia (typically unsuitable for an academic paper!), which defines home as "a dwelling-place used as a permanent or semi-permanent residence for an individual, family, household or several families in a tribe" (Wikipedia 2013). But the inquiring mind will not settle for a superficial explanation. We might look to culture within well-known quotes (e.g., "Home is where the heart is") or in the more than three hundred fifty "home" song titles ("Take Me Home," "I'll Be Home for Christmas," "My Old Kentucky Home"). We could cite famous story lines such as "There's no place like home" from *The Wizard of Oz*. Clearly, a simple dwelling-type definition of home does not suffice; our culture cherishes and romanticizes deeper notions of home. As a matter of practice, then, "homeless" immediately acquires a negative connotation.

Rather than go through the same laundry-list definitions of homeless, let's engage further in a critical-thinking exercise about the concept of homelessness. Technically—and to some extent, emotionally—I have been homeless since at least 1988 when I divorced, sold my *home*, and began the journey toward "professorship" (which came to fruition four states and ten years later). I've not owned a *home* since 1988, though I have property in Texas (the family farm), am employed in Kansas (Kansas State University), and consider California my domicile. My professional identification always reads Kansas, my driver's license is issued by Texas, and I vote and pay taxes in California. So, where and what, really, is *home*?

Similarly, let's engage the sociological imagination to examine the state of homelessness. Recall, Mills argues that the sociological imagination requires us to examine the intersection of biography and history, resulting in a shift away from over-simplistic essentialist explanations for life events (she was born that way, or it was his choice) and instead engage in a "vivid awareness of the relationship between personal experience and the wider society" (1959, 3). In the case of myself, as the homeless professor, how do details of my personal life—growing up working class on a family farm, a child of the '50s when farm girls didn't go to college, a single mother of three with overbearing responsibilities—intersect with technology (computer revolution), space and place (mobility and mass media images), and opportunity (the women's movement and role models)? With such a multifaceted lens, I became a speck on the landscape of hundreds of thousands of women who remake their lives according to both individual situations and also the larger context of political economy.

On a broader scale, the sociological imagination invites us to distinguish between personal troubles and public issues. In thinking about the stereotypical "street person," it is commonplace to perceive functional deficiencies (why don't they get a job?), lack of motivation (aren't they just lazy?), and personal failure (probably a wino). Let's look at some basic facts: By conventional definitions, among industrialized nations, the United States has the largest number of homeless women and children; homeless families comprise roughly 34 percent of the total US homeless population (estimated to be more than five hundred thousand on any given night and 1.5 million annually), with

1.6 million children experiencing homelessness over the course of a year; 84 percent of these families are headed by single females, and more than 92 percent of those have experienced severe physical and/or sexual abuse during their lifetime (Green Doors 2011). Does not this brief profile depict a different representation of homelessness in America? Can we begin to imagine homelessness as a public issue that is extremely costly to the country in terms of lost wages and human potential?

Returning to my "homeless professor" story: In no way do I suggest my circumstance is comparable to those 1.5 million who were homeless in the past year. Honestly, I had never considered myself as *home-less* until I recently decided to "walk the walk" in the same way that I ask of my students. I shopped Goodwill; gave up all my makeup, Kate Spade handbag, and Coco Chanel glasses; and covered my manicured nails, upscale tattoo, and fashionable purple-streaked hair. I became that homeless person on the streets of San Diego—an aging, white-haired, handicapped woman, with multiple bags of supplies hanging from the walker that helped me ambulate (all of this is true). In a deeply humbling experience, I faced many of my own shortcomings and biases. I felt isolation and despair, even though I knew it was temporary. I was refused service and access to basic necessities of water and restroom facilities; I alternately felt ignored and scorned. The only two people who spoke one word to me were themselves from the street population, "Miss Two Hats" (she wore them both) and "Danny," a middle-aged man who was homeless and hobbled along with painful blisters on his feet. Danny came back to me on three occasions, each time bearing some treasure from his "war chest" to give me—a can of soup, a Mountain Dew, a large candy bar, and a grocery bag of gummy bears, carefully counted out at twenty-five. For a while, I forgot it was an exercise; I felt a real connection to the street people. For a while, my identity leaned much closer to *homeless* than "professor."

As Ferrell points out, the interstitial moments of life—situated within the "drifting" from one structural space to another—reflect larger narratives of our culture:

> " ... migrant farmworkers continue to face family disruption, limited educational opportunities, and deportation; graduate students, part-time instructors, and non-tenure-track instructors now make up three quarters of college faculty; the newly homeless and unemployed drift from city to city, sleep in flood drains beneath the streets of Las Vegas, or become semi-permanent residents of cheap motels; and an economist reports that, in general, 'we're in a period where uncertainty seems to be going forever.'" (Ferrell 2012, 242)

Thus, the sociological imagination demands that we settle the particulars of the everyday within the general sociocultural milieu—global patterns of economic negotiations, legal and political tangles, and social or environmental crises—to fully understand a "shifting commonality of experience" (Ferrell 2012, 253), and thus our collective social selves. My experience as a homeless professor provides only a bare trace in grasping our connectivity, but it's a start. As Steven Tyler sings, "We're all somebody from somewhere."

It takes nuts, bolts, and forward motion.

This book is not all things to all people. The goal is to illuminate just a few of the extremely diverse and complex inner workings that hobble together everyday moments into a culture; workings that reveal instruments (and constellations) of power—the black box of society. To the extent that we understand the machinery of culture, we gain more control over our own lives; to the extent we do not, we remain a slave to the apparatus. This is not to say that I subscribe to the "bootstrap" theory of the so-called American dream (just work hard, and you, too, will be rich, successful, and president of the country); there are real barriers to attainment, and the playing field is far from equal. But knowledge is a good start. Congratulations on taking that first step!

This project is organized in four sections, each consisting of two related units. You'll soon recognize (if not already) that this project underscores the weightiness of applying what we learn to everyday interactions, intercommunications, and synergy between society and its individuals. To bolster this propensity, each section offers a few resources for your consideration. "Beyond the Book" literally reaches from these covers to connect ideas from the readings to real-world cultural objects or events. "From the Field" refers to actual research—observation, gatherings, and/or production of knowledge—and demonstrates, in some small or large way, *how* we know what we know. Each section also outlines a "Reality Check," describing basic parameters of exercises that I've used in class (to thousands of students) to provide ideas on how you might conduct your own reality check. Finally, a modest list of "OLE Resources" (Online Learning Environment) directs you to some striking and, I hope, thought-provoking resources. You never know when they might lend that just-right impetus for your next innovative piece of work!

Section I, "Imagining the Everyday," introduces the world of sociological imaginings—using specific tools of inquiry to study our selves, our society. Clearly, the sociological imagination sits center stage here and invites you to peer into "us" (see Unit 1, "The World as We Know It"). We also look at the influence of stories (we all are drawn to and learn from stories), and the power behind whose story is told and how. Unit 2, "Pathways and Culture," utilizes metaphors and everyday meanings to explore cultural symbols and certain configurations of social life. Within each unit, a "Dr. Sue to You" segment provides an overview, suggesting how various readings dovetail or contrast, and a few basic concepts to watch for. This is my way of talking to you "face-to-face"—that is, in commonsense language to "frame" (setting boundaries and perspectives) the material. Once you get through readings for that unit, I offer a wrap-up called "In Other Words … " that briefly discusses the unit and suggests at least one or two "big ideas" (general lessons or implications) gleaned from the unit. Think of these two components—"Dr. Sue to You" and "In Other Words"—as bookends that help think about the unit as a cohesive bundle of ideas.

Section II, "A Culture of Social Control," is thoroughly sociological, turning the idea of crime, deviance, and social control on its head; I'm sure you will be surprised, dismayed, delighted, or angry—perhaps all of the above! Unit 3, "Deviance, Crime, and Social Control," starts with a discussion of "being bad"—more individual-based—while Unit 4 addresses "Power of the Situation," bringing intriguing and unexpected perspectives about collective and circumstantial dynamics.

Section III is titled "Faces of Power," certainly worthy of an entire book, or a floor in the library. We touch on some of the mainstays of identity-making in Unit 5 ("Doing Identity"), including race, class, and gender. Unit 6 refers to

Dr. Sue in the Flower Fields, Carlsbad CA 2016

the adage "Everything's Political," covering a broad range of topics from cultural capital (in an academic sense) to "the butt" (in an everyday, but enlightened, sense).

"Social Inequality, Power, and Progress," in Section IV, takes a wide-lens view of society, first in Unit 7, addressing "The Rich Get Richer," and then "Power of the People" in Unit 8. We look backward a bit (e.g., "Our History Shapes Our Thinking"), and forward as we explore contemporary issues such as "green criminology" and sweatshop workers.

Section V, titled "And Finally … ", combines the spirit of Randy Pausch's (2008) remarkable *The Last Lecture* with my own "Third Act" ideas. "And Finally … " offers me the opportunity to say, "If I had one more day with you, what would I say?" An amalgamation of sober reflection, passion, and humor, this last section stands as a final reminder: you can have only one North Star.

We live in a fluid and ever-changing universe, and the key to survival is knowing not just our self, but our symbiotic relationship with the social environment. This awakening comes not in a smooth, straight-line progression, but in fits and starts, revelations that seem more as delusions, missteps, and retracing of old steps. It is my hope the collection gathered here sets you on that journey to discovery. In pulling back the curtain, be prepared to see!

Works Cited

Berger, P. L., and Luckmann, T. (1966). *The Social Construction of Reality: A Treatise in the Sociology of Knowledge.* New York, NY: Penguin Books.

Blumer, H. (1969). *Symbolic Interactionism: Perspective and Method.* Englewood Cliffs, NJ: Prentice Hall.

Brooks, K. (2014). "12 famous artists on how art can transform and inspire your life." *The Huffington Post,* July 20, 2014. Retrieved July 8, 2016, from http://www.huffingtonpost.com/2014/07/10/pbs-art-21_n_5572212.html

Ferrell, J. (2007). "For a ruthless cultural criticism of everything existing." *Crime, Media, Culture, 3,* 91–100.

Ferrell, J., and Sanders, C. (1995). *Cultural Criminology.* Boston, MA: Northeastern University Press.

Ferrell, J., Hayward, K., and Young, J. (2008). *Cultural Criminology: An Invitation.* Los Angeles, CA: Sage.

Garfinkel, H. (1954). "The origins of the term ethnomethodology." In R. Turner, ed., *Ethnomethodology* (pp. 15–18). New York, NY: Penguin Books.

Goffman, E. (1959). *The Presentation of Self in Everyday Life.* Garden City, NY: Doubleday Anchor.

Green Doors. (2011). Family homelessness facts. Retrieved July 2, 2016, from Green Doors: http://www.greendoors.org/facts/family-homelessness.php

Hamilton, J. (2008, October 2). NPR. (NPR, producer). Retrieved July 1, 2016, from http://www.npr.org/templates/story/story.php?storyId=95256794

Mead, G. H. (1934). *Mind, Self, and Society: From the Perspective of a Social Behaviorist.* Chicago, IL: University of Chicago Press.

Merton, R. (1948). "The self-fulfilling prophecy." *Antioch Review, 8,* 193–210.

Mills, C. W. (1959). *The Sociological Imagination.* London, UK: Oxford University Press.

Pausch, R., and Zaslow, J. (2008). *The Last Lecture.* New York, NY: Hyperion Books.

Ross, H. L., and Sawhill, I. V. (1977). "The family as an economic unit." *The Wilson Quarterly,* 1, 2. Retrieved from: http://www.jstor.org/stable/40255183

Ruston, M. (2016). Retrieved July 8, 2016, Maxwellrushton.com.

Schutz, A. (1944). "The stranger." *American Journal of Sociology, 49,* 499–507.

Dr. Sue and "Danny," on the street in Ocean Beach, San Diego CA 2016

Thomas, W. I., and Thomas, D. S. (1928). *The Child in America: Behavior Problems and Programs.* New York, NY: Knopf.

Watson, L. (2015, May 15). "Humans have shorter attention span than goldfish, thanks to smartphones." *The Telegraph.* Retrieved July 1, 2016, from http://www.telegraph.co.uk/science

Wikipedia. (2013, November). Home. Wikipedia. Retrieved July 1, 2016, from https://en.wikipedia.org/wiki/Home

Section I:
Imagining the Everyday

Unit 1: The Sociological Imagination

Dr. Sue to You: The world as we know it

The age-old question, "What's in a name," was made most famous in Shakespeare's *Romeo and Juliet:* "That which we call a rose by any other name would smell as sweet" (Shakespeare, trans. 1914, II, II, 47–48). The adage implies that labels are irrelevant; "essence" belongs to a thing, irrespective of its title. On the other hand, studies link names to certain life chances: easier-to-pronounce names have been linked to higher-status positions at work (Laham et al. 2012) and greater likability (Cotton et al. 2008), while a "white-sounding" name is worth as much as eight years of work experience (Bertrand and Mullainathan 2004). Names affect outcomes as diverse as restaurant reservations, stock investments, elite school entrance, and judicial elections (Delistraty 2014). Perhaps there's a reason you've never heard of Peter Gene Hernandez (Bruno Mars), Thomas Mapother IV (Tom Cruise), or Stefanie Joanne Angelina Germanotta (Lady Gaga).

The seeming diversion about names brings me to this point: the designation "Dr. Sue to You" was not chosen lightly. Long fascinated with the power of words, I believe the names of people, places, and papers take on an even more distilled sense of power. In the classroom, I've never been able to disguise my adoring fascination with students. Over the course of a semester, "Dr. Williams" or "Professor Williams" seemed stuffy and too impersonal to capture the nature of our relationship, but "Sue" or even "Susan" was reserved for friends and family status. The dilemma was exacerbated when I began to teach almost exclusively online; how could I connect with students through the digital universe? I finally settled on Dr. Sue, (not to be confused with *Dr. Phil's* hard-nosed approach or *Dr. Ruth's* love-life advice!) to convey that just-right cross between tireless teacher and life course coach. So, Dr. Sue it is. This is my corner to talk to you, pass a few tips, and share some of my thoughts before you delve into this unit. Following Goffman's and Garfinkel's cues, let's set the stage.

Unit 1 serves as a framing device (gateway to a deeper journey) for this book. I positioned "Sociological Stories and Key Concepts" first for a reason—it introduces you to sociology, defines many terms and ideas, and gives you a quick overview of the subject matter and orientation of the discipline. This is one of those core readings you may return to several times, referring to specific concepts and/or clarifying what a sociological perspective entails. This is the *lens* that assists you in deciphering the social world. By now, you also will recognize that the *sociological imagination* represents the mainstay of a sociological perspective, one you are expected to cultivate and advance as you work through the book.

The second reading, "Telling About Society," is by one of my favorite sociologists, Howard (Howie) Becker. In fact, you'll read a classic piece by him, "Becoming a Marihuana User," in Unit 4. As a young man, Becker worked semi-professionally as a musician (piano mostly) and played a lot during World War II. It was through his music that he first became exposed to the drug culture, leading to his work in deviance; the very influential theory of crime called "labeling" is attributed to Becker. A leading sociologist of our time, Becker is officially retired but hasn't slowed a bit. The author of thirteen books and more than two hundred journal articles, he is supremely prolific and splits his time between San Francisco and Paris (Goponik 2015). Becker is also well known for his contributions to sociological methodology (see his book *Tricks of the Trade*), and it is in "Telling About Society" that you will see much of this influence, related to constructionist-like techniques (akin to symbolic interactionism). In this article, pay close attention to how Professor Becker "schools" us in becoming a critical reader, always questioning, forever mindful that knowledge is constructed and partial. While the first reading constitutes the "nuts and bolts" of sociology, this piece represents the blueprint, though partial, often esoteric, and a bit elusive. Just like knowledge.

The final short reading is by William Levinson and titled "Act the Fool." Here, you will learn about "heyokas," who fill a specific role in society, often producing certain organizational and cultural functions. Some outcomes associated with heyokas may go on to become "words of wisdom" common in our culture. I'm curious to see if you can identify contemporary heyokas and recognize current words of wisdom. You may find many of these wisdoms to be a little curious, secretive, even a bit primitive—again, all descriptors that might apply to a bounded little society—encouraging you to ponder and employ new-found sociological tools of the trade!

Most of the time, the Dr. Sue to You (DSTY) corner will offer tips—some cues and clues about how to best navigate your new adventure in peeling back layers of the everyday.

DSTY TIPS for reading academic material

- Go right to the title (power of naming, right?): What content and tone does the author convey? [*Immediately provides clues to the topic and relevance.*]
- Become the audience; read with an open mind, give the writer a fair chance to develop new ideas. [*But maintain healthy skepticism.*]

- Read the introduction, then the conclusion; follow up by skimming through the remaining article, noting the subheadings. [*This orients you to the overall purpose and content.*]
- Reread the paper, beginning with the introduction. Highlight, make marginal notes; record main ideas, quotes, and definitions in a separate file. [*For core sociology articles, detailed notes will be invaluable for assignments; if reading is more peripheral, mark select quotes to provide the essence of its contribution.*]
- Reconsider the reading:
    - What is the main topic? The author's position? The overall purpose or goal?
    - How well (or not) did the author support her or his position?
    - Recall the "unpacking" exercise on the "homeless" concept in the introduction to this book? Try that on at least one main concept in the reading.
    - What are the implications? (i.e., Why is it important and what actions are implied?)
    - Identify one main strength and one limitation of the paper.
- Beginning with the title and author, write a paragraph answering these questions (referred to as annotation). This strategy engages you in critical thinking skills; much can be gleaned from these notes for review and future work/assignments.

Imagination sculpture, Kansas State University 2011

Works Cited

Bertrand, M., and Mujilainathan, S. (2004). "Are Emily and Greg more employable than Lakisha and Jamal? A field experiment on labor market discrimination." *American Economic Review, 94,* 991–1013.

Cotton, J. L., O'Neill, B. S., and Griffin, A. (2008). "The name game": Affective and hiring reactions to first names." *Journal of Managerial Psychology, 1,* 18–39.

Delistraty, C. C. (2014, July 30). "The surprising way your name affects your life." *The Atlantic.* Retrieved July 8, 2016, from http://www.businessinsider.com/how-your-name-affects-your-life-2014-7

Gopnik, A. (2015, January 12). "The outside game." *The New Yorker,* Paris Journal. Retrieved July 2, 2016, from http://www.newyorker.com/magazine/2015/01/12/outside-game

Laham, S. M., Koval, P., and Alter, A. L. (2012). "The name-pronunciation effect: Why people like Mr. Smith more than Mr. Colquhoun." *Journal of Experimental Social Psychology, 48,* 752–756).

Shakespeare, W. 1914. *Romeo and Juliet. The Oxford Shakespeare,* W. J. Craig, ed. London: Oxford University Press.

SOCIOLOGICAL IMAGINATION

READING 1

SOCIOLOGICAL STORIES AND KEY CONCEPTS

BY JEFFREY C. ALEXANDER AND KENNETH THOMPSON

The Individual and The Social

Sociology is the science (*-ology*) of society (*socio-*). This may sound either scary or pretentious. It could be scary if you think a scientific study of **society** must be all about experiments and mathematics. On the other hand, it might seem pretentious if sociology is claiming to be the only way of understanding a society with which we are already familiar. Neither is true. We would like you to think of **sociology** as offering particular kinds of commentaries or stories (though they're not the only ones available to us). As the sociologist Zygmunt Bauman puts it: "Sociology is an extended commentary on the experiences of daily life, an interpretation which feeds on other interpretations and is in turn fed into them" (Bauman 1990: 231).

As individuals we all have personal stories to tell that are unique to us. They are based on our experiences and by telling them to ourselves, and others, we give meaning to our lives. We hope that the more we think about those experiences and discuss them with others, the more we will understand them. Sociology can help us to make sense of our experiences by taking our accounts of them and comparing them with others. It can tell us how they make sense as part of a larger story—a story about groups of individuals sharing similar experiences and perhaps constituting a significant social trend. This sociological perspective is now part of our contemporary worldview and is something we encounter every day—for example, in newspaper stories and broadcast news. We may take it for granted and not stop to consider how the sociological perspective works in constructing the stories. One of the most important reasons for studying sociology at the beginning of the twenty-first century is to develop a better understanding of how we gain our knowledge of society, and perhaps gain a better understanding of ourselves as well.

Excerpt from: Jeffrey C. Alexander and Kenneth Thompson, "Sociological Stories and Key Concepts," *A Contemporary Introduction to Sociology: Culture and Society in Transition*, pp. 3-23, 26-27. Copyright © 2008 by Taylor & Francis Group. Reprinted with permission.

Although we tend to think of ourselves as unique and special, in control of our own actions, we also know that we share many characteristics with others and that we are subject to similar social pressures. The mass media are constantly presenting us with stories that make us think about these similarities and differences, and their causes. In a sense, we are all sociologists now, because we practice these skills of interpretation, comparison, and looking for causes. Normally, however, it is only when the story grabs our attention that we are motivated to do this thinking in a really serious way, perhaps because it involves people with whom we can identify.

Take the story of the Columbine High School massacre in Littleton, Colorado, where, on April 20, 1999, two teenage students, members of the self-styled "Trenchcoat Mafia," shot dead thirteen people before turning the guns on themselves. It is a story that shocked almost everyone, but it was of particular concern to students and their parents, who could readily imagine themselves in a similar situation. Many explanations were offered by the media. Some emphasized how deviant or different the killers were from "normal" students. Other commentators stressed the pressures on individuals to conform and to be like other students, especially successful students. Essayist Roger Rosenblatt in *Time* magazine (May 3, 1999) focused on cultural differences, particularly the boys' choice of clothing, noting that "[i]n an odd way, I think much can be explained by the trench coats, not because they are long and black and what the kids call gothic, but because they look alike, they conceal differences." He argued that people who are attracted to groups, such as clans and cults, seek to lose their individuality by dressing the same as the others in that group. In sociological terms, he was saying that these students were choosing to adopt the group identity of a subculture. (While **culture** refers to the symbolic and learned aspects of human society, which are socially rather than biologically transmitted, **subculture** refers to the symbols and lifestyles of a subgroup in society, often one that deviates from the "normal," more general culture of the larger society.)

The cover-story reporter for *Newsweek* (May 3, 1999), on the other hand, talked about forceful social pressures to conform to the majority, quoting students at Littleton who explained why the two killers looked "shifty" in school photographs: "They'd walk with their heads down, because if they looked up they'd get thrown into lockers and get called a 'fag.'" In other words, in addition to the official (formal) social structure of the school, there were unofficial (informal) structures and processes, which exercised constraint. (**Social structures** are the patterns of organization that constrain human behavior.)

The *Denver Rocky Mountain News* commentator covering the same story (April 21, 1999) rejected such cultural or social structural explanations, preferring a *reductionist* explanation (i.e., one that reduces a social phenomenon to a matter of individual psychology)—claiming that these were psychologically unbalanced individuals simply imitating other individuals: "Surely part of the answer is a relatively

Society A population distinguished by shared norms, values, institutions, and culture. Societies are often defined by geographic, regional, or national boundaries.

Sociology The science of society. The sociologist studies how everyday, individual stories and relationships relate to the larger, collective stories of social groups, social systems, and societies.

simple phenomenon: unbalanced, resentful kids imitating the highly publicized actions of other unbalanced kids." It dismissed the other explanations: "The influence of violent entertainment, for example, or too easy access to guns suffer[s] from the weakness of having predated the recent trend of gun-toting students invading their schools."

However, this rejection of more complicated sociological explanations, and the reduction of the level of explanation to individuals simply imitating each other, is something that sociology has always resisted. Good sociological explanations often entail constructing accounts, or stories, that involve a combination of social structural and cultural factors, and trying to calculate their respective contributions.

The mass media may offer sociological or other forms of explanation without making clear the concepts and principles on which they are based. As a knowledgeable consumer of the mass media, you are already familiar with these and have a certain amount of sociological skill, perhaps without

Culture The symbolic and learned aspects of human society. Culture is not biological but, instead, is transmitted and shared via social interaction.

Subculture The symbols and lifestyles of a subgroup in society, one that deviates from the "normal," more general (dominant) culture of a society.

Social structures Patterns of organization that constrain human behavior. These can be formal (such as school or government) or informal (such as peer pressure or trends).

knowing it! By studying a sociology course and reading this book you are building on that existing stock of knowledge and refining that skill.

Of course, there is more to daily life than puzzling over social problems in the media and thinking about what their stories have to do with us. As noted earlier, in everyday life we tend to think of ourselves as unique individuals. This means that we think, we feel, we act on the basis of our taken-for-granted conviction that our selves are separate from society. We are aware, of course, that there is a vast world outside of this self. We often talk about the world getting us down, the sacrifices it demands, our triumphs over it. From our subjective perspective as individuals, this outside world presents itself to us as resources, as objects, as other persons, as organizations. We see these as positive or negative, as sources of pleasure or pain, as things that can help us to realize our goals (no matter how vaguely sensed or defined), to express our feelings, and to satisfy or reduce the pressures we feel from our moral obligations to ideals. Sometimes, of course, we are aware that we're not really alone, that we share goals, experiences, emotional expressions, and feelings of obligation with others such as friends, fellow workers, students, or family. More often, however, we do not feel we share them, and we do not feel particularly connected. This is only natural. In the second-to-second, day-to-day sequence of our everyday lives, we are alone. It is our energy that makes things happen, and it is our responsibility, and our problem, if they do not. This may mean that, insofar as we have a perspective on everyday life, it is likely to be that of individualism. (*Individualism* is the name given to the philosophical view that sees society only as a collection of unique individuals, each with his or her own special qualities. All are responsible for their own actions, and their success and happiness are regarded as their individual achievements.)

Sociology offers a very different story to describe what is going on. From the sociological perspective, we do not see society as if it were composed simply of separate individuals, certainly not in the old-fashioned "rugged individual" sense so beloved by whose who uphold traditional American ideals. Believing that we are radically separated from others is an illusion, and sometimes a dangerous one. Indeed, according to this approach, there is no clear break between the outside world and our individual inner selves. To varying degrees we are constrained and determined in our actions by the social circumstances in which we live. Even when we think for ourselves, we do so with a language and a culture that have been given to us, the rules of which we are scarcely able to discern. However, we do not have to accept a totally deterministic view, as if individuals were parts of a big social machine. Although social structures may constrain and regulate our behavior in various ways, social life is also enabling. It provides us with the cultural resources for thinking and communication, and the social resources for cooperation and organization. Furthermore, human beings have the creative capacity to imagine the outcomes of their future actions, to choose among different strategies, and to reflect on their actions—what sociologists call *agency* or *purposive action*. Given this capacity, we should not think of structure and agency as opposites but, rather, should focus on the interplay between structural constraint and agents' creative autonomy.

Values Shared ideas of what is good/bad, desirable/undesirable, or sacred/profane in a society.

Norms Rules that prescribe correct behavior. In some cases, rules are made official (e.g., as laws). In others, they remain unofficial but commonly understood (e.g., when the Pledge of Allegiance is recited in the United States, people are expected to stand).

Status A position in social relations (e.g., mother, father, teacher, president). Status is normatively regulated; it is assumed that when a person occupies a particular status, he or she will behave in particular ways.

Roles Bundles of socially defined attributes and expectations associated with social statuses or positions (again, e.g., mother, father, teacher, president).

Within this broad sociological perspective there are many ways of giving accounts of, or telling stories about, social behavior. Sociologists sometimes speak about the society as a whole, about "our **values**" and "our way of life." At other times they focus on the parts. There are many ways in which the social whole has been broken down. For instance, sociologists may give accounts of institutions (e.g., kinship, the law, and religion) as well as their concrete organizations (e.g., schools, families, police, and churches). And, in turn, they can describe these institutions and organizations in terms of their constituent parts, such as the **norms** (or rules) that prescribe correct behavior, the **status** (or position) that people occupy, and the **roles** they are expected to play. Some institutions, such as the family and education, have a special responsibility for preparing people to take on roles and statuses in the wider society (a process known as *socialization*), although all **institutions** involve at least some socialization into their specific roles, statuses, and norms.

Roles and institutions are two of the key building blocks in the sociological conception of social structure. Roles are the expectations associated with social positions, such as those of teacher and student. And we can think of institutions as bundles of roles that are formed within a broader culture.

Institutions Patterned sets of linked social practices, such as education, marriage, or the family, that are informed by broader culture, are regularly and continuously repeated, are sanctioned and maintained by social norms, and have a major significance for the social structure.

Institutions ensure that particular actions are regularly and continuously repeated. When they aren't repeated in expected ways—when actors don't conform to the role expectations of families, schools, or workplaces—institutions typically try to sanction them, formally or informally. Culture, roles, and institutions are at the core of social structure.

It is important to keep in mind that, however much social structures and cultural factors seem to constrain and determine behavior, it is individuals who act—even when they act as the agents of institutions and organizations. Accordingly, when considering an incident like the Columbine High School massacre, we, as sociologists, would examine the various factors that might have influenced the course of events, paying special attention to the perceptions and accounts of the individuals who were involved. We would not claim that the outcome was totally socially determined, as if the individuals in question were bound to perceive and act in that particular way. However, we *are* interested in examining accounts of the troubling incident to see what they might have to tell us about wider social trends and problems.

The Sociological Imagination

In his book *The Sociological Imagination* (1959), sociologist C. Wright Mills describes some of the conditions of modern life that make the cultivation of a **sociological imagination** important for all of us. He observes that, nowadays, people often feel that their private lives are a series of traps and that they cannot overcome their troubles. And, in a sense, they are correct in this feeling, because underlying their private troubles are large-scale changes in society. Unless people develop a sociological imagination, they cannot accurately define

Sociological imagination As theorized by C. Wright Mills, the ability to understand not only what is happening in one's own immediate experience but also what is happening in the world and to imagine how one's experience fits into the larger world experience.

Troubles Personal problems, private matters having to do with the self. An individual's unemployment is an example of a trouble.

Issues Problems extending beyond the individual and local environment. These are institutional in nature and often involve crises in institutional arrangement. The high unemployment rate across the United States is an example of an issue.

the troubles they experience in terms of historical changes and the workings of the institutions of society. In other words, they lack the quality of mind necessary for grasping the interplay of individual and society, of biography and history, of self and world. Mills explains the way the sociological imagination works by distinguishing between what he calls "personal troubles" and "public issues." He says that "troubles" are "personal" in the sense that they occur within the character of the individual and his or her social environment (*milieu*); in other words, **troubles** are a private matter, having to do with the self. **Issues,** however, are public matters, transcending one's self and one's immediate social milieu—they are institutional in nature, and often involve crises in institutional arrangements:

> *Troubles* occur within the character of the individual and within the range of his [*sic*] immediate relations with others: they have to do with his self and with those limited areas of social life of which he is directly and personally aware. …
>
> *Issues* have to do with matters that transcend these local environments of the individual and the range of his inner life. They have to do with the organization of many such milieux into the institutions of an historical society as a whole, with the ways in which various milieux overlap and interpenetrate to form the larger structure of social and historical life. (Mills 1959: 8)

The distinction between private troubles and public issues can be illustrated by looking at the problem of family breakdown and divorce in America. This is often experienced as a private trouble by parents and their children—something that is personal to them and is accompanied by arguments about who is to blame. But if we compare divorce rates in various developed countries we might begin to see this as more of a public issue. As early as 1970, the United States had double the international average rate of divorce (33 percent compared with 15 percent). And by the end of the century, approximately 51 of every 100 marriages ended in divorce in the United States, compared with 14 in Greece and 12 in Italy (OECD 2002: Table GE5.1). Now, if the U.S. figure were as low as that of Greece or Italy, we might argue that the divorces in question were probably the result of the personal biographies ("troubles") of the individuals involved (one spouse or the other had misbehaved, one was neurotic, they just didn't get along). But with such relatively high figures in one country it would be absurd to conclude that all these cases were merely the result of individual/psychological troubles. Accordingly, we need to ask questions about the institution of marriage and the family in that particular society, and about the factors that might be causing the problems that make this a social issue rather than just a personal trouble. Perhaps it is the result of structural factors, such as easy divorce processes and women's greater financial independence compared with previous eras. Or maybe it is due more to changes in culture, to different standards and expectations concerning relationships, or to perceptions of divorce as normal rather than deviant. Indeed, U.S. culture offers more and more images and models of relationships, including sexual relationships, from which we can supposedly choose. As we emphasize frequently in this book, sociology is increasingly having to turn its attention to one of the defining features of contemporary society—the enormous variety of cultural images and models that are communicated through the media and that affect our perceptions of ourselves and the social world around us.

Perhaps the greatest benefit the sociological imagination can offer to students, including troubled ones like those at Columbine High School, is to teach ways of understanding how "personal troubles" may in fact be "public issues." An individual student who comes to understand that his or her feelings of alienation, boredom, and lack of respect and status are shared by a significant number of other students may begin to ask questions about the structure and culture of the educational institution. These questions, in turn, can lead to constructive strategies for changing the institution. Using the sociological imagination to distinguish between personal troubles and private issues—and, when justified, learning to translate personal troubles into public issues—empowers us to work to change the conditions that give rise to so much anguish. It is in this sense that the craft of sociology is self-enlightening and liberating.

Another example of the liberating effect of translating personal troubles into public issues is the women's movement, which developed in the 1960s and 1970s. It was only when women began to talk about what they thought of as their personal troubles of frustration and lack of fulfillment that they realized these translated into public issues concerning political power and institutions such as the economy with its inequalities of pay and career opportunities for women. Feminist sociologists have opened up areas for investigation previously overlooked, ranging from childbirth to housework, in addition to demonstrating that topics like date rape and domestic violence against women are not "private matters" but "public issues" concerning the ways men exert power over women.

Although the sociological imagination can assist us in seeing the difference between personal troubles and public issues, the problems that interest the sociologist are not necessarily limited to the everyday understanding of "problems." Sociologist Peter Berger has pointed out the difference between the sociological perspective and this common view, noting that people tend to refer to something as a **social problem** when it does not work out the way it is "officially" supposed to. They then expect the sociologist to study the "problem" as they have defined it and perhaps even to come up with a "solution" that will take care of the matter to their own satisfaction. It is important to understand that a sociological problem is something quite different from a "social problem" in this sense. For example, it would be sociologically naive to focus on crime as a "problem" simply in terms of the way law enforcement agencies define it, or on divorce solely on the grounds laid down by those who see it as a moral problem. As Berger puts it: "The sociological problem is not so much why things 'go wrong' from the viewpoint of the authorities and the management of the social scene, but how the whole system works

Social problem A situation that contradicts or violates social norms and values. Widespread drug abuse and racism are examples of social problems.

11

in the first place, what are its presuppositions and by what means is it held together. The fundamental problem is not crime but the law, not divorce but marriage, not racial discrimination but racially defined stratification, not revolution but government" (Berger 1963: 49–50).

So, asking sociological questions means being interested in looking some distance beyond the officially defined or commonly accepted accounts of actions and institutions. It means being aware that there may be different levels of meaning, some of which are hidden from our everyday consciousness. The sociological perspective is frequently concerned with seeing through the facades of social structures and debunking official interpretations. This *debunking* motif is one of four dimensions of the sociological consciousness described by Berger. The other three are unrespectability, relativizing, and cosmopolitanism.

The *unrespectability* motif of sociology, prominent in some American sociology (particularly the so-called Chicago School's studies of the urban ghetto in the 1920s and 1930s), involves a fascination with the unrespectable view of society. Berger points out that, although it is possible to distinguish between respectable and unrespectable sectors in all Western societies, "American respectability has a particularly pervasive quality about it" (Berger 1963: 56). He suggests this may be due to lingering effects of the Puritan way of life and also to the predominant role played by the bourgeoisie (middle class) in shaping American culture. In contrast to the official respectable America represented symbolically by the Chamber of Commerce, churches, schools, and other centers of civic ritual, there is an America that has other symbols and speaks another language: "It is the language of the poolroom and the poker game, of bars, brothels and army barracks. ... The 'other America' that speaks this language can be found wherever people are excluded, or exclude themselves, from the world of middle-class propriety" (Berger 1963: 56). However, it is not confined to minorities or marginal groups; even middle-class "nice people" may drop into or out of unrespectable and respectable cultures in various situations. For example, the student killers in the Columbine High School massacre were described as being completely different characters at school compared with how they were known at home— members of the Trenchcoat Mafia at school and yet sons of respectable middle-class families.

The *relativizing* motif refers to the capacity, typical of the modern mind, but especially developed in sociology, to see how identities and perspectives vary depending on the situation or context. This is sometimes contrasted with so-called traditional societies, which assigned definite and permanent identities to their members, and where it was more difficult to imagine adopting different perspectives. In modern societies, identity is more fluid and fragmented, more uncertain and in flux. Geographical and social mobility means we encounter numerous ways of looking at the world. Through the mass media we are exposed to other cultures and perspectives, which implies, at least potentially, the awareness that one's own culture, including its basic values, is relative in space and time.

Finally, there is the *cosmopolitanism* motif. The turbulent urban centers of modern times have tended to develop a cosmopolitan consciousness, a knowledge of a variety of lifestyles and perspectives, and a certain sense of detachment from them. This mentality was described in a classic sociological essay, *The Metropolis and Mental Life* (1903) by the German scholar Georg Simmel. Whereas Simmel emphasized some of the negative aspects of the cosmopolitan mind, such as its detached and calculative characteristics, Berger contrasts it with narrow parochialism and says that the sociological perspective is a "broad, open, emancipated vista on human life" and that sociologists, at their best, are people "with a taste for other lands, inwardly open to the measureless richness of human possibilities, eager for new horizons and worlds of human meaning" (Berger 1963: 67).

In *A Contemporary Introduction to Sociology*, it is this liberating vision of the sociological perspective that we will bring to our examination of the various dimensions of today's rapidly changing society. In doing so, however, we will not hesitate to draw on the accumulated wisdom of the great sociologists of the past, who sought to do the same in their own time. We will be standing on the shoulders of giants, so that we might see further. But we also must be prepared to ask whether the ways in which sociology's "founding fathers" posed their sociological questions about the transition from traditional to modern society are the most relevant for understanding today's changing society. Perhaps we need a change of focus, new concepts to describe the social forms that we see emerging today.

Society Today: So What's New?

Sociology came into being as an effort to understand and diagnose what lay behind the personal troubles and social issues that accompanied the massive changes associated with modernity. **Modernity,** in the sense used by sociologists, is not the same as its popular meaning of being up to date or contemporary. It refers to a historical period, to the culmination of the set of historical processes—economic, political, social, and cultural—that brought about the end of the traditional social order and replaced it with new and more dynamic forms. These include the rise of the nation-state and such political arrangements as parties, public life, and democracies; economic capitalism, based on the systematic pursuit of profit and the promotion of industrialization; new forms of social organization,

Modernity In sociology, a term referring to the set of historical processes that transformed the traditional order. Early sociologists (e.g., Karl Marx, Max Weber, George Simmel, and Emile Durkheim) set out to understand the social upheaval and disruption caused by these processes, which include the rise of the nation-state, economic capitalism, bureaucratization, urbanization, and secularization.

such as the modern bureaucracy based on salaried employment and recruitment on merit; urbanization, with large cities populated by recent migrants from rural areas or other nations who had suffered a loss of old community ties; and the undermining of religious belief by secular culture, especially science and technology.

Those who first laid the foundations of sociology believed that modernity automatically meant social progress. If the study of society were based on rigorous methods equivalent to those in the natural sciences, the findings could be used to ensure that further progress would follow in the future. However, the generation of sociologists who established sociology as an academic discipline in the universities toward the end of the nineteenth century (e.g., Emile Durkheim in France, Max Weber in Germany, Robert Park at the University of Chicago) could see that modernity brought with it many problems. Sociologists in the twentieth century focused on these problems: the politics of the nation-state, class inequalities and conflicts, the rigidities of bureaucratic organization, the problems of the inner city, the decline of religion, and the search for a new moral consensus.

The issues that face sociology at the beginning of the twenty-first century do not exclude such questions. The ideas we develop in this book will certainly draw on the concepts and theories that sociologists have developed before. But there are good grounds for thinking that, as this new century begins, new questions are beginning to be posed. These require new concepts and theories, or at least a revision of older ones. Before we go on to look at some of these new developments, it might be useful if you thought about your own experience of these changes. (See Exercise 1 at the end of the chapter.)

Sociologists have their own lists of significant changes, some of which are specific to particular social institutions, such as the family, economy, politics, education, religion, health and medicine, and the media. Many of these specific changes feature in later chapters. Other changes are more general, and these are the ones that pose the greatest challenge to the sociological imagination as it seeks to translate private troubles into public issues today. There is an anecdote about the American writer Gertrude Stein. As she lay dying, she asked, "What is the answer?" When no answer came, she laughed and asked: "In that case what is the question?" (See Exercise 2.)

It is the new questions that we must get right if we are to understand contemporary societies. The world's most highly developed societies are in the midst of a profound transition, one that affects less developed societies as well. Classical sociologists at the end of the nineteenth century, as well as the mid-twentieth-century creators of modern sociology, developed their models during a phase of social development that differed significantly from our own (see Table 1.1). Let's consider the main concerns of those sociologists of modernity, and then turn to some of the key issues that have begun to come into focus today.

The Sociology of Modernity

ECONOMIC LIFE

From the early nineteenth century to the middle of the twentieth, it seemed to many of the most acute social observers that industrial capitalism had turned earlier and more traditional societies upside down. Sociologists focused on the often disastrous consequences of this great transformation—specifically, on the growing inequality between economic classes as well as the physically demanding and often degrading quality of work.

SOCIAL ORGANIZATION

The shifting economic order was not by any means the only development that caught the attention of the early sociologists of modernity. They were struck by the centralizing tendencies of social organization more broadly conceived. They traced the movement of population from scattered rural settlements to urban centers and saw the future as demanding ever larger cities. They observed what they believed to be an irreversible movement away from arbitrary and personal forms of authority in "traditional" societies—rule by a king or local "strongman"—to impersonal control based on bureaucratic rules.

TABLE 1.1 Characteristics of Premodern, Modern, and Postmodern Societies		
Premodern	**Modern**	**Postmodern**
Feudalism; agricultural economy	Industrial capitalism; urbanization; material inequality	Postindustrial economy based on services and information
Arbitrary, personal forms of authority	Pressure for centralization and bureaucratization (impersonal authority)	Decentralized organization
Shared moral universe based on religion	Problem of integration	Cultural turn • dominance of mass media and popular culture • displacement of production by consumption • recognition of language, symbols, and meaning in sociological stories
Superstition; tradition	Rationalization	Derationalization
Rigid gender roles	Gender relations unchallenged	New social movements, multiculturalism, and difference
Local, ascribed identity	Public versus private life	Socialization, identity, and life cycle redefined
	Occidentalism versus Orientalism (implied superiority of the West); narrative of progress and evolution	Globalization; new forms of inequality

INTEGRATION

Alongside their preoccupations with the material inequalities of industrialism and the centralization of social organization, classical and modern sociologists were deeply concerned with reintegrating a social order they viewed as increasingly stratified and divided. Some believed that greater inclusion could be achieved through progressive and incremental reforms; others imagined that a revolutionary transformation would introduce socialism and communism. What reformers and radical sociologists shared, however, was the vision of social integration as allowing greater unity, a vision of equality that depended on increasing uniformity among people from different groups—economic, religious, ethnic, and racial.

CULTURE

The classical and modern sociologists contrasted their own societies with an earlier social order they called "traditional," "feudal," or simply "premodern." It was because they worked with this contrast in mind that they were particularly likely to see the major trend in culture as that of increasing rationality: thinking based on formal rules or calculations of efficiency rather than on tradition or emotion. Above all, they emphasized the central importance of science and the declining significance of religion. For better or worse, they believed, culture was becoming rationalized, abstract, and subjected to organized control.

GENDER AND SOCIALIZATION

As we can see so clearly from the perspective of the present, one of the most remarkable characteristics of both classical and modern sociological stories was that they took gender arrangements for granted. As women confronted the wrenching economic, political, and cultural transformations of their time, the fact that their opportunities for public accomplishment were highly restricted failed almost completely to arouse sociological interest. If the position of women inside and outside the home was noticed at all, it was seen as the result of nature. Family and child-rearing arrangements were explained in the same manner. Is there perhaps a connection between these stories and the fact that almost all of the classical and modern sociologists were men?

PUBLIC VERSUS PRIVATE

With only a few exceptions, these classical and modern sociologists paid little attention to emotion, love, friendship, recreation, and entertainment. Once again, we must look to the nature of these earlier forms of modern societies to find out why. In the transition from more traditional social orders, a stiff barrier had been erected between the private and the public spheres. (This, too, relates to the fact that the sociologists were men, whose concern was the public sphere, whereas the private sphere was more the concern of women.) The efficiency and distinctiveness of modern institutions seemed to depend upon the "rational" control of emotions and the construction of associations on universal, abstract, and universal principles. Identities that were less universal and more particularistic, structures of feeling that were more expressive and spontaneous, the pursuit of pleasure in recreation and entertainment—these were understood to be private issues. As such, they were rarely the subject of classical or modern sociological texts.

OCCIDENTALISM VERSUS ORIENTALISM

These sociological accounts were presented as part of a larger story about the distinctiveness of Western (occidental) societies as compared to non-Western (oriental) ones. Rationalization, centralization, industrialization, and the public-private split were described in evolutionary terms, as a movement of progress from East to West. They were seen as "advances" that defined the superiority of modern societies and the deficiencies of more traditional ones. This historical narrative suggested that non-Western civilizations did not possess the social capacity for modernization. Whether harshly or sympathetically, classical and modern sociologists told stories about the backwardness of societies outside the West. Could this have anything to do with colonialism as opposed to intrinsic capacities, with the political, economic, and cultural dominance of the European colonial powers as well as America's later "neo-colonial" expansion?

Beyond the Sociology of Modernity

As we enter a new century and a new millennium, we cannot help but notice how the cultural and structural facts emphasized by the sociology of modernity have been dramatically transformed. Once taken for granted as the basic foundations of any posttraditional social order, such facts have themselves fundamentally changed. These transformations have stimulated contemporary sociologists to construct new theoretical and empirical stories, accounts that raise as many questions as they answer.

POSTINDUSTRIAL ECONOMIES

By the end of the twentieth century it had become evident that technological growth had transformed the nature of economic production, at least in the most advanced economies. Because so much less time is now required to produce material goods, the workforce devoted to manufacturing—to blue-collar jobs—has dramatically declined. In its place, economic activity increasingly concentrates on nonmaterial goods. As the service economy has displaced manufacturing, the nature of work has changed. Many sociologists see this in terms of progress; they believe that education and flexibility are more important today than in the past, and that workers in service-oriented societies have much more autonomy than those in industrial societies. Other sociologists tell more depressing stories about the "deskilling of labor"—what were once the worker's skills are now programmed into the computerized machine. All agree that, in the most developed societies, the class structure is more differentiated and less homogeneous and that the overall level of material well-being has vastly increased.

DECENTRALIZED ORGANIZATION

In a postindustrial economy, information and communication are more important than the energy supplied by muscle and coal. As information becomes digitalized and communication almost instantaneous, transportation of goods, services, and people is also transformed. These economic changes have undercut the pressure for centralization. Residential patterns have changed from urban to suburban and then to ex-urban, blurring the divisions between city, suburb, and country. Shopping malls have become cities in miniature. Home-based work has become possible, contributing to the shifting balance between public and private life. Yet, while sociologists agree that these changes are occurring, they tell different stories about their effects. Some see increased opportunities for cooperation, local control, and community; others find increasing fragmentation and privatization and the creation of more artificial forms of social order. Still others have suggested that organization in general is becoming less hierarchical and bureaucratic. The contemporary sociological story about bureaucracies is much more skeptical about their efficiency. It documents vast slippage between what managers at the top of the hierarchy say happens and what the organization's working practices really are. Whether this slippage is a sign of growing irrationality or healthy decentralization is a point of heated debate.

THE CULTURAL TURN

The term *cultural turn* refers to two developments: the increasing importance of cultural industries and of knowledge more generally in the economy, and the increasing attention being given to cultural factors (such as language, symbols, and meanings) in sociological explanations.

The postindustrial organization of contemporary economies has allowed an increasingly substantial segment of social time and energy to be devoted to cultural activity. Some sociologists, in fact, have said that we live in an age characterized by "postscarcity" and "postmaterial" values—that is, in which people have less need to worry about finding the necessities of life and so can concentrate on more intellectual, emotional, or spiritual matters. In service economies, culture itself has become a gigantic industry. Popular culture, once peripheral to prestige and power, now takes center stage as the new common language spoken by people, no matter how high or low their position in society. Consumption has displaced production as the dominating experience of economic life. Increasingly large amounts of disposable income are spent on travel, entertainment, clothing, restaurants, and recreation. Knowledge itself has become an industry. For these social-economic as well as technological reasons, the mass media have become central to contemporary societies, providing not only much more immediate access to information but also more immediate forms of pleasures. The example of people watching public entertainment at home with friends and family crystallizes the manner in which the once-rigid division between public and private life has eroded. Private pleasures have become public pursuits.

It is not difficult to see how such a deep and pervasive cultural transformation of contemporary society has generated conflicting sociological stories. Everyday life is indeed now less constricted by material shortages, but has it increased in quality or become more satisfying? Has the growth of knowledge facilitated moral or artistic growth? Do we have more wisdom, or just more information?

The other important aspect of the *cultural turn* is that people, including sociologists, are increasingly aware of the ways in which language shapes our experiences, our descriptions of them, and the meanings we give to them. The sociologists of the future will be much more alive to questions of language than were even the best of the classical sociologists.

DERATIONALIZATION

Despite the extraordinary progress of contemporary science, there is now less confidence that science will displace religious and other nonscientific modes of thought. People are quite likely to be critical of the authority and effects of science, pointing to the risks its applications sometimes present to human life and the environment. New Age beliefs, religious "fundamentalism," and nationalism are just a few of the examples that have led sociologists to talk about a "return of the sacred."

NEW SOCIAL MOVEMENTS

In earlier periods, the prototypical protest was the movement of impoverished workers against the industrial system. As that earlier social order has receded, other kinds of protest movements have become more visible and more powerful, and altogether new kinds of protests have emerged. Perhaps the most visible and most successful has been the modern women's movement. Although earlier feminist protests had gained some political and social rights, they had not envisioned a fundamental shift in gender relations. Since the 1960s, precisely this has been the aim of the contemporary feminist movement, and its success has had far-reaching effects on economic arrangements, lifestyles, socialization patterns, and the public-private divide. "The personal has become political," as in controversies about women's right to control their own bodies, such as terminating a pregnancy. This issue, in turn, raises questions about the balance between individual rights and social rights and obligations.

The American civil rights movement, organized by African-American leaders and energized by African-American masses, preceded the contemporary women's movement and partly inspired it. It created the model for the growing racial and ethnic protests against exclusion that, with feminism, have marked the contemporary period. Other forms of social protest, such as environmentalism and gay rights, have emerged only in the contemporary period itself. In identifying and explaining these new social movements, most sociologists have presented them as stories of emancipation and liberation. There are some influential commentators, however, who employ these movements in a story of antiprogress. One old-fashioned radical story sees the new movements as diversions from the struggle for economic equality, whereas in a more conservative narrative these movements are described as destroying the solidarity that glued earlier societies together.

MULTICULTURALISM AND DIFFERENCE

Interacting with the forces that are undermining centralization and softening the public-private boundary, this new emphasis on race, gender, and sexuality has had the effect of introducing a new framework for social integration. Whereas modern societies in an earlier phase prided themselves on achieving color-blind unity, contemporary societies boast about their diversity and their ability to give positive recognition to difference. The idea of the melting pot, in which outgroups are assimilated into a larger national identity, has given way to a multicultural model of incorporation. Minority groups have become increasingly concerned with preserving their distinctive cultures, not in order to isolate themselves from contemporary society but, rather, to enter it in a different way and to gain recognition and respect. Because there are many possible group identities, there are constant struggles over "identity politics." Questions have been raised about whether these struggles could result in social fragmentation.

SOCIALIZATION, IDENTITY, AND THE LIFE CYCLE

The changes we have identified are producing dramatic shifts in marriage, child-rearing, and individual development. As women have moved beyond their traditional domestic roles, their financial dependence on the marriage bond has decreased. One consequence is that women now marry at a much later age, delay having children, more often decide to have children outside marriage, and, with increasing frequency, decide not to have children at all. Divorce has become more widely accepted and is now the statistical norm. In the context of dual-career couples and less stable relationships, the socialization of children has assumed a new and sometimes bewildering range of forms, from private and public daycare centers and after-school programs to much more clearly defined roles for grandparents and professional babysitters.

The growing demands for highly educated labor have extended schooling and created new life cycle stages between childhood and full adulthood, including what has recently been called "emerging adulthood," the twenty-something period when persons try on different careers and relationships without settling down. The service economy has shifted its production and marketing to these new life cycle stages, when there is more disposable income and less imperative to save for the future. The life cycle has also been stretched at the other end. With increasing wealth and leisure, the scientific transformation of medical care, and lifestyles emphasizing fitness and recreation, people are living longer and healthier lives. This trend has opened the way for new forms of human relationship, new markets for entertainment and marketing, and new challenges for socialization and care.

The expanding life cycle, increased education, new forms of consumption, the instability of marriage, and new life-styles focused on gender, race, ethnicity, and sexuality—all these changes have created a new emphasis on "identity" as central to contemporary life. Individuals today have more scope than in earlier modern societies to define themselves and their destinies. From weight-control programs and personal trainers to psychotherapies, from talk radio and reality TV to twelve-step programs for reforming everything from love to addiction, there has been an explosion of knowledge and industries devoted to improving and recasting identity. These processes of identity change and the creation of multiple identities raise questions about the stability and unity of the self. We see some of these questions raised when people talk about a "split personality" or dispute a politician's ability to be "all things to all people."

INEQUALITIES

Although modern citizens are formally equal and have certain basic entitlements, new forms of inequality have emerged. As once-marginalized ethnic groups have made use of new opportunities and the more successful members have moved out of the ghettos, they have left behind a new kind of isolated and highly vulnerable *underclass*." (As we will see in Chapter 10, this term is questionable, which is why some sociologists prefer *ghetto poor*.) Also, as women are more frequently compelled to raise children on their own, single-parent families have become a growing source of poverty, and the percentage of children living in poverty is on the rise. The postindustrial economy has had an uneven impact, producing more affluence for some but more instability and poverty for others. Even at the height of the Silicon Valley technology boom in 1999, the *San Jose Mercury News* (February 12, 1999) reported increasing poverty in the most affluent area of California, Santa Clara County. Quoting data from the U.S. Census Bureau, it specified that about 13 percent of Santa Clara County's children were impoverished. That amounts to more than 55,000 kids—or nearly one of every eight youngsters. (By comparison, 9 percent of county residents of *all* ages were living in poverty.) The problem was that the supply of relatively well-paying manufacturing jobs had dwindled, forcing many mothers and fathers to seek less lucrative wages in service-related jobs. In short, when marriages came under pressure, leading to single-parent households, child poverty in creased. Children generally have higher rates of poverty than the population as a whole because poor families tend to have more children and are more likely to have only one adult present. Also, new parents tend to be young with little work experience, and thus earn relatively low salaries.

GLOBALIZATION

The stories told by classical and modern sociologists implicitly identified "society" with the framework of the nation-state. For many contemporary sociologists, this identification seems out of date. For example, multinational business corporations are just that—*multi*national. They may have originated in a particular country, but many of them now operate out of several countries and have global connections, making it difficult for any national government to regulate and control them. Communication networks, including the Internet as well as mass media programs (ranging from CNN news and television sitcoms to movies like *Titanic* and the *Star Wars* epics), break down national boundaries. Electronic transfers of money around the world amount to more than a trillion dollars being turned over each day on global currency markets.

According to the more optimistic sociological accounts, this is all part of modern progress, of becoming "one world." A more skeptical story is presented by sociologists who see nothing very new in all this—who point to a similar emphasis on international free trade during the nineteenth century, along with trade in currencies. Or, they may say, if the scenario is new in scale, that it is still a case of richer states dominating poorer ones, either in the form of American economic and cultural imperialism or through the establishment of regional arrangements such as the European Union (EU) and the North American Free Trade Agreement (NAFTA). Some of these developments may be increasing inequalities in the world. According to the *Human Development Report 2005*, for instance, the world's richest 500 individuals have a combined income greater than that of the poorest 416 million. And the *World Development Report 2005* revealed that the 2.5 billion people living on less than $2 a day—40 percent of the world's population—account for 5 percent of global income. The richest 10 percent, almost all of whom live in high-income countries, account for 54 percent. Similarly, people in the advanced economies are increasingly "information rich" compared with their "information poor" neighbors in the global village. For example, although the Internet made possible e-mail communications among many people in the 1990s, most of those communications were confined to the United States and parts of Europe.

Even relations between economically powerful nation-states are not equal—and, rather than requiring a new concept such as **globalization,** some sociologists prefer to use older terms such as *nationalism, imperialism,* or just plain *international competition.* Certainly some sociologists outside the United States have favored these ways of telling the story. They believe *globalization* is a term that disguises inequalities in economic or cultural relations between their own country and the United States. A good example is France's efforts to resist global free trade in cultural products, out of the fear that its culture is in danger of being swamped by Hollywood movies. In 1998, French movies accounted for only 27 percent of tickets sold in France, whereas during the same year (to cite just one example) the Hollywood blockbuster *Titanic* alone accounted for 21 million of the total 170 million tickets sold. Defending its national cultural industry, the government insisted that French productions account for 40 percent of films shown on television. This may seem reasonable at first glance, but might we also feel entitled to ask whether such nation-centered thinking is practical or even desirable in an increasingly globalized world? For example, at the same time as this new national policy was unfolding in the French movie industry, a former French prime minister and two other former ministers were put on trial during a scandal over HIV-tainted blood. These French officials, it was revealed, had for months delayed national blood tests for the HIV/AIDS virus because only a U.S.-made testing device had been available. They waited to require the national test until a French-designed test emerged that could compete commercially with the American product. As it happened, both stories were published on the same day in the *New York Times* (February 10, 1999).

Globalization A social phenomenon characterized by the growing number of interconnections across the world. Rather than studying society in terms of various nation-states, sociologists today are concerned with multinational and global problems. Whether globalization is a new phenomenon marking "modern progress" toward becoming "one world," or simply a new (or even disguised) form of American imperialism, continues to be debated.

Clearly, the new concept of globalization raises as many questions as it answers. It seems to direct us to important new developments, but it may have to be complemented by other concepts such as *power geometry,* which refers to the unequal distribution of power in different parts of the world, and *world system,* which is consistent with the idea of a single global system but distinguishes between the regions at the core and those on the periphery.

How Do We Understand Today's Social World?

We have indicated some of the key themes of classical and modern sociology and also some of the new developments that raise fresh questions. Surely, you might be saying, we can now get on with finding some answers! We are about to do so, but we first need to set the scene. Specifically, we need to briefly examine some venerable philosophical debates, for our responses to them will inform all the empirical discussions that follow.

DETERMINISM VERSUS FREE WILL

Earlier we noted that, although social structures and cultural factors seem to constrain and determine behavior, it is individuals who act—even when they act as the "agents" of institutions and organization. This may seem obvious, but we need to see where sociologists stand on this issue before we can judge the adequacy of their empirical explanations. Some theorists have given compelling accounts of the forceful determinism of society and its various parts. In the middle of the nineteenth century, the revolutionary social thinker and socialist Karl Marx dramatically insisted that "it is not consciousness that determines society, but society that determines consciousness." Some fifty years later, Emile Durkheim, the French founder of modern scientific sociology, described social facts as "things" that are "objective" and "constraining" and against which individuals have little power.

Other equally influential sociologists have been appalled by such deterministic story lines. They have argued against them by creating accounts that center on the freedom of the individual. George Herbert Mead, at the University of Chicago, who exerted extraordinary influence over early American sociology, insisted that the ever creative self is at the basis of institutions. Mead conceded that inside every self there is a "me" that represents established values and attitudes, but he insisted that the self also contains an "I," which is an active, spontaneous source of creative, anticonforming activity. Erving Goffman, one of the leading American sociologists of the twentieth century, took Mead's ideas much further. He told a theoretical story that centered on the self and its ingenuity. Just because people espouse accepted social values, Goffman said, they don't necessarily believe in them. He likened people to actors for whom, as Shakespeare put it, "the whole world's a stage." Social actors present selves that can be maximally convincing to others, hiding true feelings that might get in the way.

Over the centuries, philosophers and sociologists alike have spilled a lot of ink arguing first one side of this debate and then the other. However, there is no need for us to choose a side. Very often the heat of the debate could be attributed to the fact that what was being put forward was not just a sociological theory but also a moral and emotional account. For example, the actions of students who join a subgroup that deliberately breaks school rules may be explained as the result of too much pressure in the educational system to get good grades (social determinism). Or it may be interpreted as a creative act of rebellion by individual students (free will). A full and convincing account needs to give due weight to both sides.

STRUCTURE VERSUS CULTURE

If the first dispute is about the nature of society's effects, the second one is about what exactly society is and what affects the inside of it.

Many of the greatest sociologists have made "structure" central to the stories they tell about institutions, processes, and groups. As they see it, social structure is analogous to a material or biological thing—it is a concrete, stubborn fact, located outside the individual self. Structure could be a factory or a labor market, offering financial incentives and threatening financial punishments to compel people to work. Structure could also be something less obviously material; it could be a "role" in the family or church. When sociologists describe family and religious roles as structures—"father" and "priest," for example—they focus on how performance in these roles is compelled from outside. They might point to the importance of positive and negative psychological reinforcements, such as love, anger, prestige, and ridicule, in compelling persons to become good fathers and priests.

Such structural accounts do not have to stress determinism. Just because a social element is described as a stubborn fact external to the person acting, it doesn't have to be thought of as producing automatic conformity. Indeed, theories can emphasize an individual's free will and his or her resistance to structural pressure, as in the emancipatory stories told by women, ethnic and religious minorities, and underprivileged classes. For example, some feminist sociologists have written about women's attempts to take back control of their own bodies in pregnancy and childbirth. They describe such efforts as a struggle against state governments and even doctors and husbands who use legal sanctions to force women to change their behavior—to alter their diets (stop drinking alcohol during pregnancy), modify their daily activity (be confined to a hospital throughout the last weeks of pregnancy), or undergo caesarian section—to protect the rights of the fetus (Martin 1989).

The structural approach is not the only way to account for society and its effects. A very different kind of story can be told—a story about culture rather than structure. In this account, it is values and beliefs that are central to society. From the sociological perspective, of course, values and beliefs are collective. They go beyond the wishes or ideals of a particular individual; they exist before her birth, and they will continue to exist after her death. Yet, while collective, culture is not objective. It is subjective. It is inside the mind of the individual, part of her, not outside of her. It has to do with her ways of thinking and feeling. Structure gains its effect through coercion or bargaining; culture gains its effect through persuasion and conviction. Sociologists who emphasize cultural factors are likely to focus on such topics as emotion, morality, consciousness, and belief. They need not do so, however, in a deterministic way. Culture not only constrains but enables. Creating resistance and independence, it gives us a sense of who we are, of individual worth. American individualism is a case in point. In the United States, liberty is not so much a natural fact as a cultural value. There is a great collective national story here that creates and sustains individualism, sometimes for better and sometimes for worse.

Some sociological perspectives have given more emphasis to structure; others, to culture. But to truly understand contemporary societies, we must make a renewed attempt to bring the two sides together. In this book, we will draw on concepts and insights from different perspectives as and when we need them. Structures are very much at work in every institution, group, and social process. Yet, at the same time, it is difficult to see how structures can ever really work by themselves, how they can be separated from the meanings that people attach to them. Social structures do not work like structures in the natural world. They are not mechanistic forces like gravity. What we think of as structures are, in fact, nothing more than congealed sets of beliefs that assume an objective form. As they become external rather than internal, they develop into organizations that control resources, such as money and power, that can compel people to act no matter what they believe.

In order to provide a convincing analysis of social issues, such as the increase in violent incidents in schools involving students using guns against fellow students and teachers, we have found it necessary to focus on both structural factors and cultural factors. On the one hand, it is obviously relevant to look at school structures at the microlevel and explore how they relate to wider social structures, such as the American educational institution, as well as at related structures such as the family, the economy (including the gun industry), politics, and the community. On the other hand, as we have mentioned, it is also important to take into account both the meanings that people attach to those structures and the various cultures and subcultures that supply values and symbols. None of these factors inevitably determines an individual's actions. There is always an element of choice and decisionmaking; individuals are the product of culture, too.

Conclusion

The post-tragedy conversation in the box titled "The Virginia Tech Murders" reminds us how sociological stories circulate as the mass media ask "why." It also demonstrates, in spite of itself, how careful we must be to avoid easy answers. We have seen that the sociological imagination is interested in showing how individuals' private troubles may be connected with public issues. In the chapters that follow, we will clarify this relationship by providing sociological explanations. One temptation sociologists are anxious to resist is the rush to offer readymade answers and solutions— the kind of slick, often plausible prescriptions that promise cures for all social problems, and that we find in books filling the shelves in airport shops. They range from "How to Get Rich" to "How to Solve America's Problems." They vary in quality, often mixing secondhand scientific ideas and a sprinkling of statistical "facts" with a lot of anecdotes, all of which are supposed to be explained by an all-purpose, big idea. There is usually nothing wrong with the idea itself. The problem is that it gets inflated to cover situations beyond the scope of its modest beginnings. A recent example is the term *social capital,* which was initially used to refer to the types of close family and community relations that potentially benefit adolescents' educational attainment (Coleman and Hoffer 1987). But this term has since been unwisely extended to refer, very broadly, to interpersonal and social trustworthiness, the alleged deterioration of which is then blamed for all kinds of social ills (Putnam 1995a, 1995b, 2000). In the end, it has seemed to cover just about everything and thus no longer lends itself to testable propositions.

As the American sociologist Robert Nisbet pointed out, sociology needs both the imaginative ideas of the artist and the rigor of the scientist. The ideas of a sociologist such as Emile Durkheim may be dependent upon thought processes like those of the artist, "but none of them would have survived in sociology or become fruitful for others were it not for criteria and modes of communication that differ from those of art." In particular, Nisbet mentions the need for sociologists to present their ideas in ways that others can test against the same kind of evidence. "No one asks a Picasso to verify one of his visions by repeating the process; and conversely, we properly give short shrift to ideas in science that no one but the author can find supported by experience" (Nisbet 1962: 156–157).

Yet, although sociologists are keen to establish the facts, they also appreciate that there are no facts without theories to interpret them. Facts do not speak for themselves. For example, in her study *The Time Bind* (1997), Arlie Hochschild found that statistics showed few people were taking advantage of new family-friendly employment policies allowing shorter hours, part-time work, parental leave, or flexible time. Rather than accept the conventional political explanation blaming economic pressure or organizational coercion, Hochschild drew on feminist theories about family and work in order to develop possible interpretations of the facts. She then tested these against people's testimonies as to the meanings they attached to time at home and at work. She found that for many middle-class people, work and home were changing places. Home was becoming more of a hassle. In her previous book, *The Second Shift* (1989), Hochschild had documented that, even as women were working more paid hours, they continued to receive relatively little help from their husbands at home. One of their responses has been to gradually abandon the home battle, shifting the emotional center of their lives to their work.

In the chapters that follow, we will trace the pathways of contemporary societies by presenting the newest empirical research. At the same time, we will be arranging the myriad of new social facts into theories—some big, some small. We want you to take away from *A Contemporary Introduction to Sociology* not only a bunch of new empirical facts but also new ways of thinking.

Exercises

EXERCISE 1

If you made a list of the most significant new developments in society during your lifetime, ranked in order of importance, what would it look like? (*New developments* could refer to anything of social significance: technologies, consumption, education, work, family life, attitudes toward the opposite sex or people from other ethnic groups, entertainment, politics, etc.) Jot down a few entries and then compare your list with that of your friends or classmates, if they have completed one.

It would also be interesting to ask your parents or grandparents to do the same and, again, to compare your list with theirs.

Of course, everybody's list will be different in some respects, but the similarities could provide useful clues as to what we think are the most important social changes. The comparison with parents and grandparents could also tell us something about social changes in different historical periods. For example, changes in your own lifetime might include the rapid spread of access to information and communication via the Internet and the World Wide Web. Your parents may note that more than half of all the marriages that originated in their generation now end in divorce, whereas the latter was in the minority when they were children. And your grandparents may have a long list of the changes that have taken place since they grew up in the period after World War II, such as differences in the way children relate to their parents, changes in attitudes toward sexuality, a more ethnically mixed population, and so on.

EXERCISE 2

Think about the possible links between private troubles and public issues in terms of problems affecting your own family, neighborhood, or town. Can you see how concerns that seem to arise in the private lives of individuals might be part of a bigger picture that includes changes in social structures and cultures? Are these troubles and issues different from those that might have been experienced by people living a hundred years ago?

Study Questions

1. How does the sociological perspective challenge individualism?
2. What is the difference between personal troubles and public issues? Can you think of an example that falls into both categories?
3. Briefly describe Berger's four dimensions of sociological consciousness.
4. What do sociologists mean by *modernity* and *postmodernity*?
5. What is determinism? Describe sociological arguments against this position, and explain why both sides have been heatedly debated in the field.
6. What is the difference between structural and cultural approaches? Is either deterministic?

Further Reading

Alexander, Jeffrey, C. 1995. *Fin de Siècle Social Theory.* London/New York: Verso.

Berger, Peter. 1963. *Invitation to Sociology: A Humanist Perspective.* New York: Doubleday. Reprinted in 1966.

Lash, Scott. 1990. *Sociology of Postmodernism.* London/New York: Routledge.

Loseke, Donileen, and Joel Best, eds. 2003. *Social Problems: Constructionist Readings.* New York: Aldin Transaction.

Mills, C. Wright. 1959. *The Sociological Imagination.* New York: Oxford University Press.

Newman, Katherine S., with Cybelle Fox, David Harding, Jal Mehta, and Wendy Roth. 2004. *Rampage: The Social Roots of School Shootings.* New York: Basic Books.

Ritzer, George, and Douglas J. Goodman. 2004. *Modern Sociological Theory.* New York: McGraw-Hill.

READING 2

TELLING ABOUT SOCIETY

BY HOWARD S. BECKER

I have lived for many years in San Francisco, on the lower slope of Russian Hill or in the upper reaches of North Beach; how I describe it depends on whom I am trying to impress. I live near Fisherman's Wharf, on the route many people take from that tourist attraction to their motel downtown or on Lombard Street's motel row. Looking out my front window, I often see small groups of tourists standing, alternately looking at their maps and at the large hills that stand between them and where they want to be. It's clear what has happened. The map's straight line looked like a nice walk through a residential neighborhood, one that might show them how the natives live. Now they are thinking, as a young Briton I offered to help said to me, "I've got to get to my motel and I am *not* climbing that bloody hill!"

Why don't the maps those people consult alert them to the hills? Cartographers know how to indicate hills, so it is not a restriction of the medium that inconveniences walkers. But the maps are made for motorists, originally (though no longer) paid for by gasoline companies and tire manufacturers, and distributed through service stations (Paumgarten 2006, 92)—and drivers worry less than pedestrians do about hills.

Those maps, and the networks of people and organizations who make and use them, exemplify a more general problem. An ordinary street map of San Francisco is a conventionalized representation of that urban society: a visual description of its streets and landmarks and of their arrangement in space. Social scientists and ordinary citizens routinely use not only maps but also a great variety of other representations of social reality—a few random examples are documentary films, statistical tables, and the stories people tell one another to explain who they are and what they are doing. All of them, like the maps, give a picture that is only partial but nevertheless adequate for some purpose. All of them arise in organizational settings, which constrain what can be done and define the purposes the work will have to satisfy. This understanding suggests several interesting problems: How do the needs and practices of organizations shape our descriptions and analyses (call them representations) of social reality? How do the people who use those representations come to define them as adequate? Such questions have a bearing on traditional questions about knowing and telling in science but go beyond them to include problems more traditionally associated with the arts and with the experience and analysis of everyday life.

For many years, I've been involved with a variety of ways of telling about society, professionally and out of native curiosity. I'm a sociologist, so the ways of telling that come most immediately to my mind are the ones sociologists routinely use: ethnographic description, theoretical discourse, statistical tables (and such visual representations of numbers as bar charts), historical narrative, and so on. But many years ago I went to art school and became a photographer, and in the process I developed a strong and lasting interest in photographic representations of society, which documentary and other photographers have been making since the invention of the medium. That led quite naturally to thinking about film as still another way of telling about society. And not just documentary films but fiction films as well. I'd been an avid reader of fiction since I was a kid, and like most other readers of stories, I knew that they are not just made-up fantasies, that they often contain observations worth reading about how society is constructed and works. Why not dramatic representations of stories on the stage too? Having always been interested and involved in all these ways of telling about society, I decided to take advantage of the somewhat haphazard and random collection of examples that had deposited in my brain.

To do what? To see the problems anyone who tries to do the job of representing society has to solve, what kinds of solutions have been found and tried, and with what results. To see what the problems of different media have in common and how solutions that work for one kind of telling look when you try them on some other kind. To see what, for instance, statistical tables have in common with documentary photographic projects, what mathematical models have in common with avant-garde fiction. To see what solutions to the problem of description one field might import from another.

So I'm interested in novels, statistics, histories, ethnographies, photographs, films, and any other way people have tried to tell others what they know about their society or some other society that interests them. I'll call the products of all this activity in all these media "reports about society" or, sometimes, "representations of society." What problems and issues arise in making those reports, in whatever medium? I've constructed a list of those issues from the things people who do this kind of work talk and complain about to each other, using as a basic principle of discovery this idea: if it's a problem in one way of making representations, it's a problem in every way of doing so. But the people who work in one area may have solved that problem to their own satisfaction, so that they don't even think of it as a problem, while for other people it seems an insoluble dilemma. Which means that the latter can learn something from the former.

I've been inclusive in making these comparisons, encompassing (at least in principle) every medium and genre people use or have ever used. Of course, I haven't talked about everything. But I have tried to avoid the most obvious conventional biases and have considered, in addition to reputable scientific formats and those invented and used by professionals in recognized scientific disciplines, those used by artists and laypeople as well. A list will suggest this range of topics: from the social sciences, such modes of representation as mathematical models, statistical tables and graphs, maps, ethnographic prose, and historical narrative; from the arts, novels, films, still photographs, and drama; from the large shadowy area in between, life histories and other biographical and autobiographical materials, reportage (including the mixed genres of docudrama, documentary film, and fictionalized fact), and the storytelling, mapmaking, and other representational activities of laypeople (or people acting in a lay capacity, as even professionals do most of the time).

Who Tells?

We are all curious about the society we live in. We need to know, on the most routine basis and in the most ordinary way, how our society works. What rules govern the organizations we participate in? What routine patterns of behavior do others engage in? Knowing these things, we can organize our own behavior, learn what we want, how to get it, what it will cost, what opportunities of action various situations offer us.

Where do we learn this stuff? Most immediately, from our experience of daily living. We interact with all sorts of people and groups and organizations. We talk to people of all kinds in all kinds of situations. Of course, not *all* kinds: everyone's social experience of that face-to-face kind is limited by their social connections, their situation in society, their economic resources, their geographical location. You can get by with that limited knowledge, but in modern societies (probably in all societies) we need to know more than what we learn from personal experience. We need, or at least want, to know about other people and places, other situations, other times, other ways of life, other possibilities, other opportunities.

So we look for "representations of society," in which other people tell us about all those situations and places and times we don't know firsthand but would like to know about. With the additional information, we can make more complex plans and react in a more complex way to our own immediate life situations.

Simply put, a "representation of society" is something someone tells us about some aspect of social life. That definition covers a lot of territory. At one extreme lie the ordinary representations we make for one another, as lay folks, in the course of daily life. Take mapmaking. In many situations and for many purposes, this is a highly professionalized activity based on centuries of combined practical experience, mathematical reasoning, and scientific scholarship. But in many other situations, it's an ordinary activity we all do once in a while. I ask you to visit me sometime, but you don't know how to drive to where I live. I can give you verbal directions: "Coming from Berkeley, you take the first exit on the right off the Bay Bridge, turn left at the bottom of the ramp, go several blocks and turn left on to Sacramento, keep going until you hit Kearny, turn right and go up to Columbus . . ." I can suggest you consult a standard street map along with my directions, or I can just tell you that I live near the intersection of Lombard and Jones and let you use the map to find that spot. Or I can draw my own little map, personalized for you. I can show where you would start from—"your house"—and draw in the relevant streets, indicating where you should turn, how long each leg will be, what landmarks you will pass, and how you will know when you reach "my house." These days an Internet site will tell you all that, or you can let your GPS device do it for you.

Those are all representations of a portion of society, contained in a simple geographical relationship; a simpler and better way of saying it is that these are all ways of telling about society or some portion thereof. Some of the ways, the standard automobile map or the computer description, are made by highly trained professionals using a lot of specialized equipment and knowledge. The verbal description and the homemade map are made by people just like the people to whom they are given, people who have no more geographical knowledge or ability than any ordinarily competent adult. They all work, in different ways, to do the job of leading someone from one place to another.

My own professional colleagues—sociologists and other social scientists—like to talk as though they have a monopoly on creating such representations, as though the knowledge of society they produce is the only "real" knowledge about that subject. That's not true. And they like to make the equally silly claim that the ways they have of telling about society are the best ways to do that job or the only way it can be done properly, or that their ways of doing the job guard against all sorts of terrible mistakes we would otherwise make.

That kind of talk is just a standard professional power grab. Considering the ways that people who work in other fields—visual artists, novelists, playwrights, photographers, and filmmakers—as well as laypeople represent society will show analytic dimensions and possibilities that social science has often ignored that might otherwise be useful. I will concentrate on the representational work done by other kinds of workers, as well as that done by social scientists. Social scientists know how to do their job, and that's adequate for many purposes. But their ways aren't the only ways.

What are some of the other ways? We can categorize representational activities in many ways. We could talk about media—film vs. words vs. numbers, for instance. We might talk about the intent of the makers of the representations: science vs. art vs. reportage. Such a comprehensive review would serve many purposes well, but not my purpose of exploring generic problems of representation and the variety of solutions the world has so far produced. Looking at some major, highly organized ways of telling about society means attending to the distinctions among science, art, and reportage. Those are not so much distinct ways of doing something as they are ways of organizing what might be, from the point of view of materials and methods, pretty much the same activity. Later, I'll compare three ways of using still photographs to do those three kinds of work, seeing how the same photographs might be art, journalism, or social science.

Telling about society usually involves an interpretive community, an organization of people who routinely make standardized representations of a particular kind ("makers") for others ("users") who routinely use them for standardized purposes. The makers and users have adapted what they do to what the others do, so that the organization of making and using is, at least for a while, a stable unity, a *world* (used in a technical sense I've developed elsewhere [Becker 1982] and will discuss more fully below).

Often enough, some people don't fit well into these organized worlds of makers and users. These experimenters and innovators don't do things as they are usually done, and therefore their works may not have many users. But their solutions to standard problems tell us a lot and open our eyes to possibilities more conventional practice doesn't see. Interpretive communities often borrow procedures and forms, using them to do something the originators in that other community never thought of or intended, producing mixtures of method and style to fit into changing conditions in the larger organizations they belong to.

This is all very abstract. Here's a more specific list of standard formats for telling about society, which have produced exemplary works of social representation worth inspecting carefully:

> *Fiction.* Works of fiction, novels and stories, have often served as vehicles of social analysis. The sagas of families, classes, and professional groups by writers as dissimilar in aims and talent as Honoré de Balzac, Émile Zola, Thomas Mann, C. P. Snow, and Anthony Powell have always been understood to embody, and to depend on for their power and aesthetic virtues, complex descriptions of social life and its constituent processes. The works of Charles Dickens, taken singly and as a whole, have been understood (as he intended them to be) as a way of describing to a large public the organizations that produced the ills his society suffered from.

Drama. Similarly, the theater has often been a vehicle for the exploration of social life, most especially the description and analysis of social ills. George Bernard Shaw used the dramatic form to embody his understanding of how "social problems" came about and how deeply they penetrated the body politic. His *Mrs. Warren's Profession* explains the workings of the business of prostitution as it provided the livelihood of at least some of the British upper classes; and *Major Barbara* did the same for war and munitions making. Many playwrights have used drama for similar purposes (Henrik Ibsen, Arthur Miller, David Mamet).

To say that these works and authors deal in social analysis doesn't mean that that is "all" they do or that their works are "only" sociology in artistic disguise. Not at all. Their authors have purposes in mind beyond social analysis. But even the most formalist critic should realize that some part of the effect of many works of art depends on their "sociological" content and on the belief of readers and audiences that what these works tell them about society is, in some sense, "true."

Films. In the most obvious case, documentary film—Barbara Koppel's 1976 *Harlan County, U.S.A.* and Edgar Morin and Jean Rouch's 1961 *Chronique d'un été* are well known examples—has had as a primary object the description of society, often, but not necessarily overtly, in a reformist mode, aiming to show viewers what's wrong with current social arrangements. Fiction films also often mean to analyze and comment on the societies they present, many times those in which they are made. Examples range from Gillo Pontecorvo's pseudodocumentary *Battle of Algiers* (1966) to classic Hollywood fare like Elia Kazan's 1947 *Gentleman's Agreement.*

Photographs. Likewise, still photographers have, from the beginnings of the genre, often occupied themselves with social analysis. A well-defined genre of documentary photography has had a long and illustrious history. Some exemplary works of that genre include Brassaï's *The Secret Paris of the '30s* (1976), Walker Evans's *American Photographs* ([1938] 1975), and Robert Frank's *The Americans* ([1959] 1969).

So far I have talked about "artistic" modes of making representations of society. Other representations are more associated with "science."

Maps. Maps, associated with the discipline of geography (more specifically, cartography), are an efficient way of displaying large amounts of information about social units considered in their spatial dimension.

Tables. The invention of the statistical table in the eighteenth century made it possible to summarize vast numbers of specific observations in a compact and comparable format. These compact descriptions help governments and others organize purposeful social action.

A governmental census is the classical form of such use. Scientists use tables to display data others can use to evaluate their theories. Twentieth-century social scientists became increasingly dependent on the tabular display of quantitative data gathered specifically for that purpose.

Mathematical models. Some social scientists have described social life by reducing it to abstract entities displayed as mathematical models. These models, intentionally removed from social reality, can convey basic relations characteristic of social life. They have been used to analyze such varied social phenomena as kinship systems and the world of commercial popular music.

Ethnography. A classic form of social description has been the ethnography, a detailed verbal description of the way of life, considered in its entirety, of some social unit, archetypically but not necessarily a small tribal group. The method came to be applied, and is widely applied now, to organizations of all kinds: schools, factories, urban neighborhoods, hospitals, and social movements.

Somewhere between the extremes of art and science lie history and biography, usually devoted to detailed and accurate accounts of past events but often equally given to evaluating large generalizations about matters the other social sciences deal with. (Remember that all of today's sociological reports will be raw material for historians of the future, as masterworks of sociology like the Lynds' studies of "Middle-town" have turned from social analysis into historical document.)

Finally, there are the sports, mavericks, and innovators I spoke of earlier. Some makers of representations of society mix methods and genres, experiment with forms and languages, and provide analyses of social phenomena in places we don't expect them and in forms we don't recognize as either art or science or that we see as some unusual and unfamiliar mixture of genres. So Hans Haacke, who can be called a conceptual artist, uses uncomplicated devices to lead users to unexpected conclusions. Georges Perec and Italo Calvino, members of the French literary group OULIPO (Motte 1998) devoted to esoteric literary experiments, made the novel, in one form or another, a vehicle for subtle sociological thinking. And in David Antin's "talk pieces," stories that may or may not be fictions convey complex social analyses and ideas. Like all such experiments, the work of these artists forces us to reconsider procedures we usually take for granted, [...]

Facts

I must make an important distinction, even though it is fallacious and misleading and every word involved is slippery and indeterminate. I don't think those faults make much difference for my purpose here. It's the distinction between "fact" and "idea" (or "interpretation"). One part of any report on society (of any of the kinds I've just outlined) is a description of how things are: how some kinds of things are, in some place, at some time. This is how many people there are in the United States, as counted in the year 2000 by the U.S. Bureau of the Census. This is how many of them are women and how many are men. This is the age distribution of that population—so many below five, so many aged five to ten, all the way up. This is the racial composition of that population. This is the distribution of their incomes. This is that income distribution in racial and gender subgroups of the population.

Those are facts about the U.S. population (and, of course, similar facts are more or less available for all the other countries in the world). They are descriptions of what a person who went looking for such numbers would find, the evidence that results from the operations demographers and statisticians have undertaken in accordance with the procedures of their craft.

In the same way, anthropologists tell us, for instance, how *these* people living in *this* society reckon kinship: they recognize these categories of familial relationship and think this is how people related in those ways should behave toward one another; these are, in the classical phrase, their mutual rights and obligations. Anthropologists support their analyses with accounts of the facts about how those people talk and behave, contained in the field notes that report their on-the-spot observations and interviews, just as demographers support descriptions of the U.S. population with the data produced by the census. In either case, the professionals begin with evidence gathered in ways their craft peers recognize as sufficient to warrant the factual status of the results.

Now for the caveats. Thomas Kuhn long ago persuaded me that facts are never just facts but are rather, as he said, "theory-laden" (1970). Every statement of a fact presupposes a theory that explains what entities are out there to describe, what characteristics they can have, which of those characteristics can be observed and which can only be inferred from characteristics that are observable, and so on.

Theories often seem so obvious as to be self-evident. Does anyone need to argue that you can tell a human being when you see one and distinguish such a being from some other kind of animal? Does it need arguing that these human beings can be characterized as male or female? Or as Black, white, Asian, or of another racial variety?

In fact, scientists and laypeople argue about things like that all the time, as the continually shifting racial categories in censuses all over the world make clear. Characteristics like gender and race don't appear in nature in an obvious way. Every society has ways of telling boys from girls and distinguishing members of racial categories its members think are important from one another. But these categories rest on theories about the essential characteristics of humans, and the nature of the categories and the methods of assigning people to them vary between societies. So we can never take facts for granted. There are no pure facts, only "facts" that take on meaning from an underlying theory.

Moreover, facts are facts only when they are accepted as such by the people to whom those facts are relevant. Am I indulging in a pernicious kind of relativism, or malicious wordplay? Maybe, but I don't think we have to discuss whether there is an ultimate reality science will eventually reveal in order to recognize that reasonable people, including reasonable scientists, often disagree on what constitutes a fact, and when a fact really is a fact. Those disagreements arise because scientists often disagree on what constitutes adequate evidence for the existence of a fact. Bruno Latour (1987, 23–29) has demonstrated, well enough to suit me and many others, that, as he so neatly puts it, the fate of a scientific finding lies in the hands of those who take it up afterward. If they accept it as fact, it will be treated as fact. Does that mean that any damn thing can be a fact? No, because one of the "actants," to use Latour's inelegant expression, that must agree with the interpretation is the object about which the statements of fact are made. I can say the moon is made of green cheese, but the moon will have to cooperate, exhibiting those characteristics that other people will recognize as green cheese–like, or else my fact will become an unacceptable nonfact. Worse yet, my fact may not even be disputed; it may just be ignored, so that you might say it doesn't exist at all, at least not in the discourse of scientists who study the moon. There may be an ultimate reality, but we are all fallible human beings and may be wrong, so all facts are disputable in the real world we live in. That fact is at least as obdurate and hard to talk away as any other scientific fact.

Finally, facts are not accepted in general or by the world at large, they are accepted or rejected by the particular audiences their proponents present them to. Does this mean science is situational and its findings therefore not universally true? I'm not taking a position on such ultimate questions of epistemology, just recognizing what's obvious: when we make a report about society, we make it to somebody, and who those somebodies are affects how we present what we know and how users react to what we present to them. Audiences differ—this is important—in what they know and know how to do, in what they believe and will accept, on faith or with evidence of some kind. Different kinds of reports routinely go to different kinds of audiences: statistical tables to people more or less trained to read them, mathematical models to people with highly specialized training in the relevant disciplines, photographs to a wide variety of lay and professional audiences, and so on.

Instead of facts supported by evidence that makes them acceptable as fact, then, we have facts based on a theory, accepted by some people because they have been gathered in a way acceptable to some community of makers and users.

Interpretations

It's not easy to separate interpretations from facts. Every fact, in its social context, implies and invites interpretations. People move easily and without much thought from one to the other. The same facts will support many interpretations. To say, to take a provocative example, that racial groups differ in IQ scores might well be a fact—that is, demonstrated by the use of tests commonly used by psychologists who make a business of such measurement. But to interpret such a finding as a demonstration that such differences are genetic—inherited and thus not easily changed—is not a fact, it's an interpretation of the meaning of the reported fact. An alternate interpretation says the fact demonstrates that the IQ test is culture specific and can't be used to compare different populations.

Neither do the findings about race, gender, and income we can find in the U.S. Census speak for themselves. Someone speaks for them, interpreting their meaning. People argue more about interpretations than they do about facts. We can agree on the numbers describing the relations between gender, race, and income, but the same census data might be interpreted to show the existence of discrimination, the lessening of discrimination, the joint working of two disadvantaged conditions (being female, being Black) on income, or many other possible stories.

A report about society, then, is an artifact consisting of statements of fact, based on evidence acceptable to some audience, and interpretations of those facts similarly acceptable to some audience.

READING 3

ONE GOOD IDEA
Act the Fool

BY WILLIAM A. LEVINSON

Heyokas play an important role in an organization's survival

A *Heyoka* is a sacred clown or contrarian in the Sioux and Lakota language. Using satire and farce, they ask difficult questions, help others see situations differently and open eyes to things often overlooked.[1] Almost every workplace has a few *heyokas*, and they are vital to the organization's survival.

In medieval times, a court jester was more than an entertainer or fool. The jester also played an advisory role. He was the one person who could criticize or admonish the king and speak the truth and get away with it. The jester's words could be disregarded as jokes according to social norms and customs.

The fool in tarot card decks may symbolize a similar role—the ability to challenge existing practices without constraint by calling attention to underlying assumptions and paradigms. This concept appears in a Diesel clothing company advertising campaign, "Be Stupid." The campaign encourages people to take risks, innovate and challenge established paradigms.[2]

WORDS OF WISDOM

Shigeo Shingo often acted as a *heyoka*. At a metal forming facility he asked, "Why grease scrap metal?"[3] Instead of greasing the entire piece of stock, he thought the manufacturer should only grease what came into contact with the press. This would reduce the amount of lubricant the company needed to purchase.

At a fountain pen manufacturing plant, Shingo asked, "If all you need to do is paint the pen caps, why paint the air as well?" He observed at least half of the paint sprayed missed the caps. That company paid for wasted paint twice: first in the cost of its purchase and again when it became an environmental problem.

The phrase, "keep your eye on the doughnut's hole," means to pay attention to everything that is thrown away (the hole) as well as the product (the doughnut). Phrases like "grease scrap metal" and "paint the air" put processes and waste in a new perspective. When Henry Ford said, "Pedestrianism is not a highly paid line [of work],"[4] he was commenting on jobs that required workers to walk to get tools and parts due to poor workspace organization. Ford thought walking was a waste of motion that was built into the job and taken for granted.

An effective *heyoka* uses questions and observations to challenge procedures, paradigms and organizational culture—not the people who do the jobs. This is consistent with auditing and other quality approaches that place blame on deficiencies in tasks or the work system, not the staff. **QP**

References

1. Wikipedia, http://en.wikipedia.org/wiki/Heyoka.
2. "Be Stupid," Diesel, www.diesel.com/be-stupid.
3. Shigeo Shingo, (Andrew Dillon, translator), *The Sayings of Shigeo Shingo: Key Strategies for Plant Improvement*, Productivity Press, 1987.
4. Henry Ford and Samuel Crowther, *My Life and Work*, Doubleday, Page and Company, 1922.

A LESSON FROM LEVINSON

William A. Levinson is the author of "Easy A," which features tips to ace certification exams. Check out the open-access column, which appeared in QP's July 2012 issue, at http://asq.org/quality-progress/2012/07/one-good-idea/easy-a.html.

WILLIAM A. LEVINSON is principal consultant at Levinson Productivity Systems P.C. in Wilkes-Barre, PA. He has a master's degree in engineering from Cornell University in Ithaca, NY, and an MBA from Union College in Schenectady, NY. An ASQ fellow. Levinson is an ASQ-certified quality manager, auditor and engineer, reliability engineer and Six Sigma Black Belt.

In Other Words . . .

The sociological imagination reigns supreme in this unit. The following passage sums it up: "Neither the life of an individual nor the history of a society can be understood without understanding both" (Mills 1959, 3). But by definition, a concept is a "bundle of ideas," not just one. Prepare several instances of definition, articulation, and quotes for a concept this big. Know them; use them.

One of the most important questions Becker poses consists of two words: Who tells? Instantly, the focus shifts from the story to the teller of the story. As the African proverb proclaims, until the story of the hunt is told by the Lion, the tale of the hunt will always glorify the hunter (Buabeng 2014). Every story expresses a viewpoint, a perspective; once stated, it becomes self-evident. Still, for the most part, we *acquire* information and accept it as authentic. Becker reminds us that the things we think of as "real" are all, at best, "representations of a portion of society" (Becker 2007, 6); they are partial and perhaps even blatantly false. Even so, facts are not just facts; someone speaks for them, and they are "theory-laden." We are obligated, as scholars, to interrogate methodologies and interpretations offered. Ask questions. Consider alternatives. Weigh the balance of evidence. And remember the wisdom of fallible realism: all knowledge is constructed, constructing, and constructible. These strategies undergird critical thinking—a stalwart cornerstone of an educated person.

It's hoped you now understand the point of the sociological imagination—we are a product of both our personal biography and our collective history. Once we become aware that we are peering into our own culture, we begin to understand how everything about our everyday life is constructed, and we actually *grant* it meaning. Further, sociology is a scientific discipline based on systematic observations, following specific rules and methods. Some people think sociology is all about opinions. It is not. We look to evidence, uncover patterns, and construct knowledge. But just as the *heyokas*, we sociologists continually question, interrupt, and challenge existing knowledge, testing to see if it holds up under scientific scrutiny. We want you to become well versed in this act of critical thinking—the ability to analyze, critique, and form an educated judgment about the world and its workings. How powerful that will be! In the process, I predict we will learn even more about ourselves.

The Big Idea

What we come to know about life—our reality—is a matter of perspective. Our world, our everyday lives are socially constructed; sociology concerns us with HOW that happens, the situated context and processes, and consequences thereof, both intended and unintended. With proper tools, we can discover intersections between biography and history, distinguish between personal troubles and public issues. We do this best communally. All that I've learned and taught, all I continue to discover "consists of acts of the imagination, inspired by others" (Moyers 2010).

So What?

USE these newly discovered ideas. Insert them into your assignments, surely, but also into everyday talk. Unfortunately, our country seems to be in the throes of an anti-intellectualist movement, where growing hostility is directed toward educated, philosophical, and scientific communities. This movement blindly points toward emerging discourses as contemptible. Anti-intellectualism is a common characteristic of totalitarian dictatorships and other power-mongering regimes. Some argue that in the United States corporate interests encourage anti-intellectualism, "conditioning Americans into conformity and passive acceptance of institutional dominance" (Niose 2015). It's good for business, their business. Exercising and practicing the language of learning gives you power; don't just hand it over to someone else.

Works Cited

Becker, H. S. (2007). *Telling about society*. Chicago: University of Chicago Press.

Buabeng, K. (2015, May 9). "Until the story of the hunt is told by the Lion." *Africa Redemption Magazine*. Retrieved July 9, 2016, from http://africarm.org/until-the-story-of-the-hunt-is-told-by-the-lion-1407/

Noise, D. (2015, June 23). "Anti-intellectualism is killing America." *Psychology Today*. Retrieved July 9, 2016, from https://www.psychologytoday.com/blog/our-humanity-naturally/201506/anti-intellectualism-is-killing-america

Moyers, B. 2010. *Bill Moyers Journal*, PBS transcript. Retrieved July 9, 2016, from http://www.pbs.org/moyers/journal/04232010/transcript3.html

UNIT 2 READINGS

Everyday Sociology

Self and Society

Unit 2: Pathways and Culture

Dr. Sue to You: Metaphors, meaning, and snow

Recall that in Unit 1, Howard Becker emphasized that ideas of reality are socially constructed *representations*, mere reflections, not the "thing" itself (Becker 2007). Here, I hope to give you another tool to grapple with the complexities of abstract notions rather abruptly hoisted upon you in this intellectual journey. The tool is metaphor, a figure of speech that represents a thing, but never an exact replica of the thing. Metaphors often equate a material object with an abstraction, seeking to reveal hidden and even secretive elements. Yet again, Shakespeare provides an example that has influenced centuries of intellectual endeavors: in *As You Like It*, Shakespeare declares, "All the world's a stage" (Shakespeare, trans. 1914, II, VII, 1). This metaphor is closely aligned with dramaturgy as advanced by Mead and Garfunkel. The specific metaphor I offer for this DSTY post is "snow." The abstractions I hope to elucidate are two pillars of sociological thought: a) structure and b) interaction. This introduction should prepare you to relate more consciously to material in Unit 2.

In this case, structure and interaction are referred to as *tenor* (the subject), and snow is the *vehicle* (a temporary carrier of meaning). (For more on metaphors, see *Encyclopedia Britannica*, 2016.) Thus, metaphor establishes a relationship that is not only a creation, but also one of sharing; so too are structure and interaction harnessed together.

We begin with a story of imagination. Imagine that twenty-nine of us met in, oh, Lakewood, Colorado (the "snowiest city in the United States" for 2015–16), eager to share our quest to learn about *us*—the culture within and without *us*. In following our fantasy story, we find Lakewood nestled in the Rocky Mountains, between Denver and Colorado Springs, and sporting thirteen clear, blue mountain lakes—all without the hustle and bustle of metro areas. It features a designated Arts District that houses several artist studios, galleries, and a nonprofit photography school called Working with Artists (Lakewood.org 2016*)*. Sports fans will be excited to know that pro wrestler Steve "Dr. Death" Williams (sorry, no relation!) calls Lakewood home (Wikipedia 2016). It so happens that I know someone at the Colorado campus of The Ohio Center for Broadcasting, and I've taken the liberty of leasing a nice seminar room on the top floor of its eight-story, glass-enclosed contemporary art structure. Got the picture?

Returning to our meeting in Lakewood, we engaged in a day of readings, discussion, and experiential learning exercises, all designed to whet our sociological imagination. We watched *Lars and the Real Girl*, fascinated with its teachings about socialization. Time passed so quickly; when we turned on the lights after the movie, we suddenly realized that *aqilokoq* (Inuit for "softly falling snow") had been accumulating for quite some time. Unprepared, we decided to order pizza in and wait for passages to be cleared. After more games and a little horseplay, we fell asleep in sundry places and positions.

A little stiff but in good spirits, we awoke about 5 a.m. and looked around the expansive run of glass-enclosed walls, at once captivated and a little unnerved by what we saw: Snow. Everywhere. No streets or sidewalks or signs of life in sight. A pure blanket of white, puffy snow. A recon group traipsed down the hall to raid the vending machines, and we all munched on powdered doughnuts, cold Pop-Tarts, and soda. With nothing else to do here, we headed back down for a little nap.

When we awoke again, about 11 a.m. (it was a long nap), guess what we saw? People. Lots of people. But even more evident, we observed new but distinct paths in the snow—not necessarily following the pre-made sidewalks, but tracks and passages and trails in the campus below, usually angled from one building's door to another. Some paths were a little more traveled than others, but clear-cut patterns emerged, providing a literal artery of passageways to direct "passengers" along this circuit of a little society.

By now, it should become evident to you that pathways in the snow represent structures of a social system—formed by patterns of behavior over time, with some scope and permanence. Structures do not simply appear for no reason; they are forged by people in action, for some purpose(s), and under certain conditions. We call these human actions and purposeful activity *agency*. The more entrenched the path, the more evident it has served many agents, more purposes, for longer periods. Pathways, with varying turns and twists and traits, become built institutions (family, religion, politics, economy), which also manifest institutional features (ethnocentrism, racism, sexism, homophobia, classism, ableism). Over time, these features become stubbornly fixed (institutionalized) and highly resistant to change. Sure, some brave pioneer or rebel may venture "off the beaten path," but for substantial change to occur, a crisis accompanied by a dedicated collective of people is essential. Veering off the (snow) path requires great initiative (it's cold and uncomfortable), determination (it's hard and tiring), and sustained effort.

And so, these structures of our social world become entrenched and compulsory. But that has nothing to do with you, you say? You did not participate? To the contrary, if we set one foot in that existing pathway (racism, for example), haven't we just upheld the institution? Made it a bit more hardened and secure? Contributing to these paths does not necessarily command conscious intent. By stepping into the pathway, at the very least, we participate in a system that manifests consequences, and we fail to divert to a different choice. We all participate, one way or another.

In terms of change, only a bulldozer could upend snow paths and forge new ones. Revolution?

Just as Shakespeare began this little journey with the life/stage metaphor, he also offered more life lessons about "the world": "Life is a dream in which we can never be sure of what's real and what isn't. Prospero believes that the world will one day disappear into thin air, just as dreams do" (*The Tempest, A Midsummer Night's Dream*).

Just as Shakespeare advises, life is much more ephemeral than we might think. Similarly, the snow metaphor is not a perfect representation of interaction and structure. But I hope it has given you reason to pause and consider—to work toward understanding and exploring one kind of thing in terms of another. That's the work of a good metaphor.

I do want to point to an obvious flaw in the snow metaphor—no mention of power and control. In this case, who has best access to pathways and who is blocked or diverted? Who is best served? Reiman and Leighton (2012) used the oxygen metaphor to reveal how and why workers are exploited for their labor while huge corporations reap the rewards. (Consider this social fact: in 1965, the average CEO earned twenty times that of the average worker; today the differential is more than three hundred times (Mishel and David 2015)). Yet typical citizens do not view the labor

market as exploitive or oppressive; we are conditioned to believe it is "free choice." But if we view oxygen (not labor) as the commodity being marketed, we see that the oxygen-owner holds conditions over the heads of anyone who needs oxygen to survive. The oxygen owner (corporations, primarily) controls price, conditions, and supply. The consumer (worker) has little choice but to comply, or die. Power. It's almost always about who gets what, and at whose expense.

As you read "Culture and Everyday Life," mundane, routine social habits may, it is hoped, become transparently obvious as we consider our individual part in a social system of power and distribution. Try other metaphors and tools of inquiry as well—turn the rock over, examine the other side, the context beneath, the lines in the sand. Discover the taken-for-granted qualities of our culture, because, as Inglis (2005) explains, "everyday life contains within it more significance than we might think." Culture, after all, represents "our whole way of life."

"Us, It, and Social Interaction" gets even more complex, if possible. Here we are asked to deeply explore the actual construction of *SELF*—not our body, or

Man with Guitar, cultural symbols around the world 2015

brain, or personal proclivities—but *SELF* as "an *idea* we have about our own existence" (Johnson 2014). Because we act as though it is real, it gathers real consequences. What could be more profound?

DSTY TIP: Keep your eyes on the (sociological) prize in this unit. Resist the temptation to think of *self* as only individual; self is *relational* … for the reality we create, in interaction with one another, is also decidedly repetitive and lasting; it is structural and provides statuses, roles, and the generalized other (Becker 2007).

Works Cited

Becker, H. S. (2007). *Telling about society*. Chicago: University of Chicago Press.

Encyclopedia Britannica. (2016). "Tenor and vehicle." Retrieved September 1, 2016, from https://www.britannica.com/art/tenor-literature

Inglis, D. (2005). *Culture and everyday life*. New York, NY: Routledge.

Johnson, A. (2014). "Us, it, and social interaction." In *The forest and the trees: Sociology as life, practice, and promise*. Philadelphia, PA: Temple University Press.

Lakewood.org. (2016). Lakewood, Colorado. Retrieved September 1, 2016, from https://www.lakewood.org/default.aspx#feature=news

Mishel, L., and Davis, A. (2015, June 21). "Top CEOs make 300 times more than typical workers." Economic Policy Institute, Issue Brief #300. Retrieved September 1, 2016, from http://www.epi.org/publication/top-ceos-make-300-times-more-than-workers-pay-growth-surpasses-market-gains-and-the-rest-of-the-0-1-percent/

Reiman, J., and Leighton, P. (2012). *The rich get richer and the poor get prison: Ideology, class, and criminal justice*. 10th ed. New York, NY: Routledge.

Shakespeare, W. 1914. "As You Like It." *The Oxford Shakespeare*, W. J. Craig, ed. London: Oxford University Press.

Wikipedia. (2016). Lakewood, Colorado. Retrieved September 1, 2016, from https://en.wikipedia.org/wiki/Lakewood,_Colorado

READING 1

CULTURE AND EVERYDAY LIFE

BY DAVID INGLIS

Nothing seems more transparently obvious than our day-to-day activities. All of us spend our days doing things that are so routine and mundane that it hardly seems worth talking about them—getting up, cleaning one's teeth, showering, making a cup of coffee, walking the dog, taking children to school, saying hello to the neighbors, travelling to work, watching daytime TV, taking papers to the photocopy room at work, having a quick lunch, returning home, watching evening TV, going to bed. All of these sorts of activities plus a million and one other equally banal things are the stuff from which our everyday lives are made.

Everyone's everyday life is in certain senses unique to them. But in another way, most people have the same sorts of everyday experiences, making the routines of everyday life not just "common" in the sense of mundane but also in the sense of shared by most, if not all, people.

If someone was to ask us to describe our daily lives, we might be hard pressed to find anything to talk about that we might say was at all interesting, because daily life suggests routine, and "routine" by definition involves things that are not out of the ordinary. If pressed to describe what I did yesterday, I might try to find some things that made yesterday a little bit different from other days just like it. I might mention, for example, that the bus I get to work was twenty minutes late, leaving me standing in the cold for much longer than I would have liked. If I was pressed further to describe in great detail what I did on a certain day—as sometimes is requested of witnesses in court cases—I would probably in a rather embarrassed way describe when I got out of bed and how grumpy I felt about that, exactly how long it took me to brush my teeth, what type of toothpaste I used, how diligently I brushed, and hundreds of other tiny and apparently wholly insignificant details that I would feel could hardly be of any interest to anybody, not even myself (Sumner, 1961 [1906]).

The point here is that when someone is called to reflect upon and describe their everyday existences, not only is the point of doing that probably somewhat obscure to them, but also that it is rather difficult to put into words what one takes for granted every single day of one's life. Asking people to reflect upon activities they rarely, if ever, reflect upon, can make them unsure as to what to say and how to put into words things that they generally never vocalize. As Giddens (cited at Tomlinson, 1997: 174) puts it:

> We live day-to-day lives in which for most of what we do we can't give any reason. We dress as we do, we walk around as we do [and do innumerable other everyday things] ... these things are part of a tissue of day-to-day social activity which really isn't explained. It's hard to say why we do these things except that they're there and we do them.

Society and the Everyday

If everyday life is so banal, why should we want to study it? The answer to that question is: *because everyday life contains within it more significance than we might think.* As Georg Simmel (1950: 413) put the point, "even the most banal externalities of life" are expressions of the wider social and cultural order

All human beings have everyday lives—the banal run of everyday experiences is shared by all humans across the planet. But my own everyday life as a relatively privileged, white middle class man will in some ways be rather different from, say, a Black working class woman. While we will both share the same basic routine experiences—waking up, preparing for the day, doing things during the day, eating, sleeping—that woman's version of those experiences may be very different from my own. She may have to rise at 5 in the morning to go to work, her work may be back-breaking and unrewarding, both mentally and financially. If she fails to get to work on time, she might face all sorts of sanctions, including being sacked.

My everyday routine as a university professor, by contrast, means that on days when I am not teaching, I can turn up at the office any time that I please, and if I don't appear at all then no one will really notice. And my work is far from being back-breaking, even if it involves the stress of missed publishing deadlines and the fear of boring students in lectures.

The point then is this: different people have different sorts of everyday lives; the sorts of everyday routines and activities they engage in depends on their social position; understanding how everyday life is structured for particular people requires understanding how the society in which they live is itself structured and organized. Quite simply, if we want to understand everyday life thoroughly, beyond seeing it just as a mass of dull and unremarkable activities, we have to understand how wider society and social structures make it the way it is for different sorts of people. Conversely, we cannot understand how a society, or a particular part of it, works unless we understand what goes on in everyday life for different groups of people. Sociology is the study of "society" and "social relations." Thus understanding the deeper significances of everyday life requires a sociological comprehension of the social contexts in which different sorts of everyday experiences happen, sociological understanding often seeking to go beyond the level of particular persons' perspectives and perceptions, to get at "deeper" and more hidden aspects of social structure and organisation. On the other hand, just as everyday life can tell us a great deal about society, it follows that the study of everyday life has much to teach the sociologist about how particular societies and specific aspects of those societies operate. Sociology can inform us about everyday life just as everyday life can enrich sociological knowledge, fleshing out general ideas and theories with a wealth of details and specificities.

Culture and the Everyday

However, it is not enough just to think about the connections between "society" (and "social structures," "social institutions," "social systems," and so on) on the one side, and everyday activities on the other. No human society can exist without the people within it having certain ideas, values, norms, beliefs and ways of thinking. Another way of saying that is that every society is in part made up of, runs on the basis of, and requires, "culture." Humans, unlike (many but not all) animals, are cultural beings (de Waal, 2002). What I mean is that humans do possess certain basic "in-built" and thus "natural" dispositions, like the capacity to communicate through language. But humans are not totally genetically "hard-wired" to think and act in certain ways. Unlike a lion, for example, which is instinctually predisposed to act out a limited range of behaviors, humans are not as restricted. When a lion sees an animal it regards as prey, it will be disposed to hunt it. Humans, however, do not respond automatically to particular stimuli. How they respond to it depends upon the set of ideas and attitudes—the culture—that they have been socialized into by the society and/or the particular social group they were raised within.

This means that someone brought up in one cultural context could respond to a particular thing or situation in a manner somewhat, or indeed very, different from someone brought up in another cultural context. In all places around the world where there are lions, they do very much the same sort of things. Humans too all across the world do the same kinds of things—eat, sleep, defecate, make love and so on. But the *specific ways* in which they do those things, and the manners in which they *think about* those things, vary from one society to another and from one cultural context to another. Sometimes the differences between two contexts may be very small, sometimes it may be very great. In some societies, for example, the culture is such that one can defecate and urinate in public and no one will be bothered very much, but in other societies the "toilet culture" (i.e. the ideas about how to manage urination and defecation) is such that people are appalled about such activities happening in the public eye. Lions and most other animals are not very concerned about how they void their bodily wastes. Humans, however, can be very bothered indeed about such things; but not all humans are. How a particular group thinks about and does certain things is a function not of instinct but of the culture of the group (Mead, 1938).

The upshot of all this for the understanding of everyday life is that it is not just the social position of a person that structures their everyday activities but also the cultural conditions they operate within too. The cultural conditions each person works within are, in complex modern societies, multiple and overlapping. At the most general level, we can talk about ideas, notions, dispositions and ways of thinking and feeling that are pervasive throughout all Western societies (for example, an emphasis on the importance and autonomy of the individual). We can also investigate how people's activities are related to national and regional cultures (e.g. how Protestant ideas continue to be present, albeit perhaps in disguised forms, in Scandinavia just as Catholic attitudes still are influential in many parts of Southern

Europe). At a more concrete level, we can look at how being part of a social class, an ethnic group, a professional grouping and other sorts of social belonging and affiliation, can have ramifications for how people operate in their everyday affairs, as each of these sorts of social collectivity have identifiable cultural traits. This would also be the case for different sorts of jobs and occupations, as each of these can have attached to it particular sets of attitudes, expectations and norms. Finally, at the most specific level, we could examine the ways in which the "cultures" of particular cities and towns, communities and neighborhoods, places and spaces can help to create what a person experiences as their daily business. For all of these levels of "culture," we would have to see how they intersected with "society," with the social structures and institutions which can have such a great effect on how everyday affairs are lived.

Thinking About "Culture"

To understand how culture and everyday activities are related to each other, we need to be clear from the outset what is meant by "culture" and how it might be thought about. As almost everyone who has ever written anything about culture has observed, it can mean a lot of things, some of which complement each other and some of which do not. In the early 1950s, for example, the American anthropologists Alfred Kroeber and Clyde Kluckhohn (1963 [1952]) undertook a review of all the diverse meanings of "culture" in the available literature. They found 164 separate definitions of what the word "culture" could refer to.

In the same vein, the British literary scholar Raymond Williams (1976) noted in a well-known passage that "culture" was one of the most complicated words in the English language, in that it possessed a wide range of meanings that had changed a lot over time. The main meanings of "culture" he identified as predominant in the present day were

1. "high culture," a meaning related to the words "art" and "civilization"
2. personal refinement; such as when we talk of a "cultured person"
3. cultural objects and products, such as books, films, and TV shows
4. the "whole way of life" of a given group of people; such as when we say "working class culture" or "Japanese culture." This meaning involves defining "culture" as all the ways of thinking, understanding, feeling, believing and acting "characteristic" of a particular group (and thus *not* characteristic of other groups). Such dispositions have been learned, "socialized" (or "enculturated") into an individual by being brought up as children within a particular group.

Therefore "culture" can refer to either "high culture" or "popular culture"; the ways of thinking and feeling characteristic of everyone in a given group or society, or the capacities of individuals; the attitudes and habits of the many or of the few. In sum, "culture" is a word that has a lot of work to do in the English language, because it is used to describe so many different things. This can lead to great confusion. Such a situation demands that when we talk about "culture" we make clear exactly what meaning of it we have in mind.

I will now set out what I take to be the most general aspects of "culture," conceived in Williams's fourth and most general definition of it, namely as the "whole way of life" of a given group of people.

1. *Culture comprises the patterns of ideas, values and beliefs common to a particular group of people, their "characteristic" ways of thinking and feeling.*

It does not matter whether the group is small or large, or whether it comprises a set of people within a particular "society," or everyone within that society, or people from different societies related to each other in some way across "national" boundaries. Culture is defined as being part of the collective life of given groups of human beings.

Culture comprises recurring patterns of ideas, values and beliefs. A "culture" persists to some extent over time. It has some capacities to endure over time, as well as to change and be changed.

2. *The culture of one group differentiates it from other groups, each of which has its "own" culture.*

Different types of group can be said to have "their own" cultures: the culture of a "nation" (e.g. German culture, Irish culture), of a social class (e.g. working class culture, middle class culture), of an ethnic group within a nation (e.g. Mexican–American culture), of a group outside the "mainstream" culture (e.g. a youth subculture of punks, a "criminal" subculture). Each of these types of group can be said to have *its own* culture, its own distinctive (or relatively distinctive) set of ideas, values and beliefs.

This is not, though, to claim that there are no overlaps between "different" cultures, and no elements that they might share (e.g. working class culture in the United States is part of, and shares many of the features of, more general "American" culture).

3. *Culture contains meanings. Culture is meaningful.*

These meanings are the ways through which people in the group understand, make sense of, and respond intellectually and emotionally to, the world around them.

This aspect of culture has been particularly stressed by those thinkers who have been influenced by the ideas of the 18th century German philosopher Immanuel Kant, the Kantian tradition being perhaps the mainstream way of thinking about culture in the social sciences. For example, it is a Kantian approach that animates the classical sociologist Emile Durkheim's view that a particular culture is made up of a set of *collective representations* (Durkheim and Mauss, 1969 [1903]). A particularly important set of classifications that Durkheim (2001 [1912]) identified were the ways in which each particular culture classifies things into two categories, the "sacred" on the one hand (things that are seen to be "holy," special, and literally extra-ordinary) and the "profane" (the opposite of sacred things, things that are defined as everyday, routine and ordinary) on the other.

While all cultures according to Durkheim divide things in the world up in this way, each culture has its on distinctive understandings of what fits into each category. What is regarded as "special" in one cultural context could be regarded as not at all special in another. This leads to the conclusion that there is some variance among different groups of people, living at different times and in different places, as to what counts as part of "profane" everyday life, which is the opposite of "sacred" special occasions. As Alvin Gouldner (1975) notes, different societies have had somewhat different ideas as to what counts as "everyday life." However, all of them presumably define the "everyday" as involving things that happen on a day-to-day basis and that are not especially marked out and defined as somehow "out of the ordinary."

Also in a Kantian vein, the German classical sociologist Max Weber (cited at Turner, 1996: 5) defined culture as "a finite segment of the meaningless infinity of the world process, a segment on which human beings confer meaning and significance." Both Weber and Durkheim are saying much the same thing in different ways: the culture of a group makes sense of the world for people in a particular group; culture is the framework through which they experience and understand the world around them. Humans therefore can be seen as having no direct access to "reality"; instead, their reality is thoroughly shaped by culture (Berger and Luckmann, 1967), especially through the means of the categories of the particular language they use. Culture and language are very closely connected; the way a language "carves up" reality and endows it with meaning, profoundly shapes the ways people who use that language understand things (Saussure, 1959 [1906–11])

4.   *The ideas, values and beliefs of a group are profoundly implicated in motivating people to act in certain ways.*

Max Weber's definition of sociology was "the interpretive understanding of social action" (cited at Alexander, 1983: 30). What this means is that sociology is concerned with how certain values, ideas and beliefs—that is, cultural forms—motivate people to act in the ways that they do. Functionalist sociology, at its most sophisticated in the work of the mid-20th century American sociologist Talcott Parsons (1961), looks not only at the culturally-motivated nature of people's activities, but also at how larger-scale social systems require people to act in certain ways and how such systems motivate individuals to act in those ways. As Parsons (1961: 963) puts it, "the structure of cultural meanings constitutes the 'ground' of any system of action." That is to say, culture is made up of more general values, which generate specific norms, which in turn guide people to act in ways that are in line with the "needs" of the wider social structures in which they operate.

5.   *The ideas, values and beliefs of a group are embodied in symbols and artifacts.*

These symbols can be pictorial (that is, can take the form of pictures) or can be part of a written language.

These artifacts are physical objects which are imprinted in some way with the ideas, values and beliefs of the group.

6.   *Culture is learned.*

Culture is transmitted by one generation of people in a particular social group to the next generation.

This learning process means that individuals internalize the ideas, values and beliefs of the group. These become habitual and taken-for-granted, and are generally experienced as "natural" rather than learned. This raises the issue of culturally-shaped "life-worlds," which we will examine on the next page.

7. *Culture is arbitrary.*

Culture is "arbitrary" in the sense that it the result primarily of human activities, rather than wholly the product of "nature." As culture is not completely "natural," but is instead made by human beings, it follows that it can change and be changed. Culture can always potentially be somewhat different in the future from the way it is currently. In essence, culture is mutable, even if some particular cultures can last a relatively long time.

8. *Culture and forms of social power are intimately bound up with each other.*

An influential stream of thought within sociology, that includes both Marxism and Weberianism, sees culture as always being shaped and influenced in one way or another by powerful institutions and groups in a society, whether individuals in those groups are fully aware of this or not. For Karl Marx (at McLellan, 1984: 184), the dominant culture in a society is associated with, and generated by, the ruling class(es) in that society: As he put it: "The ideas of the ruling class are in every epoch the ruling ideas: i.e. the class which is the ruling *material* force of society, is at the same time its ruling *intellectual* force." Culture on this view is synonymous with "ideology." It helps to reproduce the power of dominant classes by defining reality in ways that suit their interests. For Weber, while culture is not fully *reducible* to forms of social power, it is closely connected to them. For the late 20th century French thinker Michel Foucault (1981), different languages ("discourses") not only define the world in certain ways, but define it in ways that serve the interests and reflect the power of certain groups e.g. the language used by psychologists to define and deal with mental patients acts as a form of control by psychologists over the latter group.

Overall, a simple, brief characterization of "culture" would see as it involving *what different groups of people each believe, think and feel.*

Defamiliarizing the Familiar

How might we go about examining the ways in which cultural forces, together with social factors, influence, shape and structure our everyday activities? A key aspect of both sociological and anthropological responses to this question is to emphasize that one must take what is routine and very familiar, and try to defamiliarize oneself with it, making it seem strange and peculiar, rather than ordinary and banal.

We might usefully call the everyday circumstances in which we live the "life-world." This was a term coined by the German philosopher Edmund Husserl towards the beginning of the twentieth century. By "life-world," Husserl (1970: 380–1) meant "the always taken-for-granted ... the world that is constantly pre-given ... the world of which we are all conscious in life as the world of us all." What he meant by this was that human life can only function if the individual person has a certain sense of stability and certainty as to the world around them. We need routines and habits in order for us to function, because if everything in the world around about us kept coming as a surprise to us, as totally novel and unprecedented, we would have no bearings in life, we would be constantly dazed and confused (Sumner, 1961 [1906]: 1037). To use more modern terminology, the individual needs a certain sense of psychological security, to the effect that the world around him or her seems to be relatively predictable and understandable and is not just totally chaotic (Giddens, 1991). We need a sense of routine and stability in our everyday lives. That sense, for each person, is their life-world, their perception and experience of the orderliness and relative stability of the world around them.

However, we cannot just talk about each single person's life-world. Life-worlds are also shared; they involve expectations and ideas about, and orientations towards, the world that are shared by the members of a particular group. These groups could be akin to the ones mentioned above—nations, classes, ethnic groups and so on. In other words, the life-world for each group is shaped by the culture of the group. The life-world of a person is made up of all the intersecting cultural forces of the various different groups they belong to, and is structured by the social contexts they operate within.

The central characteristic of any life-world is its pre-reflective, taken-for-granted nature. People exist for the most part in their life-world like fish exist in water. So "natural" does the life-world seem for each person, they do not generally experience it as anything other than just "the way things are." It is only in certain situations that one can be forced out of one's life-world, where all one's routine expectations about life crumble (e.g. when a "respectable" citizen is arrested by the police for a serious crime, a situation they might find incredibly traumatic, a time when all their usual routines and ways of thinking are disrupted and challenged). As the life-world is shaped by cultural forces, but these are generally not experienced as anything but "natural," we can say that we all exist "in culture" but we are generally not aware of that fact. Thus when we are defamiliarizing ourselves with our everyday routines, what we are doing is, as it were, "escaping" from the life-world and coming to look at it "from the outside," as if it were foreign to us. We come to see the oddities and peculiarities of our life-world, as if we were looking at the thoughts and activities of a group of people who live in ways very alien to us. Just as other people's "culture" often seems very odd to us, defamiliarization means coming to see our own life-world, which we generally never realize is anything other than "natural," as not "natural" at all—we come to see that it is just *one way* of thinking and acting among a whole series of possible other ways.

Defamiliarizing your own life-world can be more difficult than investigating the nature and contours of someone else's life-world, because it is generally easier to spot the oddities and specificities of another person's way of life than one's own. Looking at the life-worlds of people who lived in the past is a good way of seeing how cultural forces, that they themselves were generally unaware of, shaped their everyday attitudes and routines. Here for example is an entry from the diary of the English diarist Samuel Pepys (2003: 87–88), dated Saturday 20th October, 1660, describing his activities in his hometown of London on that particular day:

> This morning [some]one came to me to advise with me where to make me a window into my cellar in lieu [i.e. in place] of one which ... had [been] stopped up, and going down into my cellar to look I stepped into a great heap of turds by which I found that Mr. Turner's house of office [toilet] is full and comes into my cellar, which do trouble me, but I shall have it helped. To my Lord's [the Earl of Sandwich, Pepys' former employer] by land, calling at several places about business, where I dined with my Lord and Lady; when he was very merry, and did talk very high how he would have a French cook, and a master of his horse ... among other things, my Lady saying that she could get a good merchant for her daughter Jem., he answered, that he would rather see her with a pedlar's pack at her back,

so she married a gentleman, than she should marry a citizen. This afternoon, going through London, and calling at Crowe's the upholster's, in Saint Bartholomew's, I saw the limbs of some of our new traitors set upon Aldersgate, which was a sad sight to see; and a bloody week this and the last have been, there being ten hanged, drawn, and quartered. Home, and after writing a letter to my uncle by the post, I went to bed.

For Samuel Pepys, writing in England in the latter half of the seventeenth century, all the things he describes were part of his everyday routine and seemed to him totally "normal." But for us today, living within different life-worlds, centred around somewhat different expectations and attitudes than those of Pepys's time and place, we can spot the specific cultural forces that shaped Pepys' everyday routines. On that particular Saturday, Pepys found that his neighbor's toilet facilities had spilled into his cellar. Pepys lived more than two hundred years before water-flushed toilets became the norm in England, so he has rather different attitudes as to finding a great pile of excrement ["turds"] in one's basement than you or I might today; people then were much less concerned about such matters, whereas today we have become much more intensely disgusted by human wastes. Pepys's life-world was such that, while he did say that the mess "do trouble me," he could go on to note with a shrug that "I shall have it helped," by getting workmen to come and fix the problem. A person living today, living in a cultural situation of much greater intolerance of toiletry matters, would likely not have responded to the situation in such an unconcerned way as did Samuel Pepys.

Other things can strike us as rather peculiar about the events of Pepys's particular Saturday, and the culturally-based attitudes that underpinned it. The routine talk about servants seems odd in a present-day context where widespread use of domestic servants has all but disappeared, except for the very rich. The snobbery of the Earl of Sandwich as to whom his daughter should marry—a real upper class "gentlemen" rather than a mere middle class "citizen"—also strikes us as peculiar in these apparently more egalitarian times of ours. In the same vein, while Pepys records that there have been quite a lot of public executions recently, he does not think that seeing the corpses of those who have been executed ["hung, drawn and quartered"] in the middle of London is very out of the ordinary. In a world like our own, where death is generally hidden away behind the professional screens of the medic and the mortician, such a sight would involve great unease and disgust, as well as possibly outrage about the nature of executions carried out by the government. But all of these things were quite normal in the life-world of Samuel Pepys, a condition he lived within without being reflectively aware of it, just as today we operate within culturally and socially shaped contexts we do not generally experience as anything other than the "normal" routine of life.

Approaching Culture and the Everyday

How do we get access to *"culture" in the "everyday"* and the *"everyday" aspects of "culture"*? Raymond Williams (1980 [1961]: 66) gives us a useful start in this direction. He defines culture as possessing three interrelated levels:

> There is the *lived culture* of a particular time and place, only fully accessible to those living in that time and place. There is the recorded culture, of every kind, from art to the most

everyday facts: the culture of a period. There is also, as the factor connecting lived culture and period cultures, the *culture of the selective tradition* [italics added].

The *lived culture* is made up of the ways in which a group, or groups, of people thought and felt at a particular time and place. As Williams says, in a certain way only those who were or are part of the group can know fully what it was like to live in that way (although the notion of "life-world" suggests that people tend more just to exist "inside" the lived culture than to think reflectively about it). How then can outsiders know about that lived culture?

Williams' other two levels of culture can help us in that regard. In the first place, the *culture of the selective tradition* is what is conventionally known as "high culture," the "art" and "great works" that (certain) people in a certain context have defined as being somehow more "special" than, and superior to, other forms of culture. In modern Western societies, this set includes works by the likes of great artists such as Shakespeare and Picasso, the creative works that are regarded as being the very best of their type. It is possible to see represented or imprinted in these some of the *lived culture* of the time and place in which they were created: Shakespeare's plays can be seen as, in a way, records of the customs, attitudes and ways of life in early 16th century England. We can get some sort of access to the lived culture—although obviously in a very indirect and possibly somewhat distorted fashion—through the "art" of that time and place.

The *recorded culture* of a group living at a particular time and place also allows some access to the lived culture. It encompasses all the things that record in some way how people thought and felt, not just "artworks" but everything from newspapers, films and other mass media products like posters and adverts, to bureaucratic records and official papers, to more intimate documents like personal diaries and written reminiscences. These cultural texts can give us an indirect insight into the lived culture, although obviously we have to be on our guard against thinking that what we read or view necessarily must truly represent the culture of a given time and place (Plummer, 2001). The best we can do is be skeptical about what people and records say, and never fully assume that a written or any other type of record of an everyday event totally captures what a particular event "really" was like. Any recollection of an event is both partial and created by a person with a particular way of looking at and judging things, a way of looking that is partly personal to them and partly a product of their "culture." We must be aware that all cultural texts are always created from a particular partial perspective and for particular purposes. "Everyday events" cannot be comprehensively captured and set down on paper; but what we can do is get sideways glimpses of them, partial and limited perspectives of their overall complexity and abundance.

There are other means of investigating culture and the everyday than looking at "high" and "recorded" culture, if one is dealing with people alive in the present day. Such methods include observation, participant observation and ethnography, all of which have benefits and drawbacks (Bryman, 2001). It would be a mistake to think that any of them can provide us with totally unproblematic and unmediated knowledge of everyday life and the role(s) of culture within it. As the French sociologist Pierre Bourdieu (1990: 150–55) notes, how we as social scientists construct sociological understandings of people "out there" in the "real world," the ways in which we comprehend their mundane existences, are always bound up with both our own personal dispositions and the politics of academic life. One's own social class, ethnicity, gender-orientation and other forms of social background can very much impact on how we talk about and evaluate others. We therefore have to be very aware of how our representations of "everyday life" and "culture" can reflect our own biases, likes and dislikes, and attitudes.

As an academic discipline concerned to find broad patterns of human behavior, sociology is generally in the business of stereotyping people. For the most part this is a very necessary and useful exercise—we need to draw generalisations about people so we can see general trends and not just stick at the level of particularities. We need to be able to see the forest, not just the particular trees within it. But it is absolutely crucial to remember, especially when studying "everyday life," that each person's life is both expressive of wider social and cultural forces *and* also specific and unique to them in certain ways too. Finding a balanced way of representing this fact is at the heart of good sociological thinking and research.

Discussion Questions

1. Why might it be useful to study people's everyday lives from a sociological perspective?
2. In what ways does culture shape a person's everyday activities?
3. Which cultural forces are important in shaping your own everyday life?
4. Which cultural forces might be important in structuring the everyday routines of college students?
5. In what ways might culture and forms of social power be connected?

References

Alexander, J. C. (1983) *Theoretical Logic in Sociology, Vol. III. The Classical Attempt At Theoretical Synthesis: Max Weber,* London: Routledge

Berger, P. L. and Luckmann, T. (1967) *The Social Construction of Reality,* New York: Anchor

Bourdieu, P (1990) *In Other Words,* Cambridge: Polity

Bryman, A. (2001) *Social Research Methods,* Oxford: Oxford University Press

de Waal, F. (2002) *The Ape and the Sushi Master,* Harmondsworth: Penguin

Durkheim, E. (2001 [1912]) *The Elementary Forms of the Religious Life,* Oxford: Oxford University Press

Durkheim, E. and Mauss, M. (1969 [1903]) *Primitive Classification,* London: Cohen and West

Foucault, M. (1981) *The History of Sexuality,* Vol I, Harmondsworth: Penguin

Giddens, A. (1991) *Modernity and Self-Identity,* Cambridge: Polity

Gouldner, A. (1975) "Sociology and the Everyday Life," in Lewis A. Coser (ed.) *The Idea of Social Structure: Papers in Honor of Robert K. Merton,* New York: Harcourt Brace Jovanovich, pp. 417–432

Husserl, E. (1970) *The Crisis of European Sciences and Transcendental Phenomenology,* David Carr (trans.), Evanston: Northwestern University Press

Kroeber, A. L. and Kluckhohn, C. (1963 [1951]) *Culture: a critical review of concepts and definitions,* New York, Random Ho., 1963.

Mead, G. H. (1938) *Philosophy of the Act,* Chicago: University of Chicago Press

McLellan, D. (1984) *The Thought of Karl Marx,* Basingstoke: Macmillan

Parsons, T. (1961) "Introduction—Part Four—Culture and the Social System," in Parsons, Talcott et al (eds.) *Theories of Society*, Vol. II, Glencoe: Free Press

Pepys, S. (2003) *The Diary of Samuel Pepys—A Selection*, Robert Latham (ed.), Harmondsworth: Penguin

Plummer, K. (2001) *Documents of Life 2: An Invitation to Critical Humanism*, London: Sage

Saussure, F. ([1906–11] 1959) *Course in General Linguistics*, Charles Bally and Albert Sechehaye (eds.), New York: Philosophical Library

Simmel, G. (1950) "Metropolis and Mental Life" in *The Sociology of Georg Simmel*, Kurt H. Wolff trans. and ed., New York: The Free Press

Sumner, W. G. (1961 [1906]) "On the Mores" in Talcott Parsons et al (eds.) *Theories of Society*, Vol. II, Glencoe: Free Press

Tomlinson, J. (1997) *Cultural Imperialism: A Critical Introduction*, London: Pinter

Turner, B. (1996) *For Weber: essays on the sociology of fate*, London: Sage

Williams, R. (1976) *Keywords: a vocabulary of culture and society*, Glasgow: Fontana

———(1980 [1961]) *The Long Revolution*, Harmondsworth: Penguin

READING 2

US, IT, AND SOCIAL INTERACTION

BY ALLAN JOHNSON

Having spent four chapters on social systems, those things larger than ourselves that we participate in, it's time to look more closely at the 'we' and what our participation is all about. Social systems do not happen without us, and, in important ways, we do not happen without them. On the one hand, systems contain paths of least resistance, but we are the ones who perceive, interpret, and choose among those paths. We make visible and manifest whatever power they have to shape social life. On the other hand, we live as thinking, acting beings, and yet the stuff that thoughts are made of and the meaning of our actions make sense only in relation to cultural, structural, and ecological aspects of social systems.

Self: The I Who Participates

"Take care of yourself," a friend of mine says at the end of a conversation. As I return to this work, I wonder just what that means. Who or what is this self I'm supposed to take care of, and is the 'I' who takes care of that self something other than the self that gets taken care of? Is my self something I can touch, hear, or smell? I can sense my body and what it does, but my self is more than that.

Behavioral psychologists, such as B. F. Skinner, have little interest in the self, since they cannot figure out a way to observe it scientifically.[1] And yet we think about the self as something real and thinglike that is responsible for what we do. When my 'body' does something wrong—as when my hand takes something that doesn't belong to me—no one blames my body, even though it did the deed. Nor do they blame my brain ("Bad brain!"), which directed my body to do it. They blame my self ("*You* should be ashamed of your*self*"). What that self is that I'm supposed to be ashamed of and where I am likely to find it are elusive things, because more than anything, the self is an *idea* we have about our own existence.[2] But it is a powerful idea, because we do not live it as such: we act as though the self is as real as anything we can see and touch.

Part of what makes the idea of the self so powerful is that it locates us in relation to other people and social systems. One answer to the question, 'Who am I?' is 'Allan Griswold Johnson,' three words that name me in the same way that words name an oak tree or a banana. They also serve a similar purpose. In my culture, they identify me as male (Allan being regarded as a man's name) and thereby distinguish me from females. They distinguish me from all the people I am not (except for those who have the same name). And they connect me to kin marked by common names—Griswold being my mother's family name and Johnson my father's. A person's name, then, and the self that it names have a purely *relational* purpose of marking us in relation to others. The only reason to have a name is to be able to participate in social life, and this is also why we develop ideas about the self in general and about our own selves in particular.

As philosopher and sociologist George Herbert Mead sees it, we discover ourselves as children through a process of discovering others and the ideas they have about themselves and about us.[3] Infants tend to experience the world in an egocentric way in that they cannot distinguish between the world and themselves. Everything is just one big whole, with them at the center of it all. This leaves them without a way to know that other people exist as separate people with thoughts and feelings. As an infant, I could not imagine that my mother had a point of view on things, including me. I could not see that she thought about herself in relation to me and me in relation to her or about things that had to do with neither at all. I could feel her body and otherwise sense what she did and said, but I had no way to know there was something going on beneath all that, that she had ideas about who she was or who I was or about how to be a good mother or what kind of man I would grow up to be or what to have for dinner.

If I could not imagine that my mother had a point of view on herself and the world, then I also could not imagine that I had a point of view on anything. As far as I could tell, the way I heard and felt and otherwise sensed things was simply the way things were and had nothing to do with who I was in relation to them or how I perceived or interpreted them. I was like a baseball umpire who, instead of saying, "I call 'em as I see 'em" or (confidently) "I call 'em as they *are*," says, "*Until* I call 'em, they *aren't.*"

As an infant, I could not be aware that I had a point of view on things, because I had no way to *think* about myself *as* a self, to imagine an 'Allan' who existed in the first place. Mead argues that we learn to think about ourselves as selves by discovering the inner lives of other people. We realize that other people think about us, perceive us in certain ways, expect things of us, have feelings about us, and have lives separate from our own that in many ways have nothing to do with us. This happens primarily when people use language to talk about themselves, us, and what *they* experience as reality. They use language as a bridge of meaning to connect their experience to the experiences of other people. When I was hungry, I might have experienced that as just a bodily discomfort, an empty feeling in my stomach that made me cry until it was taken care of. But when someone used words like 'I'm hungry' to describe that experience, then I could imagine how they felt and put myself in their place.

Without language, Mead argues, there is no way to be aware of that otherwise invisible realm known as the self, and without that, children have no way to construct their own ideas about who they are *as* selves. It is through language, then, that we discover the human *possibility* of a self by discovering what other people have done with that possibility. We become aware of our point of view *as* a point of view rather than as 'the way things are.'

Once we see this, we can construct all kinds of ideas about ourselves that make up the self. Because they are *about* the self, we use them to think about the self just as we would think about someone else (as in 'how to be your own best friend'). We can talk to it, have feelings about it, evaluate and judge it, believe in it or not, defend or condemn it, scold or praise it, feel proud or ashamed of it, 'get hold' of it, disown it ('I'm not myself today'), lose it, be conscious of it ('self-conscious') or not, or try to accept, understand, or 'get over' it. We can say and do things to affect how other people perceive us and how they treat us as a result. We can wade into deep pools of paradox, thinking of ourselves as unique and separate from the world around us, even though 'unique' is a cultural concept from that same world, and the self exists only in relation to other selves.

No wonder one of our most exhilarating experiences is when someone 'believes' in us. And no wonder one of the greatest crises we can experience happens when we stop 'believing in ourselves' and feel lost, cut loose with nothing to hang onto.

Note, however, that whether this experience turns into a crisis depends on the culture we live in. In many Asian cultures, thinking of the self as unique and separate from groups and society is neither a given nor an ideal of social life. In traditional Japanese culture, for example, it is a far greater crisis to lose a deep sense of attachment to the whole and be thrust from it into the uncertainties of the individual self.

To participate as selves in social systems, we have to locate ourselves in relation to them by seeing how and where we connect to them and how this reflects back a sense of who we are. Most people do not know that self my friend told me to take care of. What they do know about me are the statuses I occupy and the roles that go with them. At birth, we are known only by a handful of statuses—gender, race, age, and family position—because there is not much else about us to know. As we grow, we accumulate a social identity by occupying one status after another and using them to locate ourselves in relation to social systems and other people.

As Erving Goffman points out, when we occupy a status, the role that goes with it provides us with a ready-made self that we can adopt as a path of least resistance toward acceptance by others.[4] In this sense, most people know little about who we are on the inside. What they 'know' consists primarily of cultural images of the typical person who occupies this or that status—the typical girl, the typical student, the typical lawyer, the typical business manager, the typical politician. In social space, we are not 'who we are' in some absolute, objective sense. We are who people *think* we are, a reality they construct from cultural ideas before they know anything about us based on direct experience.

Most people, for example, know very little about the real me as I experience myself. But anyone who thinks they know about fathers, men, heterosexuals, white people, writers, grandfathers, brothers, husbands, public speakers, baby boomers, Ph.D. recipients, the middle class, and people whose households include dogs, goats, and a snake may think they know quite a lot about me. What they actually know, however, are paths of least resistance that go with statuses I occupy and the likelihood that I usually follow those paths. I may, in fact, choose quite differently, but they can't know that unless they see how I participate in social life.

Not only do other people know us primarily through role relationships, but this is also a major way for us to know ourselves. Think back for a moment to Mead's idea that we discover ourselves through first discovering others. If so, then it follows that how we see, evaluate, and feel about ourselves is shaped by the statuses we occupy, which means that as we construct the ideas and feelings about who we are that constitute the social self, we depend primarily on information that comes from outside ourselves.

These outside sources of information take the form of two kinds of 'others.' Significant others are specific people who act like mirrors, reflecting images back to us that we may incorporate into our sense of who we are.[5] 'Significant' in this case means 'specific' rather than important. If a man in the audience at one of my presentations comes up to me afterward and tells me he thinks I did a great job (or a rotten one), he becomes a significant other for me, because the information he gives comes from him as an individual. He also offers me a reflection of myself to consider as information that I may or may not include in my sense of who I am. This reflection is known as the 'looking-glass self': I use him as a mirror, and the reflection consists of what I *think* he thinks of me (which may or may not turn out to match how he actually sees me).[6]

Early in life, most information about ourselves comes from significant others, such as family members and play-mates. Only later through a complex process of socialization do we begin to grasp what is called the 'generalized other.'[7] The generalized other is not a specific person or even a group of people. It is our *perception* of how people in *general* view a social situation and the people who occupy different statuses within it.

When I go to my regular dentist, David, for a checkup, for example, I interact with someone I know as an individual. I know something about what he expects, what he's like as a person, and how he does things. This makes him a significant other to me. When I went to him for the first time, however, his name, gender, race, approximate age, and occupation were the only things I knew about him as an individual. How, then, did I know how to behave, and how did he? Without knowing each other, we had to rely on cultural ideas about dentists and their patients and what goes on between them. Until we learned about each other as significant others, these generalized others were all we had to put together some idea of what the *situation* was about and who he and I were in relation to each other. In the beginning, we knew only the statuses we occupied and the social relationship between them. In other words, we knew each 'other' only in a generalized way.

What makes the generalized other difficult for young children to grasp is that it's a purely abstract collection of ideas about status occupants. We learn what significant others expect from us by what they say and do, and children pick that up very quickly. But to distinguish between the specific woman who is my mother and 'mother' as a social status requires a level of cognitive ability that develops only as children mature.

The ideas that make up the generalized other are cultural, which encourages us to assume that we share their meanings with other people. On the basis of this belief, we also assume that people will perceive, interpret, and evaluate us in certain ways when they know which statuses we occupy. This is why people who are lesbian, gay, or bisexual may tend to be careful about revealing their sexual orientation to heterosexuals. It is also why heterosexuals feel no qualms at all about revealing theirs, to the extent that they do not experience it as revealing something at all, much less coming out or 'admitting' their sexual orientation. It is why it matters what clothes we wear when we go out in public, especially how we present ourselves as male or female, because such choices shape who other people think we are. This is why privilege and oppression based on race, gender, and disability status are so powerful. People think they know which status we occupy simply by looking at us or even just hearing our names, and, as a result, easily associate us with ideas about who we are, whether we are 'normal,' what we can and cannot do, what we are worth, and what our rights are in relation to them. In this sense, we need to extend the idea that we construct reality in a cultural sense (introduced in Chapter 2), for the reality we create is also profoundly structural in relation to statuses, roles, and the generalized other.

Since statuses and roles are elements of social systems, who we are—to ourselves and to other people—is profoundly rooted in our participation in systems and the socialization process through which we learn how to do it. This makes understanding ourselves a basic part of sociological practice and not merely the province of psychology. Statuses and roles connect us to the social world and overlap our lives with other people's lives. They locate, identify, and anchor us in social space. Without them, we do not exist in a social sense, and without that, there is little left of what we know and experience as a self or a life.

This can be a disturbing idea for people living in a culture that places a high value on being an autonomous and unique individual. But, in fact, it does not diminish our worth as people. It simply means that we (and our worth) exist in relation to something larger, that we are not the beginning and end of things. Even rebels and iconoclasts who reject society are organizing their sense of self and their lives in relation to something larger than themselves—the society they reject. And they occupy recognizable statuses within those societies, such as 'rebel' and 'iconoclast.' In most high schools and colleges, for example, a few students usually play the role of the 'nonconformist' who conforms to a cultural type by openly rejecting the idea of conforming to cultural types.

None of this means that we are nothing more than occupants of statuses and roles. Not only can we make creative choices about how to participate in social systems, but there are mysteries of human existence that are far more than social constructions. Every culture has *ideas* about such mysteries and about itself, but the best we can do with them is to construct reality second- or third-hand. Only in rare moments do we manage to shake ourselves loose from social systems and experience the mysteries of life and death more directly. But that experience can be enough to remind us that however we construct our sense of social life and ourselves, mystery piled upon mystery lie beneath it. We are not machines, and neither are social systems. Both are far more complex, elusive, and interesting than that.

Self in Systems

The key to how we participate in systems is the concept of social interaction, and the key to that is the difference between action and behavior. Everything we do is behavior, but only some behavior takes the form of action.

A baby girl's first step, for example, is a behavior but not an action. When she is older and walks across the room in response to someone saying, "Please come here," however, what she is doing is both a behavior and an action. The difference? In the first case, the behavior involves no interpretation on her part. She does not consider the meaning of what she is doing (and not doing) and how this behavior will be perceived and interpreted by someone else. She does not consider it because she lacks the language and abstract cultural ideas necessary for thinking about what she is doing or what other people expect of her and make of what she does. In the second case, she can use language to anticipate what her behavior would mean to someone else and then take this idea into account in choosing what to do. She can imagine alternatives and the most likely responses to each.

In short, behavior based on meaning is action, and actions are the building blocks of our participation in social systems and social life as we interact with other people.

On the level of individuals, interaction is the process through which social systems happen, but it is also how *we* happen as social beings. As Goffman puts it in several fascinating books, we are like actors on a stage.[8] Every social situation has its props and setting, its script and opportunities for improvisation. And every play has an audience, except that in social life we are all actors and part of someone else's audience at the same time.

As actors, we use a variety of techniques to have our performances seen as authentic, as worthy of the role we are playing, as being convincing enough for us to be accepted in that situation for who we claim to be. We usually make an effort to show up looking the part, for example, and wearing the right clothes, having the right attitude for the situation, knowing our lines, and carrying the right props. Like actors, we create impressions of who we are, what Goffman calls 'the presentation of self.'

Like every impression, the presentation of self is an ongoing process. It needs to be sustained and managed, especially when we do something that is 'out of character' or otherwise calls our performance into question. When two people go out on a date, for example, each spends time shaping the self they will present to the other—choosing what to wear, whether to shower or use deodorant or cologne, how to style their hair, the use of jewelry and makeup. Every action contributes to the impression they create—what they say and how they say it, what they order in the restaurant and how they eat it, when, how often, and how long they look at each other, and with what facial expression, what they laugh at and what they don't, how much they talk and how much they listen, and how and when they touch each other.

When they part company, each is likely to wonder about the impression made on the other, whether they said or did something that was misunderstood, taken to indicate something about the self that doesn't fit with how they see themselves or would like to be seen. Like players before an audience, as the curtain falls, they wait for the response, the volume and duration of applause, anything that might tell them how well their performance was accepted. On a date, it might be whether a kiss goodnight is forthcoming, or whether the "I had a great time" or "I'll call you" sounds sincere or merely polite (yet another way to manage impressions).

As in a play, both actors and audience in social life want everything to go as it's supposed to, because if it does not, it may compromise our own ability to play our roles effectively. Even as an audience for someone else's performance, we are never just that, for the audience has its role to play, too. This is why when actors in a theater forget their lines or otherwise ruin their performances, people in the audience often feel uncomfortable. The role of witness to someone else's failed performance is difficult to play, because the mere fact of our sitting there and watching it happen contributes to the actor's pain. We become part of the actor's failure, since if we were not there—if there were no audience—the failure could not happen.

And so we do what we can to protect the actor from failure. We don't call attention to the forgotten line, the stumble, the momentary lapse, the wooden delivery, but act as though it never happened, allowing the performance to continue with the hope that the people 'on stage' will 'get their act together.' In doing this, we protect them and ourselves as well as the integrity of the play in which we all participate. Both actors and audience have impressions to manage.

As actors, of course, there are many things we can do to protect our own performances. We can disown them with such disclaimers as "I was only kidding" or "I didn't mean it" or "I don't know what came over me." A man might say something sexist but then try to distance himself from it by saying that it doesn't mean that *he* is sexist. Or, as Goffman points out, he might react with embarrassment that lets people know that although his performance may have failed this time, he is still committed to doing better the next time around.[9] His red face and awkwardness show that he believes in the importance of what people expect of him, a display that may protect him by reinforcing his claim to the part he has in the play.

Looking at social life as theater might give us reason to wonder whether we have an authentic self at all, whether everything isn't just a cynical matter of figuring out how to make the best impression, protect performances, and play audience to someone else. The very idea of a role can seem to preclude the possibility of being authentic, as if creating impressions and trying to turn in an acceptable performance invariably mean faking it and wearing masks that conceal our 'real' selves.

But the line between who we are and how we participate in social life is not as clear and neat as it might seem. To act as though it were is to invite all kinds of trouble. If we pretend that our role behavior is somehow not connected to who we really are, for example, then we avoid taking responsibility not only for the role but also for our portion of the play.

Goffman argues that we are always being ourselves, even though we may feel uncomfortable owning up to the results and allowing them to affect how other people see us. If I play a role in a way that seems to contradict who I think I am, the person playing that role is still me and is no less real than the 'me' who rejects this performance as not reflecting the real me. If I fake it and act in ways that don't reflect how I really feel, it is still me who does the faking, who appears and behaves in ways that create a particular impression.

Whatever the performance turns out to be, it comes from somewhere in me, and any unreality in that lies in my not being aware of it and denying my connection to the consequences my behavior produces. As such, the problem of authenticity is not that we perform roles and manage impressions. The problem is that we don't embrace and own our actions for what they are as part of *who* we are. The problem is not that we have so many roles to perform that can make us appear inconsistent or other than we'd like. The problem is that we do not integrate them with an ongoing awareness of the incredible complexity of ourselves and the social life in which we participate.

Not seeing this complexity sets us up to participate unknowingly in systems that produce all kinds of consequences, both good and bad. At the same time, we cut ourselves off from our potential to do something about consequences we want to change. When white people act in racist ways, for example, they often rush to make the point that they are not themselves racist. "I didn't mean it," they say, or "I misspoke," or "I made a mistake [by saying that], and I'm sorry." They almost never respond with something like, "I guess the racism in the world gets into all of our lives, including mine, and I'd better look at that to see what that means for me."

In terms of impression management, everything said in self-defense is probably true: they did not *intend* to say or do anything that would hurt someone or add racism to the impression people have of them. But this is beside the more important point that the racist content of social action is real, and if people choose—consciously or not—to be vehicles for its expression, this says something about the systems they participate in *and* about them as participants. In a racist society, talk and action that reflect and reinforce white privilege are paths of least resistance that tell us more about society than about ourselves. But the choices we make in relation to those paths tell us something about who we are in relation to them, and if we don't see that, we cannot do anything about the paths or about ourselves.

Few things in sociological practice are as important or as tricky to grasp as the relationship between people and systems. In an individualistic society, the path of least resistance is to ignore systems altogether or to see them as vague menacing forces that threaten to swallow us up. The truth, however, is more complicated than that, and with far more potential for creative living.

Our relationship to a system's culture, for example, is dynamic and alive, with us creating the world as much as we are created by and through it. We are objects of culture—described, valued, and limited by its ideas about who we are and how we ought to think, feel, and behave. We are also subjects of culture, the ones who believe, who value, who expect, who feel, who use, who write and talk and think and dream. We are creators of culture, part of an endless stream of human experience—sensing, interpreting, choosing, shaping, making. We are the ones who make culture our own so that we often can't tell the point where it leaves off and we begin, or whether that point exists at all. We are recipients of culture, socialized and enculturated. We are the ones who internalize ideas, taking them inside ourselves where they shape how we participate in social life and thereby make it happen. And this thing we make happen is at the same time the cultural force that shapes us as *we* happen.

As a creative medium that we share with others, culture is not us, but it also is not completely external to us. It exists through us as we exist through it. It is *among* and *of* us. Our participation in it provides a way to participate in other people's lives. In this sense, there is no clear, fixed boundary that separates us from culture and, therefore, no clear, fixed boundary that separates us from other people. Culture is like the air. It is everywhere, and as humans we cannot live without it. We can live without any particular culture, but not without *some* culture.

Like the air, culture flows in and out of us in ways that make it impossible to draw a true line between 'I' or 'us' and 'it.' The air is both outside us and inside every cell of our bodies. As beings, we are of the air, but in a particular form that distinguishes us from dogs or ferns or bacteria. And since we all share this relationship with the air—as with culture—in a way we are all of one another. You are part of flowing and mixing with the same air that inhabits me.

Culture provides ideas and materials to work with as we make ourselves and social life happen from one moment to the next, but we have to decide what to do with them. Culture isn't something that can think or decide or do anything, nor is any other aspect of social systems or the systems themselves. We are not autonomous and independent in relation to systems, but we also aren't puppets on a string. We are somewhere in between in a far more creative place.

We're like jazz improvisers who cannot play without learning the basics of music. They have to know the difference between a sharp and a flat and between major and minor and how notes combine to make different kinds of chords. They have to know how to blend time, rhythm, and sound so they can shape the flow of the music and stay in sync while they play together. In other words, they need to know how symbols and ideas define and underlie jazz as a musical form and how they shape the way musicians think, hear, imagine, and relate to one another in ways both structural and ecological. But the social forms that limit them are also what they use to create, to bend and play with the 'rules,' to test the limits in ways that sound both familiar ('music,' 'jazz') and new, what it means to improvise.

This doesn't mean they can do whatever they want, even though jazz can sound that way, as if everyone is doing their own thing oblivious to everyone else. In fact, however, they are deeply aware of one another and the form within which they play all the while they're making it up as they go along. Beneath the seeming creative disorder lies an unarticulated inner discipline based on their shared participation in a social system. This is what gives the entire piece its musical integrity and its *social* integrity as something happening not merely *within* individual musicians but also *among* them. This ability to play within a form and yet improvise around and, at times, beyond it is what gives jazz its unmistakable character. As with jazz and its musicians, so also with social life and us.

Making Systems Happen

Social interaction consists of all the ways that we create and sustain a particular sense of reality out of which our lives, systems, and social life happen. Social interaction is the interplay between us and systems that works through both action and appearance. If employees in a bank, for example, dress in clown costumes and gorilla suits, customers will have a hard time identifying the bank as a company where they can confidently deposit their money. Appearance and action mirror each other. The hushed atmosphere in a typical bank and the quiet, efficient way that tellers handle transactions sustain the shared sense that this is a serious place where your money will be well taken care of. People don't laugh a lot in banks or make jokes about bank failures or embezzlement, just as airline pilots and flight attendants don't make funny remarks about crashes or bombs.

In fact, in the United States, especially since the events of September 11, 2001, you run the risk of being arrested for making jokes in an airport about possibly carrying a bomb onto a plane. This policy exists because the shared sense that flying is a safe way to travel is a fragile social reality even without the threat of terrorism and it can be sustained only by controlling anything that people might say or do to indicate otherwise. As I sit in my seat at 30,000 feet, reading a book or listening to music on my iPod, I'm usually unaware of the fine line that separates the alternate realities of safety and imminent danger, and everything around me is designed to encourage me not to. The comfort of the seats, the availability of movies, food, reading material, music, air-conditioning, heat, Wi-Fi, and phones—all create a sense of reality that, when I consider where it is taking place, is in some ways absurd. But I accept the situation and make it 'normal' and unremarkable in my mind until something happens to suggest otherwise.

Every social situation is defined by a reality that exists only as people actively shape and support it.[10] In something as simple as a conversation, we have to engage in a kind of dance of gestures, talk, and body language to sustain a shared sense that this thing we call a conversation is, in fact, happening from one moment to the next. We can use all kinds of methods, for example, to assure people that we are paying attention to what they're saying. We look at them, nod our heads now and then, murmur an occasional "uh-huh," smile or laugh at the funny parts, frown at something serious, ask a question or make a comment that's related to what they said. Without that assurance, the idea that a conversation is happening cannot be sustained as a shared reality.

A workshop exercise makes this point come alive. People pair off and one person tells a story to the other while the partner pretends to be completely oblivious to what's being said (sometimes going to sleep). It's an awful experience for the speakers, who typically cannot think of what to say next or can but cannot get their mouths to say it. In this sense, 'having a conversation' is a reality that we create and sustain between us, and everything we do or don't do figures into making it happen. The methods are something we have to learn, and they vary from one system to another.

In some societies, for example, a sign of paying attention in a conversation is looking at the other person's eyes from time to time. In other societies, however, this is considered a sign of disrespect if done by someone lower in authority toward someone higher. So, when typical middle-class white teachers in U.S. schools try to have a conversation with students from any number of Latin American or Asian societies, they find their students seeming to shirk their responsibility to help keep the conversation going (thinking, perhaps, the students are trying to conceal some wrongdoing), when what is really going on is a show of respect and politeness. What sustains a conversation in one system can have just the opposite effect in another.

We continually use our beliefs of how reality is constructed to figure out from one moment to the next what is happening and how to do our part to keep it going. At the movies, for example, I walk up to the theater and notice a line of people extending out the front door and down the sidewalk. I take this to mean that the theater hasn't started selling tickets for the next show and that I'm supposed to go to the end of the line and wait for it to move. The social reality of a waiting line is a fragile one, because most people would rather be at the front than farther back. It is so fragile that the smallest thing can make it come undone. It takes only a few people to leave the line, for example, and go into the door ahead of everyone else for people to start doubting that it is in fact a 'line' in which the rules of staying in place and waiting your turn apply. When this happens, the line can fall apart physically and as a shared social reality, which depends on certain patterns of social action to maintain a consensus that it exists.

Because the methods we use to sustain a social reality are used over and over again, they often take on a ritual quality.[11] Intimate relations between marital partners, for example, are usually based on the assumption that the two people love each other. Since an assumption is just an idea, it is sustained through rituals that call attention to it as part of the reality these two people participate in day after day. Such rituals might include saying, "Good night" before going to sleep, perhaps accompanied with a kiss, or saying, "I love you" before ending a phone conversation, or kissing as part of saying good-bye when going off in separate directions at the start of a day.

We may not think of such rituals as sustaining a reality until our partner fails to enact them, especially over a period of time. In itself, each "I love you," each kiss, each "Good night" does not amount to much, but as part of a fabric that holds together the social reality of a love relationship, it can take on much greater significance. It may not take many lapses to raise insecurity in a partner or worry that something is wrong in the relationship, that the assumption of love and commitment is weaker than it was or may never have been what they thought. Those rituals are like many interaction rituals in that we do not know they are there until someone deviates from them and we notice the hole in the social fabric that marks where they are supposed to be.

Large Structures in Everyday Life

A focus on interaction naturally draws us toward individuals, but it is important to keep in mind that almost everything we say or do happens in relation to one social system or another and often has implications for larger systems, even though we do not know it at the time.

Linguist Deborah Tannen, for example, has written several books on how women and men talk to one another.[12] She notices that men tend to talk in ways that enhance their status—they are more likely than women to interrupt during conversations, use aggressive language and tones of voice, and avoid doing anything that might suggest a lack of control, such as asking for directions or saying they do not know the answer to a question. Women, on the other hand, are more likely than men to interact in ways that support personal relationships—to listen attentively while others talk, wait their turn rather than interrupt, avoid verbal aggression, and be more open about their doubts. Tannen explains these patterns as a relatively simple matter of children playing in same-sex groups as they grow up, thereby socialized by their peers to interact in different ways. They grow up in what amounts to different cultures, Tannen argues, and behave accordingly.

The problem with Tannen's approach is that she never links such differences to the larger social context that makes them paths of least resistance. She tells us, for example, that a boy learns to interact aggressively by hanging out with other boys, but she doesn't say where *those* boys learn to interact aggressively. It's as though boys and girls invent different patterns spontaneously and all by themselves, rather than learning them as part of their socialization into the larger society they *both* inhabit.

More importantly, Tannen doesn't ask what kind of society would have paths of least resistance that lead men to seek status and women to attend to personal relationships. She barely mentions that we live in a society that is male-dominated, male-identified, and male-centered. In such a world, men who seek status and women who tend to personal relationships also reinforce male privilege and the oppressive price that privilege exacts from women.

When women and men interact along paths of least resistance, they do more than talk differently. They also play a part in making a particular kind of society happen from one moment to the next. When men interrupt and women don't object, when men answer questions even when they do not know the answer and women remain silent or say they don't know even when they do, when men argue aggressively for their point of view and women raise questions and otherwise show an openness to alternatives—this is how the system of male privilege *happens* in order to shape a major structural feature of society as a whole and all of the systems, from family to workplace, included in it.

This is true of every form of social inequality, whose patterns of inclusion and exclusion, advantage and disadvantage, reward and punishment contribute to privileging some groups over others. In all kinds of workplaces, for example, white women, people of color, people who are LGBT,* and people with disabilities find themselves on the receiving end of messages that make them feel like unwelcome outsiders. Sometimes these messages are overt and deliberate, but often they are woven into the everyday fabric of interaction.

As Rosabeth Moss Kanter has observed about corporations, for example, when men use strong language in the presence of women, they may make a point of apologizing to the women.[13] While the men may think they are being sensitive or polite, they are also sending the message that without the women there, they wouldn't have to pay such close attention to how they talk. By apologizing, men draw attention to the exceptional nature of women's presence and identify women as outsiders who interfere with what would otherwise be regarded as the normal flow of conversation.

Gays and lesbians experience this kind of exclusion all the time in the form of an ongoing assumption by heterosexuals that everyone else is heterosexual, too.[14] Since coming out carries all kinds of risks at work, for example, gays and lesbians have to be careful in the simplest everyday interactions, such as Monday morning talk about what coworkers did over the weekend. When heterosexuals try to imagine telling someone all about their family without ever using a word that indicates anyone's gender, they get some idea of what it's like to be gay or lesbian in the typical workplace. A heterosexual has nothing to lose by casually revealing a partner's gender, as when a woman refers to her partner as 'he.' But a lesbian who does the same thing could find herself in trouble, excluded if not harassed and discriminated against in ways that threaten her livelihood. Since heterosexuals have much greater freedom to talk

---

*   LGBT is an acronym for lesbian, gay, bisexual, and transgender. Some activists expand it to include 'queer' (LGBTQ), a general term that refers to those who, in various ways, reject, test, or otherwise transgress the boundaries of what is culturally regarded as normal with respect to gender, gender identity, or sexual orientation and expression. Some regard it as an umbrella term for the other four components of LGBT. 'Queer,' of course, is also routinely used as an insult directed at LGBT people.

about their personal lives, such talk becomes a form of privilege, because it is denied to others.[15] That heterosexuals are rarely aware of this is also part of their privilege.

In a society that privileges whiteness, people of many races must deal with patterns of interaction that exclude and discriminate. The messages 'You are not white' and 'You don't belong here' are sent in a variety of ways. Black men, for example, are routinely treated as objects of fear in public places, as white people hug packages and bags more tightly against their bodies as they pass by or avoid the encounter by crossing the street. Black people also often have their presence challenged, however politely.

A Black partner in a large law firm, for example, came to work early one morning and was confronted by a young newly hired white attorney who did not know whom he was talking to.

"Can I help you?" the young man asked pointedly. When told "No," he repeated the question until the senior lawyer angrily explained who he was.

A Black federal judge tells the story of waiting for a cab with several colleagues—all dressed in suits and ties—outside a prominent hotel in a major city. A white woman drove up in her car, got out, and handed the judge her keys as she strode into the hotel.[16]

In such ways, the large structures of social inequality that characterize entire societies play themselves out in everyday life. The countless ways that such systems limit and damage people's lives don't usually take the form of overt and deliberate harm. Instead, they happen through a particular choice of words, a tone of voice, the timing of a silence or an averted gaze, or a seemingly innocent question. Such patterns make it difficult for members of dominant groups to appreciate that their privilege even exists, not to mention the cost that their privilege exacts from others. And those patterns also make it difficult for members of subordinate groups to endure the small everyday exclusions and insults, no single one of which carries great weight but which accumulate into the kind of burden that gives oppression its name.

The interplay between the details of speech, gesture, and behavior on the one hand and how social systems happen on the other operates in some way at every level and in every realm of social life. This interplay gives significance to everything we do and do not do and to the choices that shape how we do it. It is, ultimately, what connects us to a social reality larger than ourselves and our own experience, a reality shaped through our participation, which, at the same time, shapes who we are.

Notes

1. See, for example, B. F. Skinner, *Beyond Freedom and Dignity* (New York: Knopf, 1971).
2. For more on the concept of the self, see D. H. Demo, "The Self-Concept over Time: Research Issues and Directions," *Annual Review of Sociology* 18 (1992): 303–326, and Morris Rosenberg, *Conceiving the Self* (New York: Basic Books, 1979).
3. George Herbert Mead, *Mind, Self, and Society* (Chicago: University of Chicago Press, 1934).
4. Erving Goffman, *Encounters* (Indianapolis: Bobbs-Merrill, 1961).

5. 'Significant others' is a term first introduced in Harry Stack Sullivan, *The Interpersonal Theory of Psychiatry* (New York: Norton, 1953).

6. Charles Horton Cooley, *Life and the Student* (New York: Knopf, 1927).

7. Mead, *Mind, Self, and Society*.

8. See the following works by Erving Goffman: *The Presentation of Self in Everyday Life* (New York: Doubleday, 1959); *Asylums* (New York: Anchor Books, 1961); *Behavior in Public Places* (New York: Free Press, 1963); *Stigma: Notes on the Management of a Spoiled Identity* (Englewood Cliffs, NJ: Prentice-Hall, 1963); *Interaction Ritual* (New York: Anchor Books, 1967); *Gender Advertisements* (New York: Harper Colophon, 1976); *Forms of Talk* (Philadelphia: University of Pennsylvania Press, 1981); and *Encounters*. See also Philip Manning, *Erving Goffman and Modern Sociology* (Stanford, CA; Stanford University Press, 1992).

9. Erving Goffman, "Embarrassment and Social Organization," *American Journal of Sociology* 62 (1956–1957): 264–271.

10. The study of methods people use to sustain the reality of a particular situation is known as 'ethnomethodology' (literally, 'people's methods'). It is most closely associated with the work of Harold Garfinkel. See his *Studies in Ethnomethodology* (Englewood Cliffs, NJ: Prentice-Hall, 1967). See also J. Maxwell Atkinson and John Heritage, *Structures of Social Action: Studies in Conversation Analysis* (Cambridge, UK: Cambridge University Press, 1984); R. A. Hilbert, "Ethnomethodology and the Micro-Macro-Order," *American Sociological Review* 55, no. 6 (1990): 794–808; and Eric Livingston, *Making Sense of Ethnomethodology* (London: Routledge and Kegan Paul, 1987).

11. See Goffman, *Interaction Ritual*.

12. See, for example, the following works by Deborah Tannen: *You Just Don't Understand: Women and Men in Conversation* (New York: William Morrow, 1990) and *Talking Nine to Five* (New York: William Morrow, 1994).

13. Rosabeth Moss Kanter, *Men and Women of the Corporation* (New York: Basic Books, 1977).

14. See Brian McNaught, *Gay Issues in the Workplace* (New York: St. Martin's Press, 1993).

15. For more on the concept of privilege, see Peggy McIntosh, "White Privilege and Male Privilege: A Personal Account of Coming to See Correspondences through Work in Women's Studies" (Wellesley, MA: Wellesley Centers for Research on Women, 1988).

16. Such stories abound in the experiences of people of color in the United States. See, for example, Lois Benjamin, *The Black Elite* (Chicago: Nelson-Hall, 1991); Ellis Cose, *The Rage of a Privileged Class* (New York: HarperCollins, 1993); Joe R. Feagin, "The Continuing Significance of Race: Antiblack Discrimination in Public Places," *American Sociological Review* 56, no. 1 (1991): 101–116; Joe R. Feagin, Hernán Vera, and Pinar Batur, *White Racism: The Basics* (New York: Routledge, 1995); Joe R. Feagin, Hernán Vera, and Nikitah Imani, *The Agony of Education: Black Students at White Colleges and Universities* (New York: Routledge, 1996); Joe R. Feagin and Melvin P. Sikes, *Living with Racism: The Black Middle-Class Experience* (Boston: Beacon Press, 1994); and David T. Wellman, *Portraits of White Racism*, 2nd ed. (New York: Cambridge University Press, 2012).

In Other Words . . .

The intent of metaphors and meaning in this unit is to provide a visual "peg for memory," one that brings to life the abstract concepts of structure and interaction. I suggest that you return to the DSTY pages a few times (now and later) to refresh your cognitive work on how a social system works dialectically. The social world does not work by some random chance, but in a process that is complicated, often reciprocal, but also uneven and one that responds to power plays in action. If this still seems fuzzy, then you're probably right on point! In fact, if anyone (or source) tries to give you a simple, unilateral explanation for complex social processes and outcomes, be very suspicious. I can assure you, it will be off base in more than one way. What we want to steer clear of are over-simplistic generalizations, essentialist (inherent, immutable) explanations, and absolutist (black/white) perspectives on how the world works. *It's never just one thing.*

An additional challenge addressed in this unit is the taken-for-granted quality of what we are studying—our culture. For example, does a fish knows it swims in water? No. Its surroundings are taken for granted, right? At least, that's true until the fish is taken out of water—then, Yikes! Fortunately, we have a somewhat larger brain capacity (though there is that whole attention span thing!) and can think consciously, accrue knowledge, and utilize scientific tools of inquiry. In short, we can engage in the sociological imagination. As Simmel (Inglis 2005, 2) reminds us, "Even the most banal externalities of life" are expressions of the wider social and cultural order.

Similarly, we are introduced to a new way of thinking about *self* and, once more, the importance of perception. The "looking glass self," a concept developed by Charles Horton Cooley (1902), posits that our self-image is shaped by interpersonal interactions and perceptions of others. But, as is typical in sociology, the concept is a little more complicated than that. Take our friend "Albert," for example. Albert has a new shirt (very colorful, with dots) that he bought just to impress Sally. Albert looks in the mirror and thinks, "I'm hot." (Don't be misled; that's not the looking glass self.) He meets Sally, who, frowning a little, thinks, "What an ugly shirt; yet, Albert seems to think he's all that." In turn, Albert reads Sally's look as astonishment and thinks, "Yeah, Sally thinks I'm *really* hot." *That* is the looking glass self—not our own perceptions, or that of others, but how we perceive how others perceive us. Thus, our socialization into society begins—a complex and often imperfect process, one that is transient and ever changing.

I hope you'll consider watching the movie *Lars and the Real Girl* (see Beyond the Book in this section). It's an outstanding illustration of socialization and the social construction of reality.

The Big Idea

Self is an idea we have about our own existence.

So What?

Culture—our whole way of life. One of the problems with this definition, though, is "whose culture?" Whose definition(s)? Whose perspective? Culture constitutes a bundle of societal norms, values, beliefs, routines, rituals, symbols, and so forth, but all become social habits carried out within certain groups. Certainly, a society shares many of those characteristics, but some are in conflict. Unfortunately, recent events (there are always "recent events," right?) of conflicts, police shootings, and violent protests demonstrate that "Black lives"—"all lives," blue lives," and so on—matter, reflect clashing viewpoints. As always, let's start with some social facts. Blacks die at the hands of police anywhere from 2.5 to 21 times (depending on data quality, which is difficult to obtain) more often than whites (Lowery 2016); much violence attributed to "race" is actually a function of socioeconomic factors; the War on Drugs disproportionately targets minority communities, resulting in an incarceration rate of 380 (per 100,000) for whites, 966 for Latinos, and 2,207 for Backs (Prison Policy Initiative 2012); and guns have killed more preschoolers than police officers in the line of duty (Turkel 2015). (For more, see the sentencingproject.org.) The typical Black household now has just 6 percent of the wealth (8 percent for Latinos) that the typical white household holds. Further, social experiments demonstrate marked employer preference for white-sounding names, and Black Americans die at higher rates than whites from most causes including AIDS, heart disease, cancer, and homicide (Cook 2015). Of course, all lives matter! But a hard look at our culture and outcomes say we do not always treat *all* lives that way; otherwise, we wouldn't need signs that read "Black Lives Matter" (also) (Roose 2015). If we dismiss the *lives matter* conflict, we ignore its associated problems. Again, we are faced with the Thomas theorem: whatsoever situations are perceived as real, are real in their consequences. Peace out.

Works Cited

Cook, L. (2015, January 5). "Why Black Americans Die Younger." *U.S. News & World Report*. Retrieved July 12, 2012, from http://www.usnews.com/news/blogs/data-mine/2015/01/05/black-americans-have-fewer-years-to-live-heres-why

Cooley, C. H. (1902). *Human nature and the social order*. New York, NY: Scribner's.

Inglis, D. (2005). *Culture and everyday life*. New York, NY: Routledge.

Lowery, W. (2016, July 11). "More whites killed by police, but blacks 2.5 times more likely to be killed." *The Washington Post*. Retrieved July 12, 2016, from http://www.chicagotribune.com/news/nationworld/ct-police-shootings-race-20160711-story.html

Prison Policy Initiative. (2012). "United States incarceration rates by race and ethnicity." Retrieved July 12, 2016, from http://www.prisonpolicy.org/graphs/raceinc.html

Roose, K. (2015, July 21). "The next time someone says 'all lives matter,' show them these 5 paragraphs." *Fusion*. Retrieved July 12, 2016, from http://fusion.net/story/170591/the-next-time-someone-says-all-lives-matter-show-them-these-5-paragraphs/

The Sentencing Project. (2016). "The color of justice: Racial and ethnic disparity in state prisons." Retrieved July 12, 2016, from http://www.sentencingproject.org

Turkel, D. (2015, October 14). "Guns have killed more preschoolers than police officers in the line of duty." *Business Insider*, Law & Order. Retrieved July 12, 2016, from http://www.businessinsider.com/guns-have-killed-more-preschoolers-than-police-officers-2015-10

Section I: Imagining the Everyday

Beyond the Book: *Lars and the Real Girl*

Lars and the Real Girl, a 2007 comedy/drama film, features the life of Lars Lindstrom, a twenties-something young man who lives in a small town, next door to his older brother Gus and wife Karin. Lars's mother died during childbirth, and his depressive father died a few years before the storyline begins. Lars is lovable but painfully shy and develops a romantic (but platonic) relationship with an anatomically correct sex doll named Bianca. As is typical among American film critics, reviews range from "miracle" to "moral fable exploring kindness, understanding, love, and the acceptance of human diversity" (Dargis 2007) to "100% pure [sappy] calculation" (Rotten Tomatoes 2007). Still, the film earned several nominations and has received even greater acclaim after the box office closed.

Regardless of the debate over cinematography, I somehow came across the movie as I was teaching Introduction to Sociology one year (around 2008); we were deep into the unit of socialization. After I could pull myself out of the storyline (it is superbly engaging), I realized the film represents perfect illustrations of the social construction of reality, including agency of individuals, power of interaction, and contributions of community in shaping our sense of self—the *how* and *why* of social interaction. I've used *Lars* as a teaching tool ever since.

Just as food for thought, here are a few questions I ask my students after they view *Lars*: What is an example of individual agency from the movie, and what is our own part in socialization? What is an example of social structure from the movie, and how are we channeled by social forces around us? Did this film, and its messages, remind you of a lesson learned in your own life? If your life were a movie, what would the title be?

Of course, the responses are as diverse as the lives they describe. Some love it and describe it as "extraordinarily creative" and "breathtaking." Others see it as "not real at all" (curious, given the title and the fact that it's fictional art!), "too fake," or "too sugary" (French 2008). The film has been compared to other works as disparate as *Harvey, Lake Wobegon, Psycho,* and *The Velveteen Rabbit.*

But most important, students overwhelmingly "get it." That is, they construct on-point and even poignant examples of sociological concepts from the movie. Two stand out in my mind as outstanding examples. Kelly observed that "Lars chose what happened in Bianca's life; whatever he willed came true through Bianca." Marlyse noticed that Bianca (the "doll") herself gained agency because "she" elicited emotion, reactions, and communal responses from the entire town. Students seemed to readily recognize social structures—not always easy for learners at this level. Students readily understand *family* (the idea of family reaches beyond Lars's "people"), *religion* (distinct from the church *per se*), and *community,* which is a social container for certain beliefs and traditions. One student even wrote about emotion itself as structure—brilliant!

So many more student responses are noteworthy. I loved that Janelle packed in the power of expectation, perception, and anxiety about norm-breaking, all into one quote from the movie: (from Gus, Lars's brother, to the psychiatrist): "We got to fix him—can you fix him, Doc?" (Aubrey 2007). Students are also able to apply abstractions to their own lives; one compared concepts to her participation in minimalism, and another to a life of abuse. They came up with imaginative titles to their own "movie," such as "Pickles and Watermelon" (Daisy), "Boats and Goats" (Jeffrey), and "A Millennial in a Million" (Stephanie).

As a poignant reminder, Roger Ebert (2007), the late and much-loved critic, proclaimed, "Only after the movie is over do you realize what a balancing act it was, what risks it took, what rewards it contains." These same words, too, mark our collective social life—one of "hurt but also hidden hope."

Works Cited

Aubrey, S. (producer), and Gillespie, C. (director). (2007). *Lars and the Real Girl* [motion picture]. Ontario, Canada: Metro-Goldwyn-Mayer.

Dargis, M. (2007, October 12). "A lonely guy plays house with a mail-order sex doll." *The New York Times,* Movies. Retrieved July 13, 2016, from http://www.nytimes.com/2007/10/12/movies/12lars.html?_r=0

Ebert, Roger. 2007. Review: *Lars and the Real Girl.* rogerebert.com. October 18, 2007. Retrieved July 12, 2016, from. http://www.rogerebert.com/reviews/lars-and-the-real-girl-2007

French, P. (2008, March 22). *The Guardian,* Movies. Retrieved July 13, 2016, from https://www.theguardian.com/film/2008/mar/23/comedy.drama

Rotten Tomatoes. (2007). *Lars and the Real Girl.* Retrieved July 13, 2016, from https://www.rottentomatoes.com/m/1175569-lars_and_the_real_girl/

Section I: Imagining the Everyday

From the Field: The Contagion Effect

A large part of critical thinking means asking well-placed questions. As within any science, it's crucial to ask, "How do we know what we know?" In social science, it becomes even more critical because we first must overcome many "common wisdoms." For example, what about attraction: Do opposites attract? Or, do birds of a feather flock together? You can find plenty of anecdotal evidence for either of these adages. So, how do we *really* know? We *do* look to evidence, but we weigh both the quality and quantity of evidence.

Several steps are involved in evaluating scientific evidence (data). First, the behavior must be observable and measurable by a qualified expert and conducted in a scientifically appropriate, systematic way (methodology). Second, observations must be in sufficient number to apply scientific principles (analysis). Once patterns are discovered, possibilities (theories) must be considered and conclusions drawn. Most researchers start with gathering relevant, known facts (literature review); some start with theory, while others look for an "emergence" of explanation.

In this section, I offer you a brief synopsis of a research project *from the field* that has produced novel, useful, and/or compelling results. It is hoped the content proves interesting or thought provoking, and just as important, that it provides you with a brief demonstration of evaluating available research results. The study reviewed here asks whether mental health, or mood, is contagious (i.e., producing a contagion effect).

Previous research on the contagion effect included mixed results. Some studies demonstrated that happy people make everyone around them happy, while others found no effect at all; rather, one's own circumstance, not that of others, was assumed to determine happiness (which, by the way, is infamously difficult to measure). Researchers from two universities, Manchester and Warwick, collaborated on the study, which was published in one of the leading journals in the UK (a peer-reviewed journal, which means it underwent blind reviews by leading experts in the field). [*So far, so good … qualified scholars within legitimate institutions of higher learning.*]

The study involved two thousand students in a range of US high schools to determine how their mood influenced one another. Using network analysis, they modeled the spread of mood similar to methods used to track the spread of infectious diseases. [*Both the numbers and methods look good.*]

The project differed from previous studies, which were prone to look at social factors such as living alone or having experienced abuse. Almost all previous studies demonstrated that social support is important for recovery from depression. In this case, researchers also examined the effect of being friends with people reporting similar or dissimilar moods. Results showed that friends count. Having "happy" friends helps one's own mood, but even "depressed" friends exert a positive effect on one's mood!

Implications are far reaching. Results suggest that "promotion of any friendship between adolescents can reduce depression since having depressed friends does not put them at risk, but having healthy friends is both protective and curative" (Phys.org 2015).

The article stated that researchers ensured the results were not confounded by "homophily," the tendency for people to be friends with others like themselves. This is known as a "control" variable. "For example, if many adolescents drink a lot of alcohol and their friends drink a lot too, it may be that alcoholic drink causes depression among the young people rather than who they are friends with" (Phys.org 2015). [*If this were the case, it would have been a "spurious" effect. Fortunately, they controlled for this factor.*]

No one study is perfect. We can't be sure these results are generalizable to other cultures, other ages, and that it is the same by gender, race, class, etc. Weigh the evidence in balance with other studies, and remain skeptical. In the meantime, enjoy your friends, depressed or not!

Works Cited

Phys.org. (2015, August 18). "Healthy Mood Spreads Through Social Contact, Depression Doesn't." Retrieved July 13, 2016, from http://phys.org/news/2015-08-healthy-mood-social-contact-depression.html

Section I: Imagining the Everyday

Reality Check: ME

Overview

The ME assignment guides application of the sociological principles addressed in Section I. It asks you to place yourself under the sociological microscope as you discuss two status positions that you occupy, one achieved and one ascribed status. Using and defining several key terms you have learned so far, discuss the two statuses and examine at least two roles associated with them. Second, choose ONE of the status positions and describe a specific example in which you can now identify influence(s) that guided you toward an appropriate role for the position. Third, reflecting on your story of ME, discuss a sociological "big idea" that you learned through this assignment. **Tip:** The *In other words …* component of Section I may give you some points of reference! Especially look for opportunities to use your sociological imagination and critical thinking.

Purpose

- To learn sociological concepts through self-exploration.
- To understand how social experiences shape who we are and how we experience society.

Introduction and Definition of Key Terms

First, introduce the topic and define key terms used in the assignment. Include at least the following terms: status, achieved status, ascribed status, and role. Make it engaging, use facts and/or anecdotes, and end this section by describing how the paper is organized.

Statuses and Roles

Achieved Status, and Corresponding Roles: Discuss one achieved status position (acquired based on merit) that you occupy and explain why it is achieved. Identify two corresponding roles (functions attached to status) and describe how you learned or adopted these roles.

Ascribed Status and Roles: Describe one ascribed status (neither earned nor chosen) that you occupy and explain why it is ascribed. Identify two corresponding roles and how you are now aware of their association with the status. How and why do you comply with these "unseen" forces?

Society's Influence on Me

Pick ONE of the statuses and describe a particular time that you can now place as instrumental in learning or adopting the appropriate roles for the status position. This example should be detailed and specific.

Conclusion

Conclude the paper by discussing a sociological "big idea" that you learned through this assignment. USE sociology!

Section I: Imagining the Everyday

OLE Resources

The techno revolution continues to expand our social world exponentially. Online learning environments (OLE) have grown by leaps and bounds in the past decade, shaping and reshaping not only what we learn, but how we learn. The Babson Group (Babson College 2016) reports that as of late 2014, 5.8 million students are taking online learning courses, and most institutes of higher learning now offer some type of distance education online. The 2016 Online Education Trends (Online Learning Consortium 2015) reports that employers are partnering with online programs, emphasizing professional development and training online. I teach 100 percent online now, and I find both challenges and rewards even more exciting than my brick-and-mortar teaching days. For these reasons and more, I offer you a few OLE resources to augment your everyday learning experience.

Bestcolleges.com. (2016). "2016 Online Education Trends." Retrieved July 12, 2016, from http://www.bestcolleges.com/wp-content/uploads/2016-trends-in-online-education.pdf

Lease, N. (2016). "Online Learning Report Shows Long-Term Higher Education Trends." edtechtimes.com. Retrieved July 12, 2016, from http://edtechtimes.com/2016/03/06/online-learning-report-shows-long-term-higher-education-trends/

This American Life: "It'll Make Sense When You're Older." (2016). Retrieved July 13, 2016, from http://www.thisamericanlife.org/radio-archives/episode/583/itll-make-sense-when-youre-older

TED Talk: "Do Schools Kill Creativity?" (2016). Retrieved July 13, 2016, from https://www.ted.com/playlists/171/the_most_popular_talks_of_all

"Is Child Marriage Legal?" (2016). Retrieved July 12, 2016, from http://www.huffingtonpost.com/entry/virginia-bans-child-marriage-illegal-underage-loophole_us_578407fae4b0ed2111d74228?

The Gods Must Be Crazy (2016). *The Gods Must Be Crazy* (full film)

Lars and the Real Girl (full film)

Works Cited

Babson College. (2015). Survey reports. The Babson Survey Research Group. Retrieved July 7, 2016, from http://www.babson.edu/Academics/faculty/provost/Pages/babson-survey-research-group.aspx

Online Learning Consortium. (2016). 2015 "Online report card: Tracking online education in the United States." Retrieved July 7, 2016, from http://onlinelearningconsortium.org/survey_report/2015-online-report-card-tracking-online-education-united-states/

Section II:
A Culture of
Social Control

UNIT 3 READINGS

Morals, Norms, and Folkways

Crime and Control

Unit 3: Deviance, Crime, and Social Control

Dr. Sue to You: Being bad

Before we delve into the substance of this unit, let us review and discuss three questions:

1. What is the distinction between deviance and crime?
2. How do we know what we know?
3. What (and who) is "bad," and who gets to define that?

Generally speaking, deviance is any behavior that violates social norms (or unwritten but expected standards) of a society (Hannon 2005). Norms involve folkways (everyday habits and lasting customs, such as a handshake), mores (strong cultural beliefs such as standing for the national anthem), and taboos (e.g., incest or cannibalism) (Sumner 1906). If norms have become codified into law, then the violation becomes a crime, though these specifications are inconsistent across time and space (e.g., consider marijuana and other drug laws and regulations) (Shepard and Blackley 2016).

How do we know what we know? The general term referring to the production of knowledge is epistemology—the investigation of what distinguishes belief from opinion (Klein 2005). As you might guess, this task becomes quite complex. For example, while the above social norm definitions may seem rather straightforward, the interpretation of how and why such norms emerge, and their role in society, varies widely, depending on the theoretical paradigm one is working within; these interpretations determine how we know what we know.

To review, I will briefly cite three paradigms (an umbrella-like perspective) within which theories (a set of ideas about how society works) can be categorized. The first paradigm is **structural-functionalism**, in which such norms serve the *function* of defining moral boundaries and emerging as an agreed-upon set of rules that "glue" together parts of a society (Durkheim 1892). Theories that fall within this general paradigm assume there is widespread agreement on the rules, and that deviance is a necessary part of the process to enforce social order. The second is the **conflict paradigm**, which sees deviant behavior and crime as the result of unequal power, usually in the form of social, political, and economic conflicts between groups (Sellin 1938). The third paradigm is **symbolic interactionism**, a perspective that frames social processes (such as deviance, identity formation, etc.) through human interaction, both between individuals (the micro level) and as people interact with social structures such as education, the economy, family structures, and so forth (the macro level) (Mead 1934). These sociological "ways of knowing" require continual verification and modification in the form of empirical investigation (research). Again, these are very broad categories of theoretical families; specific theories reside within each paradigm.

We now turn to the third question: What (and who) is "bad," and who gets to define that? For one perspective (theory) regarding this question, we turn to labeling theory, which sits astraddle the conflict and interactionist paradigms. According to labeling theory, societal reactions to so-called deviant behavior and those labeled as deviant classify these individuals as "outsiders" (Becker 1963). In turn, these outsiders react and rearrange their lives around such labels, which amplify the deviant lifestyle. As Becker succinctly states, "deviant behavior is behavior that people so label" (Becker 1963, 9). As we can see, this is not a simple answer, but it does include the question of power (who has the status and position to do the labeling), as well as the complexity of social interaction among people and institutions. The reading in this unit, "The Saints and the Roughnecks," provides an excellent glimpse of labeling theory in action.

Closely related to labeling theory is cultural criminology, which integrates certain principles of sociology, social interaction, and the "new criminology," all of which explore cultural, ideological, and material dynamics of social organization, peering in nooks and crevices to determine how certain events (and actors) become defined as criminal. As Jeff Ferrell explains:

> The many contemporary confluences of cultural and criminal dynamics force us to reconsider traditionally discrete categories of "culture" and "crime" in our research and analysis. Many social groups and events traditionally conceptualized as "criminal" are in fact defined in their everyday operations by subcultural meaning and style. At the same time, various groups and events conventionally placed under the heading of "culture" regularly suffer criminalization at the hands of moral entrepreneurs, legal and political authorities, and others. (Ferrell, 1995, 25).

In other words, crime and deviance is manufactured and interpreted locally, but in the context of historical and sociopolitical affairs. In a conversation, Professor Ferrell said he often points out the fact to his students that coffee was once illegal, punishable by death. Propaganda about its excesses blamed coffee for paralysis, impotence, and social ills such as violence and plotting against the government (Pendergrast 2010). Sound familiar? Our own patchwork past with various laws about drugs, alcohol, voting behavior, immigration laws, and curfews are only a few that come to mind.

The first reading in this unit is "Deviance," by Lonnie Hannon (2005). Hannon takes us through the development of a material manifestation of culture (Air Jordan shoes), demonstrating how a culture within a culture forms (a subculture), and how such subcultures are often viewed as deviant by others; all the while the group forms its own internal norms. Pay special attention to the distinction between formal and informal control, and how the two may produce conflicting rules. A key quote in Hannon's reading is one by Dr. Martin Luther King Jr., taken from his "Letter from the Birmingham Jail":

> The answer lies in the fact that there are two types of laws: Just and unjust. I would be the first to advocate obeying just laws. One has not only a legal but a moral responsibility to obey just laws. Conversely, one has a moral responsibility to disobey unjust laws. I would agree with St. Augustine that "an unjust law is no law at all" (1964, 82, as cited in Hannon 2005, 62).

Of the three sociological paradigms described in this DSTY piece, which does this quote from Dr. King exemplify?

The second reading in this unit, by Narvaez (2015), turns the deviance question on its head and asks, instead, why do we conform? Referring to classic studies of conformity, such as that by Solomon Asch (1951), Narvaez walks us through various research that tests ideas about social cohesion, conformity, and the risks of noncompliance. In other readings, we have explored issues of race and class; this one introduces us to the *action* of gendering, including work by Kimmel (2008) on "bro-codes." Pay attention to the empirical verification (i.e., research) of tendencies that may seem "natural" but are, in fact, social constructions.

DSTY TIPS for Critical Thinking:

- *Utilize the "because" clause.* To become more proficient at analytical thinking (as opposed to reactionary, belief-oriented traps), use the *because* clause. That is, once you define what is going on (be sure to look for verifiable facts from legitimate sources), ask *why* the situation at hand is occurring by using the *because* clause. "Women approach problem-solving skills different from men *because* … " "Conflicts

Statement Apparel; Student in class, circa 2009

occur between police and the African American community *because* ... " In addition, consider what theoretical paradigm (perspective) might best inform the analysis of the situation at hand.

- **Ask the "so what" question.** Once you determine a) verifiable facts and b) analytical reasoning, then ask c) "so what?" That is, delineating a descriptive event and a rational explanation does not necessarily mean it is relevant or noteworthy to the task at hand. Asking "so what" entails deeper attention to the situation, focusing on the immediate significance and also the wider implications of the social phenomenon under consideration.

Works Cited

Asch, S. E. (1951). "Effects of group pressure upon the modification and distortion of judgment." In H. Guetzkow (ed.) *Groups, leadership and men*. Pittsburgh PA: Carnegie Press.

Becker, H. S. (1963). *Outsiders: Studies in the sociology of deviance*. New York NY: Free Press.

Durkheim, E. (1892). *The division of labor in society*. New York NY: Free Press.

Ferrell, J. (1995). "Culture, crime, and cultural criminology." *Journal of Criminal Justice and Popular Culture*, 3, 25–42.

Hannon, L. (2005). "Deviance," 59–73, in *Life and Society*. Cognella Academic Publishing.

Kimmel, M. (2008). *Guyland: The perilous world where boys become men*. New York NY: Harper.

King, M. L. Jr. (1964). *Why we can't wait*. New York NY: Signet Classic, 2000.

Klein, P. D. (2005). Epistemology. *Rutledge Encyclopedia of Philosophy*. Retrieved September 24, 2016, from https://www.rep.routledge.com/articles/epistemology/v-2

Mead, G. H. (1934). *Mind, self, and society: From the standpoint of a social behaviorist*. Chicago IL: University of Chicago Press.

Narvaez, R. F. (2015). "Why we conform," 1–25, in *Reading the world: An introduction*. Cognella Academic Publishing.

Pendergrast, M. (2010). *Uncommon grounds: The history of coffee and how it transformed our world*. New York, NY: Basic Books.

Sellin, T. (1938). *Culture conflict and crime*. New Jersey: Social Science Research Council.

Shepard, E. M., and Blackley, P. R. (2016). "Medical marijuana and crime: Further evidence from the western states." *Journal of Drug Issues*, 46, 122–134.

Sumner, W. G. (1906). *Folkways: A study of the sociological importance of usages, manners, customs, mores, and morals*. Boston MA: Ginn and Co.

READING 1

DEVIANCE—LIFE AND SOCIETY

BY LONNIE HANNON

Introduction: The Culture of a Shoe

Nike Air Jordan or Jordans is one of the most popular brands of all time. Prior to Michael Jordan, Nike was a small, though well-known company that existed essentially to provide athletic apparel to athletes. However, much changed when the paths of Michael Jordan and Nike met.

Michael Jordan's arrival in the NBA came at a perfect time in history. The NBA had recently begun to capitalize from marketing its brand through star players, such as Julius Erving, Magic Johnson, Larry Bird, and Charles Barkley. TV networks showed more games. Attendance was good. Interest was at an all-time high. Then came Michael Jordan. Jordan's style of play emulated the "above the rim" characteristics of Julius Erving. He was exceptional on offense and defense. His acrobatic dunks were exciting. Importantly, he had what people today call "swag," a slang term short for swagger—a type of confidence that emanated from his personality. Moreover, he played in Chicago, the second or third largest market in the United States.

After entering the NBA in 1984, Michael Jordan signed a contract with Nike reportedly for $2.5 million, the richest endorsement deal for an athlete ever. Nike began manufacturing the first generation of Air Jordans. Part of the deal was that Jordan had to wear the shoes throughout the season. The NBA fined Jordan $5,000 per game for violating uniform policy. Nike reportedly paid the fines (Skidmore, 2008). The 1985 NBA All Star game featured perhaps the most famous dunk contest of all time between Jordan and Dominique Wilkins. Jordan won the contest with his now-famous dunk from the free throw line. During the All Star game, much of America got their first glimpse of the daring Air Jordans. They were colorful and uniquely designed. Importantly, because Jordan was violating NBA rules, they conveyed rebelliousness. Jordan himself represented a sort of

Figure 1 Even the retro version of Air Jordan was very popular among urbanites. These are a replica of an edition that first arrived in the late 80's. Copyright © NYR-NYG-NYY (CC by 3.0) at http://commons.wikime-dia.org/wiki/File:Air_Jordan_4_(Cement).jpg.

break from the old-school players. The endorsement deal set Jordan apart from his counterparts. He was not just a great basketball player, but he was also now a commercial icon with his brand being made larger by the day. This upset some of Jordan's more seasoned counterparts who had played in the NBA for many years without gaining the level of appeal that Jordan gained in just a few years.

Michael Jordan was perhaps the first athlete to have the level of commercial success typically associated with major movie stars. Indeed the products that he endorsed, specifically the Nike Air Jordan, have become legendary. However, can we base the legendary status of his shoe solely on his brilliant athletic play? Can we say the legendary status of his shoes is simply a function of being in the right place at the right time or is there more to it?

As we learned in the last chapter, the symbolic interactionists would argue that the meaning behind the shoes, their legendary status in other words, arose from the micro-level. It arose from people assigning a special value to the shoes and creating norms around that value. Then these norms are spread until it reaches the societal level. Interestingly, the shoe had mass appeal among young African Americans in the inner cities of America who saw Michael Jordan and basketball itself as kind of an extension of where they could go, who they were, and what could be achieved. The shoe was definitely marketed to this group. Who better to market to inner-city African Americans than Spike Lee. Lee starred as Mars Blackmon (Black man) on the acclaimed Air Jordan televisions ads of the early 1990's. He would often begin by saying "Mars Blackmon here, and nobody can cover my main man Michael Jordan … Nobody, Nobody Nobody." Lee's commercials were very popular. They were shown on sports broadcasts as well as during sitcoms and dramas with large Black audiences. Nonetheless, by the time the heavy marketing started, the appeal was already there.

Basketball itself has always been a favorite of inner-city youth of all races. Basketball was enormously popular in the inner cities because it was relatively inexpensive to participate. You did not need a lot of equipment like you do for football. You did not need a whole lot of space and people like you do for baseball. You did not need ice like you do for hockey. The rules are easy to understand. Basketball could be played virtually anywhere. All you needed was a goal and a basketball.

What we see then is basketball having a cultural impact on inner-city youth, namely African Americans. It was the first sport to raise African American stars, many of whom were from the inner city, to celebrity status. During the midst of urban decline and the economic isolation faced by many inner-city residents, ballers such as Bill Russell, Clyde Frazier, George "The Iceman" Gervin, and Wilt Chamberlain were heroes. African Americans identified with the players as well as the game. Rap songs were created: "Basketball is my favorite sport/I love the way they dribble up and down the court." These lyrics from 1980's rapper Curtis Blow are one of many. Since basketball players do not have to wear heavy equipment, you can see the personality of the players through their facial expressions, which made it easier to identify with them. A whole culture within a culture was created, terminology included: "Shook," for example, means to be faked out by someone on the basketball court, but also it means to be outwitted in business or street affairs. Also from basketball comes the phrase "from the jump," which is often used in urban communities to mean from the beginning or start of something. In total, it is logical to understand how the most prominent basketball player of a generation also resonated with this group of African Americans. Ultimately, Air Jordan became a relatively low-cost symbol of greatness.

Michael Jordan's appeal also came from his deviance. He appeared to excel by his own rules. He seemed to have little regard for the old norms of sportsmanship. He wore his own brand of shoes although they clashed with those worn by his teammates and were against NBA uniform policy. He played with his tongue out, which many people interpreted as mocking the opposition. He was cocky and brash and did not mind talking trash. By no means was Jordan radical, but he was just deviant enough to resonate with inner-city youth who were by circumstance deviant. The same youth, many of whom were African American males, had grown to appreciate deviance because in their view,

going against the mainstream norms of society was the only way they were going to survive. Many held the thought that playing by the rules (conforming) would not get them far so they, like Michael Jordan, had to play by their own set of rules and hope that the rest of society would adjust.

DEVIANCE

Deviance is a violation of formal or informal social norms. Deviance is a fundamental part of any society. Every social group, whether large or small, will have deviants. Social control is the act of enforcing the norms that society deems as valuable for its existence. Social control is a critical component of any group. It is very important that the individual members of a group adhere to the standards set forth by the group. Nonetheless, every individual to some degree is deviant. We all commit acts of deviance throughout our lives, whether it is jaywalking or starting a revolution. As we will discuss in this chapter, deviance has an important social function. In fact, it is extremely important for the growth and development of a society mainly because deviance is a primary method of gauging the quality of existing norms. When norms

Figure 2 Just like the Scarlet "A," the letter "D" (Drunkard) was often attached to offenders as a method of producing shame. Copyright in the Public Domain.

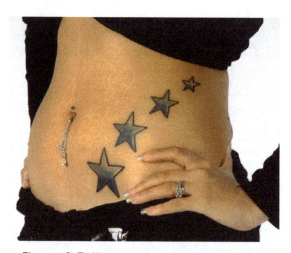

Figure 3 Tattoos are no longer seen as deviant. In fact, they are seen as conforming to the prevailing norms. Copyright © Nancy from So Cal (CC by 2.0) at http://commons.wikimedia.org/wiki/File:Woman_with_four_star_tattoos_on_her_belly,_and_a_navel_ piercing.jpg.

are challenged, society has an opportunity to determine whether the norm or the challenge to the norm is most appropriate for its cultural interests.

The obvious forms of social control involve what we know of as formal control. Formal control exists as laws and regulations. We are all familiar with traffic lights. We know that red means stop, green means go; we understand that there are speed limits; we also understand the laws that tend to preserve human sanctity—such as being honest or not murdering. Sociologists, however, are more concerned with the overall process of deviance, the outcomes, and the causes of deviance, and especially a group's response to deviance.

The group's response to these acts of deviance is referred to as sanctions. Every group, no matter how large or small, administers sanctions to those who are deviant. Most of those sanctions—just as most acts of deviance—are informal; that is, there is no written edict prescribing how a certain act should be sanctioned. Instead, every particular group has a way of dealing with deviants. The student attending a prestigious prep school who gets a tattoo of Marie Antoinette on his forehead and colors his hair purple will probably be considered deviant by his classmates and teachers. The punishment that he receives from his group may involve not being invited to join the choir. His conforming classmates may shun him. He may get invited to fewer parties. People may not want to sit next to him in the cafeteria. The social pressure that an individual receives from his or her peers is perhaps the most effective sanction. However, if the individual above were to be among others with tattoos of French royalty and colored hair, his actions won't be perceived as deviant within that group, although his deviance among larger society would persist. This points to the fact that deviance, just like other norms and values that exist in a culture, is relative to time and place and circumstance.

Deviance as a Source of Cultural Change

Sociologists are interested in the way that deviance impacts a culture. Every society must have deviance in order to grow. Dr. Martin Luther King, Jr. was one of the most famous deviants of the 20th century. His methods of protest were not well accepted by the greater American society. In fact, even the African American community did not always welcome his protests. Stories abound of African American leaders asking King "why can't you wait" for America to evolve into a country more accepting of minorities. King responded to this question in his "Letter from the Birmingham Jail":

The answer lies in the fact that there are two types of laws: Just and unjust. I would be the first to advocate obeying just laws. One has not only a legal but a moral responsibility to obey just laws. Conversely, one has a moral responsibility to disobey unjust laws. I would agree with St. Augustine that "an unjust law is no law at all." (1964 p. 82)

Following this philosophy King broke formal and informal norms. Not only did he receive social pressure from his clergy peers, he spent much time in jail for breaking laws meant to uphold de jure segregation. Furthermore, Malcolm X and other Black leaders criticized him for calling upon children to take part in violent protests in Birmingham in 1963. He was truly deviant in many ways. However, it was through his deviance that society was able to understand the adverse effects of segregation. Dr. King challenged the established norms in a way that made society question the essence of the norm. In this case, the challenge to the norm was successful and society began the process of rethinking segregation—at least lawful segregation. Now legalized race-based segregation is deviant.

Deviance has its place in society. Some acts of deviance actually help propel us forward. There are many examples of individuals changing society for the better by going against the established norms. Elon Musk is currently challenging the way that we use energy in modern society. Musk is a renowned computer programmer, engineer, and businessman. He cofounded Zip2, an innovative mapping software program that brought the city directory into the Digital Age. Zip2 quickly replaced the yellow pages as the primary source for information on local government and businesses. After selling the company, he then cofounded PayPal, which revolutionized person-to-person financial transactions. Furthermore, he cofounded SolarCity, another revolutionary company that manufactures and installs solar panels on homes and businesses. Never before could the average family affordably harness solar energy. Musk and his partners endeavor to have enough homes outfitted with panels to where society gains independence from environmentally hazardous, coal-burning electric plants. Furthermore, Musk is the creator of SpaceX, the first private company designed to accommodate space transport and eventually the exploration of Mars. Musk received a large contract from NASA to develop a transport system that could service government interests in space. However, his most ambitious project today is Tesla Motors, the first new car company that manufactures fully electric vehicles.

Figure 4 Elon Musk. Copyright in the Public Domain.

Musk has deviated from the establish norms throughout his young life. Part of being an innovator is finding a way to improve upon or redevelop that which already exists. This often involves going against the grain. This is why, as we will learn, most innovators are deviant. By definition, innovation and deviance go hand in hand. Musk invested much of the fortune he amassed from Zip2 and PayPal on Tesla. Needless to say, this was a huge risk, considering the pitfalls associated with building a car that uses battery power that performs as well as the patented internal combustion engine that uses gasoline. Most of us give little thought to the amount of energy we consume on a daily basis. The energy establishment, which includes power and oil companies, dominated energy production throughout the Industrial Revolution. While their products are highly effective and relatively cheap, the cost to the environment is staggering. Similar to what he did with SolarCity, with Tesla, Musk decided to use his immense talent and resources to deviate from the established way of doing things. Tesla's battery-powered electric cars are a direct challenge to the oil companies, car companies, and car dealers that developed the norms associated with driving automobiles today. As we learned from Dr. King when he challenged the culturally established structure of segregation and inequality, the protectors of the current value system will always put forth resistance to change. Why? Because they benefit from keeping the social order as it is. Indeed, the Vatican resisted Martin Luther; the British resisted the American patriots; and the producers of kerosene resisted J.P. Morgan and Thomas Edison's plan to introduce the electric light bulb. Similarly, Musk has found a great deal of resistance, chiefly among the auto dealers who have banded together in many states to prevent the direct sale of Tesla automobiles.

The state of New Jersey led the way in passing such legislation (Larotonda, 2014). The dealers argue that cars purchased directly from the car company would compromise age-old practices intended to protect the consumer. Specifically, they contend that dealerships have certain codes that must be followed when it comes to warranties, recalls, and lemons. These frequently occurring maladies would be very difficult for the average car owner to settle when the manufacturer is far away. In addition, the dealers maintain that unlike car manufacturers, dealerships are based locally and they are subject to local oversight. Where would a Tesla owner living in Wyoming go for routine

Figure 5 Tesla charging station powered by solar energy. Copyright © Jusdafax (CC by 3.0) at http://commons.wikimedia.org/wiki/File:Tesla_charging_station_with_so-lar_collector_trimmed.jpeg.

service or to have a recalled part replaced? Moreover, local dealers have a stronger tie to the customer. They contribute to the local economy, they support community charities, and they hire local residents (which also contributes to the local economy). The dealers make a sound point; however, the skeptics suggest that the dealers are simply protecting their own interest by limiting competition.

The banning of a product that most agree is environmentally friendly and technologically innovative suggests that society does not always immediately accept change. This leads to another point. In many cases, the challenge to the established norms fails. The resistance overcomes the deviant and society continues to adhere to the current way of operating. What do you think about the future of electric cars? Will they be the norm on our highways in the next few years? Do the auto dealers have a point?

Some acts of deviance are good for society. Dr. King and Elon Musk are past and present examples of individuals who used their work to move society forward. However, by definition, most acts of deviance are still discouraged by society. After all, there is a reason they are considered deviant. A society cannot function if there is not a high degree of adherence to its values and norms. Chaos would result otherwise. This goes for minor acts of deviance as well as the most egregious. There are, for example, certain behaviors that are universally deviant, such as murder, stealing, and child neglect. Societies put forth formal laws restricting such behaviors. Those who do not adhere to these laws tend to be severely punished, both formally and informally. However, minor acts of deviance that do not affect other individuals may be punished less severely. One form of applying group pressure to individuals is labeling. Individuals who commit a notable act of deviance that is reasonably associated with their personal character may receive a negative label called a stigma. The offender usually receives a label that symbolizes the offense. A guy who is interested in a woman only for what she can offer him sexually is labeled a "dog" because his behavior is more identifiable with basic animal instinct instead of human rationality. In another case, we can all think of classmates who may have been labeled a "nerd" in high school. He may have found it hard to get a date. He may have had to attend the prom alone. Nonetheless, everybody recognized that he was smart. After this nerd finished college, he became a top computer engineer at a leading software company. He is now labeled as "whiz kid" or even better, "innovator," and he is now more popular and successful than any of his classmates who labeled him a nerd.

Like these examples, most labels are contingent upon the behavior of the individual at the time. Such labels can be dropped if the behavior changes. The permanence of a particular label depends on the degree to which a person's behavior brings about the label. It depends on the severity of why the label was attached in the first place. Charles Manson will never be able to shake the label of "mass murderer." The severity of his actions suggests that he will always be remembered for his deviance. President Barack Obama will probably always have the label as "first African American president," regardless of what he did before or what he does after. Future textbooks may not emphasize his role as a constitutional lawyer or as a husband and father of two children. They may not refer to him as a community organizer. His master status will be associated with his being the first African American president. Deviants can also receive permanent labels if their behavior leads to a serious amount of psychological disappointment.

Bill Buckner of the Boston Red Sox will always be remembered for committing the ultimate act of deviance in baseball: taking his eye off the ball. During the 1988 World Series against the New York Mets, Buckner let a routine ground ball hit by the Mets' Mookie Wilson roll by him into right field. His error allowed the Mets to come from behind and win Game 6 of the series. The Red Sox were leading the series three games to two. A win that night would have given the Red Sox the world title. Instead, the Mets went on to win Game 7 and the world title, making Buckner's label as the guy who blew the pivotal Game 6 permanent. Buckner was a great ball player by any standards. He played twenty years in the major leagues. He won the batting title in 1980. He had a more-than-respectable career batting average of .289. He had over 2,700 career hits. Furthermore, the reality is that the Red Sox made many mistakes that night and in Game 7. Any number of players could have received the blame for losing. Nonetheless, Buckner's error happened at a crucial moment. The game had gone into extra innings. The Mets were desperately trying to rally. They needed a miracle and they got it.

The point of labeling is to evoke shame. The individual who has committed a crime and is forced to pick up litter on the side of the highway and wear an orange jumpsuit has several labels that are perfectly visible to the passersby. For one, we see that this individual is picking up trash and two the orange jumpsuit is a symbol of his labeling by society as a felon. The fact that this individual is deviant is effectively on display for hundreds of people to see. That is the purpose of the label, to inform the public that this individual is deviant and to show that such behavior will be met with a sanction that will bring shame to the perpetrator. This is a highly effective form of social control and one of the main reasons most people conform to the norms and values of society. Nobody wants to meet the ire of the group and risk being shamed.

We all remember the story of Hester Prynne. When she and the pastor committed an act of deviance, she was forced to wear the letter "A" on her clothing. Of course the letter "A" stood for their act of deviance, which was adultery. I always find it very interesting that the pastor who was an active participant never received any punishment. He never received any sanction for his acts. In fact, the pastor continued to operate in society and he was looked upon by his fellow peers as a victim of Hester Prynne's savage lust. He actually received a degree of pity from his peers. Meanwhile, Hester Prynne was forced to wear what is known as the Scarlet Letter. Of course, the purpose of her wearing this "A" was to ensure that she would be embarrassed each day that she went out into public. It was the Puritan way of evoking shame upon Hester Prynne and warning others to be mindful of their behavior.

An interesting side note of that story is that their act produced a baby, and of course Hester Prynne gave birth to the baby out of wedlock, which at that time was considered a serious offense. The baby therefore was a visual reference to her act. However, her society felt they had to enforce their own sanction—which of course was the letter "A." So society was not satisfied with the natural outcome of her act, which was the child. They wanted to ensure that *they* applied their brand of social pressure, their brand of sanctioning.

In many cases we give an individual like Dr. King or Bill Gates a negative label until their deviance proves beneficial to society and then we give it a positive label. Dr. King went from having a label attached to him by Southerners as agitator, as rabble rouser, to now his more general label as Freedom Fighter. Bill Gates exchanged the label of college dropout and nerd for pioneer of the Digital Age. Labeling does not always have to involve stigmas. Most of us have received labels that are positive or neutral. Sometimes we have many labels and it is the balance of those labels that determine how we are viewed.

There have been many theories to illustrate why deviance occurs. Robert Merton was one sociologist who created a very important explanation for deviance and the way that it plays out in society. Robert Merton is perhaps the most famous sociologist of the 20th century. He coined the phrase "American Dream." He also coined the phrase "role model." Merton believed that all individuals in a society can be categorized by their degree of deviance. He believed that most people in society are conformists.

Conformists have institutional goals. In other words, they develop goals based on what is accepted and approved by society. Also, they follow institutional means of accomplishing these goals. This is very important because following the institutional means suggests that the individual will operate within a narrower framework to accomplish his or her goals. Although this framework is narrow, most individuals in society tend to follow this pattern. Many individuals desire to be a medical doctor. That is an institutionally approved goal. In fact, it is a goal that is highly endorsed by society. The institutional means of becoming a medical doctor involves taking a very rigorous path in undergraduate school, studying biology, anatomy, and chemistry. One has to acquire a sound understanding of the natural sciences and the biomedical model. Then the student is required to complete an intense battery of classes and clinical study during medical school. Here the student is engaged in learning more about natural sciences and their effects on the body, pharmacology—the way that drugs interact with the body—and patient care. Then the future doctor has to go through a rigorous residency where they work long hours, often in places that are distant from where they went to medical school.

These are the institutional means of becoming a doctor. Most people who become medical doctors, professors, engineers, as well as people who work blue-collar jobs, such as construction, bus driver, or plumber, achieve their employment in a socially approved manner. However, the people in Merton's second category tend to take a different path. He calls these people innovators. Innovators share institutional goals with the conformists. However, they do not take the institutionally approved path to accomplishing these goals, which makes them deviant.

Most of such deviance would not be considered criminal. As far as we know, Bill Gates did not break any laws, but he certainly was deviant in his pursuit of his goals. Bill Gates and Dr. King had institutionally accepted goals. Dr. King wanted freedom that was guaranteed by the Constitution. That is a socially approved goal. But his means of acquiring it, as we discussed earlier, were deviant. He did not follow the socially prescribed path to accomplishing his goals. Some who have institutional goals but do not follow institutional means are criminal. Al Capone considered himself a normal businessman. At the heart of his operations was his adherence to the basic laws of supply and demand. The people were demanding alcohol because of Prohibition. They were demanding prostitutes and gambling. Capone was

supplying these demands. He wore a suit every day. He went to an office. He had a staff. His goal was to be a successful businessman. However, his means of accomplishing these goals were very different, very deviant. In fact, his deviance was counter to both formal and informal regulations.

Another thing that Al Capone was supplying was extortion, physical violence, and mass murder. Although Capone was a popular figure in Chicago in his early career, ultimately his brand of deviance became very unsavory to the American public and to the federal government. He was eventually sentenced to prison for tax evasion.

Merton's next category involves the retreatists. The retreatists are deviant because they do not have any goals, but they follow all the rules. These are the people who

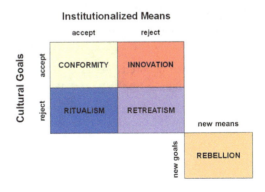

Robert K. Merton's Deviance Typology

Figure 6 Merton's Deviance Typology;
Copyright in the Public Domain.

97

Figure 7 Bob Dylan, the popular folk singer of the 1960's, used music to fight the injustices built into the American status quo. Copyright in the Public Domain.

sleepwalk through life. These are the rule followers and oftentimes they have no idea why they are following the rules. They have no purpose or goal that they are moving toward by following the rules. They are just going through the motions every day. They go to work at 8AM because they are supposed to be at work at 8AM, but getting up early in the morning has no end other than that. Their whole existence is founded upon their following rules. The retreatists are the second most represented group in society.

Finally, Merton talks about the rebels. The rebels do not have any institutional goals and they do not have any institutional means. They have to some degree withdrawn from society. They have decided to create their own subculture where they can establish their own norms and their own values. When we see certain subcultures that exist in low-income or very wealthy communities in America, this becomes evident.

In some cases the rebellion becomes so organized that a counterculture develops. This was the case in the 1960's with the hippie movement. Just like the beats and hippies were disenchanted with life in placid Middle America, the baby boomers were in search of meaning. The word "hippie" comes from "hip," so they were supposedly enlightened by what they were discovering during this quest for meaning. In many ways, the hippies rebelled against the norms of society, specifically those of Middle America. They wanted society as a whole to change, but until it did, they were content with removing themselves as much as possible. They shunned popular groups like the Four Seasons for the socially conscience, folksy rock music of Bob Dylan and The Mamas and the Papas. They used drugs. Some of them rebelled against America's core value of individualism and attempted to live communally. Their style of dress was casual and thrifty. Perhaps most visibly, they were major advocates for peace while the United States government was deeply embroiled in the Vietnam War.

Some argue that the hippies were not as rebellious as they seemed. After all, many of them were enrolled in college, an institutionally approved method of accomplishing career goals. David Brooks (2000) suggests that today it is hard to distinguish between the bohemian hippies and the conformists. Most who were considered to be hippies have increasingly adopted characteristics of the very social order that they once fought against. After returning from abroad, Brooks found it:

> …impossible to tell an espresso-sipping artist from a cappuccino-gulping banker. And this wasn't just a matter of fashion accessories. I found that if you investigated people's attitudes toward sex, morality, leisure time, and work, it was getting harder and harder to separate the anti establishment renegade from the pro-establishment company man. Most people,

at least among the college-educated set, seemed to have rebel attitudes and social-climbing attitudes all scrambled together. (2000 p. 10)

So the questions must be asked: were these hippies ever really against the core values of society, were they ever really rebels? We also have to take into consideration that perhaps the hippies achieved what they set out to accomplish. They got America to see the value of their beliefs. With this, the conformists began adopting elements of hippie core values. As a compromise, the hippies rejoined society but held on to their fundamental values, such as peace, a balance between work and leisure, acceptance of diversity, and of course, coffee houses.

Crime

Crime is the deviation from the formal norms and mores of our society. Most crimes involve the breaking of a law. Sociologists understand that there are very different degrees of crimes. Also crime is relative to time and place. What is considered a crime in the United States may not always be considered a crime in Germany. However, as we discussed before, some crimes are universal. These behaviors are against the law everywhere you go. Sociologists are more concerned with those that have a high degree of relativity. For example, we know that speaking out on controversial issues is typically not a crime in the United States. However, in some countries, speaking out or protesting is considered formally deviant, a crime. Some governments severely curtail freedom of speech.

Also, crime tends to be hierarchical. When we look at most of your high-value crimes, most of your white-collar crimes, they tend to be punished much more softly than crimes that involve less thought and less sophistication. Let's examine the act of theft. Insider trading to some degree is an act of theft. When a member of a company has access to information that is not available to other shareholders, then they can trade using an unfair advantage. Imagine for example a safe full of money. One hundred people share ownership of the safe. However, the code to the safe changed overnight and only one person has the new combination. She uses that code to withdraw money from the safe. The other owners do not have the new code yet, so they do not have any access. This is the same for insider trading.

However, white-collar crimes like insider trading are associated with light punishments. The worst cases may involve some jail time at a federal prison. Our society does not perceive such crimes as negatively as an individual who robs a local convenience store for twenty dollars. Therefore, an individual like Martha Stewart who is involved in insider trading will often get a much lighter sentence than the sentence that someone who commits a twenty-dollar robbery at the convenience store receives. White-collar crimes and street crimes are viewed very differently in our society although the white-collar crime may be far more egregious. As a result, we often reward white-collar criminals with light sanctions and we tend to punish street criminals with heavier sanctions that are intended to evoke a higher degree of shame. Many white-collar criminals may use their knowledge and social connections to reenter the workforce, whereas many street criminals are forever labeled with a criminal record that illustrates their act of deviance.

Why We Welcome Deviance

As I talked about earlier in this chapter, all individuals to some degree engage in some forms of deviance. However, most individuals are not labeled as deviant per se. Most individuals are, as Merton described, conformists. When we examine the media, various forms of entertainment, and pop culture, we see countless examples of deviance, most of which we welcome. In fact, it can be said that we are fascinated and perhaps even to some degree obsessed with various acts of deviance or with people whose lives are considered deviant. This brings us to the question of why. Why are we intrigued by the fantasy images and scripted scenarios of deviance that are often portrayed in the entertainment world?

When we listen to music or watch the news or movies, we become enthralled by deviance. We may hear the tales yarned by the rapper posing as an urban gangster rebelling against the mechanisms of law and order. The rapper may pose as an enterprising drug dealer who has now become a ghetto celebrity, but in reality this individual is in no way engaged in such behavior. Similarly, we love mafia movies like *The Godfather* and *Goodfellas* where we see deviant mob bosses and captains who commit disturbing acts of crime. Actors such as James Dean, Humphrey Bogart, Marlon Brando, and Al Pacino have achieved a fair amount of career success from portraying the "bad" guy. This is true as well in the music world. Song titles such as "Take the Money and Run" by The Steve Miller Band, "Cocaine" by J.J. Cale and Eric Clapton, "Dopeman" by NWA, and "American Gangster" by Jay-Z depict the desire of the listening public to be entertained with stories of deviance. Ultimately, we develop a level of admiration for the rebel who defies the rules as they carve out a comfortable living via their acts of deviance. Indeed *The Godfather* is consistently rated as one of the most popular movies of the 20th century right along with *Gone with the Wind* and *Casablanca*. So, why is it that we have this fascination with deviance?

Figure 8 Bonnie and Clyde's daring robberies and bloody escapes were romanticized by those who felt dispossessed by the banks and forgotten by the Federal government during the Great Depression. Copyright in the Public Domain.

There are two reasons we are captivated by deviance. The first is that watching or listening to deviance provides us with an opportunity to escape the rigidity of our society. It allows us to escape the norms and values that structure us. It is a temporary release from

Figure 10 The news is not just a source of information on world events, but it is also a source of entertainment, much of which involves highlighting deviant behavior. Copyright © Ken Lund (CC by 2.0) at http://commons.wikimedia. org/wiki/File:CNN_Center,_Atlanta,_ Georgia.jpg.

Figure 9 Through the media, we can escape the rigid norms of our society by indulging in the deviant acts of others without suffering the conse- quences. Copyright © Glenn Francis (CC by 3.0) at http://commons. wikimedia.org/wiki/File:Paris_ Hilton_2009.jpg.

the narrow expectations associated with our everyday behavior. Since most of us are conformists, we tend to go through life following a relatively strict pattern of behavior. This can sometimes be restrictive. Being entertained by individuals who appear to exist outside of these social restrictions gives us an opportunity to escape our reality without suffering the consequences of actually being deviant. It is like a roller coaster. We do not want to actually be in danger. We just want the thrill that comes along with the perception of danger, which adds a necessary degree of excitement to our lives. Thus, we like to be entertained by those engaging in deviance from the safety and comfort of our living rooms or cars without having to deal with the sanctions of actually being deviant.

The second reason we are fascinated with the media portrayal of deviance is that it provides us with a sense of superiority over the deviant individuals. This is especially true for reality T.V. For example, we tend to feel a sense of superiority over the rural and illiterate Southerner who spends his day pig hunting and drinking cheap beer. Our satisfaction comes from the fact that we can see ourselves as infinitely better than this individual. The same is true when we watch a group of women fighting on television over an issue that we may consider extremely petty. We see ourselves as superior over these individuals and it gives our general self-esteem a boost because we can compare our lives with theirs.

Moving forward, we have to also take into consideration our fascination with accounts of real-life deviance. The popularity of 24-hour news channels such as CNN is largely the result of our thirst for deviant drama. When we watch CNN and the other mass news producers, we are watching situations that actually occurred. In many cases, these behaviors can be just as exciting as fictional deviance. The caveat, of course, is that the deviance reported on the news is relatively mild and the harm is limited to hurt feelings and shame. Tragic events may interest us, but we probably will not receive a sense of enjoyment or satisfaction.

Discussion Questions

1. Provide some examples of innovators whose ideas would have been detrimental to society if adopted.
2. Most people are conformists. What are the risks involved of being an innovator in society? Why are most people not willing to take those risks?
3. Explain why labeling is such a powerful method of social control.
4. What are some examples of deviant individuals in the media who are entertaining to you? Why would their behavior be considered deviant?
5. Describe the type of deviance needed to improve society.

Key Terms Chapter 5

Deviance	A violation of formal or informal social norms.
Social Control	The act of enforcing the norms that society deems valuable for its existence. Sanctions The group's response to acts of deviance.
Label	A visible symbol of perceived character attached to an individual or group. Labels can be positive or negative; however, they are often used to engender personal shame.
Master Status	The primary characteristic by which a person is known.

READING 2

WHY WE CONFORM
BY RAFAEL F. NARVÁEZ

Human Beings Tend to Adapt to Social Circumstances

Even the most democratic societies constantly nudge people to conform to certain standards, ideas, values, fashion styles, to appropriate emotional styles (e.g., "boys don't cry"), often regardless of whether these are good or bad for us, or for our society, or for the future. In this chapter, we will study why people often comply, in different ways and by different degrees, with the broader demands of culture. We will examine research pertaining to how and why our decisions and aspects of our lifestyles may become manufactured by the broader array of social and cultural forces (not only by the market).

Solomon Asch (1951), one of the most prominent social psychologist of the 20th century, was arguably the person who pioneered research pertaining, precisely, to how and why people conform to the norms and expectations of groups. Let us discuss one of his most illustrative experiments in some detail. It took place in the mid-1950s. Asch recruited 123 male study participants who were told that they were going to participate in an experiment about visual acuity. One by one, they entered a room where they encountered five or seven males who acted as though they were also participants in the experiment, though in reality they were confederates working for Asch. The experiment consisted of showing the participant and the confederates two large cards, A and B, and asking the group to compare the contents of these cards. Card A had three parallel and perpendicular lines, marked as line one, two, and three; card B featured only one perpendicular line. All A and B cards in a stack were designed so as to make it immediately and unambiguously obvious that the single line on the B cards matched in length *only with one* of the lines on the A cards.

One by one, the confederates and the real study participant were shown pairs of A and B cards drawn from the stack, and they were asked to state which of the three lines on card A matched in length with the single line on card B. For the first couple of trials, the confederates gave the obviously correct answer; but after the fourth trial, one by one the confederates began to give obviously incorrect answers. Let us say that it was obvious that the single line on card B matched in length with line *two* on card A and yet the confederates were all in agreement that the line on card B actually matched with line *three* on card A. At this point in the experiment, something interesting began to happen. Save some exceptions, the actual participants also began to provide the obviously incorrect answers, following the cue of the confederates, even if the confederates were obviously wrong. Some participants went along with the wrong assessments of the group because they didn't want to rock the boat; they didn't want to stand out. But others, importantly, went along with the group by first denying the visual evidence provided by their own eyes; it was easier for them to think that their own eyes were conveying the wrong information, rather than to think that the group was conveying the wrong information. Solomon Asch showed that, on average, people not only tend to go along with the group but that in fact we may become blind to obvious aspects of reality simply to go along with the will of a group of peers or even strangers.

Asch's research suggests that human beings are, in general, strongly motivated by a will to conform. Human beings generally avoid transgressing the norms that govern their social surroundings. We are a very predatory species (indeed, we are responsible for the massive disappearance of other species) that, however, often acts like a herd species, often bowing to the will of the group, with individuals, in fact, often striving to dissolve themselves within the group.

Cultures That Encourage Individualism

All societies and all social groups elicit a degree of conformity from most social actors (save infants or people with socialization deficits, such as sociopaths). Indeed, as we will see in the next chapter, without a minimal degree of conformity, no society can exist. Yet, the idea that people normally tend to adapt to external demands is difficult to accept for many people, particularly for members of cultures that outwardly encourage self-reliance, self-determination, and a sense of uniqueness in individuals. So, beyond the laboratory conditions that frame Asch's research, let us begin by considering some everyday examples pertaining the phenomena of conformity and adaptation. Let us think of such occasions as weddings, funerals, parties, church functions, classrooms, your place of work, elevators—circumstances that demand a degree of conformity from all of us. It is clear that in these social environments people generally tend to abide by the expectations of the group; for example, by dress codes, codes of conduct, rules of speech, so that we behave and speak in ways that are more or less appropriate for the occasion. As many researchers have shown, we indeed tend to gesture within parameters that befit the situation, carry ourselves so as to signal a degree of agreement with the norms governing the interaction. In an elevator, for instance, people typically try to avoid displays of emotion, speak with an "appropriate" tone of voice, with appropriate manners and gestures. At a funeral we likewise tend to broadcast appropriate signals. At a job interview we tend to act and behave in a manner that generally befits the expectations of interviewers. When meeting acquaintances for the first time we yet again tend to display the version of ourselves that facilitates and eases the encounter. When on a date, we likewise tend to conduct ourselves in a manner befitting the occasion, etc.

To be sure, even members of groups who profess non-conformity—for instance, those who defy mainstream standards, values, or tastes—also tend to conform to the standards that govern their particular subcultures. Punks,

Hippies, gang members, the Amish and many other groups challenge mainstream codes. But members of these groups very much adhere to a subset of expectations and codes that govern their own subcultures. Similarly, members of highly individualistic cultures (that is to say, cultures that encourage individuals to see themselves as unique, independent, self-reliant, self-directed—cultures that value individual determination and perseverance) also tend to conform. The mainstream American culture, for example, is arguably the most individualistic in the world (Suh et al. 1998). Yet, Americans, much as members of any other society, also tend to conform and to adapt.

Bear in mind, firstly, that economic growth in the U.S. has historically hinged on consumption (among other factors, of course), which means that, as suggested, the personal desires and motives of consumers have to reflect, at least minimally, the needs of the market itself, the ideas and values engineered by it. But secondly, and more importantly, Americans undergo, much as members of any other society, a process of *socialization* whereby the person, from birth on, learns the social codes, how to display them, and what to expect if he or she violates them. Which teaches him/her how fit in, which allows him/her to partake in the social order and to become part of a larger and stronger (social) organism. Hence, as any member of any other society, Americans also undergo, and typically comply with, various mechanisms of *social control*: precisely, the social mechanisms that enforce collectively relevant beliefs, norms, and values, the mechanisms that typically punish those who infringe on these things. (If you go to a wedding wearing a t-shirt, for example, and thus infringe on the codes operant in this scenario, you will likely receive raised eyebrows and cold shoulders, be subjected to gossip, etc. which are mechanisms of social control that keep people from infringing on the norm. And of course, the law is a mechanism of social control organized and enforced by the government itself.)

Perhaps, as some researchers have argued, Americans, much as the members of other individualistic cultures, conform less when compared to members of collectivistic cultures, that is to say, cultures that encourage individuals to see themselves not as unique but as active members of larger social order, cultures that value group accomplishment over individualistic perseverance, cultures that underscore the notion that fate is a collective accomplishment. But nevertheless the point to keep in mind is that all human beings, regardless of their culture, *must* conform to at least a minimum of social demands. To conform means to accept social norms and values, to abide by them, and thus conformity legitimizes these norms and values and helps society to sustain, enforce, and maintain a civic order. Conformity thus encourages social interconnection, cohesiveness, and stability (though we will further discuss the disadvantages of conforming soon, as well). And in this particular sense, conformity, and attendant mechanisms of social control, are not only helpful but also very desirable for any society.

The Risks of Non-compliance

Again, just as some people conform more readily than others, others resist social injunctions and demands more readily and frequently than others. But anyone who resists is likely to face retaliations from society itself. At a minimal level, these involve raised eyebrows and cold shoulders, as noted, but retaliations may also involve degrees of ostracism that can be injurious, psychologically and physically. Here is a telling example: a Saudi woman named Manal al-Shari was imprisoned and endlessly harassed by Saudi authorities *and* by fellow citizens—merely because she dared to drive a car. Her son at school was bullied and bruised on account of the "unfeminine" behavior of his mother. Her brother was detained twice for giving her the keys to his car and was subsequently harassed to the point of having to quit his professional job and having to leave the country with his wife and children. Her father had to endure sermons from the local Imam, who equated women who drive with prostitutes. Manal al-Shari insisted on defending her elemental right to drive; and thus, concerned Saudi citizens retaliated and used social media—to demand that she be flogged in public! As this courageous woman says, *fighting against oppressive societal norms is often harder than fighting against openly oppressive and tyrannical regimes.* More generally, persons who transgresses the codes of gender—that is to say, those who chose *not* to deploy the gestures, the sign language, the dress-codes that men and women are expected to deploy so that others can identify them as men and women "proper"—are likely to endure more than just disapproving looks. Hate crimes against gay men and lesbians—indeed the murdering of members of these communities—tragically illustrate this idea. (In general, those who transgress the codes of gender may suffer a disproportionate burden of mental health problems, such as stress and depression, as data pertaining to the health status of gay men and women clearly show [Meyer 2003]).

To be sure, sometimes non-compliers become cultural heroes, as the example of Manal al-Shari suggests, or as the Civil Rights Movement or feminist movements illustrate. But more often, people who transgress dominant norms, rather than thereby becoming cultural heroes, tend to become handicapped: socially, they are often ostracized or scorned rather than celebrated; politically they may become disenfranchised; economically, they may carry disproportionate burdens. Transsexual men and women, for example, have a much harder time finding adequate employment, adequate housing, adequate education, adequate health care, regardless of their skills and of their character.

Even the non-compliers who eventually emerge as cultural heroes—also tend to first pay the price of non-compliance. Some of the artists who opened entire new fields of aesthetic expression and experience—from the painter Vincent Van Gogh to the poet Charles Baudelaire—also experienced the sort of daily little miseries that often punctuate the existence of *true* outsiders (who are not merely fashionable eccentrics). Indeed, many of such artistic pioneers died forsaken, even despised. The case of Nelson Mandela, who spent 27 years in prison, also illustrates this idea in the most sobering manner.

Compliance with Absurd or Belittling Social Rules

Indeed, it is important to underscore that the everyday existence of non-compliers is likely to be burdened—*even if the social codes that non-compliers violate are arbitrary, absurd, and even if these codes aim to dehumanize them.* The example of Manal al-Shari suggests that most Saudi women, save daring exceptions, had readily complied with the bizarre notion that driving was somehow unfeminine and embarrassing. As Thomas Paine, the 18th-century English-American revolutionary, argued, sometimes the will to follow "common sense" does not stem from the power of "commonsensical" ideas themselves, or from their intrinsic goodness, but simply from the fact that people tend to get used to inherited ideas, often unthinkingly abiding by the imaginations of dead generations.

The notion that people often comply with absurd or dehumanizing norms, or norms that damage their own existence, counterintuitive as it might be, warrants a full theoretical explanation, which I will provide in a subsequent chapter. But for now let us only consider a couple of additional examples closer to the U.S.

In the 1950s, American girls and women were socialized, in general and save exceptions, to believe that they would find fulfillment primarily, or even exclusively, in their God-given role as nurturers (Friedan, 2001). This particular belief-system (which Betty Friedan, the leader of the Second Wave of Feminism, termed the Feminine Mystique) postulated that women's natures had been intended for nurturing. Men and women often thought that women could therefore fulfill their biological fate primarily in the domestic sphere, nurturing the family, the children, the garden, the pets and taking care of the meals, the cleaning, etc. This belief-system postulated that women should exclude themselves from the public sphere, and from any life-path that would drive them away from their role as nurturers. Hence, from a young age, women were discouraged from pursuing careers, businesses, occupations with higher levels of responsibility (as these were seen as not feminine and indeed as unfeminine) and were thus discouraged from being financially, intellectually, and socially independent. Non-compliers—i.e., "non-feminine" women who strived to attain education and positions of power—often faced daily, petty retaliations from both men and women, from strangers and from kin. These outsiders brooked a disproportionate share of ego-attacks, precisely because they went against the *arbitrary, absurdly limiting and belittling* codes that governed femininity.

It is also worth taking a look at a contemporary example pertaining to gender. Let us turn to the work of Michael Kimmel, an American sociologist who has devoted most of his career to study masculinity in the U.S. He has similarly shown that young American men today, for example college students in their early twenties, often find themselves, much as their grandmothers in the fifties, unable to go against the codes of their gender, *however absurd and belittling these codes of masculinity might be.* Consider "bro-codes" about drinking, for instance. Kimmel (2008) describes the following scene pertaining to drinking rituals:

> Nick starts his night by ingesting some vile concoction invented solely for the enjoyment of the onlookers. Tonight the drink of choice is a 'Three Wise Men,' a shot composed of equal parts Jim Beam, Jack Daniels, and Johnnie Walker. Other variations include the more ethnically diverse (substitute Jose Cuervo for the Johnnie Walker), or the truly vomit-inducing (add a little half-and-half and just a splash of Tabasco). The next drink comes at him fast, a Mind Eraser, another classic of the power hour [the time that Nick and buddies reserve for fun]. It's like a Long Island Iced Tea except more potent, and it is drunk through a straw as quickly as possible. Shot after shot after shot is taken, the guys become all the more loud and obnoxious, and the bar manager brings a trashcan over to Nick's side, just in case. [...] Not surprisingly, the trashcan comes in handy. Nick's body finally relents as closing time approaches. He spews out a stream of vomit and the other guys know it's time to go. Fun was had, memories were made, but most importantly ... he puked. His friends can rest easy: a job well done. (Kimmel 2008, 95–96)

For many of the Nicks who inhabit Guyland, getting sick in such a manner is clearly preferable to breaking the norms that govern Guyland. As Kimmel reports, doing fraternity pledges that involve cleaning vomit, walking around grabbing the penises of other pledges while being mocked and insulted, or indeed risking being killed in hazing rituals is also preferable to breaking these norms. Every year, as Kimmel notes, about 1,400 college students aged 18 to 24, almost four students per day, are in fact "killed as a result of drinking [and] nearly half a million suffer some sort of injury" (Kimmel 2008, 106).

Note also that, much as their grandmothers, these guys have not invented these norms, the codes and rules that often guide their behavior. They have merely inherited them, without thinking too much, it would seem, about whether these make sense, or whether, all things considered, they are good or bad for them. (For the most part, they are bad. A pile of data about shows that young American men, particularly the Nicks described by Kimmel, are failing in unprecedented ways in virtually every area of achievement that is important at their age: succeeding at school, moving away from the parental house, becoming financially independent, etc. In comparison with women of their age, young American men are nearly twice as likely to live with their parents. In comparison to the previous generation, they are more likely to depend on parental money. The list is long. Philip Zimbardo, one of the most prominent contemporary social psychologists, has in fact describes this scenario as the "demise of guys.")

The examples above, in any case, illustrate the idea that men and women often fall prey to their own instinct, natural and useful as some times is, to follow the will of the larger (social) organism, not necessarily because this makes rational sense. This aspect of human nature is important for the life of a social species such as ours, but it also accounts for many of our troubles, much of our suffering, many of our delusions and humiliations. And it is therefore important for democratic societies to understand and to intervene in this aspect of social life. Let us conclude this chapter with Doris Lessing:

> Imagine saying to our children: "in the last fifty or so years, the human race has become aware of a great deal of information about its mechanisms [information provided particularly by sociologists and social psychologists]; how it behaves, how it must behave under certain circumstances. If this is to be useful, you must learn to contemplate these [social] rules calmly, dispassionately, disinterestedly, without emotion. It is information that will set people free from blind loyalties, obedience to slogans, rhetoric, leaders, group emotions. (1987, 61)

Though Lessing imagines a society where school children are encouraged to learn this sort of lesson, she also realizes that no government, no nation, no political party will actually design curricula to teach children "to become individuals able to resist group pressure" (1987, 62). Why? Because such groups often depend on group members who follow group-thinking. Thus, she suggests, it is up to us: parents, teachers, friends—it is up to the civil society to nurse these ideas, to encourage *not* fashionable eccentricity or potentially dangerous deviance but a process of psychological decolonization.

READING 3

THE SAINTS AND THE ROUGHNECKS

BY WILLIAM J. CHAMBLISS

Organizational processing, whether in the criminal justice or health care systems, tends to produce some taken-for-granted assumptions about all of the people processed. These assumptions are frequently held just as often by lay people as by professionals. It is believed that persons processed by these systems share a set of common characteristics. They are alike, not only in the offenses they have committed, but in other significant social respects as well. And, in turn, they are markedly dissimilar from all members of conventional society.

William J. Chambliss, in a study of two different high school gangs, finds variations in social responses to deviance that attest to the power and consequences of social reputation. Reputation is made up of one's past of alleged performance, social responses, and expectations for future performance. Although both of the gangs studied engaged in the same frequency of deviance, one gang received considerable official social control attention while the other one did not. In time, members of the two gangs lived up to the community's differential predictions about their future after graduation from high school. In this case study, the subsequent careers of both gangs turned out to be examples of a self-fulfilling prophecy—what people believe to be real will be real in its consequences.

Eight promising young men-children of good, stable, white upper-middle-class families, active in school affairs, good pre-college students—were some of the most delinquent boys at Hanibal High School. While community residents and parents knew that these boys occasionally sowed a few wild oats, they were totally unaware that sowing wild oats completely occupied the daily routine of these young men. The Saints were constantly occupied with truancy, drinking, wild driving, petty theft and vandalism. Yet not one was officially arrested for any misdeed during the two years I observed them.

This record was particularly surprising in light of my observations during the same two years of another gang of Hanibal High School students, six lower-class white boys known as the Roughnecks. The Roughnecks were constantly in trouble with police and community even though their rate of delinquency was about equal with that of the Saints. What was the cause of this disparity? The result? The following consideration of the activities, social class and community perceptions of both gangs may provide some answers.

The Saints from Monday to Friday

The Saints' principal daily concern was with getting out of school as early as possible. The boys managed to get out of school with minimum danger that they would be accused of playing hockey through an elaborate procedure for obtaining "legitimate" release from class. The most common procedure was for one boy to obtain the release of another by fabricating a meeting of some committee, program or recognized club. Charles might raise his hand in his 9:00 chemistry class and ask to be excused—a euphemism for going to the bathroom. Charles would go to Ed's math class and inform the teacher that Ed was needed for a 9:30 rehearsal of the drama club play. The math teacher would recognize Ed and Charles as "good students" involved in numerous school activities and would permit Ed to leave at 9:30. Charles would return to his class, and Ed would go to Tom's English class to obtain his release. Tom would engineer Charles' escape. The strategy would continue until as many of the Saints as possible were freed. After a stealthy trip to the car (which had been parked in a strategic spot), the boys were off for a day of fun.

Over the two years I observed the Saints, this pattern was repeated nearly every day. There were variations on the theme, but in one form or another, the boys used this procedure for getting out of class and then off the school grounds. Rarely did all eight of the Saints manage to leave school at the same time. The average number avoiding school on the days I observed them was five.

Having escaped from the concrete corridors the boys usually went either to a pool hall on the other (lower-class) side of town or to a café in the suburbs. Both places were out of the way of people the boys were likely to know (family or school officials), and both provided a source of entertainment. The pool hall entertainment was the generally rough atmosphere, the occasional hustler, the sometimes drunk proprietor and, of course, the game of pool. The café's entertainment was provided by the owner. The boys would "accidentally" knock a glass on the floor or spill cola on the counter—not all the time, but enough to be sporting. They would also bend spoons, put salt in sugar bowls and generally tease whoever was working in the café. The owner had opened the café recently and was dependent on the boys' business which was, in fact, substantial since between the horsing around and the teasing they bought food and drinks.

The Saints on Weekends

On weekends, the automobile was even more critical than during the week, for on weekends the Saints went to Big Town—a large city with a population of over a million, 25 miles from Hanibal. Every Friday and Saturday night most of the Saints would meet between 8:00 and 8:30 and would go into Big Town. Big Town activities included drinking heavily in taverns or nightclubs, driving drunkenly through the streets, and committing acts of vandalism and playing pranks.

By midnight on Fridays and Saturdays the Saints were usually thoroughly high, and one or two of them were often so drunk they had to be carried to the cars. Then the boys drove around town, calling obscenities to women and girls; occasionally trying (unsuccessfully so far as I could tell) to pick girls up; and driving recklessly through red lights and at high speeds with their lights out. Occasionally they played "chicken." One boy would climb out the back window of the car and across the roof to the driver's side of the car while the car was moving at high speed (between 40 and 50 miles an hour); then the driver would move over and the boy who had just crawled across the car roof would take the driver's seat.

Searching for "fair game" for a prank was the boys' principal activity after they left the tavern. The boys would drive alongside a foot patrolman and ask directions to some street. If the policeman leaned on the car in the course of answering the question, the driver would speed away, causing him to lose his balance. The Saints were careful to play this prank only in an area where they were not going to spend much time and where they could quickly disappear around a corner to avoid having their license plate number taken.

Construction sites and road repair areas were the special province of the Saints' mischief. A soon-to-be-repaired hole in the road inevitably invited the Saints to remove lanterns and wooden barricades and put them in the car, leaving the hole unprotected. The boys would find a safe vantage point and wait for an unsuspecting motorist to drive into the hole. Often, though not always, the boys would go up to the motorist and commiserate with him about the dreadful way the city protected its citizenry.

Leaving the scene of the open hole and the motorist, the boys would then go searching for an appropriate place to erect the stolen barricade. An "appropriate place" was often a spot on a highway near a curve in the road where the barricade would not be seen by an oncoming motorist. The boys would wait to watch an unsuspecting motorist attempt to stop and (usually) crash into the wooden barricade. With saintly bearing the boys might offer help and understanding.

A stolen lantern might well find its way onto the back of a police car or hang from a street lamp. Once a lantern served as a prop for a re-enactment of the "midnight ride of Paul Revere" until the "play," which was taking place at 2:00 A.M. in the center of a main street of Big Town, was interrupted by a police car several blocks away. The boys ran, leaving the lanterns on the street, and managed to avoid being apprehended.

Abandoned houses, especially if they were located in out-of-the-way places, were fair game for destruction and spontaneous vandalism. The boys would break windows, remove furniture to the yard and tear it apart, urinate on the walls and scrawl obscenities inside.

Through all the pranks, drinking and reckless driving the boys managed miraculously to avoid being stopped by police. Only twice in two years was I aware that they had been stopped by a Big City policeman. Once was for speeding (which they did every time they drove whether they were drunk or sober), and the driver managed to convince the policeman that it was simply an error. The second time they were stopped they had just left a nightclub and were walking through an alley. Aaron stopped to urinate and the boys began making obscene remarks. A foot patrolman came into the alley, lectured the boys and sent them home. Before the boys got to the car one began talking in a loud voice again. The policeman, who had followed them down the alley, arrested this boy for disturbing the peace and took him to the police station where the other Saints gathered. After paying a $5.00 fine, and with the assurance that there would be no permanent record of the arrest, the boy was released.

The boys had a spirit of frivolity and fun about their escapades. They did not view what they were engaged in as "delinquency," though it surely was by any reasonable definition of that word. They simply viewed themselves as having a little fun and who, they would ask, was really hurt by it? The answer had to be no one, although this fact remains one of the most difficult things to explain about the gang's behavior. Unlikely though it seems, in two years of drinking, driving, carousing and vandalism no one was seriously injured as a result of the Saints' activities.

The Saints in School

The Saints were highly successful in school. The average grade for the group was "B," with two of the boys having close to a straight "A" average. Almost all of the boys were popular and many of them held offices in the school. One of the boys was vice-president of the student body one year. Six of the boys played on athletic teams.

At the end of their senior year, the student body selected ten seniors for special recognition as the "school wheels"; four of the ten were Saints. Teachers and school officials saw no problem with any of these boys and anticipated that they would all "make something of themselves."

How the boys managed to maintain this impression is surprising in view of their actual behavior while in school. Their technique for covering truancy was so successful that teachers did not even realize that the boys were absent from school much of the time. Occasionally, of course, the system would backfire and then the boy was on his own. A boy who was caught would be most contrite, would plead guilty and ask for mercy. He inevitably got the mercy he sought.

Cheating on examinations was rampant, even to the point of orally communicating answers to exams as well as looking at one another's papers. Since none of the group studied, and since they were primarily dependent on one another for help, **it is** surprising that grades were so high. Teachers contributed to the deception in their admitted inclination to give these boys (and presumably others like them) the benefit of the doubt. When asked how the boys did in school, and when pressed on specific examinations, teachers might admit that they were disappointed in John's performance, but would quickly add that they "knew he was capable of doing better," so John was given a higher grade than he had actually earned. How often this happened is impossible to know. During the time that I observed the group, I never saw any of the boys take homework home. Teachers may have been "understanding" very regularly.

One exception to the gang's generally good performance was Jerry, who had a "C" average in his junior year, experienced disaster the next year and failed to graduate. Jerry had always been a little more nonchalant than the others about the liberties he took in school. Rather than wait for someone to come get him from class, he would offer his own excuse and leave. Although he probably did not miss any more classes than most of the others in the group, he did not take the requisite pains to cover his absences. Jerry was the only Saint whom I ever heard talk back to a teacher.

Although teachers often called him a "cut up" or a "smart kid," they never referred to him as a troublemaker or as a kid headed for trouble. It seems likely, then, that Jerry's failure his senior year and his mediocre performance his junior year were consequences of his not playing the game the proper way (possibly because he was disturbed by his parents' divorce). His teachers regarded him as "immature" and not quite ready to get out of high school.

The Police and the Saints

The local police saw the Saints as good boys who were among the leaders of the youth in the community. Rarely, the boys might be stopped in town for speeding or for running a stop sign. When this happened the boys were always polite, contrite and pled for mercy. As in school, they received the mercy they asked for. None ever received a ticket or was taken into the precinct by the local police.

The situation in Big City, where the boys engaged in most of their delinquency, was only slightly different. The police there did not know the boys at all, although occasionally the boys were stopped by a patrolman. Once they were caught taking a lantern from a construction site. Another time they were stopped for running a stop sign, and on several occasions they were stopped for speeding. Their behavior was as before: contrite, polite and penitent. The urban police, like the local police, accepted their demeanor as sincere. More important, the urban police were convinced that these were good boys just out for a lark.

The Roughnecks

Hanibal townspeople never perceived the Saints' high level of delinquency. The Saints were good boys who just went in for an occasional prank. After all, they were well dressed, well mannered and had nice cars. The Roughnecks were a different story. Although the two gangs of boys were the same age, and both groups engaged in an equal amount of wild-oat sowing, everyone agreed that the not-so-well-dressed, not-so-well-mannered, not-so-rich boys were heading for trouble. Townspeople would say, "You can see the gang members at the drugstore night after night, leaning against the storefront (sometimes drunk) or slouching around inside buying cokes, reading magazines, and probably stealing old Mr. Wall blind. When they are outside and girls walk by, even respectable girls, these boys make suggestive remarks. Sometimes their remarks are downright lewd."

From the community's viewpoint, the real indication that these kids were in for trouble was that they were constantly involved with the police. Some of them had been picked up for stealing, mostly small stuff, of course, "but still it's stealing small stuff that leads to big time crimes." "Too bad," people said. "Too bad that these boys couldn't behave like the other kids in town; stay out of trouble, be polite to adults, and look to their future."

The community's impression of the degree to which this group of six boys (ranging in age from 16 to 19) engaged in delinquency was somewhat distorted. In some ways the gang was more delinquent than the community thought; in other ways they were less.

The fighting activities of the group were fairly readily and accurately perceived by almost everyone. At least once a month, the boys would get into some sort of fight, although most fights were scraps between members of the group or involved only one member of the group and some peripheral hanger-on. Only three times in the period of observation did the group fight together: once against a gang from across town, once against two Blacks and once against a group of boys from another school. For the first two fights the group went out "looking for trouble"—and they found it both times. The third fight followed a football game and began spontaneously with an argument on the football field between one of the Roughnecks and a member of the opposition's football team.

Jack had a particular propensity for fighting and was involved in most of the brawls. He was a prime mover of the escalation of arguments into fights.

More serious than fighting, had the community been aware of it, was theft. Although almost everyone was aware that the boys occasionally stole things, they did not realize the extent of the activity. Petty stealing was a frequent event for the Roughnecks. Sometimes they stole as a group and coordinated their efforts; other times they stole in pairs. Rarely did they steal alone.

The thefts ranged from very small things like paperback books, comics and ballpoint pens to expensive items like watches. The nature of the thefts varied from time to time. The gang would go through a period of systematically lifting items from automobiles or school lockers. Types of thievery varied with the whim of the gang. Some forms of thievery were more profitable than others, but all thefts were for profit, not just thrills.

Roughnecks siphoned gasoline from cars as often as they had access to an automobile, which was not very often. Unlike the Saints, who owned their own cars, the Roughnecks would have to borrow their parents' cars, an event which occurred only eight or nine times a year. The boys claimed to have stolen cars for joy rides from time to time.

Ron committed the most serious of the group's offenses. With an unidentified associate the boy attempted to burglarize a gasoline station. Although this station had been robbed twice previously in the same month, Ron denied any involvement in either of the other thefts. When Ron and his accomplice approached the station, the owner was hiding in the bushes beside the station. He fired both barrels of a double-barreled shotgun at the boys. Ron was severely injured, the other boy ran away and was never caught. Though he remained in critical condition for several months, Ron finally recovered and served six months of the following year in reform school. Upon release from reform school, Ron was put back a grade in school, and began running around with a different gang of boys. The Roughnecks considered the new gang less delinquent than themselves, and during the following year Ron had no more trouble with the police.

The Roughnecks, then, engaged mainly in three types of delinquency: theft, drinking and fighting. Although community members perceived that this gang of kids was delinquent, they mistakenly believed that their illegal activities were primarily drinking, fighting and being a nuisance to passersby. Drinking was limited among the gang members, although it did occur, and theft was much more prevalent than anyone realized.

Drinking would doubtless have been more prevalent had the boys had ready access to liquor. Since they rarely had automobiles at their disposal, they could not travel very far, and the bars in town would not serve them. Most of the boys had little money, and this, too, inhibited their purchase of alcohol. Their major source of liquor was a local drunk who would buy them a fifth if they would give him enough extra to buy himself a pint of whiskey or a bottle of wine.

The community's perception of drinking as prevalent stemmed from the fact that it was the most obvious delinquency the boys engaged in. When one of the boys had been drinking, even a casual observer seeing him on the corner would suspect that he was high.

There was a high level of mutual distrust and dislike between the Roughnecks and the police. The boys felt very strongly that the police were unfair and corrupt. Some evidence existed that the boys were correct in their perception.

The main source of the boys' dislike for the police undoubtedly stemmed from the fact that the police would sporadically harass the group. From the standpoint of the boys, these acts of occasional enforcement of the law were whimsical and uncalled for. It made no sense to them, for example, that the police would come to the corner occasionally and threaten them with arrest for loitering when the night before the boys had been out siphoning gasoline from cars and the police had been nowhere in sight. To the boys, the police were stupid on the one hand, for not being where they should have been and catching the boys in a serious offense, and unfair on the other hand, for trumping up "loitering" charges against them.

From the viewpoint of the police, the situation was quite different. They knew, with all the confidence necessary to be a policeman, that these boys were engaged in criminal activities. They knew this partly from occasionally catching them, mostly from circumstantial evidence ("the boys were around when those tires were slashed"), and partly because the police shared the view of the community in general that this was a bad bunch of boys. The best the police could hope to do was to be sensitive to the fact that these boys were engaged in illegal acts and arrest them whenever there was some evidence that they had been involved. Whether or not the boys had in fact committed a particular act in a particular way was not especially important. The police had a broader view: their job was to stamp out these kids' crimes; the tactics were not as important as the end result.

Over the period that the group was under observation, each member was arrested at least once. Several of the boys were arrested a number of times and spent at least one night in jail. While most were never taken to court, two of the boys were sentenced to six months' incarceration in boys' schools.

The Roughnecks in School

The Roughnecks' behavior in school was not particularly disruptive. During school hours they did not all hang around together, but tended instead to spend most of their time with one or two other members of the gang who were their special buddies. Although every member of the gang attempted to avoid school as much as possible, they were not particularly successful and most of them attended school with surprising regularity. They considered school a burde—something to be gotten through with a minimum of conflict. If they were "bugged" by a particular teacher, it could lead to trouble. One of the boys, Al. once threatened to beat up a teacher and, according to the other boys, the teacher hid under a desk to escape him.

Teachers saw the boys the way the general community did, as heading for trouble, as being uninterested in making something of themselves. Some were also seen as being incapable of meeting the academic standards of the school. Most of the teachers expressed concern for this group of boys and were willing to pass them despite poor performance, in the belief that failing them would only aggravate the problem.

The group of boys had a grade point average just slightly above "C." Two of the boys were good football players. Herb was acknowledged to be the best player in the school and Jack was almost as good. Both boys were criticized for their failure to abide by training rules, for refusing to come to practice as often as they should, and for not playing their best during practice. What they lacked in sportsmanship they made up for in skill, apparently, and played every game no matter how poorly they had performed in practice or how many practice sessions they had missed.

Two Questions

Why did the community, the school and the police react to the Saints as though they were good, upstanding, non-delinquent youths with bright futures but to the Roughnecks as though they were tough, young criminals who were headed for trouble" Why did the Roughnecks and the Saints in fact have quite different careers after high school, careers which, by and large, lived up to the expectations of the community?

The most obvious explanation for the differences in the community's and law enforcement agencies' reactions to the two gangs is that one group of boys was "more delinquent" than the other. Which group was more delinquent? The answer to this question will determine in part how we explain the differential responses to these groups by the members of the community and, particularly, by law enforcement and school officials.

In sheer number of illegal acts, the Saints were the more delinquent. They were truant from school for at least part of the day almost every day of the week. In addition, their drinking and vandalism occurred with surprising regularity. The Roughnecks, in contrast, engaged sporadically in delinquent episodes. While these episodes were frequent, they certainly did not occur on a daily or even a weekly basis.

The difference in frequency of offenses was probably caused by the Roughnecks' inability to obtain liquor and to manipulate legitimate excuses from school. Since the Roughnecks had less money than the Saints, and teachers carefully supervised their school activities, the Roughnecks' hearts may have been as black as the Saints', but their misdeeds were not nearly as frequent.

There are really no clear-cut criteria by which to measure qualitative differences in antisocial behavior. The most important dimension of the difference is generally referred to as the "seriousness" of the offenses.

If seriousness encompasses the relative economic costs of delinquent acts, then some assessment can be made. The Roughnecks probably stole an average of about $5.00 worth of goods a week. Some weeks the figure was considerably higher, but these times must be balanced against long periods when almost nothing was stolen.

The Saints were more continuously engaged in delinquency but their acts were not for the most part costly to property. Only their vandalism and occasional theft of gasoline would so qualify. Perhaps once or twice a month they would siphon a tankful of gas. The other costly items were street signs, construction lanterns and the like. All of these acts combined probably did not quite average $5.00 a week, partly because much of the stolen equipment was abandoned and presumably could be recovered. The difference in cost of stolen property between the two groups was trivial, but the Roughnecks probably had a slightly more expensive set of activities than did the Saints.

Another meaning of seriousness is the potential threat of physical harm to members of the community and to the boys themselves. The Roughnecks were more prone to physical violence; they not only welcomed an opportunity to fight; they went seeking it. In addition, they fought among themselves frequently. Although the fighting never included deadly weapons, it was still a menace, however minor, to the physical safety of those involved.

The Saints never fought. They avoided physical conflict both inside and outside the group. At the same time, though, the Saints frequently endangered their own and other people's lives. They did so almost every time they drove a car, especially if they had been drinking. Sober, their driving was risky; under the influence of alcohol it was horrendous. In addition, the Saints endangered the lives of others with their pranks. Street excavations left unmarked were a very serious hazard.

Evaluating the relative seriousness of the two gangs' activities is difficult. The community reacted as though the behavior of the Roughnecks was a problem, and they reacted as though the behavior of the Saints was not. But the members of the community were ignorant of the array of delinquent acts that characterized the Saints' behavior. Although concerned citizens were unaware of much of the Roughnecks' behavior as well, they were much better informed about the Roughnecks' involvement in delinquency than they were about the Saints'.

Visibility

Differential treatment of the two gangs resulted in part because one gang was infinitely more visible than the other. This differential **visibility** was a direct function of the economic standing of the families. The Saints had access to automobiles and were able to remove themselves from the sight of the community. In as routine a decision as to where to go to have a milkshake after school, the Saints stayed away from the mainstream of community life. Lacking transportation, the Roughnecks could not make it to the edge of town. The center of town was the only practical place for them to meet since their homes were scattered throughout the town and any noncentral meeting place put an undue hardship on some members. Through necessity the Roughnecks congregated in a crowded area where everyone in the community passed frequently, including teachers and law enforcement officers. They could easily see the Roughnecks hanging around the drugstore.

The Roughnecks, of course, made themselves even more **visi**ble by making remarks to passersby and by occasionally getting into fights on the corner. Meanwhile, Just as regularly, the Saints were either at the café on one edge of town or in the pool hall at the other edge of town. Without any particular realization that they were making themselves inconspicuous, the Saints were able to hide their time-wasting. Not only were they removed from the mainstream of traffic, but they were almost always inside a building.

On their escapades the Saints were also relatively invisible, since they left Hanibal and traveled to Big City. Here, too, they were mobile, roaming the city, rarely going to the same area twice.

Demeanor

To the notion of visibility must be added the difference in the responses o group members to outside intervention with their activities. If one of the Saints was confronted with an accusing policeman, even **if** he felt he was truly innocent of a wrongdoing, his demeanor was apologetic and penitent. A Roughneck's attitude was almost the polar opposite. When confronted with a threatening adult authority, even one who tried to be pleasant, the Roughneck's hostility and disdain were clearly observable. Sometimes he might attempt to put up a veneer of respect, but it was thin and was not accepted as sincere by the authority.

School was no different from the community at large. The Saints could manipulate the system by feigning compliance with the school norms. The availability of cars at school meant that once free from the immediate sight of the teacher, the boys could disappear rapidly. And this escape was well enough planned that no administrator or teacher was nearby when the boys left. A Roughneck who wished to escape for a few hours was in a bind. If it were possible to get free from class, downtown was still a mile away, and even if he arrived there, he was still very visible. Truancy for the Roughnecks meant almost certain detection, while the Saints enjoyed almost complete immunity from sanctions.

Bias

Community members were not aware of the transgressions of the Saints. Even if the Saints had been less discreet, their favorite delinquencies would have been perceived as less serious than those of the Roughnecks.

In the eyes of the police and school officials, a boy who drinks in an alley and stands intoxicated on the street corner is committing a more serious offense than is a boy who drinks to inebriation in a nightclub or a tavern and drives around afterwards in a car. Similarly, a boy who steals a wallet from a store will be viewed as having committed a more serious offense than a boy who steals a lantern from a construction site.

Perceptual bias also operates with respect to the demeanor of the boys in the two groups when they are confronted by adults. It is not simply that adults dislike the posture affected by boys of the Roughneck ilk; more important is the conviction that the posture adopted by the Roughnecks is an indication of their devotion and commitment to deviance as a way of life. The posture becomes a cue, just as the type of the offense is a cue, to the degree to which the known transgressions are indicators of the youths' potential for other problems.

Visibility, demeanor and bias are surface variables which explain the day-to-day operations of the police. Why do these surface variables operate as they do? Why did the police choose to disregard the Saints' delinquencies while breathing down the backs of the Roughnecks?

The answer lies in the class structure of American society and the control of legal institutions by those at the top of the class structure. Obviously, no representative of the upper class drew up the operational chart for the police which led them to look in the ghettos and on street corners which led them to see the demeanor of lower-class youth as troublesome and that of upper-middle class youth as tolerable. Rather, the procedures simply developed from experience: experience with irate and influential upper-middle-class parents insisting that their son's vandalism was simply a prank and his drunkenness only a momentary "sowing of wild oats," experience with cooperative or indifferent, powerless, lower-class parents who acquiesced to the laws' definition of their son's behavior.

Adult Careers of the Saints and the Roughnecks

The community's confidence in the potential of the Saints and the Roughnecks apparently was justified. If anything, the community members underestimated the degree to which these youngsters would turn out "good" or "bad."

Seven of the eight members of the Saints went on to college immediately after high school. Five of the boys graduated from college in four years. The sixth one finished college after two years in the army, and the seventh spent four years in the air force before returning to college and receiving a B.A. degree. Of these seven college graduates, three went on for advanced degrees. One finished law school and is now active **in** state politics, one finished medical school and **is** practicing near Hannibal, and one boy is now working for a Ph.D. The other four college graduates entered submanagerial, managerial or executive training positions with larger firms.

The only Saint who did not complete college was Jerry. Jerry had failed to graduate from high school with the other Saints. During, his second senior year, after the other Saints had gone on to college, Jerry began to hang around with what several teachers described as a "rough crowd"—the gang that was heir apparent to the Roughnecks. At the end of his second senior year, when he did graduate from high school, Jerry took a job as a used-car salesman, got married and quickly had a child. Although he made several abortive attempts to go to college by attending night school. when I last saw him (ten years after high school) Jerry was unemployed and had been living on unemployment for almost a year. His wife worked as a waitress.

Some of the Roughnecks have lived up to community expectations. A number of them were headed for trouble. A few were not.

Jack and Herb were the athletes among the Roughnecks and their athletic prowess paid off handsomely. Both boys received unsolicited athletic scholarships to college. After Herb received his scholarship (near the end of his senior year), he apparently did an about-face. His demeanor became very similar to that of the Saints. Although he remained a member in good standing of the Roughnecks. He stopped participating in most activities and did not hang on the corner as often.

Jack did not change. If anything, he became more prone to fighting. He even made excuses for accepting the scholarship. He told the other gang members that the school had guaranteed him a "C" average if he would come to play football—an idea that seems far-fetched, even in this day of highly competitive recruiting.

During the summer after graduation from high school, Jack attempted suicide by Jumping from a tall building. The jump would certainly have killed most people trying it, but Jack survived. He entered college in the fall and played four years of football. He and Herb graduated in four years, and both are teaching and coaching in high schools. They are married and have stable families. If anything, Jack appears to have a more prestigious position in the community than does Herb, though both are well respected and secure in their positions.

Two of the boys never finished high school. Tommy left at the end of his junior year and went to another state. That summer he was arrested and placed on probation on a manslaughter charge. Three years later he was arrested for murder; he pleaded guilty to second degree murder and is serving a 30-year sentence in the state penitentiary.

Al, the other boy who did not finish high school, also left the state in his senior year. He is serving a life sentence in a state penitentiary for first degree murder.

Wes is a small-time gambler. He finished high school and "bummed around." After several years he made contact with a bookmaker who employed him as a runner. Later he acquired his own area and has been working it ever since. His position among the bookmakers is almost identical to the position he had in the gang; he is always around but no one is really aware of him. He makes no trouble and he does not get into any. Steady, reliable, capable of keeping his mouth closed, he plays the game by the rules, even though the game is an illegal one.

That leaves only Ron. Some of his former friends reported that they had heard he was "driving a truck up north," but no one could provide any concrete information.

Reinforcement

The community responded to the Roughnecks as boys in trouble, and the boys agreed with that perception. Their pattern of deviancy was reinforced. and breaking away from it became increasingly unlikely. *Once the boys acquired an image of themselves as deviants* [italics added], they selected new friends who affirmed that self-image. As that self-conception became more firmly entrenched, they also became willing to try new and more extreme deviances. With their growing alienation came freer expression of disrespect and hostility for representatives of the legitimate society. This disrespect increased the community's negativism, perpetuating the entire process of commitment to deviance. Lack of a commitment to deviance works the same way. In either case, the process will perpetuate itself unless some event (like a scholarship to college or a sudden failure) external to the established relationship **in**tervenes. For two of the Roughnecks (Herb and Jack), receiving college athletic scholarships created new relations and culminated in a break with the established pattern of deviance. In the case of one of the Saints (Jerry), his parents' divorce and his failing to graduate from high school changed some of his other relations. Being held back in school for a year and losing his place among the Saints had sufficient impact on Jerry to alter his self-image and virtually to assure that he would not go on to college as his peers did. Although the experiments of life can rarely be reversed, it seems likely in view of the behavior of the other boys who did not enjoy this special treatment by the school that Jerry, too, would have "become something" had he graduated as anticipated. For Herb and Jack outside intervention worked to their advantage; for Jerry it was his undoing.

Selective perception and labeling—finding, processing and punishing some kinds of criminality and not others [italics added]—means that visible, poor, nonmobile, outspoken, undiplomatic "tough" kids will be noticed, whether their actions are seriously delinquent or not. Other kids, who have established a reputation for being bright (even though underachieving), disciplined and involved in respectable activities, who are mobile and monied, will be invisible when they deviate from sanctioned activities. They'll sow their wild oats-perhaps even wider and thicker than their lower-class cohorts—but they won't be noticed. When it's time to leave adolescence most will follow the expected path, settling into the ways of the middle class, remembering fondly the delinquent but unnoticed fling of their youth. The Roughnecks and others like them may turn around, too. It is more likely that their noticeable deviance will have been so reinforced by police and community that their lives will be effectively channeled into careers consistent with their adolescent background.

In Other Words . . .

Judgments about human behavior labeled as "bad" remain, arguably, the most used and least understood of social interactions. Unfortunately, we are conditioned to think in dichotomous terms (i.e., it's either true or false) and visualize in black and white (literally and figuratively). Both are misleading and bereft of the complexity necessary to capture the essence of being human. These inadequacies also tend toward "othering"—categorizing certain groups as intrinsically different from "us" good people. First, such overly simplistic rationalizing is simply inaccurate and deadpan wrong. Life doesn't work that way. Second, we, ourselves, are at risk of being othered, turned from the fold and alienated from our own humanity. Surely, the "Saints and the Roughnecks" reading demonstrates lifelong outcomes from such estrangement.

So, what's the answer? Certainly, there is no one easy solution, but education is a great start. Throughout civilization we have engaged in explanations ranging from faith and superstition (witches are evil) to biological accounts (born bad) to naturalization attributions (genetic tendencies toward crime). None of these are adequate and, as such, moves us into a danger zone of intellectual illiteracy. Instead, with the assist of social science, we can prove ourselves capable of higher-order rationalization and a sensitivity to the human condition.

As one small example, I'd like to engage you in an exercise of *mitigating circumstances*. Again, considering our cultural tendency toward dichotomous rationale, we often accept certain cultural assertions as absolute. (In contrast, recall the *heyokas* from Unit 1, who question everything.) Below are a few statements that represent certain "wisdoms" in our culture. Ask yourself (or others) to think of a circumstance in which you can imagine an individual legitimately behaving in a manner that is *different from* the statement.

- Everyone should work.
- The government should stay out of private lives.
- Capital punishment is just.
- Free speech should be guaranteed.
- Do not kill.

Could you think of any mitigating circumstances that would challenge the statements? Does this exercise challenge some of your long-held beliefs about crime and deviance?

The Big Idea

The distinction between crime, deviance, and "normal" behavior varies across time and place. Crime/deviance is a particular kind of social interaction; like any social interaction, it is complex, constructed, and heavily dependent upon situational variance.

So What?

Unless and until we understand that crime/deviance is socially constructed, we risk partial (at best) and fully erroneous judgments about human behavior and how to manage our part in a civil society.

UNIT 4 READINGS

Unit 4: Power of the Situation

Dr. Sue to You: People, spaces, thoughts, and places

In Unit 3, we left off with an exercise on mitigating circumstances—situations or conditions that bring consideration of gray areas of life, rather than reliance on a simple dichotomous interpretation. In this unit, we extend that discussion to examine the power of the situation. The situation holds the capacity to control (or at least heavily influence) our behavior, even our very thoughts. The situation need not be simple physical presence or events; it preeminently incorporates the presence of others, real or imagined. It is like Jiminy Cricket (the famous character in Pinocchio that serves as his conscience) is sitting on your shoulder, whispering the norms of a culture or subculture. The content of the whisper may vary, of course, depending on your biography and history—again, the essence of a sociological imagination. But widespread cultural habits are commonplace in the United States, such as "don't cheat," "winning is important," and "good people tip." Even if you are in a room alone, you will probably hesitate before picking your nose.

The first reading in this unit, by Narvaez, demonstrates several examples of the power of the situation. The author introduces you to the work of Jane Elliott, a former teacher who became a world-renown expert on race relations in the United States. You may have seen or heard about her famous exercise with third-grade children, "Eye of the Storm" (sometimes called the blue eye/brown eye experiment), in which she used colored collars to emulate segregation and the crushing effects of racism. Not only does the exercise illustrate how a situation controls people, but also the extent of accessible power when one understands *how* to define the situation. You will find additional reference to this classic study at the end of this section.

Cast (2003) suggests that individuals can define the situation in three ways: by behaving in ways expected of their position or status (or one to which they aspire); by influencing and changing behavior of others; and by rejecting identities that others may try to impose on them. One of the most powerful experiments in social science is the Stanford Prison Experiment. In this classic study, psychologist Zimbardo constructed a situation in which volunteers (all healthy, intelligent young men) instantly *became* guards or prisoners, depending on the identity and situation assigned to them. Zimbardo (2007) eventually extended these concepts, known as the Lucifer effect, positing an explanation for why good people do bad things.

Recall, I promised you another article by Howie Becker. In this unit, Becker provides insight on "Becoming a Marihuana User." Written in 1953, the article has become timeless, not just because of waves of marijuana use and its cultural significance, but because Becker vividly demonstrates the power of the situation and the role of social learning in a process thought to be physical and biological. I think you will be surprised and intrigued by his findings!

In the third reading, George Orwell (yes, Orwell of the futuristic book *1984* fame) takes us through a grueling but revealing story, "Shooting an Elephant." I won't give it all away, but the last line is one you should thoughtfully contemplate: "I often wondered whether any of the others grasped that I had done it solely to avoid looking a fool" (Orwell 1936, 4).

Finally, I return you to Phillip Zimbardo in the last reading for this unit, "Understanding heroism." In this short piece, Dr. Zimbardo describes one of his most recent projects, studying the phenomenon of heroism. Heroism, he points out, is a social construction that has brought little attention within the social science world. Heroism seems to be the flip side of evil (the Lucifer effect), and, as such, a welcome turn. As usual, though, it is not without the multiplicity, complexity, and messiness of our constructed world. Stay tuned!

Studying the research results in this unit provides at least two avenues of power: we learn to recognize and resist some of the social forces at work in our culture; and we reduce our errors in judgment. The general idea is this: we often produce attribution errors of two kinds. In one type, we tend to attribute fault to dispositional (internal) characteristics of others, rather than considering external factors, or mitigating circumstances. This is known as the fundamental attribution error (Ross 1977). Interestingly, though, if we apply the same logic to our own behavior, we tend to underemphasize internal characteristics and overemphasize situational behavior. For example, think of the student in the classroom who often sleeps. We might think he is lazy, unmotivated, or does not value his education. If it is our own self caught in the act, we are more likely to attribute it to a heavy workload, physical exhaustion, chronic illness, or perhaps a boring professor!

The second type of error in judgment, known as the ultimate attribution error, occurs at the group level. In-group members attribute *negative* out-group characteristics as dispositional (*those* people are naturally that way), while attributing *positive* out-group behavior to luck, advantage, or as an exception (Pettigrew 1979). The result is prejudice (an attitude), which may sometimes result in discrimination (acting upon prejudice). Further, the judgments may incorporate widespread cultural values and biases. For example, one study found that regarding traditionally masculine tasks, male successes were more likely to be attributed to skill (and for females to good luck), while male failures were more likely to be attributed to bad luck (and females to inability) (Swim and Sanna 1996, as cited in UnderstandingPrejudice.org. 2016). Let me emphasize that many of these thoughts and actions can be non-intentional or even unconscious; however, recall the Thomas theorem: whatsoever situations are perceived as real, are real in their consequences (Thomas and Thomas 1928).

Works Cited

Cast, A. D. (2003). "Power and the ability to define the situation." *Social Psychology Quarterly*, 66, 185–201.

Orwell, G. (1936). "Shooting an elephant." In *New Writing*, London.

Pittigrew, T. F. (1979). "The ultimate attribution error: Extending Allport's cognitive analysis of prejudice." *Personality and Social Psychology Bulletin, 5,* 461–476.

Ross, L. (1977). "The intuitive psychologist and his shortcomings: Distortions in the attribution process." *Advances in Experimental Social Psychology* 10, 173–220.

Swim, J. K., and Sanna, L. J. (1996). "He's skilled, she's lucky: A meta-analysis of observers' attributions for women's and men's successes and failures." *Personality and Social Psychology Bulletin, 22,* 507–519.

Thomas, W. I., and Thomas, D. S. (1928). *The child in America: Behavior problems and programs.* New York NY: Knopf, 571–572.

UnderstandingPrejudice.org. (2016). "Understanding prejudice." Retrieved September 25, 2016, from http://www.understandingprejudice.org/apa/english/page9.htm

Zimbardo, P. (2007). *The Lucifer effect: Understanding how good people turn evil.* New York NY: Random House.

IT'S THE SITUATION

THE POWER OF THE SITUATION

BY RAFAEL F. NARVÁEZ

The Power of the Situation

As shown in the preceding chapter, deviance is necessary for societies; and indeed, certain forms of deviance can bring forth prosperity, creativity, justice, and hope. But of course even such positive forms of deviance present risks for those involved. And as I have suggested elsewhere, "even the great deviants, from Mandela to Van Gogh, pay the price of non-compliance" (Narváez 2012). For this reason, "it is in general easier for social actors to internalize, to mirror, and to vivify [to bring to life, to enact] aspects of the social order than to attempt to change them" (ibid. 2012). In subsequent chapters, we will see in more detail how and why people resist social norms and with what consequences. But at this point it is worth pausing to review actual data on conformity in more detail.

On April 5th, 1968, the day after Dr. Martin Luther King Jr. was assassinated, a teacher at a school in Riceville, a tiny town in Iowa, faced expectedly difficult and saddening questions from her 3rd grade students. Who was this king? And why was he killed? The teacher, Jane Elliott, who would eventually become an internationally known lecturer, provided at first some of the standard answers. The king, she explained, was actually a man named Martin Luther King Junior, and he was killed because he was fighting to end discrimination and prejudices against "Negroes." The very young, all-White, and still confused students were only vaguely capturing the idea. Concepts such as discrimination and prejudice were difficult for them, not only on account of their age (eight year olds, mostly) but particularly because these children had never actually experienced any form of discrimination. (How could you possibly understand pain, for example, without having actually experienced it?) Elliott asked the children, "Do you think you know how would it feel to be judged by the color of your skin?" A vague "yeah" is heard in the video that records the exchange. The teacher replies, "No, I don't think you know how would that feel unless you had been through it, wouldn't you?"

She decided to conduct an exercise to help the children understand racism not by reading the dictionary definition but by experiencing it (see Peters 1971). She also hoped that such an exercise might contribute to help us, as a culture, understand racial discrimination and indeed any other form of discrimination. She divided the classroom in two, with blue-eyed children on one side and brown-eyed children on the other. The first day she began by explaining that blue-eyed children were of course better than brown-eyed children. The video registers the initial resistance, astonishment even, and certain sadness among the newly labeled "brownies" (kids with brown eyes). Some of them dispute the claim. But Elliott deploys effective pseudo-logic and eventually convinces not only the resistors but the classroom, in general, that blue-eyed children might be actually better than the "lazy," "clumsy," and "not-so-smart" brownies. Moreover, she explains, as brown-eyed people are inferior, they have to receive a different kind of treatment than the hardworking and smarter blue-eyed kids; it is only fair. Hence, brownies, for example, cannot directly drink from water fountain (a reference to the "White only" water fountains that were standard under the Jim Crow laws that were superseded only in 1964). Blue-eyed children do not want to risk drinking from fountains contaminated by the darned brownies, and so brownies had to drink from a paper cup. To be sure that blue- and brown-eyed children would be easily identified, she asked brownies to wear a band around their necks (perhaps a reference to the manner in which Jewish people were marked with the Star of David by the Nazis).

Thus the day went on. Some of the minor and normal and expected little failures of the brown-eyed children, such as writing their cursives "sloppily" on the blackboard, were attributed to their inferior nature. And likewise, the minor and normal and expected little successes of the blue-eyed children were attributed to their superior nature.

The results of this experiment shocked Elliott herself; and they would eventually shock the academic world. "Marvelous, cooperative, wonderful, thoughtful" children, as the teacher calls them, began to change. In only *one single day* of being thus labeled, blue-eyed children turned into "nasty, vicious, discriminating little third graders." Imagine their recess. The formerly wonderful blue-eyed kids are now bullying the brownies, name-calling them, even though the previous day, of course, no one had noticed anyone's eye color. Some of the brownies, in turn, became submissive, subservient, but also belligerent. On the verge of tears, a brown-eyed boy confesses to the teacher that he had punched a blue-eye "on the gut," because the blue-eye had called him names.

Remarkably, the very cognitive performance of brown-eyed children was also compromised. Brownies were simply not using, and perhaps were unable to use, their brain potential. Their young brains had extra tasks to handle: coping with their "inferior" social status and with the labels now being hurled unto them, the cognitive noise that inevitably lowered their performance. Blue-eyed children performed better than brownies. The next day the roles were reversed, with blue-eyed children now assuming the inferior position, and brown-eyed children being superior. As the roles were reversed, so were their behaviors and performance, with some blue-eye children now engaging in cowed behaviors and performing at a lower level and brown-eyed children outperforming them, discriminating against them, labeling them, etc.

This experiment changed the children's understanding of discrimination dramatically. Years later, the participants were interviewed, as adults, and many reported that those two days in Ms. Elliott classroom had simply changed their view of the world. Importantly, this experiment, along with many others, also contributed to change how we view, *as a culture*, the role that discrimination, social labeling, and social positioning can have on those labeled.

Let us note also that Elliott's experiment was controversial. Some parents and concerned citizens in the little town of Riceville recriminated the teacher for putting their children in such stressful situations and plausibly argued that she had infringed on ethical standards. Eventually, she was invited to discuss her views on TV, and a viewer called the station to recriminate Elliott, arguing that Black children were "used" to being discriminated and were therefore better able to handle such situations. By contrast, White children, the caller's odd argument went, were not used to discrimination, were thus more vulnerable to it, and therefore could more easily become scarred by such situations. Elliott responded with characteristic wit, and not without causticity. She sharply asked why "we" (Whites) are quick to become concerned when White children suffer one day of discrimination, while also being quick to ignore the fact that Black children suffer *a lifetime of discrimination*. (Note that Lyndon Johnson had signed the Civil Rights Act in 1964, desegregating the country only four years before Elliott's experiment took place and that, as Elliott argued, Black children born in the fifties had in fact spent most of their lives in a legally segregated and officially racist country, routinely experiencing the sort of discrimination that Elliott's students had experienced for one day.)

Elliott's response turned out to be very important from the point of view of sociological research. If the children's behavior and performance were transformed in only one single day, what happens, then, when people experience a lifetime of discrimination? Furthermore, what happens when people experience a lifetime of negative or, by contrast, *positive* labeling? In which ways variables such as social class, gender, race, sexual identities—which are often labeled with positive and negative valences—affect us?

Golem and Pygmalion

Golems are magical creatures that populate Jewish folklore. They are often depicted as lumpy, brownish, robotic beings, usually made of clay. They are sometimes made to be protectors of the people, and they are good at first. But according to some tales, the people eventually begin to see them with suspicion. Can such odd-looking, and somehow ensouled clay creature be trusted? As people begin to grow weary, the golem, in turn, grows defensive and a bit mean in response. And thus people grow wearier, such that the golem grows meaner, and so on, in an ensuing vicious spiral, to the point that the golem, though designed to be a protector, becomes a menace that has to be destroyed. An initial lesson from such tales is that prophesies about wrongdoing sometimes become self-fulfilled. If the people expect wrongdoing from the creature, they are more likely to get wrongdoing from it. But perhaps there is a larger and tacit lesson here: labels placed upon people can become enacted by the person thus labeled, so that if a society labels these brownish, lumpy creatures a *menace*, such creatures are likely to become a menace. If we as a society label brown-eyed children "not so smart," for example, they will be more likely to perform poorly, as Elliott exercise suggested.

Social psychologists called this "the golem effect." The opposite of it is the "Pygmalion effect," the notion that positive expectations can lead those addressed by such expectations to act in a manner that fulfills them. "Pygmalion," incidentally, is the title of a play by the Irish playwright George Bernard Shaw, where Eliza, a poor, poorly spoken young woman from a tough area in London, is trained by a professor of phonetics to pass herself off as a duchess at a party. Expecting a duchess, the wealthy and snobbish partiers overlook Eliza's "mistakes," her social blunders, and focus, instead, on the signs of "nobility" that she appears to give off. The partiers thus fall for the trick. (And they also reveal, these snobby partiers, that their negative judgments about the purported lower nature of the working classes are, precisely, superficial and snobbish.) Thus, Eliza, a bedraggled peddler of flowers, *becomes* lady-like. People expect lady-like behavior from her and, thus having a green light, she delivers.

Shortly after Elliott's experiment took place, a principal at an elementary school near San Francisco, contacted a Harvard psychologist, Robert Rosenthal, who had researched aspects of the Golem and Pygmalion effects. Rosenthal, it is worth noting, had shown that owners of rats who are led to believe that their rats have been "bred for superior learning ability *obtain performance superior to that obtained by [people] led to believe that their rat had been bred for inferior learning ability*" (Rosenthal and Fode 1963, my emphasis). The school principal on the other side of the phone, Lenore Jacobson, was interested in these ideas. Would these theories, she asked Rosenthal, perhaps apply to children who are sometimes preemptively labeled as "likely achievers" and to those preemptively labeled as "likely under-achievers"? Are such labels likely to become self-fulfilled prophesies? May such labels work like magic spells that societies cast upon people to thus create, as if by magic, aspects of their lives?

Eventually, the educator and the psychologists teamed up to conduct a formal study to determine the possible effects of labeling school children (Rosenthal and Jacobson 1963). They approached an unidentified elementary school in California and asked permission to conduct a series of cognitive tests among students. Then, after assessing the abilities of the children, they gave the teachers a list of "academic bloomers," which tacitly labeled the other kids as "non-bloomers." Hence, the school children were divided between those labeled "likely achievers" and the rest. Eight months later, the research team went back to the school. They retested the students and discovered that, sure enough, bloomers had now scored, on average *10 to 15 IQ points more than their non-blooming peers*. This was really a very important gain in intelligence. Four of every five bloomers had experienced at least ten points of improvement in their intelligence tests; and, by contrast, only half of non-bloomers experienced 10 points of improvement or more. As the researchers had predicted, bloomers had indeed bloomed.

What is truly stunning about this study is that the research team had divided bloomers from non-bloomers *randomly, regardless of their intelligence*. That is to say, "bloomers" were at first *no different from "non-bloomers" except for the fact that they had been so labeled*. Much as Elliott's students, bloomers were only regular kids who were simply expected to perform in accordance with labels they had been assigned, and so they did. In fact, they *became* smarter. The teachers attributed the bloomers' small, normal, and otherwise non-surprising little achievements to their superior nature. They were less frustrated by their mistakes, which were also attributed to the natural little hurdles of the blooming process. Thus, eager teachers spent more time, patience, and mental energy ensuring that the blooming process was unfolding smoothly. And in doing so, they were instrumental in fulfilling the researchers' initial "prophecy," which said, again, that bloomers would eventually outperform their peers.

This study begged many sociological questions. What happens, then, when a society preemptively labels some children "likely achievers" on account of positive stereotypes associated, as suggested above, with their race and/or class, and/or gender? And what happens when a society, on account of negative stereotypes, labels other children as potential underachievers, or potential troublemakers, or even as likely deviants, or as potential thugs, etc.? What portion of academic success and failure among children and adults stems not from the innate potential of the students but from the ways in which the social environment addresses them? What portion of your own successes and failures might be attributable to your own innate abilities or, on the other hand, to how society perceives you?

We don't have answers to these specific questions, but we do know that the way society labels you can affect your life, in general. And we also know that stereotypes associated with race, class, or gender actually do bias people's perceptions pertaining to the potential success or failure of children (Darley and Gross 1983). Consider now the following study conducted by Princeton University researchers John Darley and Paget Gross. These researchers asked Princeton undergraduates to assess the potential success of a child, fictitiously named Hanna. Once again, students were divided in two groups. The first group watched a video of Hanna playing in stereotypically working-class settings. And the second group watched her playing in wealthy surroundings. The first group studied Hanna's "biographical information" (concocted by the researchers), which confirmed her supposedly working class background. The second group read information that confirmed Hanna's supposed upper-class upbringing. Both groups then watched another part of the video that showed Hanna at work in certain school-related tasks. This portion of the video was designed so that it could neither confirm nor disconfirm Hanna's academic ability. Sometimes Hanna was shown doing very well, and at other times she was shown doing very poorly, with no clear trend that could actually allow viewers to objectively assess her academic potential.

Then, the students evaluated how she had performed in those school-related tasks. Students who were primed to see Hanna as wealthy were more likely to see her as performing above her fourth grade level. They saw her as a potential bloomer. And those who were primed to see her as poor generally judged her to perform below her fourth grade level. They tacitly saw her as a potentially difficult student. Elliott, Rosenthal and Jacobson had allowed us to see that labels placed upon children (e.g., "bloomers," "blue-eyed") are likely to lead to differential levels of achievement in the children thus labeled. Darley and Gross helped us see that, in general, people easily label others, children included, and that we are likely to label them *not* on account of the actual potential of those being labeled—but often on account of preconceived ideas, images, biases.

On the surface, all the studies outlined above helped us see that achievement is not always innate. It can also be contextual, contingent on external circumstances. But more profoundly, they also helped us see that human beings are very malleable and indeed largely constructed by contextual and contingent circumstances often beyond our control. Only one day under the brown-eye label was enough to momentarily construct aspects of the brownies' identities, aspects of their social and academic performance. Only six months after having received a positive label, children improved in terms of their intelligence. So, to go back to a central question, what would one expect from "brownies," or from "bloomers," or from Hanna if they spent a *lifetime* addressed by such labels?[1] How would such societal perceptions affect not only their life-trajectory but also who they become as human beings?

Note

1. American sociologist Howard Becker further noted that labeling often constructs deviant behavior, deviant identities, and indeed crime. Imagine a young kid growing in a poor inner-city area. More likely than not he will dress like his peers, imitate their behaviors and speech patterns. As such displays are stereotypically seen as threatening, outsiders will likely see him a potential threat—regardless, initially, of his character. A Golem Effect may now unfold. But this time, the child is likely to grow internalizing the notion that he is, in fact, a potential threat and thus behave in a manner befitting his acquired identity. Becker also helped us see that mainstream groups often label certain *things*, not just people—clothes, music, use of certain substances, speech patterns, etc.—as deviant, regardless of whether they are objectively harmful or noxious. He argued, for example, that use of marijuana is deviant not on account of the act itself but because some cultures simply see it as bad (while other cultures see is as normal). Hence, people who engage in certain behaviors, dress in a certain manner, listen to certain kinds of music, etc. are likely to conjure up a golem effect of sort—a label, and its effects in life, regardless, again, of the objective nature of their behaviors.

READING 2

BECOMING A MARIHUANA USER*

BY HOWARD S. BECKER

ABSTRACT

An individual will be able to use marihuana for pleasure only when he (1) learns to smoke it in a way that will produce real effects; (2) learns to recognize the effects and connect them with drug use; and (3) learns to enjoy the sensations he perceives. This proposition, based on an analysis of fifty interviews with marihuana users, calls into question theories which ascribe behavior to antecedent predispositions and suggests the utility of explaining behavior in terms of the emergence of motives and dispositions in the course of experience.

The use of marihuana is and has been the focus of a good deal of attention on the part of both scientists and laymen. One of the major problems students of the practice have addressed themselves to has been the identification of those individual psychological traits which differentiate marihuana users from nonusers and which are assumed to account for the use of the drug. That approach, common in the study of behavior categorized as deviant, is based on the premise that the presence of a given kind of behavior in an individual can best be explained as the result of some trait which predisposes or motivates him to engage in the behavior.[1]

* Paper read at the meetings of the Midwest Sociological Society in Omaha, Nebraska, April 25, 1953. The research on which this paper is based was done while I was a member of the staff of the Chicago Narcotics Survey, a study done by the Chicago Area Project, Inc., under a grant from the National Mental Health Institute. My thanks to Solomon Kobrin, Harold Finestone, Henry McKay, and Anselm Strauss, who read and discussed with me earlier versions of this paper.

This study is likewise concerned with accounting for the presence or absence of marihuana use in an individual's behavior. It starts, however, from a different premise: that the presence of a given kind of behavior is the result of a sequence of social experiences during which the person acquires a conception of the meaning of the behavior, and perceptions and judgments of objects and situations, all of which make the activity possible and desirable. Thus, the motivation or disposition to engage in the activity is built up in the course of learning to engage in it and does not antedate this learning process. For such a view it is not necessary to identify those "traits" which "cause" the behavior. Instead, the problem becomes one of describing the set of changes in the person's conception of the activity and of the experience it provides for him.[2]

This paper seeks to describe the sequence of changes in attitude and experience which lead to *the use of marihuana for pleasure*. Marihuana does not produce addiction, as do alcohol and the opiate drugs; there is no withdrawal sickness and no ineradicable craving for the drug.[3] The most frequent pattern of use might be termed "recreational." The drug is used occasionally for the pleasure the user finds in it, a relatively casual kind of behavior in comparison with that connected with the use of addicting drugs. The term "use for pleasure" is meant to emphasize the noncompulsive and casual character of the behavior. It is also meant to eliminate from consideration here those few cases in which marihuana is used for its prestige value only, as a symbol that one is a certain kind of person, with no pleasure at all being derived from its use.

The analysis presented here is conceived of as demonstrating the greater explanatory usefulness of the kind of theory outlined above as opposed to the predispositional theories now current. This may be seen in two ways: (1) predispositional theories cannot account for that group of users (whose existence is admitted)[4] who do not exhibit the trait or traits considered to cause the behavior and (2) such theories cannot account for the great variability over time of a given individual's behavior with reference to the drug. The same person will at one stage be unable to use the drug for pleasure, at a later stage be able and willing to do so, and, still later, again be unable to use it in this way. These changes, difficult to explain from a predispositional or motivational theory, are readily understandable in terms of changes in the individual's conception of the drug as is the existence of "normal" users.

The study attempted to arrive at a general statement of the sequence of changes in individual attitude and experience which have always occurred when the individual has become willing and able to use marihuana for pleasure and which have not occurred or not been permanently maintained when this is not the case. This generalization is stated in universal terms in order that negative cases may be discovered and used to revise the explanatory hypothesis.[5]

Fifty interviews with marihuana users from a variety of social backgrounds and present positions in society constitute the data from which the generalization was constructed and against which it was tested.[6] The interviews focused on the history of the person's experience with the drug, seeking major changes in his attitude toward it and in his actual use of it and the reasons for these changes. The final generalization is a statement of that sequence of changes in attitude which occurred in every case known to me in which the person came to use marihuana for pleasure. Until a negative case is found, it may be considered as an explanation of all cases of marihuana use for pleasure. In addition, changes from use to nonuse are shown to be related to similar changes in conception, and in each case it is possible to explain variations in the individual's behavior in these terms.

This paper covers only a portion of the natural history of an individual's use of marihuana,[7] starting with the person having arrived at the point of willingness to try marihuana. He knows that others use it to "get high," but he does not know what this means in concrete terms. He is curious about the experience, ignorant of what it may turn out to be, and afraid that it may be more than he has bargained for. The steps outlined below, if he undergoes them all and maintains the attitudes developed in them, leave him willing and able to use the drug for pleasure when the opportunity presents itself.

I

The novice does not ordinarily get high the first time he smokes marihuana, and several attempts are usually necessary to induce this state. One explanation of this may be that the drug is not smoked "properly," that is, in a way that insures sufficient dosage to produce real symptoms of intoxication. Most users agree that it cannot be smoked like tobacco if one is to get high:

> Take in a lot of air, you know, and ... I don't know how to describe it, you don't smoke it like a cigarette, you draw in a lot of air and get it deep down in your system and then keep it there. Keep it there as long as you can.

Without the use of some such technique[8] the drug will produce no effects, and the user will be unable to get high:

> The trouble with people like that [who are not able to get high] is that they're just not smoking it right, that's all there is to it. Either they're not holding it down long enough, or they're getting too much air and not enough smoke, or the other way around or something like that. A lot of people just don't smoke it right, so naturally nothing's gonna happen.

If nothing happens, it is manifestly impossible for the user to develop a conception of the drug as an object which can be used for pleasure, and use will therefore not continue. The first step in the sequence of events that must occur if the person is to become a user is that he must learn to use the proper smoking technique in order that his use of the drug will produce some effects in terms of which his conception of it can change.

Such a change is, as might be expected, a result of the individual's participation in groups in which marihuana is used. In them the individual learns the proper way to smoke the drug. This may occur through direct teaching:

> I was smoking like I did an ordinary cigarette. He said, "No, don't do it like that." He said, "Suck it, you know, draw in and hold it in your lungs till you ... for a period of time."
>
> I said, "Is there any limit of time to hold it?"
>
> He said, "No, just till you feel that you want to let it out, let it out." So I did that three or four times.

Many new users are ashamed to admit ignorance and, pretending to know already, must learn through the more indirect means of observation and imitation:

> I came on like I had turned on [smoked marihuana] many times before, you know. I didn't want to seem like a punk to this cat. See, like I didn't know the first thing about it—how to smoke it, or what was going to happen, or what. I just watched him like a hawk—I didn't take my eyes off him for a second, because I wanted to do everything just as he did it. I watched how he held it, how he smoked it, and everything. Then when he gave it to me I just came on cool, as though I knew exactly what the score was. I held it like he did and took a poke just the way he did.

No person continued marihuana use for pleasure without learning a technique that supplied sufficient dosage for the effects of the drug to appear. Only when this was learned was it possible for a conception of the drug as an object which could be used for pleasure to emerge. Without such a conception marihuana use was considered meaningless and did not continue.

II

Even after he learns the proper smoking technique, the new user may not get high and thus not form a conception of the drug as something which can be used for pleasure. A remark made by a user suggested the reason for this difficulty in getting high and pointed to the next necessary step on the road to being a user:

> I was told during an interview, "As a matter of fact, I've seen a guy who was high out of his mind and didn't know it."
>
> I expressed disbelief: "How can that be, man?"
>
> The interviewee said, "Well, it's pretty strange, I'll grant you that, but I've seen it. This guy got on with me, claiming that he'd never got high, one of those guys, and he got completely stoned. And he kept insisting that he wasn't high. So I had to prove to him that he was."

What does this mean? It suggests that being high consists of two elements: the presence of symptoms caused by marihuana use and the recognition of these symptoms and their connection by the user with his use of the drug. It is not enough, that is, that the effects be present; they alone do not automatically provide the experience of being high. The user must be able to point them out to himself and consciously connect them with his having smoked marihuana before he can have this experience. Otherwise, regardless of the actual effects produced, he considers that the drug has had no effect on him: "I figured it either had no effect on me or other people were exaggerating its effect on them, you know. I thought it was probably psychological, see." Such persons believe that the whole thing is an illusion and that the wish to be high leads the user to deceive himself into believing that something is happening when, in fact, nothing is. They do not continue marihuana use, feeling that "it does nothing" for them.

Typically, however, the novice has faith (developed from his observation of users who do get high) that the drug actually will produce some new experience and continues to experiment with it until it does. His failure to get high worries him, and he is likely to ask more experienced users or provoke comments from them about it. In such conversations be is made aware of specific details of his experience which he may not have noticed or may have noticed but failed to identify as symptoms of being high:

> I didn't get high the first time. ... I don't think I held it in long enough. I probably let it out, you know, you're a little afraid. The second time I wasn't sure, and he [smoking companion] told me, like I asked him for some of the symptoms or something, how would I know, you know. ... So he told me to sit on a stool. I sat on—I think I sat on a bar stool—and he said, "Let your feet hang," and then when I got down my feet were real cold, you know.
>
> And I started feeling it, you know. That was the first time. And then about a week after that, sometime pretty close to it, I really got on. That was the first time I got on a big laughing kick, you know. Then I really knew I was on.

One symptom of being high is an intense hunger. In the next case the novice becomes aware of this and gets high for the first time:

> They were just laughing the hell out of me because like I was eating so much. I just scoffed [ate] so much food, and they were just laughing at me, you know. Sometimes I'd be looking at them, you know, wondering why they're laughing, you know, not knowing what I was doing. [Well, did they tell you why they were laughing eventually?] Yeah, yeah, I come back, "Hey, man, what's happening?" Like, you know, like I'd ask, "What's happening?" and all of a sudden I feel weird, you know. "Man, you're on, you know. You're on pot [high on marihuana]." I said, "No, am I?" Like I don't know what's happening.

The learning may occur in more indirect ways:

> I heard little remarks that were made by other people. Somebody said, "My legs are rubbery," and I can't remember all the remarks that were made because I was very attentively listening for all these cues for what I was supposed to feel like.

The novice, then, eager to have this feeling, picks up from other users some concrete referents of the term "high" and applies these notions to his own experience. The new concepts make it possible for him to locate these symptoms among his own sensations and to point out to himself a "something different" in his experience that he connects with drug use. It is only when he can do this that he is high. In the next case, the contrast between two successive experiences of a user makes clear the crucial importance of the awareness of the symptoms in being high and re-emphasizes the important role of interaction with other users in acquiring the concepts that make this awareness possible:

> [Did you get high the first time you turned on?] Yeah, sure. Although, come to think of it, I guess I really didn't. I mean, like that first time it was more or less of a mild drunk. I was happy, I guess, you know what I mean. But I didn't really know I was high, you know what I mean. It was only after the second time I got high that I realized I was high the first time. Then I knew that something different was happening.
>
> [How did you know that?] How did I know? If what happened to me that night would of happened to you, you would've known, believe me. We played the first tune for almost two hours—one tune! Imagine, man! We got on the stand and played this one tune, we started at nine o'clock. When we got finished I looked at my watch, it's a quarter to eleven. Almost two hours on one tune. And it didn't seem like anything.

I mean, you know, it does that to you. It's like you have much more time or something. Anyway, when I saw that, man, it was too much. I knew I must really be high or something if anything like that could happen. See, and then they explained to me that that's what it did to you, you had a different sense of time and everything. So I realized that that's what it was. I knew then. Like the first time, I probably felt that way, you know, but I didn't know what's happening.

It is only when the novice becomes able to get high in this sense that he will continue to use marihuana for pleasure. In every case in which use continued, the user had acquired the necessary concepts with which to express to himself the fact that he was experiencing new sensations caused by the drug. That is, for use to continue, it is necessary not only to use the drug so as to produce effects but also to learn to perceive these effects when they occur. In this way marihuana acquires meaning for the user as an object which can be used for pleasure.

With increasing experience the user develops a greater appreciation of the drug's effects; he continues to learn to get high. He examines succeeding experiences closely, looking for new effects, making sure the old ones are still there. Out of this there grows a stable set of categories for experiencing the drug's effects whose presence enables the user to get high with ease.

The ability to perceive the drug's effects must be maintained if use is to continue; if it is lost, marihuana use ceases. Two kinds of evidence support this statement. First, people who become heavy users of alcohol, barbiturates, or opiates do not continue to smoke marihuana, largely because they lose the ability to distinguish between its effects and those of the other drugs.[9] They no longer know whether the marihuana gets them high. Second, in those few cases in which an individual uses marihuana in such quantities that he is always high, he is apt to get this same feeling that the drug has no effect on him, since the essential element of a noticeable difference between feeling high and feeling normal is missing. In such a situation, use is likely to be given up completely, but temporarily, in order that the user may once again be able to perceive the difference.

III

One more step is necessary if the user who has now learned to get high is to continue use. He must learn to enjoy the effects he has just learned to experience. Marihuana-produced sensations are not automatically or necessarily pleasurable. The taste for such experience is a socially acquired one, not different in kind from acquired tastes for oysters or dry martinis. The user feels dizzy, thirsty; his scalp tingles; he misjudges time and distances; and so on. Are these things pleasurable? He isn't sure. If he is to continue marihuana use, he must decide that they are. Otherwise, getting high, while a real enough experience, will be an unpleasant one he would rather avoid.

The effects of the drug, when first perceived, may be physically unpleasant or at least ambiguous:

> It started taking effect, and I didn't know what was happening, you know, what it was, and I was very sick. I walked around the room, walking around the room trying to get off, you know; it just scared me at first, you know. I wasn't used to that kind of feeling.

In addition, the novice's naïve interpretation of what is happening to him may further confuse and frighten him, particularly if he decides, as many do, that he is going insane:

> I felt I was insane, you know. Everything people done to me just wigged me. I couldn't hold a conversation, and my mind would be wandering, and I was always thinking, oh, I don't know, weird things, like hearing music different. ... I get the feeling that I can't talk to anyone. I'll goof completely.

Given these typically frightening and unpleasant first experiences, the beginner will not continue use unless he learns to redefine the sensations as pleasurable:

> It was offered to me, and I tried it. I'll tell you one thing. I never did enjoy it at all. I mean it was just nothing that I could enjoy. [Well, did you get high when you turned on?] Oh, yeah, I got definite feelings from it. But I didn't enjoy them. I mean I got plenty of reactions, but they were mostly reactions of fear. [You were frightened?] Yes. I didn't enjoy it. I couldn't seem to relax with it, you know. If you can't relax with a thing, you can't enjoy it, I don't think.

In other cases the first experiences were also definitely unpleasant, but the person did become a marihuana user. This occurred, however, only after a later experience enabled him to redefine the sensations as pleasurable:

> [This man's first experience was extremely unpleasant, involving distortion of spatial relationships and sounds, violent thirst, and panic produced by these symptoms.] After the first time I didn't turn on for about, I'd say, ten months to a year. ... It wasn't a moral thing; it was

because I'd gotten so frightened, bein' so high. An' I didn't want to go through that again, I mean, my reaction was, "Well, if this is what they call bein' high, I don't dig [like] it." ... So I didn't turn on for a year almost, accounta that. ...

Well, my friends started, an' consequently I started again. But I didn't have any more, I didn't have that same initial reaction, after I started turning on again.

[In interaction with his friends he became able to find pleasure in the effects of the drug and eventually became a regular user.]

In no case will use continue without such a redefinition of the effects as enjoyable.

This redefinition occurs, typically, in interaction with more experienced users who, in a number of ways, teach the novice to find pleasure in this experience which is at first so frightening.[10] They may reassure him as to the temporary character of the unpleasant sensations and minimize their seriousness, at the same time calling attention to the more enjoyable aspects. An experienced user describes how he handles newcomers to marihuana use:

Well, they get pretty high sometimes. The average person isn't ready for that, and it is a little frightening to them sometimes. I mean, they've been high on lush [alcohol], and they get higher that way than they've ever been before, and they don't know what's happening to them. Because they think they're going to keep going up, up, up till they lose their minds or begin doing weird things or something. You have to like reassure them, explain to them that they're not really flipping or anything, that they're gonna be all right. You have to just talk them out of being afraid. Keep talking to them, reassuring, telling them it's all right. And come on with your own story, you know: "The same thing happened to me. You'll get to like that after awhile." Keep coming on like that; pretty soon you talk them out of being scared. And besides they see you doing it and nothing horrible is happening to you, so that gives them more confidence.

The more experienced user may also teach the novice to regulate the amount he smokes more carefully, so as to avoid any severely uncomfortable symptoms while retaining the pleasant ones. Finally, he teaches the new user that he can "get to like it after awhile." He teaches him to regard those ambiguous experiences formerly defined as unpleasant as enjoyable. The older user in the following incident is a person whose tastes have shifted in this way, and his remarks have the effect of helping others to make a similar redefinition:

A new user had her first experience of the effects of marihuana and became frightened and hysterical. She "felt like she was half in and half out of the room" and experienced a number of alarming physical symptoms. One of the more experienced users present said, "She's dragged because she's high like that. I'd give anything to get that high myself. I haven't been that high in years."

In short, what was once frightening and distasteful becomes, after a taste for it is built up, pleasant, desired, and sought after. Enjoyment is introduced by the favorable definition of the experience that one acquires from others. Without this, use will not continue, for marihuana will not be for the user an object he can use for pleasure.

In addition to being a necessary step in becoming a user, this represents an important condition for continued use. It is quite common for experienced users suddenly to have an unpleasant or frightening experience, which they cannot define as pleasurable, either because they have used a larger amount of marihuana than usual or because it turns out to be a higher-quality marihuana than they expected. The user has sensations which go beyond any conception he has of what being high is and is in much the same situation as the novice, uncomfortable and frightened. He may blame it on an overdose and simply be more careful in the future. But he may make this the occasion for a rethinking of his attitude toward the drug and decide that it no longer can give him pleasure. When this occurs and is not followed by a redefinition of the drug as capable of producing pleasure, use will cease.

The likelihood of such a redefinition occurring depends on the degree of the individual's participation with other users. Where this participation is intensive, the individual is quickly talked out of his feeling against marihuana use. In the next case, on the other hand, the experience was very disturbing, and the aftermath of the incident cut the person's participation with other users to almost zero. Use stopped for three years and began again only when a combination of circumstances, important among which was a resumption of ties with users, made possible a redefinition of the nature of the drug:

> It was too much, like I only made about four pokes, and I couldn't even get it out of my mouth, I was so high, and I got real flipped. In the basement, you know, I just couldn't stay in there anymore. My heart was pounding real hard, you know, and I was going out of my mind; I thought I was losing my mind completely. So I cut out of this basement, and this other guy, he's out of his mind, told me, "Don't, don't leave me, man. Stay here." And I couldn't.
>
> I walked outside, and it was five below zero, and I thought I was dying, and I had my coat open; I was sweating, I was perspiring. My whole insides were all ..., and I walked about two blocks away, and I fainted behind a bush. I don't know how long I laid there. I woke up, and I was feeling the worst, I can't describe it at all, so I made it to a bowling alley, man, and I was trying to act normal, I was trying to shoot pool, you know, trying to act real normal, and I couldn't lay and I couldn't stand up and I couldn't sit down, and I went up and laid down where some guys that spot pins lay down, and that didn't help me, and I went down to a doctor's office. I was going to go in there and tell the doctor to put me out of my misery ... because my heart was pounding so hard, you know. ... So then all week end I started flipping, seeing things there and going through hell, you know, all kinds of abnormal things. ... I just quit for a long time then.
>
> [He went to a doctor who defined the symptoms for him as those of a nervous breakdown caused by "nerves" and "worries." Although he was no longer using marihuana, he had some recurrences of the symptoms which led him to suspect that "it was all his nerves."] So I just stopped worrying, you know; so it was about thirty-six months later I started making it

again. I'd just take a few pokes, you know. [He first resumed use in the company of the same user-friend with whom he had been involved in the original incident.]

A person, then, cannot begin to use marihuana for pleasure, or continue its use for pleasure, unless he learns to define its effects as enjoyable, unless it becomes and remains an object which he conceives of as capable of producing pleasure.

IV

In summary, an individual will be able to use marihuana for pleasure only when he goes through a process of learning to conceive of it as an object which can be used in this way. No one becomes a user without (1) learning to smoke the drug in a way which will produce real effects; (2) learning to recognize the effects and connect them with drug use (learning, in other words, to get high); and (3) learning to enjoy the sensations he perceives. In the course of this process he develops a disposition or motivation to use marihuana which was not and could not have been present when he began use, for it involves and depends on conceptions of the drug which could only grow out of the kind of actual experience detailed above. On completion of this process he is willing and able to use marihuana for pleasure.

He has learned, in short, to answer "Yes" to the question: "Is it fun?" The direction his further use of the drug takes depends on his being able to continue to answer "Yes" to this question and, in addition, on his being able to answer "Yes" to other questions which arise as he becomes aware of the implications of the fact that the society as a whole disapproves of the practice: "Is it expedient?" "Is it moral?"[11] Once he has acquired the ability to get enjoyment out of the drug, use will continue to be possible for him. Considerations of morality and expediency, occasioned by the reactions of society, may interfere and inhibit use, but use continues to be a possibility in terms of his conception of the drug. The act becomes impossible only when the ability to enjoy the experience of being high is lost, through a change in the user's conception of the drug occasioned by certain kinds of experience with it.

In comparing this theory with those which ascribe marihuana use to motives or predispositions rooted deep in individual behavior, the evidence makes it clear that marihuana use for pleasure can occur only when the process described above is undergone and cannot occur without it. This is apparently so without reference to the nature of the individual's personal makeup or psychic problems. Such theories assume that people have stable modes of response which predetermine the way they will act in relation to any I articular situation or object and that, when they come in contact with the given object or situation, they act in the way in which their makeup predisposes them.

This analysis of the genesis of marihuana use shows that the individuals who come in contact with a given object may respond to it at first in a great variety of ways. If a stable form of new behavior toward the object is to emerge, a transformation of meanings must occur, in which the person develops a new conception of the nature of the object.[12] This happens in a series of communicative acts in which others point out new aspects of his experience to him, present him with new interpretations of events, and help him achieve a new conceptual organization of his world, without which the new behavior is not possible. Persons who do not achieve the proper kind of conceptualization are unable to engage in the given behavior and turn off in the direction of some other relationship to the object or activity.

This suggests that behavior of any kind might fruitfully be studied developmentally, in terms of changes in meanings and concepts, their organization and reorganization, and the way they channel behavior, making some acts possible while excluding others.

UNIVERSITY OF ILLINOIS

Notes

1. See, as examples of this approach, the following: Eli Marcovitz and Henry J. Meyers, "The Marihuana Addict in the Army," *War Medicine*, VI (December, 1944), 382-91; Herbert S. Gaskill, "Marihuana, an Intoxicant," *American Journal of Psychiatry*, CII (September, 1945), 202–4; Sol Charen and Luis Perelman, "Personality Studies of Marihuana Addicts," *American Journal of Psychiatry*, CII (March, 1946), 674–82.

2. This approach stems from George Herbert Mead's discussion of objects in *Mind, Self, and Society* (Chicago: University of Chicago Press, 1934), pp. 277–80.

3. Cf. Roger Adams, "Marihuana," *Bulletin of the New York Academy of Medicine*, XVIII (November, 1942), 705–30.

4. Cf. Lawrence Kolb, "Marihuana," *Federal Probation*, II (July, 1938), 22–25; and Walter Bromberg, "Marihuana: A Psychiatric Study," *Journal of the American Medical Association*, CXIII (July 1,1939), 11.

5. The method used is that described by Alfred R. Lindesmith in his *Opiate Addiction* (Bloomington: Principia Press, 1947), chap. i. I would like also to acknowledge the important role Lindesmith's work played in shaping my thinking about the genesis of marihuana use.

6. Most of the interviews were done by the author. I am grateful to Solomon Kobrin and Harold Fine-stone for allowing me to make use of interviews done by them.

7. I hope to discuss elsewhere other stages in this natural history.

8. A pharmacologist notes that this ritual is in fact an extremely efficient way of getting the drug into the blood stream (R. P. Walton, *Marihuana: America's New Drug Problem* [Philadelphia: J. B. Lippincott, 1938], p. 48).

9. "Smokers have repeatedly stated that the consumption of whiskey while smoking negates the potency of the drug. They find it very difficult to get 'high' while drinking whiskey and because of that smokers will not drink while using the 'weed'" (cf. New York City Mayor's Committee on Marihuana, *The Marihuana Problem in the City of New York* [Lancaster, Pa.: Jacques Cattell Press, 1944], p. 13).

10. Charen and Perelman, *op. cit.*, p. 679.

11. Another paper will discuss the series of developments in attitude that occurs as the individual begins to take account of these matters and adjust his use to them.

12. Cf. Anselm Strauss, "The Development and Transformation of Monetary Meanings in the Child," *American Sociological Review*, XVII (June, 1952), 275–86.

INFLUENCE

READING 3

SHOOTING AN ELEPHANT

BY GEORGE ORWELL

In Moulmein, in Lower Burma, I was hated by large numbers of people—the only time in my life that I have been important enough for this to happen to me. I was sub-divisional police officer of the town, and in an aimless, petty kind of way anti-European feeling was very bitter. No one had the guts to raise a riot, but if a European woman went through the bazaars alone somebody would probably spit betel juice over her dress. As a police officer I was an obvious target and was baited whenever it seemed safe to do so. When a nimble Burman tripped me up on the football field and the referee (another Burman) looked the other way, the crowd yelled with hideous laughter. This happened more than once. In the end the sneering yellow faces of young men that met me everywhere, the insults hooted after me when I was at a safe distance, got badly on my nerves. The young Buddhist priests were the worst of all. There were several thousands of them in the town and none of them seemed to have anything to do except stand on street corners and jeer at Europeans.

All this was perplexing and upsetting. For at that time I had already made up my mind that imperialism was an evil thing and the sooner I chucked up my job and got out of it the better. Theoretically—and secretly, of course—I was all for the Burmese and all against their oppressors, the British. As for the job I was doing, I hated it more bitterly than I can perhaps make clear. In a job like that you see the dirty work of Empire at close quarters. The wretched prisoners huddling in the stinking cages of the lock-ups, the grey, cowed faces of the long-term convicts, the scarred buttocks of the men who had been flogged with bamboos—all these oppressed me with an intolerable sense of guilt. But I could get nothing into perspective. I was young and ill-educated and I had had to think out my problems in the utter silence that is imposed on every Englishman in the East. I did not even know that the British Empire is dying, still less did I know that it is a great deal better than the younger empires that are going to supplant it. All I knew was that I was stuck between my hatred of the empire I served and my rage against the evil-spirited little beasts who tried to make my job impossible. With one part of my mind I thought of the British Raj as an unbreakable tyranny, as something clamped down, in saecula saeculorum, upon the will of prostrate peoples; with another part I thought that the greatest joy in the world would be to drive a bayonet into a Buddhist priest's guts. Feelings like these are the normal by-products of imperialism; ask any Anglo-Indian official, if you can catch him off duty.

One day something happened which in a roundabout way was enlightening. It was a tiny incident in itself, but it gave me a better glimpse than I had had before of the real nature of imperialism—the real motives for which despotic governments act. Early one morning the sub-inspector at a police station the other end of the town rang me up on the phone and said that an elephant was ravaging the bazaar. Would I please come and do something about it? I did not know what I could do, but I wanted to see what was happening and I got on to a pony and started out. I took my rifle, an old .44 Winchester and much too small to kill an elephant, but I thought the noise might be useful *in terrorem*. Various Burmans stopped me on the way and told me about the elephant's doings. It was not, of course, a wild elephant, but a tame one which had gone 'must'. It had been chained up, as tame elephants always are when their attack of 'must' is due, but on the previous night it had broken its chain and escaped. Its mahout, the only person who could manage it when it was in that state, had set out in pursuit, but had taken the wrong direction and was now twelve hours' journey away, and in the morning the elephant had suddenly reappeared in the town. The Burmese population had no weapons and were quite helpless against it. It had already destroyed somebody's bamboo hut, killed a cow and raided some fruit-stalls and devoured the stock; also it had met the municipal rubbish van and, when the driver jumped out and took to his heels, had turned the van over and inflicted violences upon it.

The Burmese sub-inspector and some Indian constables were waiting for me in the quarter where the elephant had been seen. It was a very poor quarter, a labyrinth of squalid bamboo huts, thatched with palmleaf, winding all over a steep hillside. I remember that it was a cloudy, stuffy morning at the beginning of the rains. We began questioning the people as to where the elephant had gone and, as usual, failed to get any definite information. That is invariably the case in the East; a story always sounds clear enough at a distance, but the nearer you get to the scene of events the vaguer it becomes. Some of the people said that the elephant had gone in one direction, some said that he had gone in another, some professed not even to have heard of any elephant. I had almost made up my mind that the whole story was a pack of lies, when we heard yells a little distance away. There was a loud, scandalized cry of 'Go away, child! Go away this instant!' and an old woman with a switch in her hand came round the corner of a hut, violently shooing away a crowd of naked children. Some more women followed, clicking their tongues and exclaiming; evidently there was something that the children ought not to have seen. I rounded the hut and saw a man's dead body sprawling in the mud. He was an Indian, a Black Dravidian coolie, almost naked, and he could not have been dead many minutes. The people said that the elephant had come suddenly upon him round the corner of the hut, caught him with its trunk, put its foot on his back and ground him into the earth. This was the rainy season and the ground was soft, and his face had scored a trench a foot deep and a couple of yards long. He was lying on his belly with arms crucified and head sharply twisted to one side. His face was coated with mud, the eyes wide open, the teeth bared and grinning with an expression of unendurable agony. (Never tell me, by the way, that the dead look peaceful. Most of the corpses I have seen looked devilish.) The friction of the great beast's foot had stripped the skin from his back as neatly as one skins a rabbit. As soon as I saw the dead man I sent an orderly to a friend's house nearby to borrow an elephant rifle. I had already sent back the pony, not wanting it to go mad with fright and throw me if it smelt the elephant.

The orderly came back in a few minutes with a rifle and five cartridges, and meanwhile some Burmans had arrived and told us that the elephant was in the paddy fields below, only a few hundred yards away. As I started forward practically the whole population of the quarter flocked out of the houses and followed me. They had seen the rifle and were all shouting excitedly that I was going to shoot the elephant. They had not shown much interest in the elephant when he was merely ravaging their homes, but it was different now that he was going to be shot. It was a bit of fun to them, as it would be to an English crowd; besides they wanted the meat. It made me vaguely uneasy. I had no intention of shooting the elephant—I had merely sent for the rifle to defend myself if necessary—and it is always unnerving to have a crowd following you. I marched down the hill, looking and feeling a fool, with the rifle over my shoulder and an ever-growing army of people jostling at my heels. At the bottom, when you got away from the huts, there was a metalled road and beyond that a miry waste of paddy fields a thousand yards across, not yet ploughed but soggy from the first rains and dotted with coarse grass. The elephant was standing eight yards from the road, his left side towards us. He took not the slightest notice of the crowd's approach. He was tearing up bunches of grass, beating them against his knees to clean them and stuffing them into his mouth.

I had halted on the road. As soon as I saw the elephant I knew with perfect certainty that I ought not to shoot him. It is a serious matter to shoot a working elephant—it is comparable to destroying a huge and costly piece of machinery—and obviously one ought not to do it if it can possibly be avoided. And at that distance, peacefully eating, the elephant looked no more dangerous than a cow. I thought then and I think now that his attack of 'must' was already passing off; in which case he would merely wander harmlessly about until the mahout came back and caught him. Moreover, I did not in the least want to shoot him. I decided that I would watch him for a little while to make sure that he did not turn savage again, and then go home.

But at that moment I glanced round at the crowd that had followed me. It was an immense crowd, two thousand at the least and growing every minute. It blocked the road for a long distance on either side. I looked at the sea of yellow faces above the garish clothes-faces all happy and excited over this bit of fun, all certain that the elephant was going to be shot. They were watching me as they would watch a conjurer about to perform a trick. They did not like me, but with the magical rifle in my hands I was momentarily worth watching. And suddenly I realized that I should have to shoot the elephant after all. The people expected it of me and I had got to do it; I could feel their two thousand wills pressing me forward, irresistibly. And it was at this moment, as I stood there with the rifle in my hands, that I first grasped the hollowness, the futility of the white man's dominion in the East. Here was I, the white man with his gun, standing in front of the unarmed native crowd—seemingly the leading actor of the piece; but in reality I was only an absurd puppet pushed to and fro by the will of those yellow faces behind. I perceived in this moment that when the white man turns tyrant it is his own freedom that he destroys. He becomes a sort of hollow, posing dummy, the conventionalized figure of a sahib. For it is the condition of his rule that he shall spend his life in trying to impress the 'natives', and so in every crisis he has got to do what the 'natives' expect of him. He wears a mask, and his face grows to fit it. I had got to shoot the elephant. I had committed myself to doing it when I sent for the rifle. A sahib has got to act like a sahib; he has got to appear resolute, to know his own mind and do definite things. To come all that way, rifle in hand, with two thousand people marching at my heels, and then to trail feebly away, having done nothing—no, that was impossible. The crowd would laugh at me. And my whole life, every white man's life in the East, was one long struggle not to be laughed at.

But I did not want to shoot the elephant. I watched him beating his bunch of grass against his knees, with that preoccupied grandmotherly air that elephants have. It seemed to me that it would be murder to shoot him. At that age I was not squeamish about killing animals, but I had never shot an elephant and never wanted to. (Somehow it always seems worse to kill a *large* animal.) Besides, there was the beast's owner to be considered. Alive, the elephant was worth at least a hundred pounds; dead, he would only be worth the value of his tusks, five pounds, possibly. But I had got to act quickly. I turned to some experienced-looking Burmans who had been there when we arrived, and asked them how the elephant had been behaving. They all said the same thing: he took no notice of you if you left him alone, but he might charge if you went too close to him.

It was perfectly clear to me what I ought to do. I ought to walk up to within, say, twenty-five yards of the elephant and test his behavior. If he charged, I could shoot; if he took no notice of me, it would be safe to leave him until the mahout came back. But also I knew that I was going to do no such thing. I was a poor shot with a rifle and the ground was soft mud into which one would sink at every step. If the elephant charged and I missed him, I should have about as much chance as a toad under a steam-roller. But even then I was not thinking particularly of my own skin, only of the watchful yellow faces behind. For at that moment, with the crowd watching me, I was not afraid in the ordinary sense, as I would have been if I had been alone. A white man mustn't be frightened in front of 'natives'; and so, in general, he isn't frightened. The sole thought in my mind was that if anything went wrong those two thousand Burmans would see me pursued, caught, trampled on and reduced to a grinning corpse like that Indian up the hill. And if that happened it was quite probable that some of them would laugh. That would never do.

There was only one alternative. I shoved the cartridges into the magazine and lay down on the road to get a better aim. The crowd grew very still, and a deep, low, happy sigh, as of people who see the theatre curtain go up at last, breathed from innumerable throats. They were going to have their bit of fun after all. The rifle was a beautiful German thing with cross-hair sights. I did not then know that in shooting an elephant one would shoot to cut an imaginary bar running from ear-hole to ear-hole. I ought, therefore, as the elephant was sideways on, to have aimed straight at his ear-hole, actually I aimed several inches in front of this, thinking the brain would be further forward.

When I pulled the trigger I did not hear the bang or feel the kick—one never does when a shot goes home—but I heard the devilish roar of glee that went up from the crowd. In that instant, in too short a time, one would have thought, even for the bullet to get there, a mysterious, terrible change had come over the elephant. He neither stirred nor fell, but every line of his body had altered. He looked suddenly stricken, shrunken, immensely old, as though the frightful impact of the bullet had paralysed him without knocking him down. At last, after what seemed a long time—it might have been five seconds, I dare say—he sagged flabbily to his knees. His mouth slobbered. An enormous senility seemed to have settled upon him. One could have imagined him thousands of years old. I fired again into the same spot. At the second shot he did not collapse but climbed with desperate slowness to his feet and stood weakly upright, with legs sagging and head drooping. I fired a third time. That was the shot that did for him. You could see the agony of it jolt his whole body and knock the last remnant of strength from his legs. But in falling he seemed for a moment to rise, for as his hind legs collapsed beneath him he seemed to tower upward like a huge rock toppling, his trunk reaching skyward like a tree. He trumpeted, for the first and only time. And then down he came, his belly towards me, with a crash that seemed to shake the ground even where I lay.

I got up. The Burmans were already racing past me across the mud. It was obvious that the elephant would never rise again, but he was not dead. He was breathing very rhythmically with long rattling gasps, his great mound of a side painfully rising and falling. His mouth was wide open—I could see far down into caverns of pale pink throat. I waited a long time for him to die, but his breathing did not weaken. Finally I fired my two remaining shots into the spot where I thought his heart must be. The thick blood welled out of him like red velvet, but still he did not die. His body did not even jerk when the shots hit him, the tortured breathing continued without a pause. He was dying, very slowly and in great agony, but in some world remote from me where not even a bullet could damage him further. I felt that I had got to put an end to that dreadful noise. It seemed dreadful to see the great beast Lying there, powerless to move and yet powerless to die, and not even to be able to finish him. I sent back for my small rifle and poured shot after shot into his heart and down his throat. They seemed to make no impression. The tortured gasps continued as steadily as the ticking of a clock.

In the end I could not stand it any longer and went away. I heard later that it took him half an hour to die. Burmans were bringing dash and baskets even before I left, and I was told they had stripped his body almost to the bones by the afternoon.

Afterwards, of course, there were endless discussions about the shooting of the elephant. The owner was furious, but he was only an Indian and could do nothing. Besides, legally I had done the right thing, for a mad elephant has to be killed, like a mad dog, if its owner fails to control it. Among the Europeans opinion was divided. The older men said I was right, the younger men said it was a damn shame to shoot an elephant for killing a coolie, because an elephant was worth more than any damn Coringhee coolie. And afterwards I was very glad that the coolie had been killed; it put me legally in the right and it gave me a sufficient pretext for shooting the elephant. I often wondered whether any of the others grasped that I had done it solely to avoid looking a fool.

1936

THE END

READING 4

UNDERSTANDING HEROISM

BY PHILLIP ZIMBARDO

Understanding Heroism

> "True heroism is remarkably sober, very undramatic. It is not the urge to surpass all others at whatever cost, but the urge to serve others at whatever cost."
>
> —Arthur Ashe

WHAT IS A "HERO" EXACTLY?

Heroes are people who transform compassion (a personal virtue) into heroic action (a civic virtue). In doing so, they put their best selves forward in service to humanity. The Heroic Imagination Project defines a hero as an individual or a network of people that take action on behalf of others in need, or in defense of integrity or a moral cause.

Heroic action is:

1. Engaged in voluntarily;
2. Conducted in service to one or more people or the community as a whole;
3. Involving a risk to physical comfort, social stature, or quality of life; and
4. Initiated without the expectation of material gain.

This is the definition of hero is what we use at HIP as the basis of our organization and as the litmus test for our research. We acknowledge that there are many interpretations of the word hero and the term heroic action as well as many varieties of heroism. We are also aware that many people can be on a heroic journey doing daily acts of goodness in preparation for enacting major heroic deeds when the opportunity arises.

Social Attributes

The very concept of heroism has been open to debate and controversy for centuries, given that it is culturally and historically contextualized. It also has been confused with related, possibly contributing factors such as altruism, compassion, and empathy, and identified with popular celebrities, role models, and media-created "fantastic heroes" of the comic book genre. Heroism and heroic status are always social attributions. Someone or some group other than the actor confers that honor on the person and the deed. There must be social consensus about the significance and meaningful consequence of an act for it to be deemed heroic, and for its agent to be called a hero.

WHY DO WE NEED HEROES?

"All that is necessary for the triumph of evil is that good men do nothing."

—Sir Edmund Burke

"We must learn that passively to accept an unjust system is to cooperate with that system, and thereby to become a participant in its evil."

—Martin Luther King, Jr.

Heroic action is the antidote to evil, and it starts with heroic imagination. At its core, it is the personal and social creation of a "bright line" of morality on a given issue that is defended, upheld and promoted despite a host of pressures to do otherwise. Perhaps those who earn the hero designation have developed a keener sense of "moral clarity," as philosopher Susan Neiman might assert. Some have described the fundamental contribution of heroes as "saving the soul of a nation."

WHAT IS EVIL?

A behavioral definition of evil:

On an individual level: the intentional exercise and abuse of power to psychologically harm, physically hurt, or mortally destroy someone else's life. It can also function to ruin someone's reputation, social status/position, or career.

On a systemic level: the intentional exercise and abuse of power by organizations to psychologically harm, physically hurt, and/or commit crimes against humanity. Institutions at systemic levels engage in immoral, fraudulent, illegal, and even genocidal actions under the cover of legal loopholes and plausible deniability for any personal accountability. Further, in both public and private administrative sectors "technical rationality" and legality have replaced ethical and moral concerns and analyses of individual responsibility. This new form of evil has been termed "administrative evil."

The most common form of evil is inaction. It's knowing you can do a necessary good deed and choosing not to.

Everyday Heroism is the Antidote to Evil

Often we imagine heroism as risking or sacrificing one's life, but there are many less dramatic acts of heroism that occur everyday in the world around us. Everyday heroism is a term we use to describe acts of heroism, however small, that are taken on a regular basis.

Do Heroes Stand Above the Rest?

The historical view of the hero suggests that there is something innately special about heroes. Historian Hughes-Hallett writes, "There are men, wrote Aristotle, so godlike, so exceptional, that they naturally, by right of their extraordinary gifts, transcend all moral judgment or constitutional control: 'There is no law which embraces men of that caliber: they are themselves law.'" One definition of heroism arises from this Aristotelian conception, "It is the expression of a superb spirit. It is associated with courage and integrity and a disdain for the cramping compromises by means of which the un-heroic majority manage their lives—attributes that are widely considered noble... [Heroes are] capable of something momentous—the defeat of an enemy, the salvation of a race, the preservation of a political system, the completion of a voyage—which no one else could have accomplished."

Traditional Emphasis on Physical Risk

Most well known examples of heroism have emphasized acts of courage that involved bravery, gallantry, and risk of serious physical injury or death; military heroes, and those who give their lives in service professions—police and fire fighters—have long been accorded special recognition in most cultures. Their acts of heroism typically involve bravery and gallantry, which combine to become courage. Their deeds involve sacrificing life and limb in the service to their country or fellows that is above and beyond the traditional standard in their profession. Currently accepted conceptions of heroism emphasize primarily its physical risk without adequately addressing other components of heroic acts, such as nobility of purpose and non-violent acts of personal sacrifice, including those individuals who challenge institutionalized injustice, deception, and fraud.

Cultural Context

Definitions of heroism are always culture-bound and time-bound. To this day, puppeteers enact the legend of Alexander the Great before children in remote villages of Turkey. In those towns where his command posts were set up and his soldiers intermarried with villagers, Alexander is a great hero, but in towns that were just conquered on his relentless quest to rule the world, Alexander is portrayed as a great villain, more than a thousand years after his death. In recent times, in San Francisco the October 12 Columbus Day parade had been time of celebrating the heroic voyage of this great explorer. It was an honor for the citizen chosen to portray Christopher Columbus. Not so anymore for some people, given the recently-discovered abuse and exploitation of his arrival on the indigenous populations. To become part of any culture's history, acts of heroism must be recorded and preserved by those who are literate and who have the power to record history or to pass it on in a persistent oral tradition. Impoverished, illiterate peoples that have been colonized retain few widely acknowledged heroes because there are few available records of their acts.

Hero Taxonomy

There are many heroic types and expressions of heroic behavior. Heroic types include whistle blowers, martyrs, military, civilian, disability, political, religious, science and technology, environmental, educational, artistic and cultural, as well as good samaritans.

For a more in-depth look at hero types, read Chapter 16 of *The Lucifer Effect* Within these types of heroes are "reactive" and "proactive" heroes. Reactive heroes are people that act in the moment, usually spontaneously. Afterwards, a reactive hero will often say something like "I didn't have time to think, I just did it." A good example of a reactive hero is Wesley Autrey, who, in 2007, saved the life of a student who had fallen on the subway tracks in New York City. A proactive hero is someone that makes continual efforts over time to expose the operation of fraud, deception, or corruption. Such heroes are more effective when they form networks with others who share their values, thereby lessening the criticism (by defenders of the evil system) that they are fanatics or misguided. Erin Brockovich is such a hero in her legal confrontation with an energy company (PG&E) whose processes were polluting local water supplies, which caused death-dealing diseases to many families living near the plant. Life-long heroes are also proactive heroes in their challenge of an entire system of injustice, such as Rev. Martin Luther King, Jr.'s confrontation with racism in the United States. Another example of proactive heroes are the many Christians who made the decision to risk their lives and that of their families to save Jews from Nazi concentration camps, and likely death. Irena Sendler was one such Polish hero, who organized a network of 20 others to successfully rescue 2,500 Jewish children from the Warsaw ghetto, where hunger and disease were rampant while they awaited deportation to concentration camps.

HOSTILE VS. HEROIC IMAGINATION

> "Every reasonable man (and woman) is a potential scoundrel and a potential good citizen. What a man is depends upon his character; what a man does, and what we think of what he does, depends upon his circumstances."
>
> —George Bernard Shaw

The Hostile Imagination

Dr. Zimbardo coined the term "heroic imagination" was because it was the opposite of the "hostile imagination", a term used by Sam Keen, in *Faces of the Enemy*, where he talks about the ways in which certain situations have the power to trigger, or activate, hatred of other people, creating a psychology of enmity. Hostile imagination includes thinking of other people as objects, as unworthy, as less than human—in short, dehumanizing others. This in turn leads to thinking about and treating those people differently than you would your own kind or kin. The end product of this hostile imagination is creating the conditions of wanting to destroy the "other", so it's not just that you have a negative perspective, you really want to destroy them and you engage in or support antisocial behavior. Here we see the bad attitude leading to destructive behavior. Another aspect of the hostile imagination is sharing the negative attitude without taking the hostile action, instead being indifferent to the hostile actions taken against the selected victims by others. This kind of indifference allows tacit approval of the hostility and thereby encourages it.

The Heroic Imagination

The very situations that inflame the hostile imagination in some can inspire in the heroic imagination in others. "Heroic imagination" is really a mindset—a set of attitudes about helping others, caring for others, being willing to sacrifice or take risks on behalf of others. Those that engage their heroic imagination are making themselves aware of opportunities where they can help others in need, and then being willing to take the appropriate action regardless of the personal risk involved. When the heroic imagination motivates pro-social behavior it becomes heroic action. This kind of behavior is labeled heroic.

The Banality of Evil

The concept of the "banality of evil" emerged from Hannah Arendt's observations at the trial of Adolph Eichmann, indicted for crimes against humanity in orchestrating the genocide of European Jews at Auschwitz Concentration Camp. In "Eichmann in Jerusalem: A Report on the Banality of Evil," Arendt formulates the idea that such individuals should not be viewed as exceptions, as monsters, or as perverted sadists. She argues that such dispositional attributes, typically applied to perpetrators of evil deeds, serves to set them apart from the rest of the human community. Instead, Eichmann and others like him, Arendt says, should be exposed in their very ordinariness. Arendt's now classic conclusion:

> "The trouble with Eichmann was precisely that so many were like him, and that the many were neither perverted nor sadistic, that they were, and still are, terribly and terrifyingly normal. From the viewpoint of our legal institutions and our moral standards of judgment, this normality was much more terrifying than all the atrocities put together, for it implied ... that this new type of criminal, who is in actual fact **hostis generis humani**, commits his crimes under circumstances that make it well-nigh impossible for him to know or feel that he is doing wrong."

And then came her punch line, describing Eichmann's dignified march to the gallows:

> "It was as though in those last minutes he was summing up the lesson that this long course in human wickedness had taught us—the lesson of the fearsome, word-and-thought-defying banality of evil."

Arendt was saying in essence that such perpetrators of evil were "normal" before and again after being embedded in evil-generating situations, such as being in charge of the mass murder of millions of Jews in Auschwitz. That situationist account in no way minimizes the accountability and guilt of the perpetrators; it simply indicts both the evil-generating situation and the person who was seduced or corrupted by it.

The Banality of Heroism and Virtue

We may now entertain the notion that most people who become perpetrators of evil deeds are directly comparable to those who become perpetrators of heroic deeds, alike in being just ordinary, average people. The banality of evil matches the banality of heroism. Neither attribute is the direct consequence of dispositional tendencies; there are no special inner attributes either of pathology or of goodness residing within the human psyche or the human genome. Both conditions emerge in particular situations at particular times when situational forces play a compelling role in moving particular individuals across a decisional line from inaction to action. There is a decisive decisional moment when a person is caught up in a vortex of forces that emanate from a behavioral context. Those forces combine to increase the probability of one's acting to harm others or acting to help others. Their decision may not be consciously planned or mindfully taken. Rather strong situational forces most often impulsively drive the person to action. Among the situational evil-action vectors are:

> Group, team pressures and group identity; the diffusion of responsibility for the action; a temporal focus on the immediate moment without consciousness of consequences stemming from the act in the future; dehumanization of the other; de-individuation (anonymity) of self; negative role models; social norms approving of the action; moral disengagement via semantic distortions of the real nature of the evil action, actor, and consequences; among others indentified by a large body of research.
>
> Zimbardo argues that the very situations that inflame the "hostile imagination" in some people, inducing them to cross the line between good and evil and become perpetrators, instill the "heroic imagination" in others, inducing them to act heroically to challenge human evil or do service to others in natural disasters. In both cases, a unique opportunity provides a call to action for evil or for good. (Social philosopher Sam Keen coined the term "hostile imagination" to describe the psychology of enmity that is fueled by national propaganda against "enemies." In his classic work, *Faces of the Enemy*, Keen reveals how the images depicting arbitrary national enemies serve to inflame citizens to hate them and soldiers to kill them.)
>
> The banality of heroism means that we are all *"Heroes-in-Waiting."* It is a choice that we may all be called upon to make at some point in time. We believe that by making heroism an egalitarian attribute of human nature rather than a rare feature of the elect few, we can better foster heroic acts in every community. Everyone has the capability of becoming a hero in one degree or another. Sometimes we might not realize it. We are all heroes to

someone when we make vital sacrifices on their behalf that enhances their quality of life. This concept acknowledges that many of us will never be "big time heroes" because we will not be given the opportunity to challenge big time evil or give aid in natural disasters, yet there is much of the social habits of heroism that can be practiced on a daily basis by each of us—as everyday heroes.

In Other Words . . .

In the book *The Person and the Situation*, Nisbett and Ross (1991) offer a way to think about the extraordinariness of ordinary situations. In the forward to the 2011 edition, Malcolm Gladwell (2011) writes that the book "has much more in common with an adventure story than a textbook." I hope this unit has given you stories to remember, for stories carry layers of meaning and lasting messages. We certainly do look at the uniqueness of ordinary situations—peering, for example, through Becker's lens to understand the unique discovery of how a "simple" act of smoking a joint is actually the product of complex layers of culture, learning, and interactions.

But we also learn commonness (or, at least, explanation of everyday acts) of what we once thought bizarre. Jane Elliott's simple application of collars brought profound results, over a span of nearly fifty years. Shooting an elephant suddenly became a lesson in group pressure and conformity. These ideas are important as we consider crime and deviance. Rather than dismissing those individuals labeled as deviant as "bad" or somehow inferior people, we can examine the behavior as situational (what would I do under the same exact circumstances, with the same history). Perhaps even more important, we might ask, is why this specific act is deemed deviant or criminal, and to whose advantage does such definition work? For example, consider the petty thief who steals a bicycle and goes to prison for fifteen years (because it was his or her "third strike") versus the large corporation that squanders millions of small investors' life savings, yet gets a (relatively) modest fine. What is it about our society, including our criminal justice system, that arranges such outcomes, and who gains privilege because of it?

This is not to say that harmful behavior should be excused; far from it. But until we discover the root causes of such behavior, and the motivation behind various parts of our institutions, we are left impoverished in dealing with such issues as a society. Left to our own devices, we often see things that are not there and fail to acknowledge the elephant(s) in the room (often there is a whole herd of them!). This unit is a small step toward providing the tools to correct some of those errors in judgment, and, in so doing, affords you the power to take control of your own situation—and life.

The Big Idea

Crime and deviance are human interactions, social constructions made by people, just as patterns in the snow. Over time they become entrenched, and the real purpose may be changed or disguised.

So What?

At the intersection of biography, history, and the situation, somewhere lies an understanding of human behavior, including crime and deviance. Look for it. Study it. Rely on social science research and sociological principles to provide bread crumbs to the answers. It's like suddenly pulling back the curtain and finding that YOU are the wizard.

It's All Situational, California Beach 2012

Works Cited

Gladwell, M. (2011). Forward. In Ross, L. and Nisbett, R. (authors) *The person and the situation: Perspectives of social psychology*. London: Pinter & Martin Ltd.

Nisbett, R. E., and Ross, L. (1991). *The person and the situation: Perspectives of social psychology*. Philadelphia PA: Temple University Press.

Section II: A Culture of Social Control

Beyond the Book: Uncommon Wisdoms

Mark Twain famously said, "Education consists mainly of unlearning what we already know" (Twainquotes.com 2016). In this section, we have explored readings and tools that help us do just that—to go beyond the so-called "common wisdom" that dictates many stereotypes, half-truths, and misconceptions about crime and deviance. Below are a few fallacies that are especially prevalent in our culture:

The dramatic fallacy: Crime in the United States is dramatic, extreme, and violent. *Actually:*

- Most crimes are ordinary, undramatic, nonviolent.
- Violent crime is estimated to be 12 times more common on TV than in real life (Hetsroni 2012); murder 1,000 times as frequent on TV (Diefenbach and West 2001).
- Of the 10 million offenses for Index I crimes (the most serious), nearly 90 percent are property crimes; homicides account for only 1.2 percent (FBI 2015).
- Of 14 million arrests, more than 80 percent are not Index I crimes (FBI 2015).
- Of 20.7 million victimizations in 2014, more than 75 percent were nonviolent (Truman and Langton 2015).

The constabulary fallacy: Police know about crimes, and the criminal justice system is the most important key to crime solutions and prevention. *Actually:*

- Most crime never comes to the attention of the police.
- Approximately 60 percent of all victimizations are not reported (BJS 2013).
- Of every 1,000 household burglaries, 390 are reported (BJS 2013); 10 result in arrests (BJS 2013b); a very small proportion of arrests get convictions, and even fewer result in incarceration (Crimeinamerica.net 2016).
- The average time between arrest for larceny and conviction is 8.5 months, despite the fact that 93 percent involve a guilty plea, and most trials are bench trials (Crimeinmerica.net 2016).
- Think of touching a hot stove that burns 1 of 500 times and it doesn't hurt until 8 months later! This metaphor describes the state of our criminal justice system.

Another effective teaching tool I use goes far beyond the book. The project is called Beyond Walls. In this learning experience, I arrange for my students to correspond every week with an inmate in a nearby state prison. At the end of the semester, we tour the prison facility, and students meet their writing partner face-to-face. This experience is, by far, a teaching tool more powerful than any text or lecture I could present. Students write me, often years later, conveying the power of the lessons they learned. Typically, the message is something like these:

"They are more than just a number."

"I discovered just how much we had in common."

"I could have been there but for a little different situation."

"They are people with hopes and dreams."

The overall lesson: statistics are just people with the tears wiped away.

Works Cited

Bureau of Justice Statistics. (2013a). For second consecutive year violent and property crime rates increased in 2012: Increases driven by simple assaults and crime not reported to police. Bureau of Justice Statistics. Retrieved September 25, 2016, from http://www.bjs.gov/content/pub/press/cv12pr.cfm

Bureau of Justice Statistics. (2013b). "Household burglary, 1994–2011." US Department of Justice, Office of Justice Programs, Bureau of Justice Statistics. Retrieved September 26, 2015, from http://www.bjs.gov/content/pub/pdf/hb9411.pdf

Crimeinamerica.net. (2016). "Crime in America." Retrieved September 26, 2016, from http://www.crimeinamerica.net/2010/01/25/crime-statistics-no-prison-sentences-for-most-felony-convictions/

Diefenbach, D. L., and West, M. D. (2001). "Violent crime and Poisson regression: A measure and a method for cultivation analysis." *Journal of Broadcasting & Electronic Media*, 45, 432–445.

FBI.gov. (2015). "Latest crime stats released." Retrieved September 25, 2016, from https://www.fbi.gov/news/stories/latest-crime-stats-released

Hetsroni, A. (2012). "Violent crime on American television: A critical interpretation of empirical studies." *Sociology Mind*, 2, 141–147.

Truman, J. L., and Langton, L. (2015). "Criminal Victimization, 2014." US Department of Justice, Office of Justice Programs, Bureau of Justice Statistics. Retrieved September 25, 2016, from http://www.bjs.gov/content/pub/pdf/cv14.pdf

Twainquotes.com. (2016). "Directory of Mark Twain's maxims, quotations, and various opinions." Retrieved September 25, 2016, from http://www.twainquotes.com/Education.html

Section II: A Culture of Social Control

From the Field: Deviance or Art?

A study by researchers at Texas Tech University reported a link between the number of tattoos a person has and his or her involvement in deviance.

As you can imagine, this report caused quite an uproar. Does this mean that tattoos *cause* deviance? Are people who sport a lot of tattoos a deviant "type"? Is there a gene that causes risk-takers to engage in both tattoos and also other kinds of deviance?

In our media-saturated, sound-bite culture, such headlines and leaps in logic abound. As an educated person, you have a responsibility to be critical-minded when reviewing research.

In this case, a cursory glance at the report (Koch et al. 2010) seems to support the notion that tattooed individuals are, in fact, more likely to "abuse alcohol, use illegal drugs, be arrested more often, have more sex partners, and engage in unprotected sexual intercourse with strangers" (p. 152). Upon closer inspection, the researchers came to a much different conclusion than the above statements suggest. The researchers maintained that those with significant body art (four or more tattoos, seven or more piercings) are more likely to belong (informally) to groups that resist the established culture. The research team used subcultural identity theory to propose that "individuals with increasing evidence of body art procurement will also report higher levels of deviant behavior in order to maintain and/or increase social distance from the mainstream" (p. 151). Here is one quote from a participant, demonstrating what researchers used to exemplify the mind-set of a "hardcore" body art enthusiast:

Dr. Sue's Tattoo. Deviance or Art?

I was walking down the street the other day and I saw this kid get out of a brand new Honda, and he had Harley-Davidson tattoos all over his arms. I mean, c'mon man, I drive a Harley and hang out with guys who take that seriously. This little puke probably lives … with mom and dad, and he's trying to act like a hardcore rebel. It makes me sick. (Koch et al. 2010, 152)

How did the researchers draw their conclusions? Using several research methods—literature, 2,000 surveys, statistical analysis—they first consulted relevant theory(s) and then triangulated (cross-verified) data to determine the strongest patterns of association. Appropriately, the authors pointed out limitations of the study and recommended further research to substantiate their tentative conclusions—that those with significant body art also report more deviant behavior in order to distinguish themselves from dominant culture.

To distinguish yourself as a critical scholar, keep these tips in mind when reviewing research:

- Do the authors hold appropriate credentials and report association with respected institutions?
- Does the research article appear in a peer-reviewed (vetted) publication?
- Does the article situate itself among other established research?
- Does it clearly document the research methods?
- Do the authors acknowledge limitations of the study?

Works Cited

Koch, J. R., Roberts, A. E., Armstrong, M. L., and Owen, D. C. (2010). "Body art, deviance, and American college students." *The Social Science Journal*, 47, 151–161.

Section II: A Culture of Social Control

Reality Check: Doing Nothing

(Credit for this idea in the social construction of reality goes to Nathan Palmer, at www.SociologySource.com. The concept originated with Karen Bettez Halnon, 2001.)

We commonly think of deviance as doing something "bad," or at least outside the norm. Critical thinking teaches us to look at an issue from another angle, to ask a different question. In this Reality Check, we ask: Is doing nothing deviant?

In this exercise, do nothing. Literally. Stand in a public place for fifteen to thirty minutes, still, with no distraction, no expression on your face. If someone approaches you, simply say, "I am doing nothing."

If possible, have a friend observe from a distance, taking notes. Record your reactions immediately after the exercise, and those of others (these observations constitute your field notes). Most likely, as Palmer explains, "All of a sudden those abstract concepts, deviance, norms, stigma, all become uncomfortably real" (p. 2). This is experiential learning; in your vulnerability, it becomes a moment to remember.

Works Cited

Bettez Halnon, K. (2001). "The sociology of doing nothing: A model 'adopt a stigma in a public place' exercise." *Teaching Sociology* 29, 423–438.

Palmer, N. (2011). "Teaching deviance by doing nothing." Retrieved April 29, 2016, from https://scatter.wordpress.com/2011/03/03/teaching-deviance-by-doing-nothing/

Section II: A Culture of Social Control

OLE Resources

At the intersection of culture and digital habitat stands the incredibly fast-growing world of online learning environments. Everything from choice of content, to communication, and learning strategies must be retooled to accommodate learning in our digital age. For example, in my online classes, I strive to create a culture that directly and purposely reflects the following (taken in part from Bates 2016):

- Mutual respect (setting tone and examples for interactions between instructor and students, and among students)
- Openness to different views and opinions (discussion boards)
- Evidence-based argument and reasoning (data and research articles)
- Experiential learning (getting out in the real world)
- Transparency in assessment (rubrics, criteria)
- Collaboration and mutual support (online groups, monitored)

Here are a few resources I have found to be particularly helpful in thinking about crime and deviance: (Tip: *The Wire* is arguably the most powerful teaching tool I've ever used!)

- Jane Elliott, "Jane Elliott's Blue Eyes Brown Eyes Exercise" http://www.janeelliott.com
- "Serial," *This American Life* https://itunes.apple.com/us/podcast/serial/id917918570?mt=2
- "Rap on Trial" http://endrapontrial.org
- "Irvine Laboratory for the Study of Space and Crime" http://ilssc.soceco.uci.edu

- *The Wire* http://www.hbo.com/the-wire
- Gulliver, G. (2015). "The Wire, Serial, and the Decline of the American Industrial Empire." http://time.com/3691610/wire-serial-baltimore/

Works Cited

Bates, T. (2016). "Culture and effective online learning environments." Retrieved September 26, 2016, from http://www.tonybates.ca/2016/05/15/culture-and-effective-online-learning-environments/

Section III:
Faces of Power

Unit 5: Doing Identity

Dr. Sue to You: Who am I and why?

Whereas other cultures (e.g., Japan, China) tend toward collectivism and group-based identity, Americans take pride in individualism, which has been identified as a cultural syndrome (Triandis 1993), or strong cultural tendency. Though some of us realize that individualism is overrated, we are nevertheless conditioned to explain events or judgments in individualistic terms. In the Section II From the Field, we briefly explored how a particular subculture forms (based on individualism) and distinguishes itself from mainstream society. Recall that in the Texas Tech research, certain people chose to set themselves apart by engaging in significant body art procurement. The study suggested they might purposely engage in certain deviant behaviors, specifically to further distance themselves from conventional society.

A problem arises when identity is tied with involuntary categorization and judgments based on non-merit standards. In American history, race and ethnicity represent two primary points of identity-making that have become entangled with political, economic, and social influence. In fact, most experts now agree that race has no biological basis and is, instead, a human invention; distinguishing characteristics vary from place to place, and over time (this concept is explored in this unit through "The Science, Social Construction, and Exploitation of Race").

The more relevant point is that race and ethnicity mark a category of difference that has gathered the moss of inequality wherever it remains uncontested. That is, throughout our history, people of color have been channeled into circumstances and positions that have worked to their cumulative disadvantage (Wilson 1990). This cumulative disadvantage becomes a very large obstinate boulder that is incredibly resistant to change. And because these elements have become embedded in our culture, ideological stereotypes abound, often resulting in prejudice and discrimination.

In this unit, we explore a few ways in which power intertwines with social constructions, becomes attached to individuals, and, by association, to group identity. In the first reading, "Making Sense of Race, Class, and Gender," Pascale reviews some facts associated with constructed inequalities and focuses on ways in which they complicate workings of social class. Pascale introduces the term *disidentification*, defined as a "process of challenging a dominant (i.e., hegemonic) discourse" (p. 6). An example would be a person with mixed ancestry refusing to check a racial box, or even "other." This process of disidentification becomes a potential source of power in dismantling some of the predominant ruling ideologies—like ways that hard-core tattoo deviants resisted mainstream culture. These actions on the part of people to control some small part of their lives is referred to as *agency*, or the capacity for self-recognition (Pascale 2008, 10), which is hoped will pave the way for social change.

Readings in this unit illustrate ways in which various categories of difference intersect and interact. That is (for example), being Black is different for men than for women, and for both sexes racial identity will likely vary by social class. Similarly, gender dynamics are different for heterosexual men than for gay men, and even that varies by race, ethnicity, and class. Taking into consideration these complications is referred to as *intersectionality* (Collins 1990).

The complexity of studying, researching, and even talking about these intersectional complications is challenging. I often refer to "shifting centers" as a learning strategy, one in which we highlight one particular dynamic for close study. In the reading titled "If Men Could Menstruate," gender takes center stage for the analysis. In this short satirical piece, note how Steinem cleverly illustrates power associated with the so-called "natural" workings of gender.

Before we turn from the topic of gender, let me offer a quick tip on how to think about gender as a social construct. We are well trained to believe that gender is biological, which would make it a "naturalization" factor, one inherent, indelible, inexpungible. Here it is important to distinguish sex (male/female) from sex role (performance expectations) from gender (social identity). Even those terms can be misleading (they are not so fixed as these definitions suggest), but the point is to understand gender as a verb, not a noun. That is, we DO gender (see Butler 1990, West and Zimmerman 1987). It is enacted, enforced, and reinforced day by day, even moment to moment. *We* enact gender. Try it as a verb: I gender, you gender, they gender … in a million ways—the way we walk, talk, work, nurture, love, think. Gender is complex, of course, and constitutes an entire field of study. But for now, the gender-as-verb strategy will help you understand that gender is not a simple either/or category; it is constructed and fluid. Now, enjoy Steinem's essay!

Finally, the last reading in this unit is "The Search for Authenticity," by Arlie Hochschild. Hochschild first became known for her work on airline attendants, described in the book, *The Managed Heart* (1983). She aptly dubbed the constant attention demanded of airline "stewardesses" (as they were called then) as emotion work. And hard work it was (and still is), as attendants must be skilled at tasks, and also at managing a mass of people packed into a small space, often in stressful situations. All the while, the attendants must stay calm, smile, and place their own needs and feelings out of sight. In this reading, Hochschild extends the concept of *emotion work* to corporations and cultural responses, in which individuals become alienated from their work and even from themselves—work that varies by gender. See what you think!

In a recent *New York Times* article, Morris (2015) argues we are deep into transition—into a post-cultural identity crisis in which "gender roles are merging. Races are being shed. … [and] we've been made to see how trans and bi and poly-ambi-omni- we are" (p. 2). Really? I'm not so sure. Yes, we have hit gigantic milestones—the first African American president, a woman presidential candidate, marriage equality legislation, transgender rights in the making—these social facts mark significant cultural progress.

But other social facts are also relevant: the racial wealth gap has widened in the last forty years (Irwin, Miller, and Sanger-Katz 2014); women are still penalized in the paid workforce (the wage gap is also widening) (Kottasova 2015) and at home (the second shift) (Hochschild 2012); Barack Obama had more death threats than any president in history (more than thirty a day) (Causes 2016); the "birther" myth of Obama's long-established birthright has been revived (Daugherty and Wuestewald 2016); the backlash with Hillary Clinton's candidacy has provoked a wave of misogyny that "may roil American life for years to come" (Beinart 2016); and Caitlyn Jenner (the transgender woman formerly known as Bruce Jenner) receives thousands of transphobic comments and death threats because of her identity (Nichols 2015).

DSTY TIP: These brief examples are, of course, the tip of the proverbial iceberg regarding social relations in our culture. Still, some evidence suggests we are transitioning into a more civil, principled society (Morris 2015). This unit provides stock to consider our place in the changing cultural landscape. Maybe we are in transition. But first we need to acknowledge that we have not yet arrived.

Works Cited

Beinart, P. (2016, October). "Fear of a female president." *The Atlantic*. Retrieved September 29, 2016, from http://www.theatlantic.com/magazine/archive/2016/10/fear-of-a-female-president/497564/

Butler, J. (1990). *Gender trouble: Feminism and the subversion of identity*. New York, NY: Routledge.

Causes. (2016). "Secret service says the number of threats against the president is overwhelming." Retrieved September 29, 2016, from https://www.causes.com/causes/350394-join-the-fight-to-stop-dishonoring-the-president/updates/620775-secret-service-says-the-number-of-threats-against-the-president-is-overwhelming

Collins, P. H. (1990). *Black feminist thought: Knowledge, consciousness, and the politics of empowerment*. New York, NY: Routledge.

Daugherty, A., and Wuestewald, E. (2016, September 19). "Obama tired of birther talk." *The Kansas City Star*. Retrieved September 29, 2016, from http://www.kansascity.com/news/politics-government/election/article102374027.html

Hochschild, A. R. (1983). *Managed heart: Commericalization of human feeling*. Oakland, CA: University of California Press.

Hochschild, A. (2012). *The second shift: Working families and the revolution at home*. New York, NY: Penguin Books.

Irwin, N., Miller C. C., and Sanger-Katz, M. (2014, August 19). "America's racial divide, charted." *The New York Times*. Retrieved September 29, 2016, from http://www.nytimes.com/2014/08/20/upshot/americas-racial-divide-charted.html

Kottasova, I. (2015). "U.S. gender pay gap is getting worse." CNN Money, November 18, 2015. Retrieved September 29, 2016, from http://money.cnn.com/2015/11/18/news/gender-pay-gap/

Morris, W. (2015, October 6). "The year we obsessed over identity." *The New York Times Magazine.* Retrieved September 29, 2015, from http://www.nytimes.com/2015/10/11/magazine/the-year-we-obsessed-over-identity.html?_r=0

Nichols, J. M. (2015, August 19). "This man turned 100s of death threats against Caitlyn Jenner into something beautiful." *The Huffington Post.* Retrieved September 29, 2016, from http://www.huffingtonpost.com/entry/this-artist-transformed-online-hate-directed-at-caitlyn-jenner-into-a-beautiful-work-of-art_us_55d4985de4b0ab468d9f28c1

Pascale, C. (2008). "Making sense of race, class, and gender: The discursive construction of class." In *Making sense of race, class, and gender: Commonsense.* New York, NY: Routledge.

Triandis, H. C. (1993). "Collectivism and individualism as cultural syndromes." *Cross-Cultural Research, 27,* 155–180.

West, C., and Zimmerman, D. H. (1987). "Doing gender." *Gender & Society* 1, 125–151.

Wilson, W. J. (1990). *The truly disadvantaged: The inner city, the underclass and public policy.* Chicago, IL: University of Chicago Press.

READING 1

MAKING SENSE OF RACE, CLASS, AND GENDER
The Discursive Construction of Class

BY CELINE-MARIE PASCALE

The gap between rich and poor in the United States has arguably exceeded the capacity to sustain meaningful democracy. Congressional Budget Office data show that, after adjusting for inflation, the average after-tax income of the top one percent of the population rose by $576,000—or 201 percent—between 1979 and 2000; the average income of the middle fifth of households rose $5,500, or 15 percent; and the average income of the bottom fifth rose $1,100, or 9 percent (Center on Budget and Policy Priorities 2003).[1] In daily, life this disparity is embodied in the struggles of African American, Native American, Native Alaskan, and Hispanic families that, according to the U.S. Census, have *median* household incomes $10–20,000 below government-based calculations for self-sufficiency. The disparity also is embodied in the struggles faced by 40 percent of poor single-parent working mothers who paid at least half of their income for child care in 2001(Center on Budget and Policy Priorities 2003); in the struggles of 4.9 million families who paid half of their income in rent in 2002 (National Alliance to End Homelessness 2002); and, in the struggles of more than 3.7 million adults with disabilities living on federal Supplemental Security Income (SSI), which now provides less than one-third the income needed for one-bedroom apartment (O'Hara and Cooper 2003:11). Minimum-wage workers, in 2002, were unable to afford a one-bedroom apartment in any city in the nation. If the increase in poverty is apparent, the tremendous increase in wealth accruing to the top 1% of the population is more extremely hard to track. While conditions of poverty may make the evening news, thorough reports on conditions of affluence are more unusual. The affluence and poverty that variously shape life in the United States are not part of a sustained or routine public conversation. In the United States, economic inequality—arguably one of the most *material* sites of 'difference'—is often one of the least visible.

If commonsense leads people to believe that we can recognize race and gender on sight, even if we might sometimes find ourselves confused or mistaken, commonsense about class operates quite differently. While people living in the extreme poverty of homeless make class visually recognizable, generally class is not apparent "just by looking" at a person, or in passing encounters. The presence of people who are homeless is arguably the most consistently clear display of class in daily life. If the observable presence of race and gender means that each can be made relevant at potentially any moment, the relative invisibility of class renders it far less likely to be made relevant.

I do not mean to suggest that wealth and poverty are simply a matter of language and representation but rather, I argue that because material conditions and discursive practices are not distinct, understandings of class need to be rooted to language, as well as economics. All objects and events are made meaningful through language. An earthquake may be understood as a geological phenomenon or an act of god; a stone may be a marker, a sculpture, or geological evidence, depending on the meaning we give to it (Hall 1997). We must interpret experience in order for it to become meaningful. The cultural discourses that enable people in the U.S. to make sense of wealth and poverty cannot be separated from the material conditions of that production. While the word "discourse" often is used as a synonym for "talk," here it has a more specialized meaning. Discourses are cultural frameworks for understanding what knowledge is useful, relevant or true in a specific context. For example, a scientific discourse enables scientists to 'recognize' a stone as a kind of geological evidence.

In my initial analysis of interviews, talk about class appeared to be so completely dislocated from economics as to lack *any* concrete mooring. Indeed, everyday assumptions about class appeared to be idiosyncratic. Scholars have often raised the specter of "false consciousness" to describe a lack of class-consciousness. Yet it is important to recall there was a time in U.S. history when cogent class analyses shaped public discourse. The disappearance of public discourse cannot be separated from a class history shaped by the U.S. government's consistent willingness to use deadly violence against workers and unions through deployment of the National Guard and federal troops between 1870 and 1930. Although we 'forget' it, we begin talking about wealth and poverty within a pre-existing discourse shaped by class struggle.

We live in a country that appears to be devoted to the ideal of democratic equality, yet is divided by disparities that are produced through a commitment to competitive prosperity. I begin by focusing my analysis on the simple questions: In what ways, and on what terms, does commonsense knowledge make class positions (our own and others) recognizable? In order for class differences to be generally invisible, there must be a systematic detachment between the social displays and economic productions of class. How is that people recognize, or fail to recognize, themselves and others as members of socio-economic classes? I examine how commonsense knowledge about class in the United States leads people to engage in practices that systematically disorganize the presence of social and economic capital. By analyzing commonsense understandings of class, I unsettle economic determinism and move toward more complex, fluid conceptualizations that incorporate discursive aspects of class

Belonging to the Middle Class

Most people I interviewed characterized themselves as middle-class—regardless of whether they were multimillionaires or blue-collar workers. While this might strike readers as itself a matter of commonsense, rather than as a point of analytic interest, it is possible to understand this information as something more than a cliché. Toward that end, let me begin by saying that four of the five multimillionaires I interviewed characterized themselves as middle class and asserted that perceptions of them as wealthy were mistaken. (I will come back to this exception a bit later.) For example, Brady, a white attorney specializing in estate planning explained: "I guess we define class by wealth since we don't have nobility here. So […] I guess I'm in the middle, based our tests, our society, probably middle class."² I found it difficult to think of Brady, with assets of nearly $5 million dollars, as "in the middle" of the economic spectrum. As Brady continued, he described upper-class people as "pretentious" and added: "I don't feel class is that important and I don't care for folks who think it is." Brady's dismissal of class is not so much a denial of his wealth but a dismissal of the "folks" who make wealth the measure of a person. Similarly, Polard, a white commercial real estate developer, distinguished his wealth from his personality. He talked about himself as "middle class" and called himself "an average kinda joe" who "eats hamburgers at McDonalds." Polard did not just call himself 'average' but invoked a discourse that links him to a certain kind of masculinity. Polard elaborated: "I don't feel a connection to I guess what one would consider upper class. I don't feel connected to that. You know, my friends—my relationships—and that, are middle America." Throughout the interview Polard, reinforced a distinction between the kind of person he is and the wealth that he has. For instance, Polard said:

> When uh you live in this house […] the average person driving down the street will view the big house with all the land sitting on an expensive street, [and think] he must be very rich. But I mean that's not me, it isn't my personality. […] I'm just an ordinary kinda guy.

Polard is not denying his wealth; on the exit interview form, he valued his assets at over $100 million. Yet Polard displaces economic considerations of class by centering personal values. From eating at McDonald's to his personal relationships, Polard lays claim to a *class* identity that stands apart, or is made to stand apart, from his wealth.

Polard and Brady talk about "being middle-class" as being *a particular kind of person*—rather than as being a particular level of income or assets. Certainly, the routine nature of daily life leads most people to think of themselves as average (Sacks 1992). While it would be quite easy to press the claim that Polard is deluding himself (or me) by characterizing himself as "middle class," such a claim would foreclose important questions. In particular, on what terms, or in what contexts, do people characterize themselves by a *class* category that is independent of their economic resources? How might such misrecognition of class (willful or not) create a cultural quarantine that prevents critical questions, and opposing interpretations, from arising, or being seriously engaged?

While the rhetoric people invoke when talking about class may be race and/or gender specific (eg., "an average joe"), I sought and examined patterns of commonsense about class that transcended boundaries of race and gender. So, it is important to note that white men were not the only multimillionaires to characterize themselves as middle class. Two women, one Latina and one American Indian, who were self-made multimillionaires expressed similar sentiments. Marisol Alegria owned two burger franchises at the time of our interview. Marisol explained:

In the community here, um, I find that there's a lotta respect for that [owning and operating fast food franchises]. Sometimes it's a misconceived respect, I think, an' especially in my case, because the perception is, "Oh my gosh, there's a lady that must be a multimillionaire." Or, you know, "That lady's just making beaucoup bucks," you know, and—and that kind of a thing. But it really, um—and there ARE some out there. I mean, because most of my counterparts throughout, are REALLY in the big buck category.

Marisol talks about herself as the object of "misconceived respect" based on a false perception. Yet, she is a self-made multimillionaire with assets just under $10 million. It seems possible that Marisol can argue that perceptions of her as wealthy are "misconceived" by comparing herself to even wealthier peers. Certainly, "beaucoup bucks" and "big bucks" are relative terms that avoid any fixed notion of wealth. However, Marisol also resists being perceived by others as a multimillionaire—a very specific category and one that is consistent with her own characterization of her assets. It seems unlikely then that Marisol is invoking a purely relative notion of wealth, or that she is trying to conceal her wealth in the interview. Since Marisol objects to the *perception* of her as a multimillionaire, it seems possible that she does not believe that she is *recognizable* as a multimillionaire—that in social environments she does not stand out as different. It is not just that class, seen from within, can be imagined to be invisible but that *markers of class can be disorganized in such a way as to make class unintelligible.* Indeed, Marisol later talked about the care that she takes with her appearance so that she does not stand out.

Marisol: I have a wonderful, and I really feel very good about this, I have a wonderful experience at mixing very well. I could be with the richest of the rich and not drop the beat, not feel intimidated, or uncomfortable.

Celine-Marie: Mmhm

Marisol: You know, I know that I have an outfit or two that would wear just as well. And if were going to ... uh, one of my employee's baptismals, out in Las Viejas I know that I could wear, you know, something there to not intimidate or feel ... you know, as though I'm out of ... out of class there

Celine-Marie: Mmhmm

Marisol: or would intimidate the guests or anything else.

Celine-Marie: Mmhmm

Marisol: I think I can do that very well. So ... for that reason, I think I ... I just kinda ... mesh very well.

Here one can better see why Marisol might object to the *perception* that she is a multimillionaire. Marisol talks about herself as someone in the middle. She can socialize with the "richest of the rich" and not "feel intimidated" and can attend a social gathering hosted by one of her fast food employees without intimidating the other guests. Marisol talks about class as a social category based on interaction; to intimidate or be intimidated is "to be out of class."

Lorraine Doe, an American Indian who worked as a tribal administrator, also talked about herself as being middle class based on being an "average" person. At the time of our interview, she held assets of over $500 million dollars. It is not just that Marisol, Lorraine, Polard, and Brady think of class in purely personal terms but that in order to maintain their 'ordinariness,' they *must* think of class in this way. And in this sense their personal identity as ordinary people is in conflict with a class location based on extraordinary wealth.

In order to produce and maintain the appearance of a class identity, people must understand and manipulate complex meanings attached to work, wealth, consumer goods and other commodified cultural forms. Recall, for instance, that Polard described himself as "an average joe who eats hamburgers at McDonalds" and Brady referred to "folks" rather than to "people."

Outside of the Middle Class

Among the five multimillionaires I interviewed, Charlie Chin, a land and business developer, stood as the exception. Charlie identified himself as a first-generation Chinese-American and talked about himself as anything BUT ordinary. Charlie, with assets over $10 million, was the only multimillionaire to categorize himself as "around the top" in terms of class. He described himself as a person who enjoys socializing among university presidents, hospital administrators, and government officials. Whereas other multimillionaires articulated a gap between the way others might perceive them based on wealth, and the kind of person they really are, Charlie made no such distinction. Charlie was also the only multimillionaire to talk about wealth as a means to overcome the vulnerabilities racism, immigration, and poverty. For instance, Charlie explained:

> I think that if you were a Mexican or Chinese immigrant and you don't have a great com-
> mand of the language or let's say you have a command of the language but you slip up a little
> bit with your words or your tenses, things like that and you go to a hospital … you're treated
> differently than if I go in there. […]
>
> So I'll go into the hospital and I'll KNOW the doctor. Ok? Or, I'll know the other doc-
> tors there. I'll know the HEAD of the HOSPITAL. Ok? […] Whereas if you go in and you
> look like you don't belong or you can't pay your bill or um or you're not going to cause them
> a problem if they leave an instrument in your stomach or something like that … it's just,
> it's just COMPLETELY different. […] I think you will live longer. […] I think you will be
> cheated less, you will be treated with more respect, you will get faster service and they will
> make sure that YOU don't die. […] That's why I work hard so I can take care of myself and
> my family and my extended family [big inhale] in that, in that manner. Also I KNOW that

> that's rotten and so I like to do things so that everybody gets a certain type of respect and care and consideration, too. Because what kind of society do you live in if it's too, too far that way?

Charlie Chin's strong identification with the experiences of immigrants, racism and poverty produces *disidentification* with dominant class discourse, even as he celebrates the benefits of wealth. Disidentification is more than a lack of identification; it is a process of challenging a dominant (i.e., hegemonic) discourse in ways that expose what the hegemonic discourse conceals. Indeed it is the work of disidentification that makes Charlie Chin's class privilege visible. His celebratory success emerges from a history of legal exclusions in the U.S. that once prevented his parents, aunts, and uncles from the rights of citizenship, property ownership, and fair employment. In addition, Charlie's family was consistently vulnerable to the physical, emotional, and economic violence of racists. While, one might say Charlie Chin is a poster child for the American Dream, in his talk about class, he does not identify with the notions of equality and fairness that permeate the mythology of the American Dream. Nor does he identify with the mythic middle class. Rather, Charlie effectively resists hegemonic class discourses and resituates the competitive prosperity of the American Dream within historical processes of racism and economic oppression. This particular practice of disidentification is possible because class identification is constituted within various, often competing, systems of representation that carry forward different parts of histories.

Excepting Charlie Chin, people who did not identify themselves as middle-class resisted characterizing themselves by class at all—regardless of whether they eventually categorized themselves as above or below 'middle class.' For example, Lana Jacobs, a highly successful artist who held assets of nearly a million dollars at the time of our interview, illustrates this point. Lana continued to make her home and studio in the working-class community of color, where she had lived before her success as an artist. While, she freely characterized herself as an artist, as Black, and as a woman, Lana refused to characterize herself by class. Lana explained:

> I guess I am a universal person. I don't see myself fitting into a group. I am not a group-minded kind of person. [...] I feel stifled by groups because I have my own ... my own attitude about uh what I feel what I know I lived. [...] I try not to judge. I work on my judgments about people.

Lana talked about class as a voluntary social category—something she could refuse to join. If Lana experiences being a woman, an artist, or Black, as a social *fact*, she talks about class as a social *judgment*. However, the unwillingness of the people I interviewed to characterize themselves as wealthy or poor should not be confused with their willingness to characterize others as such. Lana had no difficulty characterizing her grandparents as "a little below middle class." Yet being *a little* above or below the middle is an assessment comparatively free of judgment since to be 'in the middle' is to be like most other people. By contrast, if Lana were to characterize herself by assets and wealth, she would be far more than "a little above" her family and community. By resisting class categorization, Lana implicitly asserts her long-standing connections to family, neighbors, and friends.

Similarly, when I asked Cuauhtemoc, a part-time stock clerk, if he had a class identity, he explained:

I consider myself a full-blooded Mexican but as far as a class ... money's not a big thing to me, yeah we need it and everything but you know if it wasn't around or whatever, things would be a lot better. You know uhm ... I think, I don't really consider myself a class, I think I'm more, I think I'm really ... how would you say it, privilege who I am and what I have you know, because no, I don't have a lot of money but I have what I need.

Cuauhtemoc advances his identity as "full-blooded Mexican" yet, like Lana, dismisses the importance of class identification. Interestingly he explains that he "privileges" who he is and what he has *because* he doesn't have a lot of money. If "not having a lot of money" conjures images of need or poverty, Cuauhtemoc also quickly dispels those images by saying "I have what I need." The class identifications most readily available to him through U.S. hegemonic discourse would be poor or lower class—identifications more likely to diminish, than enhance, a sense of self.

All of the people I interviewed who experienced daily economic hardship resisted hegemonic class categories, sometimes by inventing new categories. Emerson Piscopo, was unemployed at the time of our interview. He offered a surprising response to my question about class.

Celine-Marie: Uh-huh. Do you have a class identity?

Emerson: Uh, meaning where, where I fit in to society?

Celine-Marie: Mhmm

Emerson: Um, I guess fore ... forefront, I'm a transsexual,

Celine-Marie: Mhmm

Emerson: transgender, transgender um, I'm since I'm still, I'm it just using hormones right now, and I have had surgery though, a hysterectomy, I guess I'm PART of the way there.

Initially, I was flummoxed by his answer. Had he misunderstood the question? Was he subverting a question he didn't want to answer? Was he refocusing the conversation to a topic more important to him? I came back to the issue later in the interview and reintroduced a question about his class identity. Emerson explained his family's economic circumstances this way:

I'm starting out, I just, I had that major surgery so I'm not backed by a year's worth of work and it affected us [short pause] financially greatly, and we are both trying to catch up. We're, we're doin' it, but we're struggling, basically. We're in the struggling class. Not, not POOR but somewhere in between poor and okay.

Emerson introduces his family's economic difficulties through news of his surgery and his loss of work; he offers an *explanation* even before mentioning the economic hardship. Emerson talks about "trying to catch up"—indicating that ordinarily, his family had more resources and then frames their efforts to "catch up" as successful, if incomplete. In this way, Emerson is able to describe economic hardship while resisting identification with poverty. He underscores this resistance by saying "Not POOR but somewhere in between poor and okay." Thus Emerson not only defines the conceptual space between being poor and okay as one of personal struggle, he constitutes the meaning of his experience in a broader economic and social context.

If Emerson's response appears to be an anomaly, or a strategy that might adopted only by people in economic transition, consider this exchange with Captain Ahab, a senior partner in a successful law firm:

> Celine-Marie: Uh-huh. Where would you place yourself in terms of class?

> Captain Ahab: I am first of all an immigrant. I moved to the United States at age six from Canada but um moved from Canada to Florida so it was a fairly long move. And so I arrived in Florida, again you know as an immigrant, and with an accent and so went through that type of displacement. Was exposed to discrimination issues at that age. I can remember very clearly driving through the southern United States and having my parents explain to me uh about the situation involving segregation in the South. This would have been in 1952. [...]

> Celine-Marie: That's interesting. Where do you put yourself today in terms of class?

> Ahab: Uh ... upper-middle class.

Captain Ahab, like Emerson, responded to my question in a way that deferred or deflected a discussion of class. Both men also displaced my question about class identity by responding with features of their identity that each felt to be more central than class: Captain Ahab as an immigrant and Emerson as a transsexual. If class is important to either man, they seem anxious to privilege a representation of self that is not class-based.

When I pursued the conversation about class, Captain Ahab described his class identity this way:

> My wife is superintendent and principal of a school district, a one-school school district. She has a master's degree. I have a BA, an MA and a JD. And probably we're more upper-middle class by education, than by finances. Uh but uh still I think in the overall scale, we'd probably be considered upper-middle class

Ahab underscores education as the determining factor in his assessment of class and then seems to capitulate to an unwanted characterization as upper-middle class. While one might argue that hegemonic notions of class can be produced through education, in Captain Ahab's talk about class, educational attainments are made to eclipse economic ones.

Overall, the people I interviewed understood class as a social judgment, not just an evaluation of someone's economic resources, but of their 'self'. When talking about their own *class* identities, everyone (except Charlie Chin) used discursive practices invoking social criteria that masked, distorted, or rendered invisible, their economic circumstances—even though they each volunteered their income and assets on the interview form. Class—construed in very personal terms, as something social—depends upon corresponding discourses of free will, personal values, and individual choices. In asserting the *primary importance* of a 'me' that stands apart from one's economic conditions, talk about class systematically hid from view the cultural, social, and economic conditions that structure access to jobs, income, and wealth.

Concluding Remarks

At stake in class identities is the capacity for self-recognition (the source of agency) and the capacity of *others* to recognize us—the capacity for collective identities. So it is especially important to note that very discourses through which people articulated class identities disorganized the presence and meaning of social and economic capital. To the extent that people can and do talk about class *as if* it is unrelated to power and wealth, they shrouded the political dimensions of daily life with commonsense knowledge. The discursive production of class obscured the networks of power that emerge through wealth. These networks of power extend beyond resources that are owned to the *potential* to control resources and people. And, in this sense the everyday "doing of class" (West and Fenstermaker 1995), and the discursive formations upon which such doing relies, occluded not only visible displays of wealth and poverty but also the history and politics of class and class struggle.

The discursive practices regarding class constituted that which they purported to describe: the relative irrelevance of class. Hegemonic discourse effectively subverts the capacity for collective identity based on class interests because class subjects are produced through discourses that conceal class positions, interests, and relationships. Class functions as it does in the United States, not because people are engaged in fictional performances of passing or because they are beset by false consciousness. Rather, class must be understood as performative precisely because discourse—as a kind of societal speech—is a practical part of what people think and feel—how we see the world.

The language of class is performative (i.e., constitutive) in that discursive practices produce the appearance of "classlessness" that they purport to describe. The relationship between material economic circumstances and the social meanings of those circumstances are not completely distinct. While capitalism has always relied on global and local relations of production, it also has produced—and required—particular forms of consciousness. Because relations of exploitation are never lived in economic terms alone, understandings of language in general—and discursive practices in particular—are critical to understanding class struggle. As mentioned at the start, we *begin* talking about class within a pre-existing discourse shaped by class struggle. Like all hegemonic discursive practices, the discursive production of class secures institutionalized relations of power. One of the most important goals of power is to prevail in determining the agenda of the struggle, to determine which questions can be raised and on what terms. Class conflict is pre-empted by the hegemonic discursive practices through which class is constituted.

Hegemonic discourse—not material circumstances—shaped class categorizations and subverted the capacity for collective identity/agency based on economic interests. While theories of class offer insight into important aspects of capitalism, within sociology much of this theory is used to reify categories of class and center debates on the adequacy and limitations of various categorization efforts. However, even if one thinks of class in purely economic terms, it exceeds existing frameworks for understanding class. Is it reasonable to think of someone with $450,000 in assets as wealthy? What if those assets are equity accrued through 40 years of real estate inflation on a small house owned by someone who works in a small factory making jewelry? How is one to understand the class position of a person who earns $70,000 a year as an independent contractor in the technology industry and who is unable to afford to buy a home because of inflated housing prices? If working-class jobs once provided workers and others with the ability to buy not only homes and cars but also boats and vacation property, this is no longer the case. Today, even people with upper-income professional careers do not necessarily experience the benefits of what was once considered wealth; rather, many now refer to themselves as "house poor" because all of their income is tied up in homeownership. This is not to equate those who are "house poor" with those who are living on minimum wage in a rented apartment, but to argue that historical categories of class are inadequate for understanding the contemporary distribution of wealth, the kinds of work and remuneration available, and the potential for social justice organizing. We are in need of new ways of conceptualizing class.

Understanding how identity and subjectivity are constituted within language provides an opportunity to re-theorize economic inequalities and the possibilities for social change. The imagined communities of class are not distinguished by truth or falsity but by the styles in which they are imagined which allow us to recognize different parts of our histories, and to construct points of identification.

The work of disindentification requires resituating the politics that personalize poverty and wealth into the historical conditions that make each possible and apparently natural. This would require the remembering of self and others by calling into question the identities we have come to inhabit as members of a "classless" nation. As scholars, one means through which we can advance an agenda of social justice is by working at the constitutive frontiers of language to imagine new socialities, new subjectivities. In the beginning of the 21st century, resistance to hegemonic economic forces in the United States requires an understanding of the performativity of language in relation to material conditions lived experience.

Discussion Questions

1. Pascale argues that material conditions and discursive practices are not distinct. What does this mean?
2. Why does Pascale place the word *recognize* in single quotes when she writes "… a scientific discourse enables scientists to 'recognize' a stone as a kind of geological evidence"?
3. What discourse(s) do you use to describe your own (or your parents') class location? Does this reading challenge any assumptions that you have held?
4. Have you ever experienced class location used as a social judgment against your-self or others? Have you ever used it as a social judgment?

Notes

1. The Census Bureau does not publish data on the incomes of the top one percent; the Congressional Budget Office supplements Census data with IRS data to capture gains and losses among the top one percent of the population.
2. My racial characterization of interviewees comes from self-identifications on the interview exit form. All names a pseudonyms chosen by the interviewees.

References

Hall, Stuart. 1997. "The Work of Representation." Pp. 1–74 in *Representation: Cultural representations and signifying practices*, edited by S. Hall. Thousand Oaks: Sage Publications, Inc.

Homelessness, National Alliance to End. 2002, Retrieved 2005 http://www.endhome-lessness.org/).

O'Hara, Ann and Emily Cooper. 2003, "Priced Out", May. Retrieved July 7, 2005 (http://www.tacinc.org/).

Priorities, Center on Budget and Policy. 2003, "Poverty Increases and Median Income Declines for Second Consecutive Year", Retrieved Fall 2005, 2006 (http://www. cbpp.org/9-26-03pov.htm).

Sacks, Harvey. 1992. "On Doing "Being Ordinary"." Pp. 413–440 in *Structures of Social Action: Studies in conversation analysis*, edited by J. M. Atkinson and J. Heritage. Cambridge: Cambridge University Press.

West, Candace and Sarah Fenstermaker. 1995. "Doing Difference." *Gender and Society* 9:8–37.

DOING RACE AND CLASS

READING 2

THE SCIENCE, SOCIAL CONSTRUCTION, AND EXPLOITATION OF RACE

BY RASHAWN RAY

The Sociohistorical Context of Race—highlights how the social construction of race, based on the falsifying of the science of race, is used to justify the exploitation of race for economic gains. In this section, race is situated within a sociohistorical context to discuss the origins and central outcomes of race. Since race is real in its consequences (i.e., outcomes), individuals assume that race must be real in its circumstances (i.e., origins) (Zuberi 2001). Therefore, it is important to convey that race is indeed a social construct that has real structural consequences for individuals (Feagin 2001). Furthermore, it must be made clear that race is an organizing principle that is ingrained in the institutions of society that marginalizes and exploits minority group members (Drake 1987; Bonilla-Silva 1997).

The Science of Race

Race can be conceptualized as ethnoracial, historically rooted distinctions or social constructions. Ethnicity, on the other hand, can be classified as a subgroup that shares a common ancestry, history, and/or culture (Bobo and Fox 2003). While numerous studies show that no biological or genetic differences exist among races that have significant psychological, mental, or physical origins, most individuals profess that there are innate racial differences between groups (Zuberi 2001). These include stereotypes such as Asians being short yet intelligent, Blacks being physically superior yet intellectually inferior, and Whites being the standard and epitome of humanity.

Humans are one species regardless of skin color, dialect, eye shape, and/or hair texture. In fact, individuals show more genetic variation within races than among them. In other words, a Black person and a White person can be genetically more similar to each other than two White people or two Black people. While differences seem to develop through health disparities (Gilbert 2010), IQ tests (Lewis 2010), and physical prowess, most of these differences are rooted in socialization, environmental factors, cultural variation, and perceptions of opportunities. Altogether, the science of race is only skin deep and instead differences between groups are based upon structural consequences.

The Invention of Race

So if race is indeed a social construction, how was race invented, and by whom? As Zuberi (2001) discusses, race was formally posited in the mid 1700s by Carolus (Carl) Linnaeus, a Swedish taxonomist, who asserted that people looked different. Linnaeus argued that because people looked different, there had to be psychological traits associated with these physical differences related to skin color. Accordingly, Linnaeus split humans into four subspecies—americanus, europaeus, asiaticus, and afer—each associated with a major continent. The German naturalist Blumenback introduced five racial categories—American, Caucasoid, Malay, Mongoloid, and Ethiopian—with each race associated with a color (i.e., white, yellow, red, brown, Black). It should be noted that Negroid, which means Black, later replaced the term Ethiopian. In turn, many of the Biblical associations with Ethiopians were lost. It should also be noted that Whites were the group doing the racial classifying. Some scholars argue this explains why Whites were placed on top of the racial hierarchy and used whiteness as the pure marker of perfection. Subsequently, other groups fall in line based on skin color from lightest to darkest. This was of course about 150 years after American slavery, thus a system of racial groupings already existed before Linnaeus' formal classification.

In *The Origin of Species*, Charles Darwin (1859) developed the theory of evolution, which asserts that through survival of the fittest, the most superior species will evolve and adapt to its environment. This is where the term race is such an intriguing choice of words. By classifying groups as races, it insinuates that groups are indeed competing and racing to be the fittest. Similarly, eugenics, which was developed in 1865 by Sir Francis Galton, a cousin of Charles Darwin, asserts that through a unique combination of nature versus nurture whereby various interventions are constructed, the perfect human can be created to enhance intelligence levels, save society's resources, and decrease human suffering. Some of these interventions include selective breeding, genetic engineering, in vitro fertilization, and forced sterilization. Eugenics movements have been criticized for justifying state-sponsored discrimination and human rights violations. Recently, some researchers have called for a resurgence into the study of eugenics through new forms of technology. Critics of eugenics insinuate that the "perfect human" will leave out the actual racial pluralism that exists in the world.

As a result of these theories and their implications for race, external physical characteristics (e.g., skin color, hair color and texture, eye color) came to be accepted as reflecting psychological and mental abilities that imply racial superiority or inferiority (Ray 2010). These assumptions, however, are refuted by researchers who note that individuals of every racial group have the same characteristics. More importantly, researchers have never found a gene for race. British fraternal twins are a good example. In 2005, a mixed race couple (that most would classify as Black on skin color alone) gave birth to one brown-skinned, brown eyed, and black haired girl and one fair-skinned, blue eyed, and blond haired girl. In other words, a Black couple had a Black *and* White baby at the same time. While these types of births are rare, they are not uncommon. These twins are validation for those who claim that the science of racial separatism is only skin deep. Still, stereotypes regarding physical characteristics persisted through the falsifying of cranium weight and facial angles as determinants for intelligence. Scientists constructed White brains to be larger than Black brains and used this form of pseudoscience to shape public opinion and public policy.

Through the formulation of theories and concepts to describe and categorize humans, race moved from being a rumor to being a social reality and became a means to separate groups. Darwin's theory of evolution and natural selection became the scientific basis for justifying that differences exist among racial groups. Galton's eugenics theory became the scientific basis to carry out preserving so-called racial purity. "Color prejudice thus became fused with beliefs in biological determinants to produce White racism" (Drake 1987). Collectively, these theories spurred Social Darwinism where scientific studies sought to justify the classification of racial groups.

The Social Construction of Race

Phenotypic features such as skin color, hair color, hair texture, and eye color that have been purported as classifying racial groups actually change over the life course based on how these genetic features interact with the environment. Ask yourself a few simple questions:

- Has your hair color or eye color changed from birth?
- Does your skin color change with exposure to light?
- Does your hair color or eye color change from season to season depending on the temperature of your environment?

If you answered yes to some or all of these questions, you are not alone. Most individuals' phenotypic features change over the life course. And yet, these features that change within each of us were/are used as justification for racial classification and exploitation.

We can even think about the simple definitions of White and Black. White is classified as purity, cleanliness, and innocence. It is the color that brides, doctors, and nurses traditionally wear. Altogether, white is the absence of color and the essence of what is considered good and positive. On the contrary, black is classified as evil, bad, and satanic. Black is the color people wear at funerals and symbolizes death.[a]

Images of Barbie and Aunt Jemima display this White/Black duality. Barbie is traditionally portrayed as pretty, queen-like, and angelic, while Aunt Jemima is frequently portrayed as dark-skinned, overweight, and ugly. In the 1950s and 1960s, Barbie and Aunt Jemima were some of the few caricatures of White and Black women seen by youth across racial lines. Messages that individuals receive about race from social institutions such as the media shape how

---

a   If you take a historical perspective on the color Black, it actually symbolized authority, power, and royalty.

individuals are socially constructed to view race, currently and historically. We receive unconscious messages on a daily basis in all facets of our lives that reinforce the ideology of race. Thus, the ideology of race shapes attitudes and perceptions and all aspects of social life that have real consequences for individuals' opportunities and social interactions. Even children are continuously subjected to messages and images that racially classify groups.

For example, Drs. Kenneth and Mamie Clarks'[b] doll experiments found that Black children often preferred to play with White dolls compared to Black dolls and often classified their own skin color as a lighter shade than it actually was. Additionally, children often viewed White as good and pretty and Black as bad and ugly. The Clarks concluded that racial identity and self-awareness develop as early as 3 years old. Although it would seem as though this form of racial identity among Blacks is a thing of the past, unfortunately it is not. In a 2005 documentary, entitled *A Girl Like Me*, Kiri Davis replicated the Clarks' doll study and found similar results. *A Girl Like Me* is a short, intriguing documentary that captures how stereotypes affect the racial identities of minority group members.

Another documentary that should be of interest to those studying the social construction of race is *A Class Divided*, which is a compelling film about the establishment of ingroups/outgroups and the socialization of internalized prejudices, stereotypes, and discrimination. Third grade teacher Jane Elliott's "Blue Eyes/Brown Eyes" exercise, which was originally conducted following the assassination of Dr. Martin Luther King, Jr. in 1968, places a hierarchical distinction between blue-eyed and brown-eyed students. The documentary shows how quickly prejudice attitudes and discriminatory behavior can commence. Years later the students return as adults to discuss their experiences with the exercise and how it has shaped their beliefs about race and privilege. In part three of the documentary, Elliot conducts the study with adults.

The Exploitation of Race

The social construction of race based on the falsifying of the science of race lead to the exploitation of race. Three examples are fitting here. First, Nazi Germany's "racial hygiene" programs during the 1930s and 1940s sought to preserve the human race by exterminating all Jews. The Aryan nation, commonly associated with Nazi Germany and Adolf Hitler, categorized themselves as the pure breeds. While the Nazis could not find consistent recognizable physical characteristics to distinguish Germans from Jews, they resulted to forcing Jews to wear yellow armbands and have only traditional Jewish names. Germans were told to only marry and breed with blue-eyed and blond-haired humans. As part of the sterilization process, over 40,000 individuals including Jews, Gypsies, Jehovah witnesses, Blacks, and homosexuals were sterilized from 1934–1937. The Holocaust formally lasted from 1933–1945 and more than 5.7 million Jews were killed in Germany. Interestingly, Adolf Hitler, the leader of Nazi Germany, had brown hair and dark eyes.

---

b   Dr. Kenneth Clark was the first Black to obtain a PhD from Columbia University in 1940 with his wife right behind him as the first Black woman to obtain a PhD from Columbia University in 1943. Dr. Kenneth Clark became a full professor in 1942 at City College in New York City and later became the President of the American Psychological Association. Collectively, Drs. Kenneth and Mamie Clark founded the Northside Development Center for Child Development in Harlem. The Clarks were expert witnesses in the Brigg v. Elliot case, which was one of the influential cases that set the tone for the infamous Brown v. Board of Education Supreme Court case.

Second, the U.S. Public Health Service conducted an experiment on 399 Black male farmers in Alabama from 1932–1972. Known as the Tuskegee Syphilis Experiment, these men were never told that they had syphilis and instead told that they had "bad blood" so that doctors and researchers could document the effect syphilis has on the human body. In turn, these farmers were denied proper care for the disease. This tragic event did not come to light until after the experiment was over with one doctor stating, "As I see it, we have no further interest in these patients until they die" (Jones 1993).

Third, The Transatlantic Slave Trade lasted formally in the U.S. from 1619–1865 and led to the deaths of over 20 million Africans. While slavery and bondage existed in human history, until the Transatlantic Slave Trade, the racialization of slavery did not exist (Zuberi 2001). Approximately 8 million Africans died during the Middle Passage, which was the transport voyage from Africa to the Americas. On the slave ships, Africans were hand-cuffed and shackled next to other Africans who did not speak their language so that they would not be able to communicate. Africans would go for days without seeing sunlight. In turn, they were forced to urinate and defecate on themselves and one another. When Africans were brought to the deck of the ship, they had cold, salt ocean water thrown on them and their wounds from whippings and beatings.

Once brought to the Americas, they were publicly sold at an auction like a piece of equipment such as a vehicle or appliance. Africans were then broken down like one would break a horse or a wild animal. Whites would take the African male who they considered to be the strongest mentally and physically and mutilate and murder him in front of the other slaves. White slave owners and caretakers would beat the African male to a pulp instilling fear in the other slaves. After that, they would tie each of his arms and legs to a horse. They would beat the horses in opposite directions until they ripped the African's body in separate pieces. Subsequently, Whites would select the second strongest African slave and beat him to a pulp until he yelled out his newly selected name by the slave owner. This established a precedent that African males had lost their power and would be beaten brutally for exerting any form of agency. Additionally, African women were savagely raped by White slave owners and caretakers. Altogether, if any individuals should be classified as embodying "the survival of the fittest," survivors of atrocities such as the Transatlantic Slave Trade and the Holocaust should be in that category.

In sum, race started out as a rumor, as a myth. This myth of racial difference was transmitted across media outlets, pulpits, classrooms, and stages. In turn, race has become one of the main social structural factors to determine life chances and opportunities. Subsequently, the social construction of race, based on the falsifying of the science of race, is continuously used to justify the exploitation of race for economic gains.

Supplemental Readings and Resources

A Class Divided (Blue Eye/Brown Eye Experiment). Frontline PBS Documentary.
Anderson, Margaret L. and Patricia Hill Collins. 2001. *Race, Class, and Gender; An Anthology, 4th Edition*. Belmont, CA: Wadsworth.

Bobo. Lawrence and Cybelle Fox. 2003. "Race, Racism, and Discrimination: Bridging Problems, Methods, and Theory in Social Psychological Research." Social Psychology Quarterly, *Special Issue: Race, Racism, and Discrimination* 64: 319–332.

Davis, Kiri. 2005. *A Girl Like Me.* Independent Documentary.

Du Bois, W. E. B. [1899] 1995. *The Philadelphia Negro: A Social Study.* Philadelphia: University of Pennsylvania Press.

Du Bois, W. E. B. 1903. *The Souls of Black Folk.* New York: Dover.

Du Bois, W. E. B. 1939. *Black Folk, Then and Now: An Essay in the History and Sociology of the Negro Race.* New York: Henry Holt.

Havard's Implicit Association Tests. https://implicit. harvard.edu/implicit/demo/

Muhammad, Khalil Gibran. 2010. *The Condemnation of Blackness: Race, Crime, and the Making of Modern Urban America.* Cambridge: Harvard University Press.

Williams, Juan. 1987. *Eyes on the Prize. America's Civil Rights Years (1954–1965).* PBS.

Wilson, William Julius. 1978. *The Declining Significance of Race: Blacks and Changing American Institutions.* Chicago: University of Chicago Press.

READING 3

IF MEN COULD MENSTRUATE

BY GLORIA STEINEM

A white minority of the world has spent centuries conning us into thinking that white skin makes people superior—even though the only thing it really does is make them more subject to ultraviolet rays and wrinkles. Male human beings have built whole cultures around the idea that penis-envy is "natural" to women—though having such an unprotected organ might be said to make men vulnerable, and the power to give birth makes womb-envy at least as logical.

In short, the characteristics of the powerful, whatever they may be, are thought to be better than the characteristics of the powerless—and logic has nothing to do with it.

What would happen, for instance, if suddenly, magically, men could menstruate and women could not?

The answer is clear—menstruation would become an enviable, boast-worthy, masculine event:

Men would brag about how long and how much.

Boys would mark the onset of menses, that longed-for proof of manhood, with religious ritual and stag parties.

Congress would fund a National Institute of Dysmenorrhea to help stamp out monthly discomforts.

Sanitary supplies would be federally funded and free.

Military men, right-wing politicians, and religious fundamentalists would cite menstruation ("*men*-struation") as proof that only men could serve in the Army ("you have to give blood to take blood"), occupy political office ("can women be aggressive without that steadfast cycle governed by the planet Mars?"), be priests and ministers ("how could a woman give her blood for our sins?"), or rabbis ("without the monthly loss of impurities, women remain unclean").

Male radicals, left-wing politicians, and mystics, however, would insist that women are equal, just different; and that any woman could enter their ranks if only she were willing to self-inflict a major wound every month ("you *must* give blood for the revolution"), recognize the preeminence of menstrual issues, or subordinate her selfness to all men in their Cycle of Enlightenment.

Street guys would brag ("I'm a three-pad man") or answer praise from a buddy ("Man, you lookin' *good!*") by giving five and saying, "Yeah, man, I'm on the rag!"

Men would convince women that intercourse was *more* pleasurable at "that time of the month." Lesbians would be said to fear blood and therefore life itself—though probably only because they needed a good menstruating man.

Of course, male intellectuals would offer the most moral and logical arguments. How could a woman master any discipline that demanded a sense of time, space, mathematics, or measurement, for instance, without that in-built gift for measuring the cycles of the moon and planets—and thus for measuring anything at all? In the rarefied fields of philosophy and religion, could women compensate for missing the rhythm of the universe? Or for their lack of symbolic death-and-resurrection every month?

Liberal males in every field would try to be kind: the fact that "these people" have no gift for measuring life or connecting to the universe, the liberals would explain, should be punishment enough.

And how would women be trained to react? One can imagine traditional women agreeing to all these arguments with a staunch and smiling masochism. ("The ERA would force housewives to wound themselves every month": Phyllis Schlafly.) Reformers and Queen Bees would try to imitate men, and *pretend* to have a monthly cycle.

All feminists would explain endlessly that men, too, needed to be liberated from the false idea of Martian aggressiveness, just as women needed to escape the bonds of menses-envy. Radical feminists would add that the oppression of the nonmenstrual was the pattern for all other forms of oppression. ("Vampires were our first freedom fighters!") Cultural feminists would develop a bloodless imagery in art and literature. Socialist feminists would insist that only under capitalism would men be able to monopolize menstrual blood. . . .

In fact, if men could menstruate, the power justifications could probably go on forever.

If we let them.

READING 4

THE SEARCH FOR AUTHENTICITY

BY ARLIE RUSSELL HOCHSCHILD

> In a social system animated by competition for property, the human personality was metamorphosed into a form of capital. Here it was rational to invest oneself only in properties that would produce the highest return. Personal feeling was a handicap since it distracted the individual from calculating his best interest and might pull him along economically counter-productive paths.
>
> —Rousseau (Berman's paraphrase)

When Jean-Jacques Rousseau observed that personality was becoming a form of capital he was writing about eighteenth-century Paris, long before there were stewardess training schools and long before the arts of bill collecting were standardized and mass produced.[1] If Rousseau could sign on as a flight attendant for Delta Airlines in the second half of the twentieth century, he would doubtless be interested in learning just *whose* capital a worker's feelings are and just *who* is putting this capital to work. He would certainly see that although the individual personality remains a "medium of competition," the competition is no longer confined to individuals. Institutional purposes are now tied to the workers' psychological arts. It is not simply individuals who manage their feelings in order to do a job; whole organizations have entered the game. The emotion management that sustains the smile on Delta Airlines competes with the emotion management that upholds the smile on United and TWA.

What was once a private act of emotion management is sold now as labor in public-contact jobs. What was once a privately negotiated rule of feeling or display is now set by the company's Standard Practices Division. Emotional exchanges that were once idiosyncratic and escapable are now standardized and unavoidable. Exchanges that were rare in private life become common in commercial life. Thus a customer assumes a right to vent unmanaged hostility against a flight attendant who has no corresponding right—because she is paid, in part, to relinquish it. All in all, a private emotional system has been subordinated to commercial logic, and it has been changed by it.[2]

It does not take capitalism to turn feeling into a commodity or to turn our capacity for managing feeling into an instrument. But capitalism has found a use for emotion management, and so it has organized it more efficiently and pushed it further. And perhaps it does take a capitalist sort of incentive system to connect emotional labor to competition and to go so far as to actually advertise a "sincere" smile, train workers to produce such a smile, supervise their production of it, and then forge a link between this activity and corporate profit. As the sticker on a TWA computer (facing the ticket agent) in the San Francisco Airport read: "When people like you, they like TWA too." It takes considerable sophistication for a company to make this into an ordinary, trivial thought for a worker to be urged to bear in mind.

The Human Costs of Emotional Labor

Massive people-processing—and the advanced engineering of emotional labor that makes it possible—is a remarkable achievement. It is also an important one, for a good part of modern life involves exchange between total strangers, who, in the absence of countermeasures and in the pursuit of short-term self-interest, might much of the time act out suspicion and anger rather than trust and good will. The occasional lapses from the standard of civility that we take for granted remind us of the crucial steadying effect of emotional labor. But like most great achievements, the advanced engineering of emotional labor leaves new dilemmas in its wake, new human costs, and I shall focus now on these. For without a clear understanding of these psychological costs, we can hardly begin to find ways of mitigating or removing them.

These are three stances that workers seem to take toward work, each with its own sort of risk. In the first, the worker identifies too wholeheartedly with the job, and therefore risks burnout. In the second, the worker clearly distinguishes herself from the job and is less likely to suffer burnout; but she may blame herself for making this very distinction and denigrate herself as "just an actor, not sincere" In the third, the worker distinguishes herself from her act, does not blame herself for this, and sees the job as positively requiring the capacity to act; for this worker there is some risk of estrangement from acting altogether, and some cynicism about it—"We're just illusion makers." The first stance is potentially more harmful than the other two, but the harm in all three could be reduced, I believe, if workers could feel a greater sense of control over the conditions of their work lives.

The first kind of worker does not see her job as one of acting. She has little or no awareness of a "false self." She is likely to offer warm, personal service, but she is also warm *on behalf of* the company—"when people like you, they like TWA too." She offers *personalized* service, but she herself becomes identified with the *-ized* part of it. She is not so good at depersonalizing inappropriately personal behavior toward her. For these reasons, she is more likely to suffer stress and be susceptible to burnout. Instead of removing the idea of a "self" from the job either by will or by art, such a person often reacts passively: she stops caring and becomes remote and detached from the people she serves. Some flight attendants who describe themselves as poor at depersonalizing reported periods of emotional deadness: "I wasn't feeling anything. It was like I wasn't really there. The guy was talking. I could hear him. But all I heard was dead words."

This sense of emotional numbness reduces stress by reducing access to the feelings through which stress introduces itself. It provides an exit from overwhelming distress that allows a person to remain physically present on the job. Burnout spares the person in the short term, but it may have a serious long-term cost. The human faculty of feeling still "belongs" to the worker who suffers burnout, but the worker may grow accustomed to a dimming or numbing of inner signals.[3] And when we lose access to feeling, we lose a central means of interpreting the world around us.

As a precaution against burnout many experienced workers develop a "healthy" estrangement, a clear separation of self from role. They clearly define for themselves when they are acting and when they are not; they know when their deep or surface acting is "their own" and when it is part of the commercial show. They may sometimes feel "phony"—because at a given moment they feel that they shouldn't be acting at all or that they are not acting well enough. But by differentiating between an acting and a nonacting side of themselves, they make themselves less vulnerable to burnout.

Now when the company institutes a speed-up—when it maintains its call for emotional labor but sets up conditions that make it impossible to deliver—the worker may become estranged from the acting itself. She may refuse to act at all, thus withdrawing her emotional labor altogether. Since the job itself calls for good acting, she will be seen as doing the job poorly. She may respond to the constantly negative consequences of this by trying not to take any consequences at all, by trying not to *be* there. If in the first stance the worker is too much present in the role, in the third stance, she is not present enough. In all three, the essential problem is how to adjust one's self to the role in a way that allows some flow of self into the role but minimizes the stress the role puts on the self.

In all three cases, the problem of adjusting self to role is aggravated by the worker's lack of control over the conditions of work. The more often "tips" about how to see, feel, and seem are issued from above and the more effectively the conditions of the "stage" are kept out of the hands of the actor, the less she can influence her entrances and exits and the nature of her acting in between. The less influence she has, the more likely it is that one of two things will occur. Either she will overextend herself into the job and burn out, or she will remove herself from the job and feel bad about it.

Worker control over the conditions of good acting boils down, in the end, to practical politics. The San Francisco base manager for United Airlines gave an example: "The company wanted to take two flight attendants off each San Francisco-Honolulu crew, but the union was adamantly opposed, and they won. Now that's a multimillion dollar decision. But maybe it was a good thing they won. They felt they could have some control over that decision. It wasn't just money they wanted. They wanted some say over their work lives so they could do the job like they wanted."

But even such actions by organized workers cannot solve the whole problem. For whenever people do acting for a living, even if they have some control over the stage, they inhabit their own stage faces with caution: behind the mask, they listen to their own feelings at low volume. Cheerfulness in the line of duty becomes something different from ordinary good cheer. This applies much more to the flight attendant, who must try to be genuinely friendly to a line of strangers, than to the commissary worker, who can feel free to hate packing the three-hundredth jello cup onto a lunch tray.

The Culture's Response

Estrangement from display, from feeling, and from what feelings can tell us is not simply the occupational hazard of a few. It has firmly established itself in the culture as permanently imaginable. All of us who know the commercialization of human feeling at one remove—as witness, consumer, or critic—have become adept at recognizing and discounting commercialized feeling: "Oh, they have to be friendly, that's their job" This enables us to ferret out the remaining gestures of a private gift exchange: "Now *that* smile she really meant just for me." We subtract the commercial motive and collect the personal remainders matter-of-factly, almost automatically, so ordinary has the commercialization of human feeling become.

But we have responded in another way, which is perhaps more significant: as a culture, we have begun to place an unprecedented value on spontaneous, "natural" feeling[a] We are intrigued by the unmanaged heart and what it can tell us. The more our activities as individual emotion managers are managed by organizations, the more we tend to celebrate the life of unmanaged feeling. This cultural response found its prophets in late eighteenth-century philosophers like Rousseau and its disciples in the Romantic movement of the nineteenth-century; but widespread acceptance of the view that spontaneous feeling is both precious and endangered has occurred only recently, in the mid-twentieth century.

According to Lionel Trilling, in his classic work *Sincerity and Authenticity*, there have been two major turning points in the public evaluation of expressed feeling. The first was the rise (and subsequent fall) of the value that people put on sincerity. The second was a rise in the value placed on authenticity.[4] In the first case, the value attached to sincerity rose as its corresponding flaw, insincerity or guile, became more common. In the second case, I think the same principle has been at work: the value placed on authentic or "natural" feeling has increased dramatically with the full emergence of its opposite—the managed heart.

Before the sixteenth century, Trilling says, insincerity was neither a fault nor a virtue. "The sincerity of Achilles or Beowulf cannot be discussed; they neither have nor lack sincerity."[5] It simply had no relevance. Yet during the sixteenth century, sincerity came to be admired. Why? The answer is socioeconomic. At this period in history, there was an increasing rate of social mobility in England and France; more and more people found it possible, or conceivable, to leave the class into which they had been born. Guile became an important tool for class advancement. The art of acting, of making avowals not in accord with feeling, became a useful tool for taking advantage of new opportunities. As mobility became a fact of urban life, so did guile and people s understanding that guile was a tool.[6]

Sincerity for its part came to be seen as an inhibition of the capacity to act before a multiplicity of audiences or as an absence of the psychic detachment necessary to acting. The sincere, "honest soul" came to denote a "simple person, unsophisticated, a bit on the dumb side."[7] It was considered "dumb" because the art of surface acting was increasingly understood as a useful tool. When mobility became a fact of urban life, so did the art of guile, and the

---

[a] People want to be their "authentic" selves. As Marshall Berman has put it: "To pursue authenticity as an ideal, as something that must be achieved, is to be selfconsciously paradoxical. But those who seek authenticity insist that this paradox is built into the structure of the world they live in. This world, they say, represses, alienates, divides, denies, destroys the self. To be oneself in such a world is not a tautology but a *problem*" (1970, p. xvi).

very interest in sincerity as a virtue declined.[b] Modern audiences, in contrast to nineteenth-century ones, became bored with duplicity as a literary theme. It had become too ordinary, too unsurprising: "The hypocrite-villain, the conscious dissembler, has become marginal, even alien, to the modern imagination of the moral life. The situation in which a person systematically misrepresents himself in order to practice upon the good faith of another does not readily command our interest, scarcely our credence. The deception we best understand and most willingly give our attention to is that which a person works upon himself?"[8] The point of interest has moved inward. What fascinates us now is how we fool ourselves.

What seems to have replaced our interest in sincerity is an interest in authenticity.[9] In both the rise and the fall of sincerity as a virtue, the feeling of sincerity "underneath" was assumed to be something solid and permanent, whether one was true to it or betrayed it. Placing a value on guile amounted to placing a value on detachment *from* that solid something underneath.[10] The present-day value on "authentic" or "natural" feeling may also be a cultural response to a social occurrence, but the occurrence is different. It is not the rise of individual mobility and the *individual* use of guile in pleasing a greater variety of people. It is the rise of the *corporate* use of guile and the organized training of feeling to sustain it. The more the heart is managed, the more we value the unmanaged heart.

Rousseau's Noble Savage was not guided by any feeling rules. He simply felt what he felt, spontaneously. One clue to the modern-day celebration of spontaneous feeling is the growing popularization of psychological therapies, especially those that stress "getting in touch with" spontaneous feeling.[11] Consider them: Gestalt, bioenergetics, biofeedback, encounter, assertiveness training, transactional analysis, transcendental meditation, rational-emotive therapy, LSD therapy, feeling therapy, implosive therapy, EST, primal therapy, conventional psychotherapy, and psychoanalysis. Therapy books, as the linguist Robin Lakoff has said, are to the twentieth century what etiquette books were to the nineteenth. This is because etiquette has itself gone deeper into emotional life.

The introduction of new therapies and the extension of older ones have given a new introspective twist to the self-help movement that began in the last century.[c] To that twist is now added the value on unmanaged feelings. As practitioners of Gestalt therapy put it: "The childish feelings are important not as a past that must be undone but as some of the most beautiful powers of adult life that must be recovered: spontaneity, imagination."[12] Again, in *Born to Win*, two popularizers of transactional analysis collapse a more general viewpoint into a simple homily: "Winners are not stopped by their contradictions and ambivalences. Being authentic, they know when they are angry and can listen when others are angry with them."[13] Winners, the suggestion is, do not *try to know* what they feel or *try to let themselves* feel. They just know and they just feel, in a natural, unprocessed way.

---

[b] "If sincerity has lost its former status, if the word itself has for us a hollow sound and seems almost to negate its meaning, that is because it does not propose being true to one's self as an end but only as a means" (Trilling 1972, p. 9).

[c] The significance of the growth of new therapies cannot be dismissed by the argument that they are simply a way of extending jobs in the service sector by creating new needs. The question remains, why *these* needs? Why the new need to *do* something about how you feel? The new therapies have also been criticized, as the old self-help movement was, for focusing on individual solutions to the exclusion of social ones and for legitimating the message "Look out for Number One" (Lasch, 1976b). This critique is not wrong in itself, but it is partial and misleading. It is my own view that the capacity to feel is fully analogous to the capacity to see or hear; and if that capacity is lost or injured, it is wise to restore it in whatever way one can. But to attach the cure to a solipsistic or individualistic philosophy of life or to assume that one's injury can only be self-imposed is to contribute to what I have called (with optimism) a "prepolitical" stance.

Ironically, people read a book like *Born to Win* in order to *learn* how to *try* to be a natural, authentic winner. Spontaneity is now cast as something to be *recovered*; the individual learns how to treat feeling as a recoverable object, with ego as the instrument of recovery. In the course of "getting in touch with our feelings," we make feelings more subject to command and manipulation, more amenable to various forms of management.[14]

While the qualities of Rousseau's Noble Savage are celebrated in modern pop therapy, he did not act in the way his modern admirers do. The Noble Savage did not "let" himself feel good about his garden. He did not "get in touch with" or "into" his resentment. He had no therapist working on his throat to open up a "voice block." He did not go back and forth between hot and cold tubs while hyperventilating to get in touch with his feelings. No therapist said to him, "Okay, Noble Savage, let's try to really get into your sadness." He did not imagine that he owed others any feeling or that they owed him any. In fact, the utter absence of calculation and will as they have become associated with feeling is what nowadays makes the Noble Savage seem so savage. But it is also—and this is my point—what makes him seem so noble.

Why do we place more value now on artless, unmanaged feeling? Why, hopelessly and romantically, do we imagine a natural preserve of feeling, a place to be kept "forever wild"? The answer must be that it is becoming scarce. In everyday life, we are all to some degree students of Stanislavski; we are only poorer or better at deep acting, closer or more remote from incentives to do it well. We have carried our ancient capacity for gift exchange over a great commercial divide where the gifts are becoming commodities and the exchange rates are set by corporations. Jean-Jacques Rousseau as a flight attendant for Delta Airlines might add to his eighteenth-century concern for the faceless soul beneath the mask a new concern for the market intrusion into the ways we define ourselves and for how, since his day, that intrusion has expanded and organized itself.

The False Self

Both psychoanalysts and actors, from different perspectives, have spoken about a "false self," which is a disbelieved, unclaimed self, a part of "me" that is not "really me." To the psychoanalyst, the false self embodies our acceptance of early parental requirements that we act so as to please others, at the expense of our own needs and desires. This sociocentric, other-directed self comes to live a separate existence from the self we claim. In the extreme case, the false self may set itself up as the real self, which remains completely hidden. More commonly, the false self allows the true self a life of its own, which emerges when there is little danger of its being used by others.

The actual content of feelings—or wishes, or fantasies, or actions—is not what distinguishes the false self from the true self; the difference lies in whether we claim them as "our own." This claiming applies to our outward behavior, our surface acting: "I wasn't acting like myself." It also applies to our inner experience, our deep acting: "I made myself go to that party and have a good time even though I was feeling depressed."

Professional actors think of the false self as a marvelous resource that can be drawn upon to move audiences to laughter or tears. They find some margin of unclaimed action and feeling to be wonderfully helpful in getting into the part. The danger for the actor lies in *becoming* the part he plays, in feeling that he *is* Hamlet.[d]

Among ordinary people, the false or unclaimed self is what enables one to offer the discretion, the kindness, and the generosity that Noble Savages tend to lack. It is a *healthy* false self. By giving up infantile desires for omnipotence, a person gains a "place in society which can never be attained or maintained by the True Self alone."[15]

Christopher Lasch has recently speculated that our culture's latest model of an unhealthy false self may be the narcissist.[16] The narcissist feeds insatiably on interactions, competing desperately for love and admiration in a Hobbesian dog-eat-dog world where both are perpetually scarce. His efforts are self-perpetuating because he must discount the results: what admiration he does receive, after all, is offered to his false self, not his real one.

But our culture has produced another form of false self: the altruist, the person who is overly concerned with the needs of *others*. In our culture, women—because they have traditionally been assigned the task of tending to the needs of others—are in greater danger of overdeveloping the false self and losing track of its boundaries. If developing a narcissistic false self is the greater danger for men, developing an altruistic false self is the greater danger for women. Whereas the narcissist is adept at turning the social uses of feeling to his own advantage, the altruist is more susceptible to being used—not because her sense of self is weaker but because her "true self" is bonded more securely to the group and its welfare.

Added to the private sexual division of emotional labor is now the trend toward organizing the ways in which public-contact workers manage emotion. Organizations do this in hopes of having the worker's *true* self come to work. They hope to make this private resource a company asset. Yet the more the company offers the worker's true self for sale, the more that self risks seeming false to the individual worker, and the more difficult it becomes for him or her to know which territory of self to claim.

Given this problem, it becomes all the more important to have access to feeling itself. It is from feeling that we learn the *self*-relevance of what we see, remember, or imagine. Yet it is precisely this precious resource that is put in jeopardy when a company inserts a commercial purpose between a feeling and its interpretation.

For example, flight attendants in Delta's Recurrent Training classes were told: "When you get mad at some guy for telling you that you owe him a smile, you're really mad only because you're focusing on yourself, on how *you* feel. Get your mind off yourself. Think about how the situation looks to *him*. Usually he doesn't mean a thing by it. And anyway that kind of behavior isn't going to change for a long, long time. So don't get mad at that." When a flight attendant feels angry at a passenger in this situation, what does her anger signal? According to the teacher in Recurrent Training, it indicates that she is *mis*locating herself in the world, that she is seeing the man who demands a smile in the wrong sort of way—that she is oversensitive, too touchy. It does not signal a perception about how emotional display maintains unequal power between women and men, and between employees and employers. It indicates something wrong with the worker, not something wrong with the assumptions of the customer or the company. In this way the company's purposes insinuate themselves into the way workers are asked to interpret their own feelings. It raises questions for

---

[d]   Stanislavski warned: "Always act in your own person, as an artist. You can never get away from yourself. The moment you lose yourself on the stage marks … the beginning of exaggerated false acting. For losing yourself in the part, you kill the person whom you portray, for you deprive 'him' of the real source of life for a part" (1965, p. 167).

them at every turn. "Is that how I should think about my anger? Is this how the company wants me to think about it?" Thus the worker may lose touch with her feelings, as in burnout, or she may have to struggle with the company interpretation of what they mean.

Coping with the costs of emotional labor calls for great inventiveness. Among themselves, flight attendants build up an alternative way of experiencing a smile or the word "girl"—a way that involves anger and joking and mutual support on the job. And in their private lives—driving back home on the freeway, talking quietly with a loved one, sorting it out in the occasional intimacy of a worker-to-worker talk—they separate the company's meaning of anger from their own meaning, the company rules of feeling from their own. They try to reclaim the managed heart. These struggles, like the costs that make them necessary, remain largely invisible because the kind of labor that gives rise to them—emotional labor—is seldom recognized by those who tell us what labor is.

On Broadway Avenue in San Francisco there was once an improvisational theater called The Committee. In one of its acts, a man comes to center stage yawning, arms casually outstretched as if ready to prepare himself for bed. He takes off his hat and lays it methodically on an imaginary bureau top. Then he takes off his hair, a wig apparently. He slowly pulls off his glasses and massages the bridge of his nose where his glasses had rubbed. Then he takes off his nose. Then his teeth. Finally he unhitches his smile and lies down to sleep, a man finally quite "himself."

This insinuation of the "false" into the "true," of the artificial into the natural, is a widespread trouble. One main cause of it, as it applies to feeling, is that people are made increasingly aware of incentives to *use* feeling. Those who perform emotional labor in the course of giving service are like those who perform physical labor in the course of making things: both are subject to the rules of mass production. But when the product—the thing to be engineered, mass- produced, and subjected to speed-up and slowdown—is a smile, a mood, a feeling, or a relationship, it comes to belong more to the organization and less to the self. And so in the country that most publicly celebrates the individual, more people privately wonder, without tracing the question to its deepest social root: What do I really feel?

Notes

Epigraph: This, in Marshall Berman's words, is what Rousseau concluded about the impersonality of personal relations in the eighteenth century (Berman 1970, p. 140).

1. As Berman goes on to note, Rousseau saw the modern man of Paris both as the victim of self-loss and as the more astute judge of just what modern life had made him lose. "Modern conditions created a moral imagination which could define inauthenticity as a problem," for "among so many prejudices and false ... passions, it is necessary to know how to analyze the human heart and to disentangle the true feelings of nature" (p. 158). *"La Nouvelle Heloise* had succeeded so splendidly in decadent Paris which it denounced but had been rejected so coldly in solid Switzerland whose virtues it celebrated" (p. 157). The injured attend more to the cure.

2. Geertz (1973) has noted that when believers came to uphold Islam *in order to* build nationalism, the traditional beliefs themselves changed meaning; when seen as means, they functioned less as ends. The same thing happens when feelings are made to serve external ends; and the more remote these ends, the more the managed heart becomes "not me" and "not mine"

3. Christina Maslach interviewed burnout victims, who told her such things as, "I don't care anymore. I don't have any feelings left. I've nothing left to give, I'm drained. I'm exhausted. I'm burned out." For further work on burnout, see Maslach (1978a, 1978b, 1978c, 1979).

4. Just when this rise in the value of authenticity occurred will surely maintain itself as a point of lively historical debate. For example, Berman (1970) contends that even in the late eighteenth century, Rousseau and his Parisian readers saw authenticity as a problem born of "modern life."

5. Trilling (1972), p. 9. Speaking of English literature before and after the sixteenth century, Trilling continues: "But if we ask whether young Werther is really as sincere as he intends to be, or which of two Dashwood sisters, Elinor or Marianne, is thought by Jane Austen to be the more truly sincere, we can confidently expect a serious response in the form of opinions on both sides of the question." Sincerity did not become a relevant virtue until insincerity or guile became a common temptation. The very term *sincerity changed* in meaning: "As used in the early sixteenth century in respect of persons, it is largely metaphorical—a man's life is sincere in the sense of being sound or pure, or whole; or consistent in its virtuousness. But it soon came to mean the absence of dissimulation or feigning or pretense" (p. 13).

6. The rising value placed on detaching feeling from semblance is strikingly illustrated in Trilling's discussion of Diderot's "The Nephew of Rameau." ("Nephew" was written some time between 1761 and 1774. It was translated by Goethe and touted by Hegel as a paradigm of the modern cultural and spiritual situation.) This is a dialogue between the philosopher, Diderot, who defends sincerity, and the nephew of Rameau, who celebrates liberation from sincerity. The nephew is a "presenter of self in everyday life," a true Goffman man in his capacity to act (though not in his ability to calculate personal advantage). He not only is but sees himself as an actor on the everyday social stage. Demonstrating his capacity to fool people in an exhibition for Diderot, the nephew is, in succession: "furious, mollified, lordly, sneering. First a damsel weeps and he reproduces her kittenish ways; next he is a priest, a king, a tyrant. Now he is a slave, he obeys, calms down, is heartbroken, complains, laughs, singing, shouting, waving about like a madman, being in himself dancer and ballerina, singer and prima donna, all of them together and the whole orchestra, the whole theater; then redividing himself into twenty separate roles, running, stopping, glowing at the eyes like one possessed, frothing at the mouth. He was a woman in a spasm of grief, a wretched man sunk in despair." Quoted in Trilling (1972), p. 45.

7. *Ibid.,* p. 9.

8. *Ibid.,* p. 16.

9. Trilling points out several meanings of the overly inclusive term *authenticity.* One is shamelessness, inauthenticity being the conduct of life in the fear of shame or guilt—emotions through which we honor propriety. In this sense "authentic heroes and heroines" put themselves beyond the proper limits, and the obligations they do accept have a certain fascinating weightlessness. Authenticity also refers to having an extreme degree of power over something, including oneself. What most interests and appalls Trilling is authenticity as a legitimized exit from one's moral community, and the use of the term as a glow word that lends moral credence to illusions of narcissistic grandeur and social detachment. R. D. Laing's invitation to go mad is Trilling's case in point: "Who that finds intelligible in the sentences which describe madness ... in terms of transcendence and charisma will fail to penetrate to the great refusal of human connection that they express, the appalling belief that human existence

is made authentic by the possession of a power, or the persuasion of its possession, which is not to be qualified or restricted by the coordinate existence of any fellow man" (ibid., p. 171).

The problem is that with this stroke of disapproval, Trilling dismisses the very question to which his whole analysis leads: *why has authenticity as a value supplanted sincerity*? This he never answers. Ironically, it is the sensibility and analysis of R. D. Laing, the very person who bids us all go mad, which, for reasons quite separate and detachable, help answer the question that Trilling himself poses. Authenticity can supplant sincerity because it is understood to refer to spontaneous, natural, artless feeling.

10. The very notion of *disguising* feeling in order to play a role implies, as Trilling puts it, that "somewhere under all the roles [that] have been played, [one] would like to murmur, 'Off, off you lendings!' and settle down with his own original actual self' (ibid., p. 10). This Trilling calls the immutable "English" self, a self about which one can fool the world, but not oneself. Trilling distinguishes between an English self and an American one. The English self is "private, solid, intractable" (p. 113). This is Trilling's fantasy of a self in an immobile society—a fantasy he locates for some reason in England. The American self he conceives as thinly composed and correspondingly more malleable.

11. For an excellent essay on this subject, see Turner (1976).

12. Peris etal. (1951), p. 297.

13. James and Jongeward (1971).

14. The ego detachment necessary to do emotion work is fostered by many modern therapies that aim, in part, to increase control over feelings. The individual is inducted into the belief that he or she *already has control over feeling*, a control that simply has to be brought to awareness. For example, Brown (1974) reports that in bioenergetic therapy, "The subject is told that various colored lights are actually operated by his own brain waves ... and that these are controlled by his own feelings and thoughts and moods. The subject is told that he himself can control the lights by the way he feels and thinks" (p. 50). Again, in transcendental meditation, the patient is told that by manipulating his inner thoughts or images, he can maintain "alpha wave activity" as he wishes. The individual is inducted into the belief that he *already has control* by being asked to distinguish between ego and id, framer and framed- upon, director and actor.

15. Winnicott (1965), p. 143. The early development of a false self is an asset for the actor. As Winnicott notes, "It can easily be seen that sometimes the False Self defense can form the basis for a kind of sublimating, as when a child grows up to be an actor" (p. 150).

16. Lasch (1978). We have an accumulation of literature now on the new "modern self' adapted to conditions of modern society: for example, Riesman (1953), Lasch (1978), Lifton (1970), Turner (1976), Zurcher (1972). These theorists suggest a general link between conditions of modern life (living in transient social worlds or being transient in stable ones, the decline of kinship ties, social mobility) and the development of a more outwardly attuned (Riesman), more protean (Lifton), more malleable self. In other words, their conclusion seems to be that conditions conspire to foster in us more false selves, which are more flexibly related to what we conceive as our illusive "true self."

In Other Words . . .

The title of the last reading in this unit, "The Search for Authenticity," might suggest that a "pure" self exists. Sociologically speaking, our *selves*, just as with every element of society, is constructed and ever changing. This is not to say that Hochschild's piece is off the mark. Indeed, she provides great insight into how we construct and use emotion, and how it often becomes co-opted by other groups and institutions in our society.

In this short segment, though, I'd like to focus on personal identity. Envision for a moment that you were born in Uganda, in 1984. Who would you be? What language would you speak, how would you support yourself (and a family, perhaps), and what would be your attitudes toward work, war, politics? What food would you eat, how would you travel, and how would you raise your children? How would you value (or not) and obtain (or not) an education? This short foray into fantasy quickly brings to surface assumptions about our self, our personality, our very existence, assumptions we seldom stop to consider.

George Herbert Mead, a distinguished forebear in sociology, gave us the classic work *Mind, Self and Society* (1934), asserting "the individual mind can exist only in relation to other minds with shared meanings" (Mead 1982, 5). Mead's work stands responsible, in large measure, for the symbolic interactionist perspective in which meaning emerges only in interaction and interpretation. Symbolic interactionism centers on five basic principles (Charon 2004): 1) human beings are social actors, created through interaction; 2) humans are thinking beings, always considering and conversing with ourselves and others; 3) humans do not experience environment directly, but define the situation they are in; 4) the cause of human action is the result of the current situation; and 5) human beings are not passive but actively construct their relation to the environment.

Mead (1934) begins his discussion with *Mind*. Mind develops as a building block, based on "communication by a conversation of gestures in a social process or context of experience" (p. 50); Mind exists outside the body, as a set of communication and symbols. *Self* develops through Mind and becomes a reference point for events, emotions, and sensations (p. 136). As a child grows, *significant others* (closely related) become defined and, eventually, a *generalized other* (wider, societal reference points) emerges as a social self. All of these human acts are socially mediated by *Society*, which organizes relations in which humans are able to take the perspective of others. *You*, whether in your current position or as a child in 1984 Uganda, do not preexist outside interactions with others.

With this brief consideration of *self*, the artificiality of race, class, gender, and other constructed differences becomes more apparent. Though we may be born with a certain DNA, the meaning of those characteristics emerges only through interaction with other humans. This happens over time and space, in different ways for distinct cultures. Unfortunately, irrational patterns emerge (such as racism and sexism), and these sociocultural traditions become entrenched in nonsensical ways that take on real and often tragic consequences.

The Big Idea

Racism, sexism, and other harmful "isms" are human constructions with real consequences. They are societal institutions that reach far beyond individual intent.

So What

It could be you; we are all involved in social construction. The good news: negative behavior and institutionalized harm can be deconstructed.

"This country isn't a melting pot. Think of this country as a stir fry. That's what this country should be. A place where people are appreciated for who they are."—Jane Elliott

Individual. Just Like Everybody Else.

Works Cited

Charon, J. M. (2004). *Symbolic interactionism: An introduction, an interpretation, an integration*. Boston, MA: Pearson.

Elliott, Jane. (2016). "Jane Elliott's Blue Eyes Brown Eyes Exercise." Retrieved October 4, 2016, from http://www.janeelliott.com

Mead, G. H. (1934). *Mind, Self and Society*. Chicago, IL: University of Chicago Press.

Mead, G. H. (1982). *The individual and the social self: Unpublished essays by G. H. Mead*. Edited by D. L. Miller. Chicago, IL: University of Chicago Press.

UNIT 6 READINGS

Culture and Power

Diversity and Work

The Personal and the Political

Unit 6: Everything's Political

Dr. Sue to You: Unlearning what we know

When we say "everything's political," we most often do not pause to consider what that really means. In this unit, I've compiled a number of readings highlighting issues that may initially seem unrelated—everything from the very abstract *cultural capital* concept of Bourdieu (the first reading in this unit), to the monetarily hard dollar, to personal body parts. What is the common denominator? Power. Not just overt power, which is typically issued with some force, resulting in A causing B to do something against its will, but much more complex dimensions of power. At the core of political power lies the "capacity of persons or collectivities 'to get things done' effectively, in particular when their goals are obstructed by some kind of human resistance or opposition" (Parsons 1963, 232).

For a much more nuanced consideration of three-dimensional power, I will introduce you to Lukes's (1974) three faces of power. The first "face" of power refers to the exertion of power just described—overt, decision-based, and behavioral. The second face of power is organizational and agenda-setting. Through institutional rules, behavior, and regulations, A succeeds in setting the agenda and putting up barriers detrimental to B's set of preferences. Much of this is assumed and carried out behind the scenes.

The third face of power is by far the most potent, covert, and dominating; it is ideological in nature, creating a hegemonic mind-set that controls actual perceptions and preferences of actors. As Lukes explains:

Is it not the supreme and most insidious use of power to prevent people, to whatever degree, from having grievances by shaping their perceptions, cognitions, and preferences in such a way that they accept their role in the existing order of things, either because they can see or imagine no alternative to it, or because they see it as natural and unchangeable or because they value it as divinely ordained and beneficial (Lukes 1974, 24).

We could illustrate Lukes's ideas with almost any public issue. To make the point clearer, let's take the current example of global warming. In the simplest of terms, a parent can control the use of energy in the household by curtailing use of long hot showers, turning the thermostat up, and eliminating the use of clothes dryers. That's the first face of power. The second face of power is much more complex, involving regulations such as fuel-efficient cars, emission standards, and car-pool lanes. But a domineering aspect of power comes with publicly expressed manifestations of ideas about global warming, expressed through media and other public coverage, which may take a positive form of informing the public about evidence and urgency of global climate change, or a negative form, declaring global warming a hoax or even a conspiracy, even though "scientific evidence for warming of the climate system is unequivocal" (NASA 2016).

These contradictions to scientific evidence often come through social media and other informal networks, or through officials or public figures who have some vested interest in weighting public opinion one way or another. This is the third face of power.

We could use the same logic to evaluate other controversial public issues such as abortion rights, gun safety, immigration, drug legalization, free trade, legalized prostitution, gay marriage, and national health care. Unit 6 affords a few examples of political power being attached to a diverse range of issues.

Works Cited

Lukes, S. (1974). *Power: A radical view*. Macmillan: London.

NASA.gov. (2016). "Climate change: How do we know?" Retrieved October 3, 2016, from http://climate.nasa.gov/evidence/

Parsons, T. (1963). "On the concept of political power." *Proceedings of the American Philosophical Society*, 107, 232–262.

Politics on Display

READING 1

THE SOCIOLOGY OF PIERRE BOURDIEU

BY DAVID SWARTZ

At the heart of Bourdieu's sociological inquiry is the question of why forms of social inequality persist without powerful resistance. The answer, Bourdieu argues, lies in how cultural resources, practices, and institutions function to maintain unequal social relations. The relationship of culture to power stands at the center of Bourdieu's intellectual project. Bourdieu's analysis of how culture obscures class power and provides the tools for social distinctions represents a key contribution to contemporary sociology of culture. Indeed, Bourdieu's reformulation of the problem of ideology and false consciousness stands as one of his central contributions to the study of class and power in modern societies.

The tremendous growth of education and cultural markets in the advanced societies has fostered the increased use of more subtle and elusive cultural mechanisms of domination than was the case during the period of nascent capitalism. In formulating his political economy of symbolic power, Bourdieu insightfully addresses this change in modes of domination. Bourdieu's work demonstrates that a general shift from physical coercion to softer forms of social control nonetheless fosters the reproduction and legitimation of inegalitarian social relations. His political economy of symbolic power is perhaps the most ambitious and consequential project for the study of the symbolic realm since that of Talcott Parsons (1951). Indeed, Bourdieu tries to do for the cultural realm what Marx attempted for the economic realm: to understand the fundamental structures and dynamics of power in cultural life. Key elements of his conceptual language, such as social and cultural reproduction, cultural capital, habitus, field, and symbolic violence have already become part of the working vocabulary of many social scientists.

Bourdieu's Sociology of Culture in Comparative Perspective

In many respects, Bourdieu's ambitious program spans the four principal traditions and their key theorists that Wuthnow et al. (1984) identify as decisively shaping contemporary approaches to the study of culture. Bourdieu draws upon phenomenology as does Peter Berger (1967; Berger and Luckmann 1966); cultural anthropology—particularly the Durkheimian influence—as does Mary Douglas (1966, 1970, 1982); French neostructuralism, as does Michel Foucault (1972, 1978a, 1980); and critical theory, as does Jürgen Habermas (1970, 1971, 1973). While it would be presumptuous to suggest that he provides a synthesis, the complexity and richness of his approach does incorporate key elements of each of these separate traditions. Like Foucault, Bourdieu searches for deep structures of cultural and social life that are linked to power. The dynamics of power intersect with all aspects of cultural life. Like Douglas, Bourdieu sees culture in terms of categories of social classification; cultural distinctions euphemize underlying social distinctions. Like Habermas, Bourdieu examines critically received cultural categories, and shares with Habermas a concern for the epistemological status of a science of culture. And like Berger, Bourdieu shows that macro structures are also objects of social construction by actors.

More generally, Bourdieu contributes to the current shift in orientation toward the study of culture at the institutional level (Wuthnow 1987). Though he rejects the bifurcation of human behavior into distinct realms—one subjective, having to do with thoughts, beliefs, and ideas, and the other objective, entailing concrete observable behaviors—his overall effort can be seen as part of a broader swing from subjective to more institutional approaches to the study of culture. He focuses on categories of classifications and practices rather than emphasizing rich description of behavior or empathic understanding of actor sentiments and intentions as does the phenomenological tradition. His institutional emphasis can be seen particularly in his concept of field which calls attention to the positions of actors, organizations, resources, and their struggle in the production, transmission, and consumption of culture.

Compared with other leading contemporary cultural theorists, Bourdieu alone manages to combine abstract theory reflecting his Continental philosophical heritage with empirical research and an explicit reflection upon method. He reaches out in both directions—toward the abstract and the concrete—in ways no other contemporary social scientist does. This is all the more remarkable in a sociologist at a time when the social sciences—sociology in particular—are becoming more and more fragmented and internally differentiated by competing specializations in method, theory, and substantive areas of inquiry (Swartz, 1988).

Bourdieu is a source of inspiration to those who labor in social sciences, for he demonstrates that doing social theory is not incompatible with carrying out empirical research. Immersion in data need not mean loss of theoretical grounding; on the contrary, it may solidify it. His ethnographic research on peasant households in colonial Algeria, which is reported in *Outline of a Theory of Practice* (1977c) and *The Logic of Practice* (1990b); his study of consumer and lifestyle patterns in contemporary France, which is present in *Distinction* (1984a); his study in *Les regies de Part* (1992) of French literature; and his research into the various mechanisms of inter- and intra- institutional stratification in French higher education, reported in *Reproduction* (Bourdieu and Passeron, 1977), *Homo Academicus* (1988b) and *La Noblesse d'Etat* (1989c)—to mention only some of the most comprehensive and notable bodies of work—are all empirical exercises in rigorous social theorizing. Each of these publications will undoubtedly serve as a benchmark for future work in its respective field.

Culture as Power

Of all his concepts, *cultural capital*, which calls attention to the power dimension of cultural resources in market societies, undoubtedly has thus far found the widest reception. This concept is a powerful one, and has stimulated considerable research in the sociology of education, culture, and stratification. By calling attention to the subtle and pervasive ways in which language, knowledge, and cultural style shape interactions, it improves our understanding of the processes through which social-background effects are translated into unequal school performance and subsequent career chances. In the sociology of education, the concept has fostered detailed examination of kinds of cultural resources children bring from families to classrooms that affect academic performance (DiMaggio 1982; Lareau 1989). In the sociology of the arts, the concept has also been employed usefully to show how cultural socialization in families and schools shapes attitudes and behavior toward the arts (DiMaggio 1977; DiMaggio and Useem 1978, 1982; Zolberg 1989).

The concept of cultural capital stands at the midpoint of two radically opposing intellectual traditions in Western thought. On the one hand, in identifying culture as a form of capital, Bourdieu breaks with the Marxist tradition by holding that culture is a power resource standing in its own right; it cannot be reduced to some superstructural derivative of underlying economic factors. On the other hand, Bourdieu also breaks with the humanist tradition that lauds the universal value of the classical canon; he argues that ideas and aesthetic values embody the practical interests of those who produce and appropriate them. Bourdieu thus bridges two radically different intellectual traditions by means of his theory of culture as a form of power.

Bourdieu makes a convincing case that the opposition between cultural capital and economic capital operates as a fundamental differentiating principle of power in modern societies. It distinguishes among elites who base their claim to power on cultural resources and those who rely more on economic resources. Particularly in *Distinction* do we see Bourdieu's effort to conceptualize and empirically display class and intraclass groups in terms of their respective configurations of different types of capital and their corresponding lifestyles as a bold and original approach to the study of stratification. Conceptualizing social classes in terms of their volume and composition of capital and social trajectory through fields gives a multidimensional and dynamic perspective on class hierarchies not captured in mainstream status-attainment research.

At a time when Marxism as a theory of advanced industrial societies appears less compelling, Bourdieu provides an attractive alternative, for he focuses attention on those knowledge and service occupations that are gaining in number and importance in late capitalism. But unlike postindustrial society theorists, such as Daniel Bell (1973, 1988), Bourdieu shows how these new cultural practices embody new forms of domination and social interests. Moreover, Bourdieu's theory and empirical research on the unequal distribution of cultural capital and its intergenerational transmission through schooling have produced an important insight into the internal differentiation of elites in modern societies: the primary beneficiaries of the expanded educational meritocracy are not members of the capitalist class but the children of professional families with cultural capital.

217

Bourdieu's meticulous efforts to demonstrate how cultural resources mediate class differences, particularly in the realm of tastes and lifestyles, stands in critical opposition to postmodern theories of consumer culture that posit a waning of class differences in consumer patterns in postindustrial societies (Baudrillard 1981). Despite growth in mass consumer markets, Bourdieu contends that cultural practices continue to be markers of underlying class distinctions in the case of France. His analysis invites comparisons with other national contexts, such as the United States, where differences in consumer choices may be perceived more as the result of differences in income than as disguised status distinctions of social honor, as Bourdieu claims. Moreover, the kind of class-culture distinctions Bourdieu stresses may be more characteristic of upper- and lower-class groups than of middle-class groups where consumer choices may be more directly influenced by mass-market product standardization.

Culture as a form of capital is a useful conceptualization for analyzing stratification processes in advanced societies, where market mechanisms penetrate virtually all realms of modern life. The concept seems less useful for societies where market mechanisms are less developed. Its currency appears less promising in societies with a less imposing high-culture tradition and with more cultural diversity than France. In addition, the concept suggests a view of agency that reduces actors to strategizing investors driven to maximize their investment opportunities regardless of where they are located in the stratification order. The culture-as-capital metaphor works best for certain professions in the media, the arts, and academe, where individuals seek to convert their valued cultural resources into economic rewards, and for those families who seek out valued types of education for their children. The concept is less useful for analyzing groups with few power resources.

Bourdieu is able to extend and reformulate with particular insight both Weber's idea of legitimation and the Marxian concept of ideology when he analyses how cultural practices assume symbolic value and obscure their role in justifying social inequality. However, Bourdieu's emphasis on the legitimating aspects of power, particularly their indirect and hidden effects, leave him with relatively little to say about the continued importance of sheer economic power or physical coercion in modern societies. The stress he places on misrecognition probably overstates the role that false consciousness has in maintaining groups in subordinate positions. Individuals and groups often see clearly the arbitrary character of power relations but lack the requisite resources to change them. And his insightful analyses of the important role that intellectuals play in providing cognitive classifications for ordering society probably overstates the importance of intellectuals to governing elites in some modern societies.

Social Change

Bourdieu was an early and key architect of the widely influential theory of social reproduction. His focus on the role of culture in social reproduction, however, leaves the important question of social change undeveloped. While Bourdieu is not rigidly deterministic, as some critics charge, his conceptual framework is clearly more attentive to patterns of continuity than to change. The concepts of habitus, cultural capital, and field stress the tendency to perpetuate structures inherited from the past. The propensity of habitus is clearly to address new situations in habituated ways, it takes capital to accumulate more capital, and field permits an impressive mapping of social positions and their continuity over time. His framework does not encourage researchers to seek out forms of change. Sources of change, as I point out in chapter 8, are suggested here and there in his work but never mobilized into a convincing demonstration of their dynamics. One conceptual possibility for resistance and change rests on the mismatch between the expectations of habitus and the opportunities offered by fields. Yet the conditions under which disappointed expectations might turn into effective motors of change remain to be specified.

Habitus

One of Bourdieu's main contributions is to propose a framework that addresses the agency/structure problem in contemporary social theory. He in fact was one of the first poststructuralist sociologists to bring actors back into structural models of stratification by showing that the idea that structures reproduce and function as constraints is not incompatible with the idea that actors create structures. Bourdieu's actors are strategists, though he does not think of strategy primarily as conscious choice but as a tacit calculation of interest and pursuit of distinction. His concept of habitus both offers a programmatic research agenda for addressing the agency/structure issue and points to an ideal-typical pattern of action. The research agenda derives from his theory that action is generated by the encounter between opportunities or constraints presented by situations and the durable dispositions that reflect the socialization of past experiences, traditions, and habits that individuals bring to situations. An adequate account of human behavior needs to combine the observed regularities of human behavior and the representations of individuals and groups. His programmatic agenda mounts a challenge to academic sociology by claiming that micro and macro, and objective and subjective levels of analysis are not to be separated by forms of theoretical or methodological specialization. He argues that theory and empirical research must proceed simultaneously on both levels rather than, as is the frequent practice today, confining attention to just one type of data or level of analysis.

Though difficult to specify empirically, habitus also points to an ideal-type of action that is habituated, practical, tacit, dispositional, and at the same time structured. Culture is conceptualized as practices following common master patterns that range over cognitive, corporeal, as well as attitudinal dimensions of action. Some of Bourdieu's most suggestive analyses point to such common dispositions, as in the case of the aristocratic asceticism among French university teachers who display cultivated restraint in sports, diet, entertainment, and bodily care. While I criticized Bourdieu in chapter 5 for being reluctant to specify conditions in which one dimension prevails over the other, I nonetheless believe that his understanding of individual action comes much closer to conceptualizing the complexity of human conduct than simplified rational-actor or structural models that attribute action to either calculated choice or to external constraints. Yet he also criticizes interpretative and phenomenological approaches for not situating action with respect to broader structural constraints. Bourdieu's idea that action is generated by the *interaction* of the opportunities and constraints of situations with actor dispositions—the repository of past experience, tradition, and habit—seems to constitute a considerable advance over these alternative views.

While habitus calls attention to the dynamics of self-selection in competitive social processes, the internalization of objective chances into expectations and the adaptation of aspirations to actual opportunities are often more complex and contradictory processes than the concept suggests. Moreover, both adaptation to external constraints and distinction from competing actors are two distinct types of agency juxtaposed in Bourdieu's concept without their exact relationship being clarified. Bourdieu calls upon one or the other dynamic depending on the issue he is addressing and without specifying the conditions in which one assumes the more prominent role.

Field

If habitus provides a valuable orientation for conceptualizing and researching relations between agency and structures, the concept of field is useful for studying the operation of culture at a more institutional level. His field-analytic framework contributes to our understanding of ways that culture mediates class relations at an institutional level. It offers a political economy of culture by identifying areas of production, transmission, and consumption of various forms of cultural capital. Of all his concepts, field is currently the least well understood and yet the most promising for future sociological work.

Bourdieu's concept of field draws on his insight that social units develop their identity in opposition to others and that an adequate grasp of their sociological character requires that they be situated within this broader arena of opposing forces. The concept points to arenas of conflict and struggle that develop with the emergence of particular kinds of valued resources, and shows how forms of social closure result from structures and processes that engage individuals and groups in competition for valued cultural resources as fields gain in autonomy. Bourdieu's field concept encourages the researcher to seek out sources of conflict in a given domain, relate that conflict to the broader arenas of class and power, and show what opposing parties actually share, but rarely acknowledge.

Bourdieu's effort to define some of the structural properties of fields gives this concept more analytical promise than the concept of markets for the analysis of culture. Fields indicate much more than the "invisible hand" of the market. They specify power relations and hierarchy. The ideas of structural polarities, hierarchial positions, competition for scarce resources, struggle between heterodoxy and orthodoxy, and a shared *doxa* among competitors indicate mechanisms of internal structuring that generate fields and contribute to their autonomy and functioning. They offer a much richer analysis of producer-consumer relations than does the image of a market.

The idea of the relative autonomy of cultural fields goes beyond both instrumentalist and structuralist views of how social classes, markets, and government shape cultural life, particularly education, in modern societies. By calling attention to the internal structuring mechanisms as groups of specialists develop, transmit, and control their own particular status culture, the idea of relative autonomy usefully stresses how particular organizational and professional interests can emerge and come into conflict with outside demands. Here Bourdieu's thinking intersects with issues raised in the debate over the relative autonomy of the state (see Block 1977; Skocpol 1979: 24–32). Bourdieu's contribution to the debate is to call attention to the cultural and professional as well as structural interests that give to central institutions, such as education or the state, some autonomy from capitalist class interests.

The idea of relative autonomy leads Bourdieu to give priority to the internal analysis of cultural fields. In so doing Bourdieu leaves undeveloped the important question of interfield contradictions as a possible source of crisis and change. To suggest that works of art or curriculum in schools reflect as much patterns of hierarchy and conflict among artists and educators as they do broader social, economic, or political interests is a useful rejection of class reductionism. Yet, by concentrating on the internal structuring mechanisms of fields, Bourdieu's concept gives short shrift to potential sources of conflict between cultural fields and their external demands.

Bourdieu's field analysis of intellectuals substantiates his framework by showing how intellectuals are situated in competitive arenas that have their own structures and dynamics that shape both their intellectual and political behavior. Field analysis is useful, for it suggests dimensions of influence on intellectual behavior that are not fully tapped by social-class background or position, *Zeitgeist*, or location in an organization. Rather, field analysis requires the researcher to move through all of these levels in search of the mechanisms of struggle for scarce resources and symbolic recognition that are important to the intellectual milieu. This important shift in focus for the study of intellectual and cultural life can be seen in Fritz Ringer's (1992) comparative analysis of German and French intellectual history.

The idea of cultural field sidesteps the old debate between idealism and materialism by offering a mediation concept that anchors intellectual life socially but avoids class reductionism. The contribution of field analysis of intellectuals suggests that New Class theories mistakenly try to assess the political significance of the highly educated largely in terms of their class position. Field analysis suggests that we can better understand the political behavior of intellectuals by situating them within their professional milieu. Yet the problem of reductionism does not go away, but reemerges in a kind of field reductionism as individual ideas and artistic styles reduce to their field positions. Indeed, there seems to be little chance for Bourdieu's cultural producers to transcend their field interests.

Field analysis provides an attractive structural mapping of arenas of struggle over different types of capital for power and privilege. It offers an insightful way of charting cultural as well as economic resources that can be mobilized in the politics of modern life. Bourdieu uses it to make many perceptive observations on political relations between culturally rich intellectuals and economically subordinate groups. He shows that both intellectuals and workers occupy subordinate positions relative to capitalists (though in different fields of struggle) and argues that this creates a basis for political alliance, albeit a precarious one. Yet, this powerful analytic technique leaves unexamined the social processes through which such an alliance might be formed. The difficulty is that many groups occupy homologous positions in their respective fields, but not all of them form alliances with one another. To conflate an observation of the homologous relations with an explanation of the formation of an alliance runs the risk of what I observed in chapter 6 as a form of "structuralist mystification." Bourdieu's field analysis needs a sociology of politics that would examine the actual processes of political action and mobilization.

Reflexivity, Science, and Politics

We have seen that Bourdieu rejects scientific positivism in favor of a thoroughly reflexive practice of sociology. For Bourdieu, the organization and analysis of empirical data, the use of both commonsense and scientific categories, professional interests, and the attitude of the social scientist toward the subject of inquiry all embody fundamental value orientations that prohibit a fully objective grasp of that world. Indeed, Bourdieu maintains that it is only by subjecting the full range of research procedures and professional interests to critical examination that the sociologist can gain a measure of freedom from their distorting influence.

Bourdieu believes that by doing a sociology of sociology he, as a researcher, can achieve a significant measure of freedom from the distorting effects of competition within the academic field rather than simply reproduce them. Nevertheless, a tension emerges between this vision for a reflexive practice of sociology and his analysis of possible sources of resistance to the cycle of reproduction. In Bourdieu's framework, the conceptual possibility for resistance and change rests on the mismatch between habitus and the opportunity structures of fields rather than on the power of reflexive thought. Yet Bourdieu articulates a vision of sociology as a source of human emancipation that seems to emphasize the power of theory as well as the structural underpinnings for resisting the status quo. If the source of change indeed derives from a structural dislocation between habitus and field, then what critical role can Bourdieu claim for the social sciences, or for himself? If, on the other hand, scientific reason, in spite of its interested quality, holds a measure of hope for gaining some greater control over the social forces that shape our behavior, then the view of culture as a form of capital seems too limiting. Bourdieu affirms both the power of reason and the necessary material conditions under which it finds expression as science. But these affirmations reside in uneasy tension and as of yet remain unreconciled in his work.

Bourdieu believes that the critical thrust of social science can help subordinate groups in their struggle against elites and he sees his sociology as a form of political intervention against all forms of domination. Yet he has very little to say on the central questions of when subordinate groups will have the inclination and capacity to act upon the critical findings of social science to actively resist domination. This suggests an idealized political role that Bourdieu envisages for the sociologist but one that remains to be grounded in a genuine political sociology.

If Bourdieu himself does not fully free himself from the competitive struggle for recognition in the scientific field, his efforts nonetheless give him an exceptional degree of critical distance from and insight into the French academic world. *Homo Academicus* identifies the institutional basis of the sharply critical posture of many contemporary French intellectual superstars, including Barthes, Derrida, Foucault, and Bourdieu himself; they are all marginalized from the center of organizational power within the French university system and teaching profession. Not since Gouldner's *The Coming Crisis in Western Sociology* appeared more than two decades ago have sociologists been so challenged to submit their own practices to the same critical examination they apply to others. While certainly not free of either analytical or moral dilemmas, Bourdieu's call for reflexivity speaks to one of the most pressing tasks for social scientists today: the need to gain a more objective, albeit not objectivist, grasp on the social world—including our own.

DIVERSITY AND WORK

DIVERSITY = DOLLARS

BY CEDRIC HERRING

Companies That Recruit, Retain and Reward a More Diverse Workforce are More Profitable. Now It's Time for Latin American Corporations to Catch Up.

For many people, gender diversity is important because it removes barriers that have historically prevented women from taking their rightful places in the corridors of power. But there's also a specific business case to be made: including more women in the corporate setting will help meet customers' needs, enrich understanding of the pulse of the marketplace and improve the quality of products and services.

The business case rests on what should be an obvious point: companies cannot effectively sell to women if they do not understand and value women, whether as customers or as employees. Therefore, increasing gender diversity in Latin American companies, especially in mass consumer-oriented sectors where women form large portions of the actual or potential customer base, will help boost their bottom line.

In the United States, proponents of diversity commonly make the claim that diversity pays. The greater the diversity among employees, the broader their perspectives, resulting in an ability to marshal a wider array of intellectual and cultural resources to solve problems. Diversity also is a source of creative conflict that can lead to a re-examination of assumptions that would otherwise be dominated by male points of view. The putative competitive advantages—fresh ideas, positive outreach and communication with customers, more qualified workers—have persuaded many companies that diversity can produce greater profits.

How It Works

These claims about gender diversity and business outcomes are well-supported in the United States. For example, using a random sample of business organizations, a 2009 study showed that higher average sales revenues are associated with higher levels of gender diversity.[1] The study revealed that the average revenues of businesses with low levels of gender diversity were roughly $45.2 million, compared with $299.4 million for those with medium levels of gender diversity, and $644.3 million for businesses with high levels of gender diversity. [**see figure below**]

Higher levels of gender diversity were also associated with greater numbers of customers.

The average number of customers for businesses with low levels of gender diversity was 20,500, compared to 27,100 for those with medium levels, and 36,100 for businesses with high levels. The analysis also showed that 62 percent of businesses with high levels of gender diversity reported higher than average market share, compared with 45 percent of those with low levels of gender diversity and 58 percent of businesses with medium levels of gender diversity.

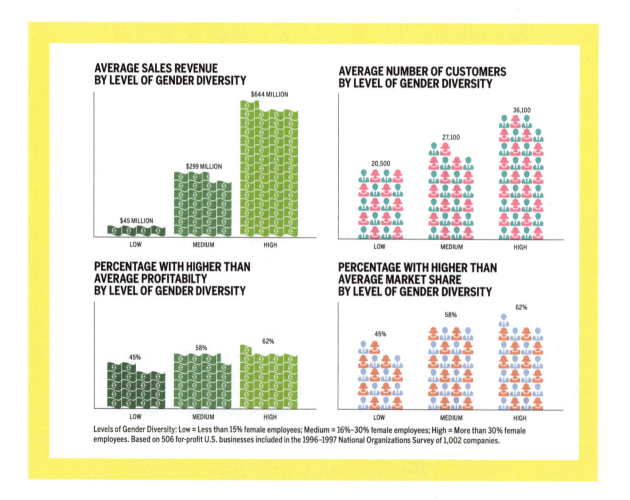

Levels of Gender Diversity: Low = Less than 15% female employees; Medium = 16%–30% female employees; High = More than 30% female employees. Based on 506 for-profit U.S. businesses included in the 1996–1997 National Organizations Survey of 1,002 companies.

The same was true in terms of reporting higher than average profitability. Fewer than half—45 percent—of businesses with low levels of gender diversity reported higher than average profitability. This compares with 62 percent of establishments with high levels of gender diversity and 58 percent of those with medium levels of gender diversity. While studies documenting the link between gender diversity and business outcomes in Latin America are not as prevalent, there is little reason to believe that these patterns differ from the United States.

How the Latin American Private Sector is Behind and What Can Be Done About It

Latin American companies lag behind North American and European companies in the area of gender diversity. Although increasing numbers of women in Latin America work in management jobs, they continue to confront glass ceilings. Latin American women constitute 10 percent of corporate presidents or vice presidents.[2] Women hold less than 7 percent of companies' board seats in Mexico, 5 percent in Brazil, 7 percent in Argentina, 7 percent in Venezuela, and less than 2 percent in Chile.[3] In contrast, women hold more than 16 percent of the corporate board positions in the U.S, and 73 percent of Fortune 500 companies in the U.S. have at least one female executive officer.[4]

By increasing their focus on gender diversity, and by implementing the kinds of pro-women policies and programs that are becoming commonplace in other parts of the world, Latin American companies could reap great benefits. But a number of steps must be taken, by governments as well as companies.

First, while there have been steady improvements in the quantity of education—such as expanded enrollment and more years of schooling—there are gaps in the type of education available for women. Latin American governments can join in public-private partnerships to train women so their skills better match the needs of the market.

A good example is WE Americas (Women's Entrepreneurship in the Americas)—a recently launched public-private partnership to increase women's economic participation and to remove barriers women face when starting and growing businesses. The goal is to provide support to women entrepreneurs throughout Latin America and the Caribbean, expand women-led initiatives, and improve women's access to credit and other financial services."[5] Such an initiative can help give companies a competitive advantage in the global market as well.

A second goal should be to promote gender equality in political participation. This can be accomplished by undertaking electoral reforms and making political parties more inclusive. For example, by encouraging parties to include an equitable number of female candidates in their slates, governments can also allocate resources and information to facilitate greater participation by women in the political process—and, in turn, greater attention to gender equality in public policies.

A third strategy for catalyzing the effects of gender diversity is to enact gender equity policies for the workplace, including for recruitment and retention. Offering job training opportunities for women and encouraging them to keep their skills current so that they can advance appears to pay dividends. Companies that offer formal job training are more diverse than those that do not; those that proactively select women for job training rather than let employees self-select are also more diverse. And those that offer family-friendly policies have the opportunity to do even better.

Also, employers can take advantage of transparency. Those that do things as simple as posting information about job vacancies and making use of internal hiring strategies (and presumably promote women from within) are more gender diverse. These strategies are consistent with the idea that organizations that foster woman-friendly climates have more success in retaining them. Many of these recruitment and retention efforts go hand in hand with signaling the importance of fairness in employment practices and providing job benefits that make it easier for companies to be inclusive.

Caterpillar, the U.S.-based maker of agricultural machinery, illustrates the point. Historically, Caterpillar was a laggard in terms of gender diversity. But after the 1980s, when it came close to bankruptcy, it stepped up its recruitment of women. By 2004, the company reported record-breaking profits and sales.

However, the company's diversity policies were not universally welcomed by its own employees. Male workers complained that women were getting promoted above men into management. In response, an internal educational program was established to promote greater understanding of company goals and practices. In 2006, Caterpillar also created the Women's Initiatives Network (WIN) to promote cultural awareness, mentoring, employee recruitment and retention, career development and community outreach—which increased support for its diversity programs.

By 2009, Caterpillar was ranked number 44 in the Fortune 500, and since 2010 the company has consistently been named one of the "Top 50 Employers" by *Woman Engineer* magazine. It has worked in Latin America as well. In 2011, Caterpillar-Brazil was recognized by *HSM* magazine as one of the "Top 50 Best Places to Work For" in Latin America.

Caterpillar also illustrates the fourth and final point. Companies must develop strategies to overcome the often stiff internal resistance to broadening diversity practices. Effective management of such disputes is important if companies want to reap the full benefits of bringing more women into their workplaces.

Governments in Latin America can respond to low levels of gender diversity by encouraging more of it, discouraging it, or ignoring it. Those working through such processes must be willing to confront the hard issues, and will need to recognize the distinct historical and cultural experiences that have set different paths for men and women in different countries. Today, reaping higher profits and competing with the rest of the world means that companies, and the countries in which they are based, must abandon policies that have stunted their growth and potential.

Cedric Herring *is professor of sociology and public policy at the University of Illinois at Chicago. His forthcoming book is* Critical Diversity: The New Case for Inclusion and Equal Opportunity.

FOR SOURCE CITATIONS SEE:
WWW.AMERICASQUARTERLY.ORG/HERRING

Notes

1. Herring, Cedric, "Does Diversity Pay? Race, Gender, and the Business Case for Diversity," American Sociological Review 74 (2009): 208-224.

2. Maxfield, Sylvia, "Ligar las prácticas de género y diversidad en los negocios con la ciudadanía corporativa: las implicaciones para Latinoamérica," Academia, Revista Latinoamericana de Administración 38 (2007): 65-80.

3. Quick Takes: Women on Boards (New York: Catalyst, 2012).

4. Soares, Rachel, et al, 2010 Catalyst Census: Fortune 500 Women Executive Officers and Top Earners (New York: Catalyst, 2010).

5. U.S. Department of State. 2012. Diplomacy in Action located at www.state.gov/r/pa/prs/ps/2012/04/187904. htm. Last accessed June 1, 2012.

READING 3

TRANS-CORPORATION
A Benefit Analysis of a Transgender Man in a Corporate Setting

BY CT WHITLEY

I'm hunkering down. My bunker is a tan particleboard desk enclosed by five-foot grey fabric partitions. I've become a corporate cadaver, entombed in my three-walled office illuminated in a fluorescent hue. A harsh voice bellows from the conference room. "You motherfuckers! You need to pull your heads out of your asses!" I take a deep breath. I've had my first lesson in high profile corporate interactions: learn to communicate so it isn't your ass getting chewed on the other side of that door.

This is not the touchy-feely environment I'd grown accustomed to during my liberal arts education in Sociology and Ethnic Studies. It's not an environment where I can capitalize on my queer theory and gender research by challenging the perception of gender norms in the work place. It's not a non-profit that holds diversity trainings or recognizes and values an array of differences. This is a company that records racial categories only to boost its EEO chart ratings, reducing the names on the chart to square boxes of Black, White, Asian, and Hispanic. Privilege is the sweat from management's pores, bonuses are the incentive, performance is everything, and cash reigns king.

During my two-year tenure as a financial officer in New York City, I grew increasingly aware of the gendered nuances of professional interactions in corporate culture, which reinforce binary systems, hamper communication between men and women, and frequently limit women's advancement. With this awareness, I moved at the periphery of categorized gender, shifting and shuffling through the expected communication patterns of my past and present genders. As a gender outlaw long accustomed to carving my own path, I learned to communicate in ways that were unavailable and unidentifiable to my non-transgender male and female coworkers, catapulting my own transgender status from corporate cost to corporate benefit. My female past and male present provided valuable reference points for negotiating interactions with both men and women. These days I rarely notice when I switch communication styles, sometimes even among different participants within a single conversation.

Just a few nights ago my partner asked, laughing, "You were talking to a man on the phone, weren't you?" I nodded, puzzled.

"How did you know?"

"When you talk to women, your voice is higher, you use more intonation, and you're more emotive," she said, "It's not that you become a woman, but you take on the communication style of one." She's right. In my journey, I have learned to call up elements of my past female life into my current male one when that style will strengthen my position. My masculine and feminine vocabularies meld to create negotiation platforms where I can understand and be understood without gendered limitations, expressing myself freely and clearly across sexes and genders.

While I understand sex and gender as socially constructed labels, I also understand that those labels are made real by their enforcement in dominant culture. Gendered behavior patterns were the key to at least half of miscommunication in my office. Therefore, this is not a deconstructive analysis, but rather a discussion of the realities of the gendered professional world. That world is built on the dominant culture's definitions of male, female, masculinity, femininity, and gay and straight, complete with the misogynist assumptions and biases the dominant culture bequeaths. While I neither believe in nor fit into these binary identity platforms, they nonetheless frame the corporate world. As a transgender man who has used my female past and male present to navigate an unknown world, I used my multi-gendered experience to challenge and manipulate the paradigm rather than to reinforce it; I was able to improve my office environment as well as to propel my career.

Thanks to my time in the queer spaces and liberal enclaves I've been a part of, I was able to view with fresh eyes the heteronormative world I worked in and its heavily gendered corporate interactions. In a corporate world where the infinite possibilities of sex, gender and sexuality went unnamed and unnoticed, gendered stereotypes about communication quickly proved useful. To be heard by men, brevity was key and intonation was a frivolous indulgence I could not afford, but cultivating the all-important air of dominance was well worth my while.

Part of my job was contract management; I would call directors and inform them of their ending contracts. When calling a man, I would say a quick hello and get to the point. "We have twenty-seven clients who need new contracts. I will bump up the value of the contracts, assuming you are okay with that?" They would answer a quick yes or no and I would return the phone to the receiver. By contrast, my female coworker would start with a friendly greeting, then scold him for not answering her emails or calling her back more quickly. After eight or nine minutes she would hang up the phone, excitedly reporting, "They said yes, yes, yes to everything I asked!" only to be livid later when nothing actually materialized. Her conversation partner had stopped listening after the first "so how are the kids?" and hadn't heard any part of her real request. Lost in the material element of the call, the male colleague had missed the human element in the conversation, the point of real connection where community is developed. In this instance and others, my understanding of female and male communication styles allowed me to avoid the pitfalls of my more seasoned coworker, and my conscious study, awareness, and embodiment of male interactions facilitated my success with upper management.

In another instance, my department was tasked with a project that would have made Einstein sweat. In response to the stress, the non-transgender men hunkered down, stopped returning phone calls and focused solely on the task at hand, as though they were each an army of one. The women searched for reassurance from others, found community with other women by discussing their frustrations, made plans to go out at the end of the week, and leaned on social networks. These disparate responses, while effective for the individuals, created huge problems for the whole as neither side understood the other's stress-management techniques. I found that I could play the middleman, deftly switching roles so that in the presence of men I was isolated and hardworking and in the presence of women I was cooperative and sympathetic. The men stormed into my office grumbling, "She can't get anything done because she has to take time to talk to everyone. We have deadlines, can't she see that?"

Similarly, the women rushed in complaining, "He's so irritating, I try to talk to him to take the edge off and he shuts me down. He's so uncooperative!"

I listened sympathetically to each side's complaints, and then I worked my communication magic. With each side seeing me as an insider, I could venture a guess about what was going on across the gender divide, smoothing the tumultuous, gendered waters that threatened to flood the office with rage and dysfunction.

Interestingly, I was the first person in my position to receive high marks from both male and female coworkers. When I talked to male supervisors about past female employees in my position, they would say things like, "The men didn't find her to be effective. She made too many phone calls bothering directors about little stuff. The women liked her style, but I guess it's just because women tend to get along." When I asked about past male employees in my position, the same dynamic presented itself. Men found the male employee to be "more effective," but women found him to be "less connected." Both communication styles had something important to offer. Most importantly, because of the heteronormative patriarchy reinforced in those office spaces, it was often the communication styles of my female colleagues that were deemed frivolous, when in fact, their sense of community and collaboration reinforced cohesion, a sense of belonging, and unity among staff. Ironically, despite my openness about my transgender status, management didn't notice the bridge I was building over the gender divide. Nonetheless, I was getting promoted, even if my boss couldn't see that my success had one foot carefully balanced in the male world and the other in the female realm.

Despite the professional advancements women have made and continue to make since the 1960s, I think it is safe to say that many still hit a glass ceiling. My office was no exception. It is widely understood that "male" and "female" are constructed well before birth, which means that by the time a person enters the workforce he or she has had twenty to thirty years of standard gender construction and reinforcement woven into every fiber of the individual's life. This becomes a huge disadvantage for women. Women who are strong, determined, and free-willed are labeled 'lesbians' or 'bitches,' rejected for promotion because their deviation from socially accepted gender norms makes others uncomfortable. Women who present as feminine and communicate in a typically feminine manner see no upward mobility, regardless of their inputs into projects and discussions. Of course, outliers exist: women who can alter their performance of masculinity and femininity to interact with key people so that their outward performance is feminine, but their communication employs carefully selected "masculine" traits, like brevity and curtness. In my male-managed company, these women excelled.

Understanding socialized gender differences in communication is not merely about men expecting women to interact on their terms. It requires an ongoing discussion and assessment of office culture, politics, and engagement. It's not a one-day training on diversity, but a continual process of resocializing the self to use and understand various communication styles within and outside of a gendered context. Through this experience, I learned to value my journey as a transgender man by strategically utilizing my past and present to affect change and promote personal gain.

Over the past two years, I have challenged myself to articulate the communication differences in my office. I have experimented with changing my posture, tone, and style to address the men in management. I notice that in meetings where I was once invisible I am now addressed by management over my supervisor, a woman who has held her position for twenty-five years. It's a bittersweet moment, one where I realize I have mastered a new language. I am a bi-gender communicator. This is a point of joy in my life as a transgender male. I have crossed over to be heard as male by other men. However, power has infused me with a sense of responsibility as I have not always been in this position and can easily recognize the shift in power. In this recognition it is my responsibility to speak up when others are being silenced, to challenge the corporate communication style nested in a masculine paradigm. Knowing how to utilize and maximize communication styles between men and women helps me to be a better advocate, to assert my voice when others are being silenced.

In my years of transitioning, I often underestimated the complexity of my journey. I never imagined that I would be uniquely positioned to rise up the corporate ladder through my manipulation of gender. For those of us who have second-guessed ourselves, questioned our value, or been confronted with harassment and violence, I offer up this unlikely refuge: we can learn powerful life skills from our negotiation of gender divisions. Our differences are a powerful resource to reshape the social systems we are forced to engage in, even if we remain undercover.

Unfortunately, my corporate management not only perpetuated serious gender issues, but also fell victim to a severe lack of self-reflection, ultimately missing the invaluable perspectives of its employees. If they had recognized the bridge I represented between gendered communication styles, asked for advice, or simply acknowledged that my gender differences created a unique opportunity for them to learn, I could have been not just a behind-the-scenes asset, not just a self-promoter, but a visible, tangible proponent of the company's growth. My life's calling has since led me out of the corporate environment and into academia, but it is my hope that other gender outlaws working in corporations throughout the country will rise up out of their dimly lit cubicles to hold strategic conversations that directly challenge the cultural and political structures of their workplaces. Our voices, speaking from our breadth of experience, can transform dysfunctional companies into pinnacles of gendered bliss. Recognizing the heteronormative communication systems in the corporate world, we can challenge these dynamics from the inside. Becoming the medium of translation between the dual gendered system, we can begin to create spaces where those who have become silenced can speak.

READING 4

THE GIRAFFE AND THE ELEPHANT—A MODERN FABLE

BY R. ROOSEVELT THOMAS, JR., 1999

In a small suburban community just outside the city of Artiodact, a giraffe had a new home built to his family's specifications. It was a wonderful house for giraffes, with soaring ceilings and tall doorways. High windows ensured maximum light and good views while protecting the family's privacy. Narrow hallways saved valuable space without compromising convenience. So well done was the house that it won the National Giraffe Home of the Year Award. The home's owners were understandably proud.

One day the giraffe, working in his state-of-the-art wood shop in the basement, happened to look out the window. Coming down the street was an elephant. "I know him", he thought. "We worked together at PTA committee. He's an excellent woodworker, too. I think I'll ask him in to see my new shop. Maybe we can even work together on some projects." So the giraffe reached his head out the window and invited the elephant in.

The elephant was delighted; he had liked working with the giraffe and looked forward to knowing him better. Besides, he knew about the wood shop and wanted to see it. So he walked up to the basement door and waited for it to open.

"Come in, come in", the giraffe said. But immediately they encountered a problem. While the elephant could get his head in the door, he could go no farther.

"It's a good thing we made this door expandable to accommodate my wood shop equipment", the giraffe said. "Give me a minute while I take care of our problem." He removed some bolts and panels to allow the elephant in. The two acquaintances were happily exchanging woodworking stories when the giraffe's wife leaned her head down the basement stairs and called to her husband: "Telephone, dear; it's your boss."

"I'd better take that upstairs in the den", the giraffe told the elephant. "Please make yourself at home; this may take a while."

The elephant looked around, saw a half-finished project on the lathe table in the far corner, and decided to explore it further. As he moved through the doorway that led to that area of the shop, however, he heard an ominous scrunch. He backed out, scratching his head. "Maybe I'll join the giraffe upstairs", he thought. But as he started up the stairs, he heard them begin to crack. He jumped off and fell back against the wall. It too began to crumble. As he sat there disheveled and dismayed, the giraffe came down the stairs.

"What on earth is happening here?" the giraffe asked in amazement.

"I was trying to make myself at home", the elephant said.

The giraffe looked around. "Okay, I see the problem. The doorway is too narrow. If you'd take some classes there, we could get you down to size".

"Maybe", the elephant said, looking unconvinced.

"And the stairs are too weak to carry your weight", the giraffe continued. "If you'd to go to ballet class at night, I'm sure we could get you light on your feet. I really hope you'll do it. I like having you here".

"Perhaps", the elephant said. "But to tell you the truth, I'm not sure that a house designed for a giraffe will ever really work for an elephant, not unless there are some major changes."

READING 5

THE BUTT
Its Politics, its Profanity, its Power

BY ERIN J. AUBRY

Unlike the face with its mixture of trickery and pretense, the behind has a genuine sincerity that comes quite simply from the fact that we cannot control it.

—*Jean-Luc Herring*, Rear View:
A Brief But Elegant History of the Bottom

I have a big butt. Not wide hips, not a preening, weightlifting-enhanced butt thrust up like a chin, not an occasionally saucy rear that throws coquettish glances at strangers when it's in a good mood and withdraws like a turtle when it's not. Every day, my butt wears *me*—tolerably well, I'd like to think—and has ever since I came full up on puberty about twenty years ago and had to wrestle it back into the Levi's 501s it had barely put up with anyway. My butt hollered, *I'm mad!* at that point and hasn't calmed down since.

But my butt is quite my advocate: introducing me at parties, granting me space among strangers when I am too timorous to ask for it. It retreats with me only when I am at my gloomiest, when it has no choice, and even then it does so reluctantly, a little sullenly, crying out from beneath the most voluminous pants I own: *When can we go back?* It has been my greatest trial and the core of my latest, greatest epiphany of self-acceptance, which came only after a day of clothes shopping that yielded the Big Three—pants, skirt, another pair of pants. (Floating out the mall doors with bags in hand, I thought, *Veni, vidi, vici!*) I think of my butt as a secret weapon that can be activated without anyone knowing: In the middle of an earnest conversation with a just-met man, I shift in my seat or, if I am standing, lean on one hip, as though to momentarily rest the other side. *Voilà!* My points are suddenly more salient, my words more muscled, and the guy never knew what hit him.

I have come to realize that my butt makes much more than a declaration at parties and small gatherings. Its sheer size makes it politically incorrect in an age in which everything is shrinking—government, computers, distances between people. In a new small-world order, it is hopelessly passé. Of course, not fitting—literally and otherwise—has always been a fact of life for Black women, who unfairly or not are regarded as archetypes of the protuberant butt, or at least the spiritual heirs to its African origins.

Now, many people will immediately cry that Black women have been stereotyped this way, and they'd be right—but I'd add that the stereotype is less concerned with body shape than with the sum total of Black female sexuality (read: potency), which, while not nearly as problematic as its male counterpart, still makes a whole lot of America uneasy. Thus, an undisguised butt is a reminder of that fact, and I have spent an inordinate number of mornings buried in my closet trying to decide whether I should remind other people, and myself, of yet another American irresolution about Black folks.

Women tend to talk freely about butt woes—it is simply another point along the whole food-exercise-diet continuum that dominates so many of our conversations, especially in my hometown of Los Angeles. But Black women do not so readily consign their butts to this sort of pathology, because that is like condemning an integral part of ourselves; even *talking* disparagingly about butts, as if they existed separately from the rest of the body, is pointless and mildly amusing to many of us.

Sounds like this would be the healthiest attitude of all—but it's not the end of the story, says Gail Elizabeth Wyatt, an African-American psychologist at the University of California at Los Angeles who recently published a book about Black female sexuality, *Stolen Women: Reclaiming Our Sexuality, Taking Back Our Lives.* As you might guess from the title, her book—the first comprehensive study of its kind—is an all-out assault on a host of misperceptions and stereotypes about Black women, many of which Wyatt believes are rooted in slavery and notions of sexual servitude. Not to my surprise, one survey she cites found that the Black woman/big butt association is among the most enduring of female physical stereotypes; it was the only thing the majority of the women polled—Black, white and other—agreed upon as being characteristic of Black women.

All right, I ask, but don't most Black women *have* good-sized butts? Is that, in and of itself, a bad thing? Wyatt says no, explaining that what she objects to is not the butt per se, but how it is negatively perceived by the mainstream and by ourselves. We have all, she says, effectively reduced the Black woman to either the "she devil," a purely sexual object, butt prominently in place, or the long-suffering "workhorse" and caretaking "mammy" types, who have no real sexual presence to speak of. To complicate things further, Wyatt says that American culture is increasingly sexualizing its young. "Unfortunately, the very sexual image has moved from magazine pages to school campuses," she says. "But when, say, Madonna puts on that image, it's understood that it's an image. She can move between being a ho' and being a film genius. We don't move that easily." In other words, Black women have little or no context to work with.

I recognize the truth of Black women's unfortunate history, but I am nonetheless dispirited. If in fact we spend so much time battling myths other people created, if we are always put on the butt defensive, as it were, we'll never have the psychic space to assess how we *really* feel about wearing Lycra—and a woman with a sizable butt *must* have an opinion about it. Another one of Wyatt's findings was that Black women, when it comes to the body parts they like most, tend to focus on hair, nails and feet; everything in between is virtually ignored. "We're not dealing with our bodies at all," Wyatt says, by way of interpretation. "We're very conscious of the fact that our image is so bad. We're not dealing with ourselves individually."

The moment of butt reckoning always comes with a mirror—if it's a three-way mirror, you're pretty much standing at the gates of hell. It is a bad day. I freeze my eyes on a spot in the middle mirror that's well above my waist, with no more gut left to suck in or butt left to pull under. I'm trapped with my own excess, which commands my attention though I will myself not to look. The butt swallows my peripheral vision and sops up reserve confidence like it's gravy; it doesn't merely reject my hopes for a size six, it explodes them with a nearly audible laugh that forces the ill-fated jeans back into an ignominious heap around my ankles. My butt looms triumphant, like Ali dancing over Liston: *Don't you know who I am?*

My butt refuses to follow the current trend of Black marginalization, nor does it care that we are heading into the millennium with the most collective uncertainty as a people since we first stumbled up out of the dark holds of the slave ships and onto American soil. It proclaims from the miserable depths of the sofa where I lie prone, in a stirring Maya Angelou rumble: *I rise! I rise! Still I rise!* My butt has a reserve of esteem and then some; like the brain, it may even have profound, uncharted capacities to heal.

It also has a social conscience. When I pass a similarly endowed woman in public I relax into a feeling of extended family; I know we are flesh and blood, not Frank Frazetta cartoons.

Recently I got a very gratifying bit of news from an African friend who called to say she had spotted supermodel Tyra Banks in the Century City Bloomingdale's. I was mildly curious: What was Tyra like? There was a significant pause. "Erin," my friend said solemnly, "she has a *big butt.*"

"Oh," I said. "You mean, big by model standards."

"No, no. I mean she has a *big* butt."

"What?"

"Yes. Let me tell you." The finality in her voice had a residue of awe. "A Big Butt."

It took a few moments for it to sink in: She was one of us. She was a famous model. *And* she was rumored to be dating Tiger Woods. I could have wept.

As has happened in many other instances, Black people have taken a white-created pejorative of a Black image—a purely external definition of themselves—and made it worse. Big butts thus offend a lot of Black people as being not just improper, but low-class and ghettoish, the result of consuming too much fried chicken and fatback. "Look at that!" one Black woman will hiss in the direction of another shuffling past, wearing bike shorts with abandon. *"Mmm-mmm-mmmh.* Criminal. Now you know she needs to do something about that." In the mind of the Black upwardly mobile, the butt may connote a dangerous lack of self-analysis, a loose, unrestricted appetite for food, sex, dances like the Atomic Dog. It's like having a big mouth or no table manners.

Now, we will accept, even expect, generous butts in a select group of Black people—blues and gospel singers, for example, whose emotional excess can and should be physically manifest—but for most of us who are trying to Make It, butts are the first to hit a glass ceiling.

I have a friend who's been trying to elevate the butt's social status by publishing a classy pinup calendar called "The Darker Image." It's the Black answer to the *Sports Illustrated* version—airbrushed skies, tropical settings—but its models are notably endowed with butts that Kathy Ireland could only dream of, butts that sit up higher than the surf rolling over them and render a thong bikini ridiculously beside the point. My friend said it was hell to get distribution from mainstream bookstores—Black, by definition, is a specialty market, Black beauty off the retail radar completely—but he finally got it with Waldenbooks and Barnes & Noble. It's a small but potentially significant victory for the butt, a public admission of its beauty and influence that hasn't been seen since the days of the "Hottentot Venus." I want to give America the big payback: posing next year as Miss January.

Let's face it: Sexual sophistication is one of those Black stereotypes, like dancing prowess, that is not entirely bad. It implies a healthy attunement to life, a knowingness. At the age of thirteen or so, though becoming acutely butt-conscious, I also became aware of the implicit power in a figure, how it shaped an attitude and informed a simple walk around the block. In sloping my back and elongating my stride, my butt was literally thrusting me into the world, and I sensed that I had better live up to the costume or it would eventually wear me to death. For me this didn't mean promiscuity at all, but a full-blown statement of the fact that I *stood out,* that I made a statement that might begin with my body, but that also included budding literary proclivities, powers of observation, silent crushes on boys sitting two rows over. Which is not to say—which is never to say—that my shifting center of gravity wasn't cause for alarm. I started a lifelong pattern of vacillating between repulsion and satisfaction: My butt branded me, but it also made me more womanly, not to mention more identifiably Black. I may have been a shade too light for comfort, but my butt confirmed my true ethnic identity.

As one of those physical characteristics of Black people that tend to differ significantly from whites', like hair texture and skin color, the butt demarcates, but also, in the context of the history of racial oppression, stands as an object of ridicule. Yet unlike hair and skin, the butt is stubborn, immutable—it can't be hot-combed or straightened or bleached into submission. It does not assimilate; it never took a slave name. Accentuating a butt is thumbing a nose at the establishment, like subverting a pinstriped suit with waist-length dreadlocks. And the butt's blatantly sexual nature makes it seem that much more belligerent in its refusal to go away, to lie down and play dead. About the only thing we can do is cover it up, but even those attempts can inadvertently showcase the butt by imparting a certain intrigue. (Hmmm, what is that thing sticking out of the back of her jacket?)

It was tricky, but I absorbed the better aspects of the butt stereotypes, especially the Tootsie-Roll walk—the wave, the undulation in spite of itself, the leisurely antithesis of the spring in the step. I liked the walk and how it defied that silly runway gait, with the hips thrust too far forward and the arms dangling back in empty air. That is a pure apology for butts, a literal bending over backward to admonish the body for any bit of unruliness. Having a butt is more than unruly, it's immoral—the modern-day equivalent of a woman eating a Ding Dong in public.

But there are those cases where a healthy butt is an essential endowment. Take Selena, the *tejana* superstar: Would she have been as big a phenom if not for her prodigious, cocktail-table behind, the whispers of possible African origins surrounding it, the mystery? Mexicans complained when Jennifer Lopez was cast as the lead in the Selena biopic two years ago, but what else could Hollywood have done? A butt was of prime concern, and Lopez's butt, courtesy of her Puerto Rican heritage, was accordingly considered.

What impressed me most was how Selena so neatly countered that butt—which was routinely fitted in Lycra pants and set off, like dynamite, by cropped tops—with a wholesome sweetness, a kind of wonder at finding herself in such clothes in the first place. She strutted her stuff, but more dutifully than nastily; she was the physical parallel but the actual opposite of young R&B singers like Foxy Brown and Lil' Kim, who infuse new blood into that most enduring (but least discussed) Black-woman image of the sexually available skeezer.

Grounded in butt size, this image is too potent to be complicated by wholesome sweetness or benign intent. No matter the age or station of the Black woman who dares to wear revealing dress—Foxy Brown, Aretha Franklin, En Vogue, hell, even octogenarian Lena Horne—they're all variations on a dominant theme of sexiness that is hard-wearing, full but embittered somehow; sexiness with a worldly sneer, that dangles a cigarette from its lips and rubs the fatigue from its eyes before it is fully awake. It's Sister Christian vs. the streetwalking Creole Lady Marmalade. Selena bounded from one end of the stage to the other ruminating on the grand possibilities of love, embodied in her boundless rear; Foxy Brown gyrates her hips and grinds all possibility into dust. One seeks knowledge of eros; the other already knows. To the world at large, the Black butt tells the entire sordid story.

Black men are famous for their audacity with women, even more famous for their predilection for healthy butts. The celebratory butt songs of the last ten years testify: "Da Butt," "Rump Shaker," "Baby Got Back," more brazen versions of such '70s butt anthems as "Shake Your Booty," "Shake Your Groove Thing" and, of course, the seminal "Bertha Butt Boogie." These songs are plenty affirming—especially the irreverent "Baby Got Back," in which Sir Mix-A-Lot rightly condemns *Cosmo* magazine *and* Jane Fonda for deifying thinness—but they are also vaguely troubling, because most of the praises are being sung these days by rappers, many of whom are as quick to denigrate Black women as they are to celebrate them; indeed, some of these artists don't bother to distinguish between the two. As pop music has segregated itself, the ruling butt democracy of the dance floor (over which the explicitly inoffensive KC and the Sunshine Band presided) has given way to a butt oligarchy run by self-proclaimed thugz and niggaz 4 life. Call me classist, but my butt deserves a wider audience. So to speak.

But sometimes all that matters is a captive audience, and Black men rarely disappoint. Recently, as I was walking in comfortable anonymity through a clean section of Hollywood, I passed by a homeless Black man pushing a shopping cart. He took a look at me, stopped dead in his tracks and shouted in a single breath: "Honey, don't let the buggy fool you! I got means! How about I take you to lunch? Are you married?" I didn't take him up on it, even after he trailed me for half a block, but I had to admire his nerve; I was in fact grateful for it. For all the much-discussed Black angst about our war between the sexes, approbation from Black men is still very much food for my soul, even from the ones with no means. It breaks the lull of assimilation and makes me remember that, for all the dressing-room nightmares I've lived and will live, I'd rather be successful at fitting comfortably into my own skin than into clothes meant to cover someone else's.

Recently, I had an epiphanic flash: My figure is still the soul of the feminine ideal. It *has* been through the ages. In the '90s it has merely run afoul of this trend of casting what is good and perfectly logical as something suddenly without currency, something that was once a nice idea, but ... (cf. affirmative action, civil rights, TVs without remotes).

I'll admit: For all of my hand wringing, I'm growing accustomed to my butt. It's a strange and wonderful development of the last six years or so—as I've gotten heavier I've actually gotten more comfortable with how I look. Perhaps it's a function of maturity or a realization that fashions aren't likely to bulk up anytime soon, but I'm much more inclined to reveal myself now than I ever was before. I've finally concluded that there's no clever way around my butt, as there never seems to be a clever way around the truth—whatever you try leads to the most fantastic lies. In the interest of honesty, my butt now gets accent—a lot of stretch, slouch pants, skirts that fall below the navel, platform shoes that punch up my walk. I don't do big and shapeless anymore, not even in the complete privacy of home. I have finally glimpsed the full, unadulterated length of me and don't want to obfuscate the image any more than I already do on bad mornings. I must burn myself into my own memory; my butt is more than happy to help.

So what if America, in its infinite generosity, wants to help me get rid of this bothersome behind with its *Self* magazines and *L.A. Times* "Celebrity Workouts" and the demonizing of complex carbohydrates. More and more, my response has been: I *am* going to eat cake. I *will* wear the things that fit—whatever ones I can find—with impunity. I *will* walk this way. I don't have an issue, I have a groove thing. Kiss my you know what.

In Other Words . . .

The personal is political; the political is personal. The interlocking nature of these terms was first used as a rallying cry for two concurrent movements in the 1960s and 1970s—student activism and second-wave feminism (Oliver 2007, and Pekar and Buhle 2009). Both movements focused on how widespread social and political trends affected the most personal aspects of private lives, ways that had seldom been acknowledged. The slogans were used to challenge traditional values that brought disadvantage to young people, women in general, sexual minorities, and people of color.

Actions of these organizations were first engaged through small group gatherings referred to as "consciousness raising" meetings (Brownmiller 1999). The power of these groups was at least threefold. They brought to light the political nature of issues seldom questioned (such as household division of labor). They established the fact that many voices previously had been unheard and unheeded (such as student organizers). And, most important, they demonstrated that organizing collectively meant that issues formerly perceived as isolated and individual were now recognized as widespread, political, shared, and exploitive (Napikoski 2016). At last, people could find common ground with others in similar situations instead of turning self-blame inward.

This unit has brought together many of those issues often assumed to be personal, casual, or random, but now acknowledged as organized, politicized, and employed as strategies to gain power and unfair advantage over other people. We have seen that the circles in which one travels translates into capital (Bourdieu), that diversity is not a liability but a lucrative asset (Herring), and that a transgender individual can help to challenge and transform chasms in the workplace (Whitley). The giraffe and the elephant (Thomas) teach us, through fable and metaphor, that we are most successful when we think empathetically and creatively about change. And finally, we learn, with some degree of comic relief, not to take ourselves—and cultural mirrors—so seriously (Aubry). Indeed, everything may be political, but with a little introspection we can raise our own consciousness.

The Big Idea

Whenever ideas, however unintentional, distort reality in a way that justifies the prevailing distribution of wealth, power, and privilege; hides society's injustices; and thus secures uncritical allegiance to the prevailing social order, we have … ideology. This definition is adapted from Reiman's (2012) *The rich get richer and the poor get prison*. Study every word. Contemplate what it means. How does this fit with Lukes's three faces of power?

So What?

Once we understand the power of ideology, we gain power over it; until then, we remain its slave.

Works Cited

Brownmiller, S. (1999). *In our time: Memoir of a revolution*. New York, NY: The Dial Press.

Napikoski, L. (2016, August 31). "Feminist consciousness-raising groups." Retrieved October 4, 2016, from http://womenshistory.about.com/od/feminism/a/consciousness_raising_groups.htm

Oliver, S. (2007). *Betty Friedan: The personal is political*. New York, NY: Pearson.

Pekar, H., and Buhle, P. (2009). *Students for a Democratic Society: A graphic history*. New York, NY: Hill and Wang.

Reiman, J., and Leighton, P. (2012). *The rich get richer and the poor get prison: Ideology, class, and criminal justice*. 10th ed. New York, NY: Routledge.

Beyond the Book: News, Fake News, and "Alternative" Facts

Following our theme of "unlearning what we already know," I'd like to recommend a few sources to encourage new habits in your quest to reeducate yourself. Amazingly, a recent Pew poll reports that nearly one-half(!) of American adults get their news from Facebook (Lichterman 2016). "Two-thirds of Facebook users access news on the social platform, and with 67 percent of U.S. adults active on Facebook, that translates to 44 percent of the overall U.S. population which accesses news on the social platform" (p. 1). According to the report, 62 percent of American adults access news on social media (including YouTube, Twitter, Reddit, Instagram, Snapchat). This is up from 47 percent in 2013 (Lichterman 2016).

Why is this important? First, even "big social media" such as Facebook or Google News are not news organizations, have no news mission, and are not regulated (Schlesinger 2016). News content may be repeated or suppressed and is sometimes tailored to a user's preferences or political leanings (Tennery 2016). Social media sources deny bias, and there is some evidence to support their claims. For example, Zoomph, a social media analytics firm, concludes that while some differences occur in the number of postings, "If you dig below the surface, it's really about the audiences that interact with these entities" (WYMT 2016). Still, implicit biases proliferate in such unregulated sources, and it's up to us, as consumers, to find well-rounded news channels that keep us well informed.

One way to do that is to check stories from various (legitimate) sources, looking to see how facts line up with the "slant" of the story. Also, refer to more than one source among fact-check organization to see how they compare. Finally, look for what is referred to as alternative press channels—that is, those outside the mainstream or corporate-owned world. Some examples include *Mother Jones, The Progressive, Utne Reader,* and *Alternative News.*

As Bill Nye, the "Science Guy," says: "It's important that our children are raised to be educated, well-rounded tax-paying citizens that understand the importance of technology and science" (IMDb 2016).

Works Cited

IMDb.com. (2016). Bill Nye Quotes. Retrieved October 4, 2016, from http://m.imdb.com/name/nm0638557/quotes

Lichterman, J. (2016, May 26). "Nearly half of U.S. adults get news on Facebook, Pew says." NiemanLab. Retrieved October 4, 2016, from http://www.niemanlab.org/2016/05/pew-report-44-percent-of-u-s-adults-get-news-on-facebook/

Schlesinger, R. (2016, May 27). "The new too big to fail." U.S. News & World Report. Retrieved October 4, 2016, from http://www.usnews.com/opinion/articles/2016-05-27/why-we-should-care-about-facebook-and-google-having-political-bias

Tennery, A. (2016, May 9). "Report claiming bias in Facebook 'trending' topics sparks social media outcry." Reuters. Retrieved October 4, 2016, from http://www.reuters.com/article/us-socialmedia-facebook-idUSKCN0Y02EY

WYMT.com. (2016, May 21). "Does Facebook have an anti-conservative bias?" Retrieved October 4, 2016, from http://www.wymt.com/content/news/Does-Facebook-have-an-anti-conservative-bias-380349001.html

Section III: Faces of Power

From the Field: Implicit Bias

Implicit bias refers to attitudes or stereotypes that affect our judgments and decisions unconsciously. Also known as implicit social cognition, implicit bias works very differently from explicit bias. While explicit bias is deliberate and often stated or demonstrated openly, implicit bias occurs outside of our conscious awareness and control. Most often, we may be fully surprised that it works behind the scene to influence our judgments and behavior.

Research provides solid and consistent evidence that implicit bias exists in almost every realm of life where judgments and decision making take place (see Levinson 2007). It is also widespread among humans; all of us are at risk because we *unconsciously* base judgments on a bundle of experiences and attitudes that influence our cognitive processes. Here are a few myth-busters about implicit bias (from Staats et al., with the Kirwan Institute 2015):

- **Myth:** Implicit bias is nothing more than beliefs people choose not to tell others; these people just hide their feelings.
- **Busted:** Implicit biases are activated involuntarily and work beyond our awareness or intentional control
- **Myth:** I am not biased; I have diverse friends and I believe in equal treatment.
- **Busted:** Actually, we all have implicit biases. All individuals are susceptible to harnessing implicit associations about others based on characteristics including race, skin tone, income, sex, and even attributes such as weight and accents.

- **Myth:** Having implicit biases makes me a bad person.
- **Busted:** No one is a "bad" person for harboring implicit biases; these are normal human processes that occur on an unconscious level.
- **Myth:** If bias is "natural," there is obviously nothing we can do about it.
- **Busted:** Unwanted implicit biases can be mitigated. Various intervention strategies, such as intergroup contact, perspective-taking, and exposure to counter-stereotypical exemplars are effective, according to solid research.

Several excellent sources help test for hidden bias. Teaching Tolerance, a project of the Southern Poverty Law Center, is an excellent one. Please see the source below. Acknowledgement is the critical first step!

Works Cited

Levinson, J. D. (2007). "Forgotten racial equality: Implicit bias, decision making, and misremembering." *Duke Law Journal,* 57, 345–424.

Southern Poverty Law Center. (2016). Teaching tolerance. Retrieved October 4, 2016, from http://www.tolerance.org/Hidden-bias

Staats, C., Capatosto, K., Wright, R.A., and Contractor, D. (2015). State of the science: Implicit bias review 2015. The Kirwan Institute. Retrieved October 4, 2016, from http://kirwaninstitute.osu.edu/wp-content/uploads/2015/05/2015-kirwan-implicit-bias.pdf

Section III: Faces of Power

Reality Check: Crayons

Overview:

Research indicates that students learn concepts more effectively when applied to everyday activities. As Ray points out in the Unit 5 reading, "The Science, Social Construction, and Exploitation of Race," Jane Elliott's *Blue Eyes/Brown Eyes* documentary is useful in considering the social construction of race. The *Crayons* exercise provides an opportunity to view a film related to race/ethnicity and to apply key sociological concepts to these films: *The Essential Blue Eyed* (in most university libraries) and/or *Angry Eye* (found on YouTube). Also, you can find the original documentary *A Class Divided* on the PBS website.

While viewing the film(s), take notes on the key points of the film(s) and think about how they apply to the following key concepts: race, discrimination, racism, stereotyping, and prejudice.

Purpose:

- To demonstrate understanding of principles in one of the Elliott films.
- To define key concepts related to race/ethnicity.
- To apply sociological concepts to the film(s).

Introduction and Definition of Key Terms:

Introduce the topic and define the following terms: race, racism, discrimination, prejudice, and stereotyping. Bring in both historical and contemporary social facts about race (and/or gender and other points of identity).

Application of Key Terms:

Apply each of the above concepts to one of the films. Please thoroughly discuss how each concept applies, using specific examples from the film(s).

Reaction to the Film:

Answer at least three of the following questions: How did you *feel* after watching the film? Did your reaction to the film change over time? What was the most memorable part of the film for you? Would you recommend this film to one of your friends? Why or why not? Should this film be shown to high school (or earlier) students? Why or why not?

Conclusion:

Conclude the paper by discussing both the "So what?" question of this assignment and also a sociological "big idea" demonstrated in the documentary.

Works Cited

"Jane Elliott's Blue Eyes Brown Eyes Exercise." Retrieved October 4, 2016, from http://www.janeelliott.com
The Angry Eye. Retrieved October 4, 2016, from https://www.youtube.com/watch?v=tAE3UqxIhfE
A Class Divided. Retrieved October 4, 2016, from http://www.pbs.org/wgbh/frontline/film/class-divided/

Section III: Faces of Power

OLE Resources

Student engagement in the online learning environment is a hot-button topic in twenty-first-century education. The connection between engagement and retention is especially critical in the digital classroom. Fortunately, research is now providing valuable feedback in this area, and we gain increasingly valuable insights from students who are involved in studies. Here are some tips we've learned recently:

- Students expect direct interaction from the instructor and timely feedback. Faculty strategies include presence in discussion forums, blogs, announcements, and personal communication. Video feedback is even more effective.
- Students relate to real-world applications that are relevant to their concerns. Faculty members who take time to know students are more aware of their interests and concerns.
- Motivation and interest are key. Instructors who provide opportunities for hands-on exploration, schedule meetings, and arrange instructive tools and resources enhance these qualities.

Below are a few sources to supplement material in Section III:
- *The State of Arizona*. An Independent Lens documentary http://www.pbs.org/independentlens/films/state-of-arizona/
- Immigration Quiz, an interactive exercise.
- http://www.pbs.org/independentlens/blog/immigration-quiz-2/
- For Your Reconsideration. This American Life podcast reviews door-to-door canvassing on how voters change their minds.
- http://www.thisamericanlife.org/radio-archives/episode/584/transcript

"One woman, five characters, and a sex lesson from the future." Sarah Jones, Ted Talk 2015. https://www.ted.com/talks/sarah_jones_one_woman_five_characters_and_a_sex_lesson_from_the_future

"Why gender equality is good for everyone—men included." Michael Kimmel, Ted Talk 2015. https://www.ted.com/talks/michael_kimmel_why_gender_equality_is_good_for_everyone_men_included

Section IV:
Social Inequality, Power, and Progress

Unit 7: The Rich Get Richer

Dr. Sue to You: What everybody else gets

In the last section, we learned that various characteristics such as race, gender, sexuality, age, weight, etc. get entangled in stereotypes and, sometimes, discrimination. While we sometimes get caught up in either a) political correctness, or b) the shunning of political correctness, the truth is that these patterns matter in real people's lives.

In this short treatise, I will briefly address three questions: 1) Do the rich really get richer? And if that's true, what does everybody else get? 2) Are these patterns relevant today? and 3) Are we making progress?

Do the rich really get richer? Yes.

- Since 1979, the top 1 percent has increased its income earnings more than four times faster than the bottom 20 percent (Inequality.org 2016).
- The mega-rich—the top one-tenth of 1 percent—controls more wealth (cumulative holdings) than the bottom 90 percent (Inequality.org 2016).
- The ratio between pay for large-company CEOs and worker pay has grown from 42:1 in 1980 to 335:1 in 2015 (Inequality.org 2016).
- By 2015, the wealthiest twenty people owned more wealth than half the American population (Parramore 2016).

- Economic inequality has been growing markedly, by every major statistical measure, for about thirty years (Inequality.org 2016).
- At 1979 income distribution levels, today all Americans would experience income increases of at least $3,000 across all quintile levels, with the bottom quintile owed an additional $17,311 (Inequality.org 2016).
- Rising poverty rates disproportionately affect young parents and young children (Child Trends 2016).
- Poverty levels among children have remained high, while poverty levels among the elderly have declined (Peter G. Peterson Foundation 2016).

Are these patterns relevant today? Yes.

- Income inequality is growing at an extremely fast rate. Multinational studies illustrate the result: the United States now ranks at the bottom of ten well-off countries in the world in terms of overall economic health (Gursky, Mattingyl, and Varner 2016). This is an example of quantitative evidence; the supporting research in this area is strong and consistent.
- For an outstanding graphic of how inequality patterns have changed over time, please go to the *L.A. Times* (Hiltzik 2016) website, listed in the reference section below. It clearly illustrates the growing gap between the well-off and everyone else.
- We also have qualitative evidence that demonstrates continuing and growing inequality. As one brief example, Quigley's reading in this unit clearly states that our history shapes our current attitudes and practices. The old vagrancy laws, it seems, are being revived. In Florida, a 90-year-old man and two ministers were arrested (and subsequently rearrested) for breaking an ordinance that severely restricts public feeding of the homeless. CBS news (2014) reports that "The city believes the sight of the homeless is affecting tourism, nearby businesses and tarnishing the city's image."

Are we making progress? Depends/not much/no.

This is a hard one. All of the patterns described vary by race, class, gender, age, sexual orientation, geography, and other points of difference. Yes, we've made strides in some ways but not others. As the *facts* demonstrate, we have lost ground in inequality in this country. It is a myth to think that we've arrived, or even that we're competing well in many of these categories. Yet, we DO live in a powerful nation with the capacity and potential to solve these problems. Will we? What will it take? Do we have the political will to do so?

Section IV addresses these very questions. I won't pretend to have all the answers, or even to give you enough material to solve all of the problems. But we are a country of problem-solvers, and none so much as the young generation. Educate yourself, seek facts, show up. It gives us great promise!

DSTY TIPS: It's never just one thing. If anyone tries to give you a black/white version of the problem, or a single-step answer, don't buy it. It's never just one thing.

Woman on street

Works Cited

CBS News. (2014, November 5). "90-year-old man, 2 pastors charged with feeding homeless in Florida." Retrieved October 5, 2016) from http://www.cbsnews.com/news/90-year-old-man-2-pastors-charged-with-feeding-homeless-in-florida/

Child Trends. (2016). "Rising poverty rates take a toll on two generations." Retrieved October 5, 2016, from http://www.childtrends.org/news-release/rising-poverty-rates-take-a-toll-on-two-generations/

Grusky, D. B., Mattingly, M. J., and Varner, C. E. (2016). "The poverty and inequality report." The Stanford Center on Poverty and Inequality. Retrieved October 5, 2016, from http://inequality.stanford.edu/sites/default/files/Pathways-SOTU-2016.pdf

Hiltzik, M. (2016, March 20). America's explosion of income inequality, in one amazing animated chart. *Los Angeles Times*. Retrieved October 5, 2016, from http://www.latimes.com/business/hiltzik/la-fi-hiltzik-ft-graphic-20160320-snap-htmlstory.html

Inequality.org. (2016). A project of the Institute for Policy Studies. Retrieved October 5 2016, from http://inequality.org

Parramore, L. S. (2016, April 14). "The .1 percent are the true villains: What Americans don't understand about income inequality." *Salon*. Retrieved October 5, 2016, from http://www.salon.com/2016/04/14/the_1_percent_are_the_real_villains_what_americans_dont_understand_about_income_inequality_partner/

Peter G. Peterson Foundation. (2016, January 11). "Poverty levels among children have remained high, while poverty levels among the elderly have declined." Retrieved October 5, 2016, from http://www.pgpf.org/chart-archive/0193_poverty_age_groups

WHAT DO YOU THINK?

OUR HISTORY SHAPES OUR THINKING

BY WILLIAM QUIGLEY

"Unless you start saving your money, you're going to end up in the poorhouse!" Ever heard someone say that? Where does that saying come from?

My students generally do not know that the United States was dotted with government and private poorhouses in the early part of the twentieth century.[1]

Poorhouses were real, and the fear of landing in the poorhouse was also real. That is where that warning comes from. The fear of ending up in the poorhouse has been handed down orally from generation to generation, even after the poorhouses disappeared. Yet poorhouses continue to shape our consciousness about poverty and behavior.

There are plenty of other examples of how our shared history and culture unconsciously shapes our outlook on poverty. To properly analyze poverty and work, we have to consider that we have some preconceived notions already imprinted on our thought process.

In the mid-1990s, some politicians declared that they had a new idea—it was time to "get tough" on poor people, time to "force poor people to work." It was time for welfare reform.

It may come as a surprise that their efforts were nothing new, that, in fact, our laws have been trying to "get tough" on the poor for more than 650 years.

In 1349 England enacted the first law to get tough on poor people. What the English did to their poor people is important because the United States inherited many of our basic legal principles of how we deal with poverty and poor people from the English. Our American colonies essentially adopted the English laws about poor people, and those colonial poor laws became the basis for many of our state laws.[2]

In the mid-1300s, the English government was becoming concerned that there were too many poor people wandering around. Too many poor people who appeared to be able to work were choosing to beg. Therefore, England made it illegal to give alms to beggars who were able to work by enacting its first law to classify who among the poor was worthy of help and who was not.

This is what the law of 1349 said:

> Because that many valiant beggars, as long as they may live of begging, do refuse to labour, giving themselves to idleness and vice, and sometimes to theft and other abominations; none, upon the said pain of imprisonment shall, under the colour of pity or alms, give any thing to such, which may labour, or presume to favour them towards their desires, so that thereby they may be compelled to labour for their necessary living.[3]

Translation? There are too many homeless beggars roaming around who could work if we were only tougher on them. These folks are lazy and probably petty criminals. They will only work if we force them. So, we are now making it illegal to feed them or give them any more help, and that way they will be forced to work. The law was sent to each of the bishops, who were asked to order people in their communities to obey it.[4]

Sound familiar? It should. It is familiar. This old English law, enacted more than 650 years ago, and some of the ones that the English enacted later, sound quite a bit like the "welfare reforms" enacted by the Congress in the 1990s.

Nearly two hundred years later, in the 1530s, England continued to be concerned about the number of poor people, beggars, and vagrants. English law was changed to allow only "the aged poor and the impotent" (so severely disabled that they were unable to work) to beg for alms or charity. Even then, the aged poor and the disabled were not allowed to beg unless they were given official written permission, and they were limited to certain locations. Everyone else under age sixty who was poor but who could work was prohibited from begging and was forced to work, even children. Those of whatever state or condition who violated the law were whipped. Repeat offenders were subject to having their ears cut off.[5]

Poor children? The local justice of the peace was given the responsibility of taking poor children, ages five to fourteen, away from their families if the children were found begging and place them as apprentices.[6]

This was England's welfare reform of the 1500s. The English thought that helping the poor only encouraged dependence and actually increased the number of poor people. On grounds quite similar to those raised by contemporary opponents of public assistance to the poor, some even criticized religious monasteries for feeding the poor:

> It is obvious ... the monastic institutions ... had the effect of increasing tenfold the evil which they were designed to cure.[7]

Translation? Helping poor people only hurts poor people. What the poor need is not the tender help of generosity, but tough love.

These English poor laws of 1349 to 1601 share several common themes with U.S. welfare "reforms" of the mid-1990s.[8]

First, poor people can work and are choosing not to, so they must be forced to work. Second, helping poor people actually hurts poor people, so it is time to get tougher on them for their own sake. And third, poor parents are likely bad parents, and we should take their kids away from them.[9]

Is it a coincidence that these laws, hundreds of years apart, are so similar? No. These old English laws became the primary basis for the laws enacted in the American colonies when colonial legislatures decided how to handle the problems of poverty on the continent. These laws, and the assumptions they contain, became part of the unconscious backdrop of how we view poverty. And they are such good scenery that we often do not consciously understand how they set the tone for the current actions that take place.

These old English laws are like the poorhouses. They are not actually here anymore, but they continue to influence our thinking.

Many other important forces shaped colonial and early American thought about poverty, including Puritanism, Calvinism, and our national sense of the frontier culture. All of these influences were, like the English poor laws, pretty intolerant and skeptical of poor people.[10]

The "reforms" in welfare at the end of the twentieth century resulted from decades of concerted conservative attacks on the principle that government can or should assist poor and working people.[11] These campaigns increasingly relied on stigmatizing, shaming, and stereotyping poor people as immoral, undermotivated, urban, nonworking, overpopulating, living in and creating a culture of poverty, and dark-skinned. Think tanks and institutions tapped into the historical roots of antagonism against poor people and the age-old proposition that helping poor and working people only ended up harming them. Poor people were analyzed and categorized by those who had no accountability to poor and working people.

In these campaigns, life was simple. Government was bad. Business was good. Rich people were righteous and productive. Poor people were immoral failures. The market was free and self-regulating. Public laws to regulate for the common good were unrealistic and counterproductive. The smaller and less intrusive the government, the better off we all are.

The relentless efforts of conservatives to undercut public assistance to the poor were matched by similar efforts to undercut government regulation in other areas of the economy that were characterized as "antibusiness." Systematic dismantling and decreased funding of government agencies was not just good for business interests, but was in the common good.

Laws were changed accordingly. Not surprisingly, the changes reflected some old themes.

Anyone who has ever heard a talk radio discussion of welfare will be familiar with what the 1834 English Poor Law Commission called "less eligibility." In the English welfare "reform" of the 1830s, "less eligibility" meant that in order for the poor relief system to work, the living standards of the best-situated nonworking poor person must be worse than the worst-situated working person. Translation: the best welfare can never be better than the worst job, or else why would anyone take the bad jobs?

As the twentieth century closed, nonworking poor people were the most visible group to lose welfare. But less publicized cutbacks occurred in many other areas as huge holes were systematically cut in the government safety net.

Working people lost just as much. The real value of the minimum wage dramatically declined. The influence of organized workers in unions declined. The gap between the rich and the rest increased.

In thinking about a public response, we must be constantly aware of these historical themes that are often deeply embedded in our unconscious views and stereotypes about poverty. These old themes and laws are like the poorhouses our parents warned us about. The poorhouses are not here anymore, but they continue to influence our thinking.

The challenge for those who want to engage in serious discussion about these issues is to first acknowledge our ingrained presumptions and then examine them to see what is actually true and what is not.

Part of that discussion has to include an examination of the official definition of poverty.

Notes

1. Michael B. Katz, *In the Shadow of the Poorhouse: A Social History of Welfare in America* (Basic Books, 1986), 3–109; David J. Rothman, *The Discovery of the Asylum: Social Order and Disorder in the New Republic* (Little, Brown & Co., 1971), 180–205.

2. For a more detailed history of these English laws, see William P. Quigley, "Five Hundred Years of English Poor Laws, 1349–1834: Regulating the Working and Nonworking Poor," *Akron Law Review* 30(1) (Fall 1996): 73–128.

3. Statute of Laborers, 1349, 23 Edward 3rd (Eng.), Chapter 7, reprinted in *Statutes at Large*, Vol. 2, ed. Danby Pickering (London, 1762), 26, 29.

4. Quigley, "Five Hundred Years," 88.

5. Ibid., 92–98, discussing 22 Henry 8th, Chapter 12 (1531), and 27 Henry 8th, Chapter 25 (1536).

6. Children between the ages of five and fourteen who "live in idleness, and be taken begging, may be put to service … to husbandry, or other crafts or labours." Quigley, "Five Hundred Years," 97.

7. Ibid., 96.

8. English laws about poor people were codified in a comprehensive way in 1601 under Queen Elizabeth. Quigley, "Five Hundred Years," 100–103, discussing 43rd Elizabeth, Chapter 2 (1601).

9. William P. Quigley, "Backwards into the Future: How Welfare Changes in the Millennium Resemble Poor Law of the Middle Ages," *Stanford Law & Policy Review* 9 (1998): 101–13.

10. Those wishing more details on poor laws in these times should look, for starters, at: Walter I. Trattner, *From Poor Law to Welfare State: A History of Social Welfare in America*, 5th ed. (Free Press, 1994), and Sidney and Beatrice Webb, *English Local Government—English Poor Law Policy*, Volume 10, 1910, reprinted 1963.

    My other works on the poor laws predating this time period include "Five Hundred Years"; "Work or Starve: Regulation of the Poor in Colonial America," *University of San Francisco Law Review* 31 (1996): 35; "Reluctant Charity: Poor Laws in the Original Thirteen States," *University of Richmond Law Review* 31 (1997): 111; "The Quicksands of the Poor Law: Poor Relief Legislation from 1790 to 1820," *Northern Illinois University Law Review* 18 (1997): 1; and "Rumblings of Reform: Northern Poor Relief Legislation in Antebellum America, 1820–1860," *Capital University Law Review* 26 (1997): 739.

11. See Joel F. Handler, *The Poverty of Welfare Reform* (Yale University Press, 1995); Michael B. Katz, *The Price of Citizenship: Redefining the American Welfare State* (Metropolitan Books, 2001); and Frances Fox Piven and Richard A. Cloward, *The New Class War: Reagan's Attack on the Welfare State and Its Consequences* (Pantheon Books, 1985).

READING 2

WHY THE RICH ARE GETTING RICHER
American Politics and the Second Gilded Age

BY ROBERT C. LIEBERMAN

The U.S. economy appears to be coming apart at the seams. Unemployment remains at nearly ten percent, the highest level in almost 30 years; foreclosures have forced millions of Americans out of their homes; and real incomes have fallen faster and further than at any time since the Great Depression. Many of those laid off fear that the jobs they have lost—the secure, often unionized, industrial jobs that provided wealth, security, and opportunity—will never return. They are probably right.

And yet a curious thing has happened in the midst of all this misery. The wealthiest Americans, among them presumably the very titans of global finance whose misadventures brought about the financial meltdown, got richer. And not just a little bit richer; a lot richer. In 2009, the average income of the top five percent of earners went up, while on average everyone else's income went down. This was not an anomaly but rather a continuation of a 40-year trend of ballooning incomes at the very top and stagnant incomes in the middle and at the bottom. The share of total income going to the top one percent has increased from roughly eight percent in the 1960s to more than 20 percent today.

This is what the political scientists Jacob Hacker and Paul Pierson call the "winner-take-all economy." It is not a picture of a healthy society. Such a level of economic inequality, not seen in the United States since the eve of the Great Depression, bespeaks a political economy in which the financial rewards are increasingly concentrated among a tiny elite and whose risks are borne by an increasingly exposed and unprotected middle class. Income inequality in the United States is higher than in any other advanced industrial democracy and by conventional measures comparable to that in countries such as

Ghana, Nicaragua, and Turkmenistan. It breeds political polarization, mistrust, and resentment between the haves and the have-nots and tends to distort the workings of a democratic political system in which money increasingly confers political voice and power.

It is generally presumed that economic forces alone are responsible for this astonishing concentration of wealth. Technological changes, particularly the information revolution, have transformed the economy, making workers more productive and placing a premium on intellectual, rather than manual, labor. Simultaneously, the rise of global markets—itself accelerated by information technology—has hollowed out the once dominant U.S. manufacturing sector and reoriented the U.S. economy toward the service sector. The service economy also rewards the educated, with high-paying professional jobs in finance, health care, and information technology. At the low end, however, jobs in the service economy are concentrated in retail sales and entertainment, where salaries are low, unions are weak, and workers are expendable.

Champions of globalization portray these developments as the natural consequences of market forces, which they believe are not only benevolent (because they increase aggregate wealth through trade and make all kinds of goods cheaper to consume) but also unstoppable. Skeptics of globalization, on the other hand, emphasize the distributional consequences of these trends, which tend to confer tremendous benefits on a highly educated and highly skilled elite while leaving other workers behind. But neither side in this debate has bothered to question Washington's primary role in creating the growing inequality in the United States.

It's the Government, Stupid

Hacker and Pierson refreshingly break free from the conceit that skyrocketing inequality is a natural consequence of market forces and argue instead that it is the result of public policies that have concentrated and amplified the effects of the economic transformation and directed its gains exclusively toward the wealthy. Since the late 1970s, a number of important policy changes have tilted the economic playing field toward the rich. Congress has cut tax rates on high incomes repeatedly and has relaxed the tax treatment of capital gains and other investment income, resulting in windfall profits for the wealthiest Americans.

Labor policies have made it harder for unions to organize workers and provide a countervailing force to the growing power of business; corporate governance policies have enabled corporations to lavish extravagant pay on their top executives regardless of their companies' performance; and the deregulation of financial markets has allowed banks and other financial institutions to create ever more Byzantine financial instruments that further enrich wealthy managers and investors while exposing homeowners and pensioners to ruinous risks.

In some cases, these policy changes originated on Capitol Hill: the Ronald Reagan and George W. Bush tax cuts, for example, and the 1999 repeal of the Glass-Steagall Act, a repeal that dismantled the firewall between banks and investment companies and allowed the creation of powerful and reckless financial behemoths such as Citigroup, were approved by Congress, generally with bipartisan support. However, other policy shifts occurred gradually and imperceptibly.

Hacker and Pierson's second important point is that major policy shifts do not always happen in such obvious ways. Many of the policies that have facilitated the winner-take-all economy have just as often come about as a result of what Hacker and Pierson call "drift," which occurs when an enacted policy fails to keep up with changing circumstances and then falls short of, or even subverts, its intended goal. The American system of separated powers—with its convoluted procedures and bizarre rules, such as vetoes and the filibuster—is especially conducive to drift, particularly compared to more streamlined parliamentary systems in other countries that afford majorities relatively unimpeded dominance over the policymaking process. Policies in the United States, once made, tend to be hard to overturn or even to modify.

Sometimes drift occurs through simple neglect or inertia. An example is the phenomenon known as "bracket creep," the process by which prior to the indexing introduced in 1981, inflation pushed incomes into higher tax brackets. But Hacker and Pierson particularly zero in on instances of intentional policy drift, when policymakers deliberately sidestepped or resisted available policy alternatives that might have reduced inequality. Allowing corporate executives to be compensated with stock options is one such case; stock-option compensation tends to bend incentives toward the short-term maximization of share prices rather than planning for long-term growth. Consequently, such compensation has allowed top managers to capture jaw-dropping gains despite their companies' often dismal performances. The long-term cost of corporate failure is borne not by ceos and their executive minions, of course, but by rank-and-file employees, who get laid off when companies need to cut costs and whose pension investments are wiped out when companies' stocks sink.

In the 1990s, the Financial Accounting Standards Board, which regulates accounting practices, noticed this practice, correctly predicted the damage it would do to the economy, and then sought to curtail it. But Congress, spurred on by the lobbying efforts of major corporations, stopped the FASB in its tracks. As a result, Americans spent the 1990s and the first decade of this century living under 1970s accounting rules, which allowed top executives to more or less help themselves and, through the mutual back-scratching habits of corporate boards, help one another.

Similarly, labor law has failed to keep up with the times. Policymakers have repeatedly failed to enact reforms that would have accommodated new union-organizing techniques and empowered unions to counter the growing power of business to resist labor's demands. In this realm, the United States is running a twenty-first-century economy under 1940s rules. A clearheaded understanding of the power of drift in policymaking puts the Republican congressional minority during President Barack Obama's first two years in a fresh light. Obsessive obstructionism is not just a symptom of general crabbiness; it is a shrewd and sensible part of a larger strategy to enrich corporations while gutting longstanding protections for the middle class.

The dramatic growth of inequality, then, is the result not of the "natural" workings of the market but of four decades' worth of deliberate political choices. Hacker and Pierson amass a great deal of evidence for this proposition, which leads them to the crux of their argument: that not just the U.S. economy but also the entire U.S. political system has devolved into a winner-take-all sport. They portray American politics not as a democratic game of majority rule but rather as a field of "organized combat"—a struggle to the death among competing organized groups seeking to influence the policymaking process. Moreover, they suggest, business and the wealthy have all but vanquished the middle class and have thus been able to dominate policymaking for the better part of 40 years with little opposition.

The Business Backlash

In pursuing this argument, Hacker and Pierson revive the old academic tradition of pluralism to shine a bright light on some of the pathologies of American politics. The contemporary study of American politics emerged from pluralism, the post–World War II view that in the shadow of the two totalitarianisms of midcentury Europe—communism and fascism—democracy could be rendered stable and progressive through a politics of mutual accommodation among relatively evenly matched groups. Rather than titanic conflict between workers and capitalists, so the argument went, pluralist democracy would produce solid incremental policy changes that would inch American society forward toward security and affluence. The dramatic and decidedly nonincremental events of the 1960s and 1970s—the civil rights movement, the Vietnam War, and broader cultural upheaval—punctured this view.

Critics of pluralism began to note its limitations, emphasizing the primacy of individual motivations rather than group affiliations. Since then, the study of American politics has largely turned away from questions of organized interests and their role in policymaking and has focused instead on the ways in which individual attitudes and behavior combine to produce policy. Yet if one assumes that people vote based on their economic interests and that election outcomes influence policy through something like majority rule, how can one account for a generation of policies that promoted the interests of the wealthy few at the direct expense of everybody else?

Another critique of pluralism is that it underestimated the lopsidedness of political organization. As the great political scientist E. E. Schattschneider wrote in 1960, "The flaw in the pluralist heaven is that the heavenly chorus sings with a strong upper-class accent." Schattschneider, it turned out, did not know the half of it. To most observers, the 1960s seemed the height of American liberalism, and the decade's policy developments—upgrading the basic New Deal package of social protection and labor rights to include extensive protection of civil rights and civil liberties and additional benefits such as limited health insurance—seemed to bear out this view. But to business elites, the 1960s marked the nadir of their influence in American society, and they did not react passively. The era saw the stirrings of a conservative counterrevolution marked by ideological, political, and organizational developments, and particularly by the political awakening of business.

American conservatives, increasingly empowered by effective organization and lavish funding from their patrons in the business community, began to actively resist the politics of pluralist accommodation. Rather than accepting the basic contours of the New Deal and the Great Society and seeking to adjust them step by incremental step, conservatives assumed a newly confrontational posture and turned their efforts toward dismantling the legacies of Franklin Roosevelt and Lyndon Johnson.

The economic crisis of the 1970s, which heralded the end of a generation of U.S. economic dominance, helped their cause by laying bare the limitations of the New Deal order. The country's economic and social policy regime—which relied heavily on the private provision of important social protections, such as pensions and health insurance—may have been adequate for a globally dominant industrial economy that generated 30 years of widely shared growth and stable employment for millions of industrial workers. But in the 1970s, it began to prove thoroughly inadequate for an era of globalization, deindustrialization, and economic dislocation, as displaced workers found themselves unable to rely on the government for economic protection. This, in Hacker and Pierson's parlance, was policy drift on a massive scale.

Ascendant conservatives seized on this state of affairs to argue that the whole New Deal edifice of social protection, financial regulation, progressive taxation, and civil rights should be dismantled rather than reinforced. Beginning with the Carter administration, the expanding business lobby successfully defeated proposal after reform proposal and aggressively promoted an opening round of tax cuts and deregulation—mere down payments on the frenzy to come.

Curing the Disease

If there is a flaw in their telling of this grim tale, it is that Hacker and Pierson perhaps underestimate the actual discontent of the American middle class over the period they discuss. In the 1960s and 1970s, Americans came increasingly to distrust their government, and not without reason. Their leaders had led them into a distant war that proved unwinnable and tore the country apart; a criminally corrupt president was exposed and forced to resign; cities were going up in flames, exposing the deep racial rift that remained in American society despite the triumphs of the civil rights movement. Democrats and Republicans began to diverge on racial issues. The Republicans became the party not only of the wealthy but also of the whites (no Democrat since Johnson has received a majority of the white vote in a presidential election).

Even in the age of Obama, racial inequality remains an acute and intractable problem, and the forces of racial resentment, mingled with legitimate discontent over the government's abandonment of the middle class, infect American politics down to the present day (as the Tea Party movement's more lurid fulminations suggest). So by the late 1970s, dissatisfaction with the state of the government, politics, and policy was rampant across the board, among the wealthy and the middle class alike, and the conditions were ripe for a turn against the political status quo. Conservatives, on behalf of the wealthy, were ready with ideas and organization to seize the moment. Progressives and the middle class were not, and so began the spiral toward the winner-take-all game that Hacker and Pierson describe.

Like many social critics, Hacker and Pierson are long on diagnosis and rather short on treatment. Not surprisingly, they emphasize rebuilding the organizational capacity of the middle and working classes as the place to start repairing the infrastructure of American politics, neither a terribly precise prescription nor a route to a quick cure. But if they are right—and theirs is a compelling case—the task of restoring some sense of proportion and balance to the winner-take-all political economy is essential if the American body politic is to recover from its current diseased condition.

THE OTHER AMERICA

A SCANDAL IN THE MAKING

BY SASHA ABRAMSKY

Fifty years after the social critic Michael Harrington published his ground-breaking book *The Other America*, in which he chronicled the lives lived of those excluded from the Age of Affluence, poverty in America is back with a vengeance. It is made up both of the long-term, chronically poor and the newly impoverished, the victims of a broken economy and a collapsed housing market.

The saga of the timeless poor, of individuals immersed in poverty for decades, of communities mired in poverty for generations, is something of a dog-bites-man story: It's sad, but it's not new. The tale of the newly poor, however, is more akin to the man-bites-dog story: It is surprising and counterintuitive. It is the narrative of millions of Americans who had economic security, enjoyed something of the comforts of an affluent society, and then lost it. Not since the Great Depression have so many millions of people been so thoroughly beaten down by vast, destructive forces. Yet while the story of the more recent poor has more of a sensation factor to it, in reality the stories of the long-term poor and the newly destitute increasingly blend together, creating a common set of experiences that pummel the bodies and minds of those who live them; that corrode communities; and that, all too often, obliterate optimism.

As with the men and women Harrington wrote about in 1962, too frequently these poor Americans are invisible. "Here are the unskilled workers, the migrant farm workers, the aged, the minorities, and all the others who live in the economic underworld of American life," Harrington wrote in his opening chapter. "The other America, the America of poverty, is hidden today in a way that it never was before. Its millions are socially invisible to the rest of us. ... The new poverty is constructed so as to destroy aspiration; it is a system designed to be impervious to hope."[1]

Sasha Abramsky, "Prologue: A Scandal in the Making," *The American Way of Poverty: How the Other Half Still Lives*, pp. 1-13, 331-332. Copyright © 2013 by Perseus Books Group. Reprinted with permission.

Harrington was a Jesuit-educated political activist, born and raised in St. Louis during the years between the world wars. Over several decades he carved out a reputation for himself as a longtime chronicler of the American condition. In the run-up to his book's publication, he had spent years in poor communities as a volunteer with Catholic Worker and as a left-leaning political organizer—hardly the most fruitful of pursuits in the conservative, affluent era following the end of World War II. In fact, *The Other America* hit a raw nerve at least in part because so many Americans, living comfortably in suburbias miles from the epicenters of hardship, thought their country had already solved the poverty conundrum. With many having a mind-set of out of sight, out of mind, poverty simply wasn't a part of the national political discourse in the 1950s. Indeed, the Harvard Kennedy School of Government lecturer and author Richard Parker, in his biography of the progressive economist John Kenneth Galbraith, noted that when the Joint Economic Committee of Congress commissioned University of Wisconsin economist Robert Lamp man to put together "a complete bibliography of postwar books and articles by economists on modern poverty, his typed list required only two pages."[2] That the Gordian knot of poverty hadn't actually been unraveled, and that it could continue to exist alongside the Affluent Society, was a source of tremendous national embarrassment for many. In the wake of *The Other America*'s publication, a critical mass of policy makers doubled down, using Harrington's writings as a Virgil-like guide to America's hidden underbelly and laying the foundations for an all-out assault on the causes and conditions of poverty that would fundamentally impact American social policy for a generation.

Liberal America's belief during the 1960s that with one more great push the scourges associated with poverty could be forever eradicated from America's shores was naïve, possibly even disingenuous. After all, no society in human history has ever successfully banished poverty; and no polity with a modicum of respect for individual liberty has entirely negated the presence of inequality. But it did reflect a confidence in America's innate sense of possibility; in an era of space travel and antibiotics, computers and robots, poverty was just one more frontier to be conquered, one more communal obstacle to be pushed aside. When it turned out to be an order of magnitude more complicated, Americans quickly grew tired of the effort. In 1968, four years after the War on Poverty was launched, Richard Nixon won election to the White House, in part by stoking popular resentment against welfare recipients. Twelve years after that, Ronald Reagan was elected president on a platform of rolling back much of the Great Society. Today, after four decades during which tackling economic hardship took a distant backseat to other priorities, one in six Americans live below the poverty line, their lives as constricted and as difficult as those of the men, women, and children who peopled the pages of *The Other America* in the Kennedy era. And this is despite the fact that the president, Barack Obama, is a onetime community organizer who understands the impact of poverty on people's lives better than almost any other of his predecessors.

Too poor to participate in the consumption rituals that define most Americans' lives, too cash-strapped to go to malls, to visit cafés or movie theaters, to buy food anywhere other than dollar stores, these men and women live on America's edge. The poorest of the poor live under freeway ramps and bridges in out-of-the-way neighborhoods such as the Alphabet district of northern Las Vegas or Los Angeles's Skid Row. Others live in trailer parks far from central cities. Then there are those living in apartment buildings and even suburban houses, who for a variety of reasons have lost their financial security; their deprivation remains hidden behind closed doors. All of these people share an existential loneliness, a sense of being shut out of the most basic rituals of society.

In mid-2011, the Open Society Foundation's Special Fund for Poverty Alleviation gave me a grant to chronicle the faces and voices of economic hardship in America. To do so, I began traveling around the country interviewing and photographing people on the economic margins—Harrington's "economic underworld"—and the environments in which they lived.

As the stories accumulated, three things struck me with particular force.

The first is the sheer loneliness of poverty, the fact that profound economic hardship pushes people to the psychological and physical margins of society—isolated from friends and relatives; shunted into dilapidated trailer parks, shanties, or ghettoized public housing; and removed from banks and stores, transit systems and cultural institutions. The poor live on society's scraps—a few dollars in government assistance or charity, donated food, thrift-store clothes. They can afford neither transport to venture out of their communities nor simple luxuries such as movies or a cup of coffee with friends in a café. They cannot afford to vary the routines of their daily lives. Embarrassed by their poverty, worried about being judged failures in life, and humiliated by that judgment, many told me that they have essentially withdrawn from all but the most necessary, unavoidable social interactions.

The second thing that one realizes in telling this story is the diversity, the complexity, of poverty. Its causes, and therefore its potential solutions, cannot meaningfully be reduced to a pat list of features. There are people with no high school education who are poor, but there are also university graduates on food bank lines. There are people who are poor because they have made bad choices, gotten addicted to drugs, burned bridges with friends and family—and then there are people who have never taken a drug in their lives, who have huge social networks, and who still can't make ends meet. There are people who have never held down a job, and others who hold down multiple, but always low-paying, jobs, frequently for some of the most powerful corporations on earth. There are people who have never had a bank account and use payday loans and other predatory lending sources whenever they need access to extra cash, and there are others who, during more flush times, owned huge suburban houses and expensive cars. There are children whose only hot meals are what they are given at school, and young adults who have nothing now and never really had anything earlier in life either. There are military veterans who have struggled to find a place in civilian life, middle-aged and once-middle-class people falling down the economic ladder as the recession fails to fully lift, and elderly people cascading into destitution as savings evaporate and expected equity in their homes fails to materialize.

Poverty is, in other words, as diverse as the United States itself. What the poor have in common, however, is an increasingly precarious existence in a country seemingly unable—or at least unwilling—to come to grips with their collective despair.

Yet if the lives of America's poor are increasingly desperate, the desire to make something of those lives remains a force to be reckoned with. That leads to the third thing that fascinated me in my travels around the country: the sheer resilience of people who, battered by tough economic times, could be excused for thinking that life never gives them any breaks. Instead, many of the men and women I talked to were doing everything they could to ensure that their futures would look brighter than their pasts. They were going to school, taking job-training classes, looking for any and every source of income, and struggling to make sure that their kids had enough food to eat and little extras to enjoy. It was, in many ways, a humbling, inspiring experience.

Whose Future?

The poverty being stockpiled in the early twenty-first century, at the back end of a forty-year stampede toward ever-greater economic inequality, will leave generational legacies affecting current workers, their children, and as likely as not their children's children. What starts off as a temporary hiccup too often results in a permanent downgrading of family prospects.

How we as a society deal with this challenge will determine what kind of a country we become in the years and decades ahead.

As I detail in the second part of this book, we already have the contours outlined for a credible and fair new social compact. That the first Obama administration didn't focus on poverty to the extent that the issue deserved was, I believe, largely the product of a political calculus. Assuming power in the midst of a financial system meltdown, the new administration had to stabilize a collapsing economy early on; they did so, but in so doing they churned up a roiling, ugly opposition. As a result, by the time the free-fall stopped, they had to swiftly start navigating one of the most treacherous political landscapes in modern history en route to the 2012 election. Now that that election is over, however, in his second term Obama will have to not simply enact technocratic anti-poverty measures but also take the country with him as he explains the moral imperative of a fairer social compact. He will have to employ all of his extraordinary narrative powers to craft a new American story in which tens of millions of citizens feel that they have a stake. If Obama accomplishes this, he will secure for himself a legacy as one of the country's great progressive presidents. If he doesn't, it will be a serious blot on his tenure in the White House.

Were we as a society to implement this new story in affordable and equitable ways, the result would be a fundamental reimagining of the American economic landscape. We can use four major revenue sources: (1) a public works fund to protect against mass unemployment; (2) a new educational opportunity fund to dramatically expand access to, and affordability of, higher education; (3) a poverty-mitigation fund built up from the introduction of a financial transaction tax and energy profit taxes; and (4) money to stabilize Social Security and start reducing the national deficit, made available from higher taxes on capital gains, high-end inheritances, and the income of the most affluent of wage earners. I detail the mechanisms of these in Part Two. If we used these revenue sources, we could change both our expectations of society and our long-term financial calculus in a way beneficial to tens of millions of people.

Too often in recent decades, our political leaders have ignored what's staring them in the face and instead enacted policies that make economic hardship worse for those already on the margins or starting the long slide into destitution. As detailed in this book, they do so because America's political process is increasingly beholden to powerful financial interests, its priorities shaped by what used to be seen as Southern mores: a belief not just in the inevitability of inequality, but in the *desirability* of oligarchy as a social structure, in the usefulness of poverty as a social control mechanism, its reaction to that poverty punitive and unforgiving. Increasingly, it is a democracy in which the voices, and the basic economic needs, of ordinary Americans are drowned out by the noise generated by advocates and lobbyists for the well-heeled and already-influential. It is an economy that, to a large extent, revolves not around the making of things but around the shuffling of money—hence the overblown impact of financial sector, insurance, and real estate instability on the broader economic system. And it is one in which, for the last several decades, ordinary Americans have borrowed against home equity, run up credit card debt, and taken out loans to go to school, all just to survive on a daily basis. Data compiled by the Federal Reserve show that just before the financial crash of 2008, the average American household was spending nearly 19 percent of its disposable income servicing debt.[3]

Increasingly, our leaders either ignore the scale of poverty present in our midst—or, tacking to the Southern winds, they seek to blame or to punish those who fail to economically thrive. For proof of the former, witness the fact that throughout the three televised presidential debates in 2012, the plight of the tens of millions of Americans living below the poverty line was *never* meaningfully addressed, nor were the implications of proposed cuts to Medicaid, food stamps, and other safety net programs properly teased out.

That Obama's first administration was unable to fully break out of this mold after 2008, leaving largely untouched the scourge of poverty and inequality that as an insurgent, grassroots candidate he had talked about tackling, was a source of bemusement to many of his supporters. The election of 2012 gave him a new opportunity to so do, which can only be a source of hope. After all, few political leaders are given the sort of second chance to rewrite their story that Obama was granted by the electorate. Unhappy with the status quo, voters nevertheless reelected him as president. One can argue that they did so, at least in part, in the expectation that his second term would deliver on promises never followed through on in the first four years.

The Miners' Canary

Shake a stick in post–financial collapse America, and one hits poverty. It's everywhere: tent cities in municipal parks, under freeway overpasses, along river walks. Food lines stretching down city blocks. Foreclosure signs dotting suburban landscapes. Overstretched free clinics providing a modicum of healthcare to people no longer insured. Elderly people whose pensions have vanished and whose hopes for a decent old age have evaporated. Unemployed men and women looking for clothes for their kids at thrift stores and food for their families at pantries. Mothers begging for free turkeys from churches so they can at least partially partake in the national ritual of Thanksgiving.

By the end of 2010, according to the U.S. Census Bureau, 15.1 percent of Americans were living below the federally defined poverty line, an increase of approximately fifteen million people since the start of the century. Fully 34.2 percent of single mothers and their children were in poverty, up from 28.5 percent in 2000. Some of the poor lived in traditionally deprived communities; many others lived in the suburbs. In fact, according to Georgetown University's Peter Edelman, in his book *So Rich, So Poor*, in the first decade of the twenty-first century, suburban poverty increased by fully 53 percent.[4] Much of that was due to an extraordinary collapse in the worth of assets owned by middle-class African American and Hispanic families. In 1984, the median value of household asset ownership for African American families was $6,679. By 2009, as the recession destroyed the worth of homes, that number had declined to a mere $4,900—thirty years of asset accumulation vanished. White households, despite suffering during the recession, by contrast still had a median net worth of $92,000.[5]

The disparate impact of the crisis could be measured in soaring regional unemployment numbers and age- and race-specific poverty data. In Imperial County, California, for example, residents were experiencing a collapse on a scale that most of the country didn't witness even at the height of the Great Depression. Nearly one in three workers were unemployed, and for the 68 percent of the working population in the county who had jobs, average income was abysmally low, hovering not far above the poverty line.[6]

In Detroit, more than one-third of the total population was in poverty, and upward of two-thirds of children were in families living below the poverty line.[7] New Orleans fared almost as badly: there, more than four in ten kids were in poverty, and, in the African American community, fully 65 percent of children five and under lived below the poverty line.[8] These numbers were so extraordinary that they made Philadelphia's abysmal data look almost good in comparison: there, a mere one in three children lived at or below the poverty line.[9] In Indiana, nearly one in ten kids lived in "extreme poverty," meaning their family incomes didn't even reach half of the poverty line threshold.[10] In northern St. Louis in 2010, the poverty rate for kids stood at a dispiriting 30 percent.[11]

Not surprisingly, in May 2012, UNICEF reported that of the world's developed countries, the United States had the second highest rate of child poverty, with more than 23 percent of its kids officially poor. Only Romania, still struggling to shed itself of the awful legacy left by Nicolae Ceauşescu's dictatorship, had worse numbers.[12]

We look at the scale of misery unleashed; shake our heads; listen to that inner voice saying sadly, "What a tragedy"; and then, assuming we're fortunate enough not to be poor ourselves, we try to get on with our lives. Yet, if we thought a little harder, we'd realize that what we're witnessing isn't so much a tragedy as a scandal.

It's a subtle difference, but an important one. What turns poverty into a scandal rather than a tragedy is the political landscape out of which it bubbles. "It makes a difference if we treat it as a bug or a feature," argued longtime community organizer and Harvard Kennedy School of Government senior lecturer Marshall Ganz. "Is it a bug in the system for which we provide a safety net, or a *feature* of the system? It's a moral, political, and economic crisis. It's a process of suicide. When countries stratify themselves into a wealthy few and an impoverished many, they go down the tubes."

For Ganz, poverty was akin to the "miners' canary." It was the warning signal of a more general malaise—of school systems in disrepair, healthcare delivery mechanisms that were no longer delivering healthcare to large swaths of the population, a degraded environment, and more. "As long as people think poverty is the problem," Ganz explained, "they're missing the whole point. Poverty is *evidence* of a problem; it's not the source of the problem. They're all based on the weakening of collective institutions—the decline of labor, of common interests. The core question is not about poverty, it's really about democracy. The galloping poverty in the United States is evidence of a retreat from democratic beliefs and practices."

When people go hungry because of, say, drought or a plague of locusts; when thousands die in an epidemic; when natural disasters convert whole countries into wastelands, religious people say these are acts of God—the less religious might say they are acts of nature. But the process of casting around for someone to blame takes a back seat. Tragedy is, somehow, beyond the realm of the deliberate, the product not so much of malign decisions as of confounded bad luck, of happenstance.

By contrast, when poverty flourishes as a direct result of decisions taken, or not taken, by political and economic leaders, and, either tacitly or explicitly, endorsed by large sectors of the voting population, then it acquires the rancid aroma of scandal. It is a corrosive brew, capable of eating away at the underpinnings of democratic life itself.

My aim in writing *The American Way of Poverty* is to shine a light on this travesty; to bring poverty out of the shadows; and, ultimately, to suggest ways for moving toward a fairer, more equitable, and more truly American social compact. For what is caused by human choices can, mostly, be solved by human choices. Tragedies, quite legitimately, tend to generate hand-wringing; scandals, by contrast, ought first and foremost to lead to action.

The American Way of Poverty is a plea for a more morally cogent political approach to poverty, for an acknowledgment of a crisis that existed *before* the 2008 financial collapse and shows every sign of continuing to exist even as the broader economy slowly recovers *from* that collapse. It is more than a technocratic discussion of poverty; rather, it is a portrait of a political system in crisis, of a democracy that has ceased to be able to address the basic needs of a growing proportion of its population.

At the same time, my book also offers a blueprint for change, exploring how a new politics could emerge that prioritizes poverty as a moral challenge, and how once that politics takes root, we could retool our welfare systems; better craft our tax policies; set up new social insurance systems as ambitious as that of Social Security; rethink our strategies on private and public debt; invest more thoroughly in education, housing, healthcare, and other vital parts of the public commons; and set in place wage and pension protections all aimed squarely at providing basic security to the American population.

It is, after all, of little use to identify problems if one doesn't also spend time exploring solutions. The second part of *The American Way of Poverty* details a comprehensive, and creative, set of policies to be rolled out over a period of years, which would not only tackle the consequences of wholesale poverty but would go a long way toward dealing with its underlying causes. I explain how support for such policies can be generated—how many of the organizing methods and outreach used by Barack Obama's campaign team in both 2008 and 2012 lend themselves to just such a mission—and how the rigid anti-government, anti-tax rhetoric popularized by conservatives over the past few decades can over time be successfully neutralized.

Fifty years ago, Michael Harrington warned his readers that unless attention was paid, another journalist decades in the future would end up writing about the exact same conditions that he had chronicled. "After one read these facts, either there are anger and shame, or there are not," he opined. "And, as usual, the fate of the poor hangs upon the decision of the better-off. If this anger and shame are not forthcoming, someone can write a book about the other America a generation from now and it will be the same, or worse." It was, Harrington believed, a moral outrage that in a country as wealthy as America, so many people could be so poor, and so many other people could turn blind eyes to their plight.[13]

Fifty years on, I am chronicling these conditions, as alive today as they were in the early 1960s. For unfortunately, Harrington's prophecy has come true: conditions are again getting worse for a vast number of Americans, yet for millions of others, it is all too easy to downplay, or to simply ignore, these dire straits.

Notes

1. Michael Harrington, *The Other America: Poverty in the United States* (New York: Touchstone, 1997).
2. Richard Parker, *John Kenneth Galbraith: His Life, His Politics, His Economics* (New York: Farrar, Straus and Giroux, 2005), 481.
3. See http://www.federalreserve.gov/releases/housedebt/.

4. Peter Edelman, *So Rich, So Poor: Why It's So Hard to End Poverty in America* (New York: The New Press, 2012), 29.

5. Jeannette Wicks-Lim, "The Great Recession in Black Wealth," Amherst, Massachusetts, Political Economy Research Institute, January 29, 2012.

6. See http://www.kpbs.org/news/2011/aug/22/imperial-valley-unemployment-rate-tops-30-percent/. For a good discussion of Imperial County's economic condition and the prevalence of low-wage employment, see also http://www.rohan.sdsu.edu/~jgerber/docs/Explaining_low_income.pdf.

7. Patricia Lesko, *Huffington Post*, August 22, 2012. Available at http://www.huffingtonpost.com/patricia-lesko/detroit-childhood-poverty_b_129 9269.html.

8. See http://louisianajusticeinstitute.blogspot.com/2011/10/poverty-sky rockets-in-new-orleans-65-of.html. For a more general display of New Orleans's poverty data, see http://www.nationofchange.org/blogs/bill-quigley/katrina-pain-index-2012-7-years-after-1346013999.

9. For a discussion of Philadelphia's child poverty rates, based on U.S. Census Bureau data, see work done by Witnesses to Hunger: http://www.witnessestohunger.org/News-Highlights/News-Highlights/72/vobId__285/.

10. See http://www.in.gov/legislative/igareports/agency/reports/CCP02.pdf.

11. American Community Survey estimates, 2010. Northern St. Louis corresponds to Missouri's Congressional District 1.

12. Peter Adamson, UNICEF, *Measuring Child Poverty*, 2012. Available at http://www.unicef-irc.org/publications/pdf/rc10_eng.pdf.

13. Harrington, *The Other America*, 159.

READING 4

MYTHS AND FACTS ABOUT POVERTY AND WORK

BY WILLIAM QUIGLEY

It's not what we don't know that hurts us,
it's what we know for certain that just ain't so.

—Mark Twain

The very first time I taught my course Law and Poverty, I asked my students midsemester to anonymously suggest a person they'd like to have as a guest speaker. Some students, no doubt intending to challenge my liberal perspective, asked me to invite David Duke, then a Louisiana state representative, to speak about poverty to my class. Duke had just lost a close election to the U.S. Senate in Louisiana, even though he had received hundreds of thousands of votes. I was surprised by the suggestion and frankly did not know how to respond. Since I was a brand new teacher I went to talk it over with Loyola's dean and my friend, Louis Westerfield. Louis was Loyola's first African-American dean and was personally not too thrilled with the idea of a visit to the law school by Duke, but he reminded me that I was in a university and that we needed to be open to controversial ideas and people. I agreed to invite Duke to speak to my class, and he promptly accepted.

Duke was very articulate. As an experienced and able speaker, he spoke at some length about poverty. He spoke about the problems of the welfare underclass, the need for tough love, the need to put welfare recipients to work, the need for drug testing of all welfare recipients, and other issues that had not yet achieved the national acceptance that they would later achieve.

David Duke was great at answering questions, even the challenging ones, with quick and easy responses. He had spoken all over the world hundreds of times and was very comfortable with the give and take of questions about poverty.

Except one.

A student asked, "We've heard what you'll do about the poor who aren't working—you'd put them to work—but what do you propose to do about those who are working but are still poor? Hundreds of thousands of workers in our state aren't on public assistance, but they're so poor that their kids still qualify for subsidized school lunch. What are we to do about those people who are poor?"

For the only time in the nearly one-hour session, Duke was at a loss for words. He stopped, a slight bit flustered, and then uncharacteristically fumbling for a response, he told of his allegiance to the cause of the working poor. Then, he switched gears and launched into a criticism of those who cheated in order to qualify for free or reduced-cost school lunch.

Like Duke, few of us think of people who work when we think about the poor. Yet most of the people in poverty live in homes where someone is working. Few of us consider that for many Americans, work and poverty go hand in hand.

In fact, when I speak to groups I often start by asking people to close their eyes to summon a picture of poverty in the United States. They report common visions.

A homeless person begging for money.

A dark-skinned welfare mother with kids living in inner-city public housing.

A lonely widow in an empty apartment.

Of course, there are poor people like this in America, but these visions are seriously inadequate when it comes to describing the poor in a comprehensive way. Further, if these are the visions of poverty, then the proposed solutions to the poverty they exemplify are also likely to be, and indeed have been, inadequate.

Most of what the general public believes about poverty and work is inaccurate. Common understanding of poverty is built on myths instead of facts. Unfortunately, statements that are not actually true can still be thought of as accurate if they are repeated often enough. Let's take a brief look at some of the most common myths and facts about poverty and work.

Myth #1 Most poor people do not work.

The fact is that most poor people live in families where someone is already working. In 1998, seven out of every ten of the able-bodied *employable poor people worked at least part-time. One of every four worked full-time, year-round.*[1]

Myth #2 There are plenty of jobs out there for those who want to work. Just look at the want ads!

A university study in Washington, D.C., checked the accuracy of this often-heard assertion. Researchers looked at the number of job openings in the *Washington Post* and found there were more than 3,000 jobs advertised. At the same time, there were 36,400 people reported unemployed and another 28,000 adults receiving some sort of public assistance payments. Close examination revealed that most of the jobs advertised required educational or prior employment experience that the poor just did not have. The study concluded that only 354 of the advertised jobs were obtainable by the low-skilled poor, and those were usually filled immediately by job seekers.[2]

The reality of the job market is more like the situation at the city-sponsored job fair in New York City, held at the height of the booming economy in late 1999, where forty companies agreed to accept résumés. Approximately five thousand people showed up, and some waited more than three hours in line to put in a résumé. The line included everyone from welfare mothers to recent college graduates. Many said they had been job hunting for months. As one employment expert said, "There is a huge pool of people with entry-level skills and not enough jobs for them."[3]

Myth #3 Unemployment is at a very low level and few people actually need jobs.

Unemployment is often twice as high as people think, even using official government information. For example, in May 2002, the U.S. Department of Labor (DOL) reported that the unemployment rate was 5.8 percent and 8.4 million people were unemployed. That in itself is a real reason to be concerned—more than 8 million people out of work. But the real number of people in May 2002 who needed work, numbers also reported by the DOL, was actually more than 17 million.

Here is how it works. Every month the DOL releases information on the unemployment rate and the number of people who were unemployed. But this number does not count millions of other people who need work. In the same May 2002 report, in data rarely picked up by the media, the DOL reported an additional 3.8 million persons who were working part-time but wanted to be working full-time, and another 5.4 million people were unemployed and wanted jobs but were classified as no longer actively looking for them. Some were classified as "discouraged" workers, people who wanted to work and were available to work but could not find work and have given up looking for work. Others were unable to seek work because of disability or home responsibilities. Thus, the number of people who are either out of work or not working full-time and who would like to be is around 17.6 million, well more than double the total usually reported by the media. And instead of an unemployment rate of 5.8 percent in May 2002, our nation was really facing an unemployment and underemployment rate of more than 12 percent.[4]

Myth #4 If people would just work, even at minimum wage, they would not be poor.

The fact is that full-time minimum-wage work has not been enough to lift most families over the poverty line in years. With the minimum wage at $5.15 per hour, the full-time minimum-wage worker earns $10,712 per year. That has not been above the poverty level for a family of three since 1990, or for a family of four since 1984. Even when the minimum wage is inevitably raised, full-time minimum-wage work will not likely lift a family out of poverty. For a single parent with two children, the official poverty guideline for the year 2002 was a yearly income of $15,020. For a parent with three children, the yearly income was $18,100. A parent with two children working full-time would have needed to make at least $7.22 per hour, and a parent with three children would have needed to earn $8.70 per hour, to at least earn enough to be over the 2002 official poverty threshold.[5]

Myth #5 Minimum wage is not important because hardly anyone except teenagers earns minimum wage.

Not true. If the minimum wage had been raised in 2001 by $1 an hour, more than 10 million workers, or 8.7 percent of the entire workforce in the United States, would have seen a direct increase in wages and another 9.7 million workers, who earned up to $7.15 an hour, would have also likely seen an increase. Despite the prevailing wisdom that only teenagers and part-time employees work for minimum wages, 68.2 *percent of the workers affected would have been over twenty years old and close to half, 45.3 percent of the workers, would be full-timers. The majority of the affected workers would have been women, 60.6 percent, and African American and Hispanic workers would disproportionately benefit.*[6]

Myth #6 Minimum-wage and other low-wage jobs are important to the community because they give unskilled people training opportunities and experience at wages employers can afford, which in turn allows the workers to improve their skills in order to move into better-paying jobs.

The fact is that more than one out of every four workers in the United States earns low wages—too little an hour to lift a family of four over the official government poverty line. That translates into more than thirty million people in this country who work and earn less than $8.19 an hour. These are not entry-level workers who are moving on up the economic ladder. Sixty-three percent of these folks are over twenty-six years old. One in four has attended college. Certainly there are some who are temporarily in these jobs on their way to higher-skilled, better-paying jobs, but most are not. Low-wage work is a permanent fact of life for millions of workers.[7]

Myth #7 There are really not that many poor people out there.

There were between thirty million and forty million people living below the unrealistically low official poverty line during the last ten years. This means that there are more officially poor people in the United States than all the people who live in El Salvador, Haiti, Honduras, Ireland, New Zealand, and Nicaragua combined.[8] Put another way, the official total American poor represent more than the total combined populations of the states of Alabama, Arkansas, Iowa, Kansas, Kentucky, Maine, Minnesota, Mississippi, Nebraska, North Dakota, Oregon, South Dakota, and Tennessee.[9]

If you add in the numbers of people below 125 percent of the official poverty level, a modest increase that some researchers suggest is a more realistic poverty line, there are between forty-five million and fifty million people living in poverty.[10] That is more than the total combined populations of all the states mentioned above plus the total populations of the states of Delaware, Hawaii, Montana, New Hampshire, New Mexico, Rhode Island, Vermont, West Virginia, and Wyoming—a total of twenty-two states.[11]

Myth #8 Apart from the poor, most people in the United States are doing pretty well.

The fact is that more than one in every four workers in the United States, more than thirty million people, earns poverty-level wages. These people are all adults, and not counted in this number are the millions of children in their families. The Economic Policy Institute calculates "poverty-level wages" as those that would still leave a full-time year-round worker earning less than the official poverty threshold for a family of four. The institute's 1999 calculation found that full-time year-round workers earned poverty-level wages if they made less than $8.19 an hour. In 1999, 26.8 percent of all workers—more than thirty million workers—earned less than that.[12] The effects of these low wages are serious. The U.S. Conference of Mayors identified low-paying jobs as the number one cause of hunger in urban America.[13]

Myth #9 Most poor people are African American or Hispanic.

The fact is that there have always been many more poor white people than poor African-American or Hispanic people. Poverty afflicts a much higher percentage of Hispanic and African Americans than whites, but in actual numbers there are more white poor people.

For example, the 2001 *Statistical Abstract of the United States*, published by the U.S. Census Bureau, reported on the details of poor people in 1999. Of the thirty-two million people below the official poverty line in 1999, approximately twenty-two million were white, eight million were Black, and seven million were Hispanic. Thus, approximately 10 percent of whites were poor compared with 24 percent of Blacks and 23 percent of Hispanics.[14]

You cannot realistically discuss poverty without discussing race and the effects of racism. Unfortunately, the media do a disservice in this area when they repeat and reinforce unconscious racial stereotypes by portraying poverty as primarily a problem for minority Americans. For example, a Yale University study showed that television and print news was much more likely to portray Black people as poor than other racial groups.[15]

There are some clear racial patterns in poverty. The rate of joblessness in many urban minority poor areas in the 1990s was as high as 66 percent.[16] Median incomes of white families are much higher than those of Black, Hispanic, or Native Americans.[17] When looking at savings and retirement, the situation is worse; white families have as much as twenty times the accumulated wealth of Black families.[18]

While among all children one of every five or six lives in a poor family,[19] one of every three African-American and Hispanic children are poor.[20] The infant mortality rate for Black babies in the 1990s was more than two times the rate for white babies.[21]

As with children, the poverty rate for those over age sixty-five is also much higher among minorities. Nationwide one in nine or ten persons over age sixty-five is poor, but one in every four African Americans and one in every five Hispanics over age sixty-five is poor.[22]

Myth #10 Most of the poor are nonworking, middle-aged, panhandling bums.

Even though "can-you-spare-some-change" men may be more visible than others who are poor, they are really a very, very small part of poverty.

Gender and age are important predictors of poverty, but not for middle-aged men. In fact, women are more likely than men to be victims of poverty. Approximately one-third of all female single-parent households live under the poverty line, and these mothers and children accounted for around fourteen million people in poverty in the mid-1990s.[23] The poverty rate for women in the labor force is higher than men.[24] The *Wall Street Journal* reported in 1995 that women in the United States earned 75.9 cents for every dollar earned by men; by 1999 that figure had risen by 1 cent.[25] Women earn substantially less than men, even when comparing women and men with similar educational backgrounds.[26] Child support is of limited help; researchers for the DOL estimate that only just over one-third of all the children of absent fathers receive child support.[27]

Of all people, children bear the highest burden of poverty. One of every five or six children lives in a poor family.[28]

Of those over age sixty-five, one in about every nine or ten are poor.[29] Those over age sixty-five represent the one group where the antipoverty efforts of the twentieth century (primarily Social Security, Medicare, and Medicaid) have really worked. In 1959, 35.2 percent of those over age sixty-five were poor; by 1970 this declined to 25 percent; and by 1998 poverty among those over age sixty-five was down to 11 percent.[30]

Myth #11 Poverty is really just an inner-city problem.

The fact is that wherever there are people, there are poor people. Percentagewise, there is not much difference in the presence of poor people in the country, the suburbs, or the cities. Nationwide in 1998, poor people made up just over 12 percent of all persons in metropolitan areas with populations over fifty thousand, 18 percent of persons living in central cities, and 14 percent of all persons living outside metropolitan areas.[31]

Myth #12 The United States provides more help to poor people than any other country in the world.

The United States ranked twentieth of ninety-six nations in percentage of government expenditures on social security and welfare, behind, among others, the United Kingdom, Italy, Canada, Finland, Norway, the Netherlands, Denmark, Switzerland, and Sweden. Of the ten developed nations in the international Luxembourg Income Study, the United States is the only one without a child allowance. Compared to ten other industrialized nations, the United States has the highest percentage of its population with incomes less than half of the median income level. And, it ranks first in the percentage of poor families with children and second only to the United Kingdom in the percentage of elderly people who are poor.[32]

In a study of fifteen prosperous nations, children in the United States had the highest percentage of poverty, the second lowest standard of living, and the highest gap between rich and poor than any of the nations.[33]

The World Bank reports that the United States ranks behind all other developed nations in how much of its economy it devotes to international development aid to poor countries, one-tenth of 1 percent of our gross national product. Other countries are pretty stingy too, most giving substantially less than 1 percent—Britain 0.23 percent, Germany 0.26 percent, Japan 0.35 percent, France 0.39 percent, the Netherlands 0.79 percent—but the United States is at the bottom.[34]

One of the realities about poverty and work is that poor people rarely have input in the laws that affect them. If laws about prescription drugs are being considered, there are many people involved—the drug makers, the research community, pharmaceutical retail outlets such as drug stores, and health insurance providers. The same is true for most other areas of law; there are built-in lobbies of people who will help push and pull and shape the laws regulating their area. That is not usually true about laws affecting poor people.

Poor people are fairly powerless in the political arena not only because they have insufficient funds to contribute to candidates, but also because voter participation is closely correlated with income. The poorer the person, the less likely he or she is to vote. In a 1996 study of registration and voting behavior between naturalized and native-born Americans, the U.S. Census Bureau found a correlation between income and voter participation:

- 41 percent of those with incomes of less than $9,999 voted
- 49 percent of those with incomes between $10,000 and $14,999 voted
- 53 percent of those with incomes between $15,000 and $24,999 voted
- 56 percent of those with incomes between $25,000 and $34,999 voted
- 62 percent of those with incomes between $35,000 and $49,999 voted
- 69 percent of those with incomes between $50,000 and $74,999 voted
- 76 percent of those with incomes over $75,000 voted[35]

Thus, most of the laws about working and nonworking poor people are formulated by nonpoor people, debated by nonpoor people, and mostly enacted due to lobbying that is not conducted by poor people.

Often these laws are formulated based on the common myths that are described above and are not really in the interest of poor people, but are part of some other political or religious or cultural agenda.

Any realistic discussion of poverty in the United States must look to the facts about who lives in poverty. While numbers and statistics are not everyone's favorite topic of discussion and are as subject to spin and manipulation as any other facts, they are important. The official poverty numbers, as reported by the Census Bureau, change every year. For the latest statistics, check the poverty link at the bureau's web site at www.census.gov. While the precise numbers change each year, there are some general trends which do not change and are reflected in the figures given above.

The facts are important. If our common idea of poverty is flawed, then our proposed solutions are also likely to be, and frequently have been, flawed.

In a very real way our commitment as a nation regarding how we address the problem of poverty comes out of our history. That history, going back to the English poor laws, is a very big part of the unconscious background that has shaped our current poverty-fighting policies. Let's take a brief look at what we can learn from our history of dealing with poverty and poor people.

Notes

1. Lawrence Mishel, Jared Bernstein, and John Schmitt, *The State of Working America, 2000/2001* (Cornell University Press, 2001), 318.

    According to researchers at George Washington University, in the 1990s 5.5 million poor people lived in families where there was at least one full-time, year-round worker; 14.5 million poor people, nearly 60 percent of all the nation's poor, lived in families where someone worked at least part-time; nearly 9.3 million workers were poor; of the working poor, 2 million worked full-time, year-round. Sar A. Levitan, Frank Gallo, and Isaac Shapiro, *Working but Poor: America's Contradiction* (Johns Hopkins University Press, 1993), 15–19, 46.

2. Bradley R. Schiller, *Economics of Poverty and Discrimination*, 7th ed. (Prentice Hall, 1998), 59–60.

3. Amy Waldman, "Long Line in the Bronx, But for Jobs, Not the Yankees," *New York Times*, October 20, 1999.

4. The official employment and unemployment figures are published monthly by the Bureau of Labor Statistics, U.S. Department of Labor, www.bls.gov/schedule/schedule/2003/monthsched.htm. The *Monthly Labor Review* is published by the Bureau of Labor Statistics (BLS) of the U.S. Department of Labor. In the "Notes on Current Labor Statistics," at the beginning of each month's report, the BLS advises that it does not count within its definition of employed or unemployed "discouraged workers, defined as persons who want and are available for a job and who have looked for work sometime in the last 12 months (or since the end of their last job if they held one within the past 12 months) but are not currently looking, because they believe there are no jobs available or there are none for which they could qualify."

    The real numbers of unemployed people are usually reported in full on the web site of the National Jobs for All Coalition, www.njfac.org/jobnews.html.

For more on "discouraged workers" and others outside the labor force who want to work, see Monica D. Castillo, "Persons Outside the Labor Force Who Want a Job," *Monthly Labor Review* 121(7) (July 1998): 34. Castillo reported that in 1997, 4.9 million people fit this category.

5. See official poverty guidelines at the web site of the U.S. Department of Health and Human Services, www.aspe.hhs.gov/poverty/01poverty.htm.

6. Edith Rasell, Jared Bernstein, and Heather Boushey, "Step Up, Not Out: The Case for Raising the Federal Minimum Wage for Workers in Every State," Economic Policy Institute, Issue Brief #149, February 7, 2001, p. 2.

   Other research organizations arrive at similar figures. For more information see the web sites of the Economic Policy Institute, Minimum Wage Facts at a Glance, www.epinet.org/Issueguides/minwage/minwagefacts.html, and Making Wages Work, www.financeprojectinfo.org/mww/minimum.asp #strategies.

7. Mishel, Bernstein, and Schmitt, *State of Working America, 2000/2001*, 325, Table 5.19.

8. In 1995, there were 36.4 million people in poverty in the United States. *Statistical Abstract of the United States, 1997*, 477, Table 741. According to the 1997 *World Almanac*, the populations of the countries mentioned, in millions, are: El Salvador, 5.8; Haiti, 6.7; Honduras, 5.6; Ireland, 3.5; New Zealand, 3.5; Nicaragua, 4.2.

9. In 1995, there were 36.4 million people in poverty in the United States. *Statistical Abstract of the United States, 1997*, 477, Table 741. The populations of the states mentioned, in millions are: Alabama, 4.2; Arkansas, 2.5; Iowa, 2.8; Kansas, 2.5; Kentucky, 3.8; Maine, 1.2; Minnesota, 4.7; Mississippi, 2.7; Nebraska, 1.6; North Dakota, .6; Oregon, 3.2; South Dakota, .7; Tennessee, 5.3. *Statistical Abstract of the United States, 1997*, 28, Table 26.

10. *Statistical Abstract of the United States, 2000*, 475, Table 754. In 1998, more than forty-six million people (17 percent of all people in the United States) lived below 125 percent of the poverty level. The number was as high as fifty-one million—a full 20 percent of the population—in 1993.

11. The additional populations of these states are, in millions: Delaware, .7; Hawaii, 1.1; Montana, .9; New Hampshire, 1.2; New Mexico, 1.7; Rhode Island, .9; Vermont, .6; West Virginia, 1.8; Wyoming, .5. *Statistical Abstract of the United States, 1997*, 28, Table 26.

12. Mishel, Bernstein, and Schmitt, *State of Working America, 2000/2001*, 325, Table 5.19.

13. "Summary: A Status Report on Hunger and Homelessness in American Cities—1998," U.S. Conference of Mayors. Available at www.usmayors.org/uscm/homeless/hhsummary.html.

14. *Statistical Abstract of the United States, 2001*, 441, Table 676.

15. "Study: Media Portrays Poor as Black," Associated Press, August 19, 1997, as cited in Gwendolyn Mink, *Welfare's End* (Cornell University Press, 1998), 161n58.

16. William Julius Wilson, *When Work Disappears: The World of the New Urban Poor* (Knopf, 1996), 66.

17. For example, in 1994, the median income for white families was $39,308; for Black families it was $21,548. *Statistical Abstract of the United States, 1995*, 48, Table 49. For both whites and Blacks, median income fell from 1990 to 1994: for whites it fell from $41,922 to $39,308; for Blacks it fell from $23,550 to $21,548. *Statistical Abstract of the United States, 1995*, 48, Table 49. For Hispanic families, the 1992 median income was $23,912. *Statistical Abstract of the United States, 1995*, 51, Table 53. For American Indians the 1989 median family income was $21,619. *Statistical Abstract of the United States, 1995*, 50, Table 52.

Black men earned less, on average, in 1989 ($14,182) than in 1979 ($14,619), while the average earnings of white men increased (from $20,564 to $21,361), according to data from the U.S. Census Bureau. Lisa Saunders, "Relative Earnings of Black Men to White Men by Region, Industry," *Monthly Labor Review* 118(4) (April 1995): 68.

18. Relative income of African-American households held steady at about 60 percent of white income in the 1980s, but the relative wealth position of most Black families deteriorated. In 1983, the median white family had eleven times the wealth of the median nonwhite family. By 1989, this ratio had grown to twenty. Middle-class Blacks did succeed in narrowing the wealth gap with whites, but most nonwhite families moved even farther behind. More than one in three nonwhite households now have no positive wealth at all, in contrast to one in eight households. Edward N. Wolff, *Top Heavy: A Study of the Increasing Inequality of Wealth in America* (Twentieth Century Fund Press, 1995), 2.

19. *Statistical Abstract of the United States, 2000*, 475, Table 755. Since 1970, the poverty rate among all children in the United States has ranged from a low of 14.9 percent in 1970 to a high of 22 percent in 1993. In 1998, the child poverty rate was 18.3 percent.

20. *Statistical Abstract of the United States, 2000*, 475, Table 755.

    Since 1970, the poverty rate among white children has ranged from a low of 10 percent in 1970 to a high of 17 percent in 1993. In 1998, the poverty rate among white children was 14.4 percent.

    Since 1970, the poverty rate among African-American children has ranged from a low of 36.4 percent in 1998 to a high of 46.3 percent in 1992.

    Since 1970, the poverty rate among Hispanic children has ranged from a low of 27.2 percent in 1978 to a high of 41.1 percent in 1994. In 1998, the rate was 33.6 percent.

21. Robert Pear, "Infant Mortality Rate Drops but Racial Disparity Grows," *New York Times*, July 10, 1995, p. A8.

22. *Statistical Abstract of the United States, 2000*, 476, Table 758. The poverty level for African Americans over age sixty-five was 26.4 percent in 1998 and for Hispanics over age sixty-five 21 percent.

23. Mishel, Bernstein, and Schmitt, *State of Working America, 2000/2001*, 306, Table 5.11, analyzed Census Bureau data and found that the poverty rate among female-headed households in the last year for which data was available was 33.1 percent. See also *Statistical Abstract of the United States, 1997*, 478, Table 742.

24. Jennifer Gardener and Diane Herz, "Working and Poor in 1990," *Monthly Labor Review*, 115(12) (December 1992): 20, note that while the working poor include more men than women, the poverty rate for women in the labor force was higher than that for men. The higher rate for women was largely the result of two factors: women were much more likely to head families on their own, and, on average, women supported their families with lower earnings than did men.

25. Paulette Thomas, "Success at a Huge Personal Cost," *Wall Street Journal*, July 26, 1995, p. B1.

    In 1999, working women earned 76.9 percent of what working men did. Mishel, Bernstein, and Schmitt, *State of Working America, 2000/2001*, 127.

26. *Statistical Abstract of the United States, 2000*, 437, Table 752.

    The gender-pay gap (defined as the ratio of women's to men's median annual earnings for full-time, year-round workers) has closed considerably in the past several decades. Paul Ryscavage, "Gender-Related Shifts in the

Distribution of Wages," *Monthly Labor Review,* 117(7) (July 1994): 3, 6, footnote 15 (citing *Money Income,* B-37, Table B-10).

27. Jonathan R. Veum, "Interrelation of Child Support, Visitation, and Hours of Work," *Monthly Labor Review,* 115(6) (June 1992): 40. The composition of families has changed significantly over the past fifteen to twenty years. Families headed by women grew from 21.1 percent in 1970 to 31.1 percent in 1988. The growth in the number of such families is occurring for two reasons: there has been a large increase in marital separation and divorce, and there has been a rise in the number of unwed mothers. Research shows that young mothers who receive child support payments are more likely to work than nonrecipients and are apt to work longer hours and have higher earnings if their children are visited by their father; young fathers who pay child support are more likely than nonpayers to visit their children.

28. *Statistical Abstract of the United States, 2000,* 475, Table 755. In 1998, the child poverty rate was 18.3 percent.

29. *Statistical Abstract of the United States, 2000,* 476, Table 758. The poverty level of people over age sixty-five was 10.5 percent in 1998.

30. *Social Security Bulletin,* 1995 Annual Statistical Supplement, 163, Table 3E2. In 1995, 10.5 percent of the elderly were poor. *New York Times,* September 27, 1996, p. A11.

    Older Americans are now the chief beneficiaries of federal money, receiving about a third of federal outlays, roughly $13,000 per person over age sixty-five per year. Robert J. Samuelson, *The Good Life and Its Discontents: The American Dream in the Age of Entitlement, 1945–1995* (Times Books, 1995), 143, 161.

31. *2000 Green Book,* U.S. House of Representatives Committee on Ways and Means, 1293, Table H-8.

32. Linda F. Alwitt and Thomas D. Donley, *The Low-Income Consumer: Adjusting the Balance of Exchange* (Sage Publications, 1996), 7.

33. "There have been significant changes in the welfare system, yet a rise in child poverty rates is now a real risk in the US." Jeff Madrick, Economic Scene, *New York Times,* June 13, 2002.

34. This is despite the tremendous widening of the gap between nations. "In 1820, the richest country had only three times as much income per person as the poorest; today, the richest nation has 30 times the income." Jeff Madrick, Economic Scene, *New York Times,* November 1, 2002.

    To illustrate, one American or European consumes as much in food, goods, and services as forty-three Rwandans. John L. Allen Jr., "Make Globalization User-Friendly Is Catholic Plea," *National Catholic Reporter,* July 27, 2001.

    More than one-fifth of the world's population, 1.3 billion people, live on less than a dollar a day. United Nations, *Human Development Report 2000* (Oxford University Press, 2000), 4.

35. Loretta E. Bass and Lynne M. Casper, "Are There Differences in Registration and Voting Behavior Between Naturalized and Native-Born Americans?" U.S. Census Bureau, Population Division Working Paper No. 28, February 1999, Table 1, Reported Voting and Registration among Citizens, by Nativity Status: November 1996. Available at www.census.gov/population/www/ documentation/twps0028/twps0028.html.

In Other Words . . .

The nineteenth century French author and critic, Jean-Baptiste Alphonse Karr, said, in 1849, "The more things change, the more they remain the same" (Chisholm 1911). Unit 7 echoes this sentiment. Abramsky's article ("A Scandal in the Making") chronicles the trend in the American way of life, citing Harrington's (1962) *The Other America*, which described poverty in the United States predating social programs such as the War on Poverty. In fact, Harrington's work is credited with inspiring President Johnson to enact the programs associated with the war on poverty. In his State of the Union Address, in 1964, Johnson declared:

> This administration today, here and now, declares unconditional war on poverty in America. I urge this Congress and all Americans to join with me in that effort. It will not be a short or easy struggle, no single weapon or strategy will suffice, but we shall not rest until that war is won (Johnson, L. B. State of the Union Address, 1964, as cited by PBS.org).

Indeed, the great War on Poverty brought relief to many Americans. Analyzing the ebb and flow of the poverty rate is incredibly complex, and I suggest you read (at the least) a review by Jencks (2015), which outlines some of its successes and failures. But, at the very least, that era gave us some of our most important social programs, such as food stamps, Supplemental Security Income, Medicaid, Section 8 rent subsidies, and Head Start. Unfortunately, other programs fell away; our society hasn't established a good track record in maintaining programs long enough to prove their effectiveness. As one comparison, France claims a long history in supporting national childcare for families that dates to the nineteenth century (Fagnani 2012); their premier childcare system remains unparalleled today.

We again find ourselves at the head of the pack in inequality; the gap between the rich and poor continues to widen. Marked gains of the wealthy have escalated since the economic "trickle down" policies of the Reagan era (Stone, Trisi, Sherman, and Horton 2016). Why? Of course, the answer is neither singular nor simple, but national polices heavily influence the trend.

Why don't we do something? Almost everyone—even fiscal conservatives and the wealthy elite—typically say they support a fairer distribution of resources. A great problem lies in misinformation, myths, and lackadaisical efforts to find answers. And ideologies die hard. McNamee and Miller (2013) point out that Americans widely believe that success comes with individual talent and effort, despite hundreds of studies to the contrary. As Fitz (2015) reports, George Carlin once joked that "the reason they call it the American Dream is because you have to be asleep to believe it."

The Big Idea

Policies matter. With political will, we can turn the train around.

So What?

Are we stumbling over our own individualism? As Martin Niemoller famously declared:

First they came for the Socialists, and I did not speak out because I was not a Socialist.

Then they came for the Trade Unionists, and I did not speak out because I was not a Trade Unionist.

Then they came for the Jews, and I did not speak out because I was not a Jew.

Then they came for me—and there was no one left to speak for me. (Mayer 1966).

Works Cited

Chisholm, H. (ed.) (1911). Karr, Jean Baptiste Alphonse. *Encyclopedia Britannica* (11th ed.). Cambridge, UK: Cambridge University Press.

Fagnani, J. (2012). "Childcare policies in France: The influence of organizational changes in the workplace." In Kamerman, S., Phipps, S., and Ben-Arieh, A. (eds.) *From child welfare to child well-being: An international perspective on knowledge in the service of policy making.* 2010 ed., 385–402. New York: Springer.

Fitz, N. (2015, March 31). "Economic inequality: It's far worse than you think." *Scientific American.* Retrieved October 10, 2016, from https://www.scientificamerican.com/article/economic-inequality-it-s-far-worse-than-you-think/

Harrington, M. (1962). *The other America: Poverty in the United States.* New York, NY: Macmillan.

Jancks, C. (2015, April 2). "The war on poverty: Was it lost?" *The New York Review of Books.* Retrieved October 10, 2016, from http://www.nybooks.com/articles/2015/04/02/war-poverty-was-it-lost/

Mayer, M. (1966). *They thought they were free: The Germans, 1933–45.* 2nd revised edition. Chicago, IL: University of Chicago Press.

McNamee, S., and Miller, R. Jr. (2013). *The Meritocracy Myth.* 3rd ed. New York, NY: Rowman & Littlefield Publishers.

PBS.org. (2016). Primary resources: State of the Union Address, 1964. *American Experience.* Retrieved October 10, 2016, from http://www.pbs.org/wgbh/americanexperience/features/primary-resources/lbj-union64/

Stone, S., Trisi, D., Sherman, A., and Horton, E. (2016, September 30). "A guide to statistics on historical trends in income inequality." Center on Budget and Policy Priorities. Retrieved October 10, 2016, from http://www.cbpp.org/research/poverty-and-inequality/a-guide-to-statistics-on-historical-trends-in-income-inequality

UNIT 8 READINGS

Mixing It Up

Everyday Moments

The Personal and the Political

Unit 8: Power of the People

Dr. Sue to You: When librarians march . . .

I love to watch people, and I love photos of people. During the protests of 2011 (associated with Occupy Wall Street and other economic issues) I started collecting protest photos. I have thousands of them. I'm particularly attracted to faces and the signs they carry (whether literal or implied through expression), and one struck me as especially salient for this unit. It pictures a face in the crowd, an unremarkable brown-haired woman in navy blue, with black-rimmed glasses, holding a sign with very neatly lettered words that read: "You know things are messed up when librarians start marching" (Bodylit 2011). Indeed, the Great Recession of 2008 hit millions and millions of Americans (spreading to global markets), and many citizens started fighting back (even librarians!), questioning the shadow banking system (Grusky, Western, and Wilmer 2011) and its lack of regulation.

In this final unit, I hope you find some positive messages. Sometimes that seems difficult. Sociology tends to look at problems because we see ourselves as problem-solvers—or at least the discoverers and un-coverers of root problems. How else do we adjust, correct, reconstruct, as a society? We ARE a great nation, with a pioneering, can-do spirit. So in this unit, we look at just a few ways in which everyday moments become sites of resistance, and how issues become social movements.

In the first reading, "Tangled Up in Green," we return to a cultural criminology lens (recall we employed that theory in Section II). Jeff Ferrell introduces us to the question, when do harms become criminal? And who are the power mongers who define it? Perhaps even more important, how do we all participate in the consumer culture that defines the very future of our planet? Suddenly, we find ourselves amid "[r]uined rural landscapes, fake plastic trees and gas-powered leaf blowers, middle-class lawns made a deeper shade of green by overdoses of water and fertilizer, sedentary children driven to and from schools three blocks away … " (Ferrell 360). The environmental movement in the United States has grown in breadth and number since the late 1940s (PBS 1989), but it recently has taken a hit. In 1991, 78 percent of Americans identified as environmentalists; in 2016, that number was down to 42 percent (Gallop 2016). The backlash seems to reflect heated debates based on corporate interests, and spotted resistance among certain populations, especially working-class white Americans (McCright and Dunlap 2011).

Just as Ferrell points to widespread consequences, so too does Ballinger ("How Civil Society Can Help"). Ballinger outlines the human fallout when global supply chains became a common response to labor costs in capitalist markets. The reading estimates the astronomical number of workers in forced labor (more than ten million), with Asia and the Pacific region bearing the brunt of this growing trend. Yet, we seldom hear the term "forced labor," much of which involves children. In this reading, the author recommends several steps to alleviate such "work without consent," including global regulation through the World Bank and leadership from rich countries.

The final two readings revisit the personal/political consanguinity, which we talked about in Unit 6—the intertwining of individual experiences and political issues. In "A mixed race memoir: The personal is political," Sherry Lee Quan poignantly reveals how becoming vulnerable can be a courageous act of resistance. It gives me shivers every time I read it. Finally, "The Family History Project" challenges us to get personal ourselves, to delve into our own family background to discover and uncover "doings" that may foster a deep understanding of "cultural differences, civic ideals and practices, power and privilege, development and identity" (McCrary 2008, 167).

And so, that brings us full circle. We started with identity, and we end with, I hope, a much deeper understanding and appreciation of our differences, our sameness, our shared culture. And just like that, you have become a budding sociologist!

DSTY TIPS: Think about some basic sociological principles as you study this unit's material. Here are three. Can you think of ways to apply them?

- *Unintended consequences*: popularized by sociologist Robert Merton, who emphasized that purposive social action may also result in unexpected results. Intervention into a complex social system can have unintended consequences (Merton 1936).
- *The Thomas Theorem*: Whatever situations are perceived as real, are real in their consequences; the social construction of reality (Thomas and Thomas 1928).
- *The Matthew Effect*: Coined by Merton in 1968, the Matthew Effect refers to cumulative advantage, or unearned credit, that accrues by matter of inheritance or position (Merton 1995).

Works Cited

Bodylit.com. (2011, October 8). "Can you read my sign?" Retrieved October 10, 2010, from https://bodylit.com/tag/march/

Gallup. (2016, April 22). "Americans' identification as 'environmentalists' down to 42%." Social Issues. Retrieved October 10, 2016, from http://www.gallup.com/poll/190916/americans-identification-environmentalists-down.aspx

Grusky, D. B., Western, B., and Wimer, C. (2011). *The great recession*. New York, NY: Russell Sage Foundation.

Merton, R. K. (1936). "The unanticipated consequences of purposive social action." *American Sociological Review* 1, 894–904).

Merton, R. K. (1995). "The Thomas Theorem and The Matthew Effect." *Social Forces* 74, 379–424.

McCrary, N. E. (2008). "The family history project: Uncovering the personal as political." In J. D. Alexander and K. Thompson (eds.), *A contemporary introduction to sociology: Culture and society in transition*, 3–28). Boulder, CO: Paradigm Publishers.

McCright, A. M., and Dunlap, R. E. (2001). "Cool dudes: The denial of climate change." *Global Environmental Change*, 21, 1163–1172).

PBS.org. (1990, April 22). *Timeline: The modern environmental movement*. Retrieved October 10, 2016, from http://www.pbs.org/wgbh/americanexperience/features/timeline/earthdays/1/

Thomas, W. I., and Thomas, D. S. (1928). *The child in America: Behavior problems and programs*. New York, NY: Knopf.

MIXING IT UP

TANGLED UP IN GREEN
Cultural Criminology and Green Criminology

BY JEFF FERRELL

The past two decades have seen the development of two new types of criminological analysis: green criminology and cultural criminology. Both remain emergent perspectives, still in the process of sharpening their theoretical and substantive focus—though in the case of cultural criminology at least, this inchoate state is itself valued for its anarchic and inclusionary dynamics, for keeping cultural criminology "a loose federation of outlaw intellectual critiques" (Ferrell 2007: 99). Even in this emergent stage, though, particular orientations can be indentified—orientations that create some potentially fertile ground for the intertwined growth of green criminology and cultural criminology. By the nature of their subject matter, both green criminology and cultural criminology push against the conventional boundaries of criminology, and so tend to upset the definitional and epistemic order of the discipline. Likewise, both are open to exploring a range of social harms and social consequences, whether these harms are conventionally defined as "criminal," currently left outside the orbit of law and criminality, or even themselves propagated by the criminalization process. At their best, both link their overt substantive concern—environmental harm in the case of green criminology, meaning and representation in the case of cultural criminology—with broader issues of power and inequality. And certainly both attempt to situate their subject matter historically, both in terms of its long-range development and its current residency within the crisis of late modernity and late capitalism.

This potential for a convergence of green criminology and cultural criminology has already been anticipated with, for example, South's (1998) invocation of a green cultural politics, Brisman's (2010) work on the criminalization of pro-environmental activities and activism, and White's (2002) linking of environmental harm to the political economy of capitalist consumption. As these works on criminalization, activism, and consumption suggest, cultural criminology is an orientation attuned to the various intersections of crime, crime control, and cultural dynamics. In particular, cultural criminology attempts to theorize the ongoing interplay of popular culture, subcultures, crime, and crime control in everyday life. In this context, cultural criminology argues that both crime and crime control operate as cultural processes—processes whose consequences emerge from contested symbolism and collective interpretation. An analysis of "crime" or "criminal justice," then, necessitates also an analysis of mediated anti-crime campaigns, alternative notions of justice circulating within subcultures and social movements, public displays of law and policing, and the cultural conventions of everyday life. Of particular importance for the convergence of cultural criminology and green criminology, this approach explores seemingly "objective" or "taken-for-granted" phenomena—public concerns over crime, the amount of damage done by one sort of crime or another, the characteristics of "criminals" or "nature" or "society"—as cultural and political constructions. Refusing to accept the objective reality of law and crime, cultural criminologists investigate the ways in which political institutions determine which acts are to remain legal or illegal; media institutions portray (or ignore) particular acts in such a way as to spawn more or less fear of them; and law enforcement agencies negotiate social situations in ways that determine rates of arrest, incarceration, and conviction, and thus the ongoing identities of those labeled criminal. From this view, cultural dynamics construct the reality of crime, crafting its meaning and consequences, and charging crime and crime control with the energy of power, conflict, and resistance.

In this way, cultural criminology casts a particularly critical eye toward official explanations of crime and crime control, and toward popularly accepted narratives regarding crime and criminals. Likewise, cultural criminologists question academic or governmental accounts that reduce the various experiences of criminality and criminal victimization to statistical summaries. Such accounts, they argue, rest on a series of questionable epistemic and methodological assumptions, and in any case, miss the situated meaning and emotion, the mix of pleasure, pain, and outrage, that animates crime and crime control. In all of this, cultural criminology, like green criminology, also seeks to attune criminology to the particular structures, processes, and problems of the late modern/late capitalist world. As White's (2002) work argues, for example, the global reach of contemporary consumerism necessitates not only a broad analysis of "culture and crime," but a focused examination of consumer culture as a locus of criminality and social harm. Similarly, Brisman's (2010) work suggests that the global degradation of work and the dislocation of global populations, coupled with the emergence of a punitive, neoliberal state, point to the necessity of exploring new forms of late modern political activism, and new forms of punishment and political repression as well. Of equal significance for cultural criminologists, the incursion of multiple media forms into everyday life—indeed, the saturation of everyday life by media technology, advertising images, and manufactured political discourse—means that any contemporary criminology must account for an ongoing process in which criminal events, their mediated images, and public perceptions of crime spiral around and amplify one another. If "real" is taken to mean real effects and real consequences, then the cultural construction of crime and crime control is now as real as crime and policing itself—to the extent that the two remain distinguishable at all (Ferrell 1999; Ferrell, Hayward and Young 2008; Ferrell and Sanders 1995).

Across this range of concerns, cultural criminology can be seen to share with green criminology a deeper agenda as well: the revitalization of the criminological imagination. Following from C. Wright Mills's (1959) classic conceptualization of the sociological imagination, cultural criminologist Jock Young (2011: 2, 5) has recently called for the return of "the criminological imagination," noting that "for Mills, the key nature of the sociological imagination was to situate human biography in history and in social structure," and arguing that, "surely, in a late modern world of heightened insecurities and competing fundamentalisms, the necessity for a sociological imagination becomes that much greater" if we are to "connect together personal troubles in various parts of the world with collective issues across the globe, to make the personal political." At the same time, green criminologist Rob White (2003: 483–4), writing on "environmental issues and the criminological imagination," has noted that green criminology "demands more than simply talking about the environment in general and what needs to be done to protect or preserve it"—instead, it requires "an appreciation of how harm is socially and historically constructed [and] understanding and interpreting the structure of a globalized world; the direction(s) in which this world is heading; and how diverse groups' experiences are shaped by wider social, political and economic processes." For both cultural and green criminologists, then, the criminological imagination means situating the personal in the social and the historical, and the local in the global—but equally, it means an imaginative reconsideration of criminology's contemporary subject matter and modes of analysis. With each new historical period, with each shift in the social composition of everyday life and the cultural construction of crime, the criminological imagination must itself be re-imagined if criminologists are to regain the "capacity for astonishment" (Mills 1959: 8). As emergent perspectives, green criminology and cultural criminology seem well-positioned to assist in reviving this criminological imagination, and in restoring the criminological capacity for astonishment, analysis, and critique.

Consumer culture as ecological harm

Green criminologies of capitalism and its complicity in environmental harm have followed a number of analytic paths, each critically important to locating cases of environmental destruction within the exploitative dynamics of contemporary economic arrangements. Some research, for example, addresses corporate pollution and the pervasive corporate violation of health and environmental regulations (for example Shuqin 2010). Other research explores the increasing commodification of nature—from farm animals to genetically modified seed stock—and the concomitant privatization of essential natural resources like water (for example Brisman and South in press; South 2007; White 2002, 2003). Still other research attempts to expose the dynamics of corporate "greenwashing" campaigns, whereby dangerous corporate practices are recast as environmentally beneficial or genuine pro-environmental activism is co-opted in the service of corporate profit and legitimation. In each of these arenas, green criminology's task is to connect particular corporate practices and their representations—profit-taking, privatization, unregulated manufacturing processes—to the particular environmental harms that are their consequence.

While these are indisputably essential areas for green criminological inquiry, a cultural criminological perspective can perhaps contribute a different frame for approaching them. This analytic framework begins with the understanding that contemporary capitalism—globalized "late capitalism"—operates as an essentially *cultural* enterprise, one "whose economic and political viability, and its crimes and transgressions, rest precisely on its cultural accomplishments" (Ferrell 2007: 92–3; see Ferrell, Hayward and Young 2008). This later form of capitalism manufactures physical products less than it manufactures and markets the meanings of these products and the images of their appropriate use; in this process, the advertising industry operates not as an adjunct to capitalist dynamics, but as capitalism's essential motor force. Moreover, advertising itself is designed not to address existing needs but to create new ones, then to be filled, allegedly, by the advertised product. This ongoing creation of meaning, need, anxiety, and status insecurity produces a predictable consumer insatiability, and with it elastic markets potentially expandable with each new advertising campaign. Widening markets further still is the planned obsolescence of contemporary consumer goods; importantly, this obsolescence is accomplished not only by building in technical limitations, but by creating ever more rapid cycles of fashion trends and product "improvements," such that yesterday's purchase is certain to be out of style or out of date come tomorrow. "Planned obsolescence of desirability"—Vance Packard (1960: 71) memorably refer to this cultural process the ability "to wear the product out in the owner's mind." Within this late capitalist universe, a phenomenon that Thorstein Veblen (1953 [1899]: 61, 64, 70) first identified amidst an emerging "leisure class" a century ago now comes to pervade everyday life as a general "norm of reputability for the community": consumption as status acquisition. Here, consumption takes on a "ceremonial character," becomes "honorific," more a matter of displaying and confirming one's status than of addressing an innate need for, say, shelter or warmth. With this "conspicuous consumption," as Veblen called it, consumer items come to be purchased and displayed for the status that they carry and communicate—and so, once this status evaporates, so does their social and cultural worth.

As a result of these processes, late capitalism promotes both consumption and, more to the point, a pervasive *culture of consumption*—an increasingly globalized consumerist way of life defined by advertised meaning, constructed need, cycled fashion, and conspicuously acquired status. This consumer culture can usefully be investigated for the social harms it produces—for the syndromes of personal and bodily insecurity, ontological vacancy, and financial indebtedness it spawns. But it can also be investigated for its environmental harms, in two primary dimensions. First, as a carefully orchestrated constellation of meanings and perceptions, this late capitalist consumer culture serves to mask the environmental abuses (and labor abuses) that underpin the manufacture of its products. With the globalized divorcing of production from consumption, and the wall of corporate advertising that is erected between the two, widespread corporate pollution and degradation of natural resources are made all but invisible to privileged consumers. Inside the swirl of first-world status associated with Nikes or iPhones or DeBeers diamonds, the conditions of their third-world production are rendered all but unimaginable (see Redmon 2005). In this sense, consumer culture itself operates as the ongoing, everyday machinery of corporate greenwashing. On occasion focused corporate greenwashing campaigns may be needed to finesse particular environmental abuses that come to light—but in general, the pervasiveness of corporate advertising and the consumer culture it engenders is such that no such campaigns are needed. In such a cultural climate, the greenwash is ongoing; ecological harm remains, in Jenkins's (1999) terms, "unconstructed." Every advertisement hides its own ecological crisis—and taken collectively, the ongoing saturation of everyday life by corporate advertising ensures that, for consumers, the environmental harms endemic to consumer products exist as vague abstractions, if they exist in the minds of consumers at all.

A second environmental harm is the consumer waste that this system produces—waste as pervasive as it is predictable. The endless, advertised construction of new needs and insatiable insecurities not only promotes the (over) consumption of whatever products are presently being marketed as their resolution, but the discarding of products accumulated by the consumer once those products come to be reconstructed as inadequate in the next round of marketing. The planned obsolescence built into poorly made goods, and promoted by carefully engineered fashion cycles, likewise spawns a throw-away culture of ongoing dissatisfaction and disposal. The microwave oven imported from China might be repaired, but where, and by whom, and likely at a cost greater than that of a newly imported one; the tear in last year's Italian dress pants might be sewn, but why bother, when the pants are already out of style anyway? And if, as Veblen suggested, an item is purchased in the first place primarily for the status it can confer—for the sheen of its newness and the cultural desirability of its design—then the exhaustion of the item's status leaves it culturally worthless, and so disposable, no matter its remaining physical utility. Indeed, Veblen (1953 [1899]: 71, 77) contended that waste is inherent in the process of conspicuous consumption; the "element of waste," the "waste of goods," he argued, is the key to "demonstrating the possession of wealth" to others:

> Throughout the entire evolution of conspicuous expenditure, whether of goods or of services or human life, runs the obvious implication that in order to effectually mend the consumer's good fame it must be an expenditure of superfluities. In order to be reputable it must be wasteful. No merit would accrue from the consumption of the bare necessities of life, except by comparison with the abjectly poor who fall short even of the subsistence minimum; and no standard of expenditure could result from such a comparison, except the most prosaic and unattractive level of decency.

Waste is at the heart of consumer culture, and triply so; conspicuous consumption builds from the wasteful over-exploitation of natural resources, promotes the wasteful over-consumption of manufactured items beyond basic human need, and then spawns these items' widespread disposal, sooner than later, as social waste (see Varul 2006; White 2002). The designer coat, bought not for its warmth but for its fashionable status, will not be kept for its warmth, either; it will be wasted once its value as a status symbol wears thin.

Here the criminological imagination offers insights into otherwise inexplicable individual behaviors, and into the deep roots of consumerism's ecological crisis as well. The consumer's willingness to purchase a product with origins in human and environmental destruction—and thus to partake in that destruction by way of the product—may well reflect the sort of mindset that emerges amidst the shallow, self-centered satisfactions of consumer culture; but it as much so reflects the power of that culture, and the advertising that animates it, to successfully mask such destruction behind ideologies of status, style, and convenience. Likewise, the consumer's decision then to dispose of that product wastefully, unnecessarily, with no regard to its remaining utility for the consumer or others in need, may well reflect the hurried, insatiable, and status-driven nature of consumerist identity; but this decision also echoes and exists within the larger patterns of waste that are built into a consumerist society. No matter how calloused the consumer, the ecological crisis of late capitalism does not begin with her poor choices; it begins amidst a globalized system of production and distribution, and inside the cultural dynamics and consumerist ideologies that structure these choices, and the system itself.

The material consequences of this system are mountainous. Across the globe, in developed and developing societies, the removal and disposal of waste present intractable problems, and result in engorged landfills, sprawling illegal dump sites, and the consequent pollution of land and water. The problems of consumer waste reinforce and reproduce other social problems as well, producing particularly virulent forms of environmental racism and ecological injustice—ranging from the disproportionate disposal of consumer waste in impoverished pockets of American cities to the illegal transport of Northern Italian waste to southern Italy. These patterns cut across global capitalism as well with, for example, the shipping of U.S. and European electronic consumer waste to China and West Africa, there to be "reclaimed" through open-air burning and other environmentally destructive practices, and the illegal shipping of discarded automotive batteries from the U.S. to Mexico, where the poorly regulated extraction of lead from them exposes both workers and residents to soaring levels of toxicity and those aboard (Gibbs et al. 2010; Pellow 2004; Rosenthal 2011; South 2010; Takemura 2010). The particular content of the trash that accumulates within consumerist economies, that fills these sprawling landfills and spreads out across global dump sites, confirms the profligate wastefulness of contemporary consumerism. Within consumer culture, "trash" is conventionally associated with filth, decay, and dysfunction—in no small part because such association serves, once again, to push the consumer back towards the new and the immediately marketable. But as my ongoing research has shown, a large proportion of everyday consumer waste is neither decayed nor dysfunctional. Instead, it is made up of commodity packaging, like-new clothing, functional appliances—even many purchased items that retain their wrappers, having never been worn nor used (Ferrell 2006; http://empireof-scrounge.blogspot.com/). In what is now a decade of daily trash picking and trash sorting—a decade dedicated to an ongoing archeology of consumer waste—I have consistently found that waste to be defined less by its physical deterioration than by its cultural contamination.

In formulating his theory of conspicuous consumption among the leisure class, Veblen (1953 [1899]) anticipated—in a sense, predicted—what would become this particular form of wastefulness within a larger late capitalist consumer economy. In his analysis of clothing and fashion, for example, he argued that:

> No one finds difficulty in assenting to the commonplace that the greater part of the expenditure incurred by all classes for apparel is incurred for the sake of a respectable appearance rather than for the protection of the person [...] And the commercial value of the goods used for clothing in any modern community is made up to a much larger extent of the fashionableness, the reputability of the goods than of the mechanical service which they render in clothing the person of the wearer [...] That the alleged beauty, or "loveliness," of the styles in vogue at any given time is transient and spurious only is attested by the fact that none of the many shifting fashions will bear the test of time.

(Veblen 1953 [1899]: 119, 125)

Failing to bear the test of time, their fashionableness made obsolete by the next cycle of marketing and consumption, wearable clothes as a result accumulate in trash bins and curbside trash piles. Not surprisingly, given that women remain the primary target of the fashion industry, women's clothes in particular are discarded; in fact, they constitute the single most common type of discarded consumer goods that I have collected and documented over the past decade. Notably, these and other trashed clothes are often found with their price tags still attached; never worn, purchased perhaps as part of an "impulse buy" whose impulsivity was in reality an orchestrated consequence of consumer culture, their fashionableness having over time worn out even if they have not. In this sense, the "ecocidal tendencies" (South 2010: 228) of the fashion industry are not confined to wildlife trafficking and the fur and leather trades; such tendencies are put into play with every change in the height of hem lines, the width of lapels, or the soles of sports shoes.

Likewise, Brisman (2010; Brisman and South in press), Croall (2007, this volume), South (2007), White (2002, 2003), and other green criminologists have highlighted the pervasive corporate privatization and commodification of water, as well as animals, plants, seeds, and the food that comes from them. As they have shown, such privatization and commodification spawn social harms ranging from animal abuse, food adulteration, and deprivation of essential human resources to the destruction of local knowledge and local economic sustainability. This commodification has consequences for waste as well, and for its content. The commodity chains through which global capitalism manufactures and moves these products mean that they arrive at their destinations not in their "natural" state, but encased in cardboard, bubble wrap and plastic—all to be discarded upon arrival. Water as a bottled commodity embodies, among other social harms, a wasted bottle. A sandwich as corporate product—enclosed in its cardboard and plastic shell, lined up alongside a hundred others at an airport food shop or motorway convenience store—differs from a homemade sandwich not only in flavor and freshness, but in the amount of attendant packaging waste. Commodified food itself is also more likely to be wasted: manufactured and shipped in large quantities, bought in mass by retailers, it is disposed of en masse as a result of expiration dates or overstocking. To the many "food crimes" that Croall (2007, this volume) documents, then, can be added another one: the foundational crime of food commodification itself, and with it the inevitable waste of food and packaging alike.

As a whole, contemporary consumer culture produces any number of social harms—insecurity, insatiability, inequality—but certainly central among them is a "constant and escalating pressure on the world's nonrenewable resources," and with this "a huge waste of existing human and natural resources and potentials" (White 2002: 88). This advertising-driven culture of consumption serves both to mask initial environmental harms of extraction, exploitation and commodity production, and to ensure the subsequent and ongoing environmental harms of waste and misuse. Significantly, the pervasively wasteful logic of this system is such that it is more than capable of engulfing any alternatives that do not confront it directly—even green alternatives. Green shopping is, after all, still shopping, and even within a "greener" system of consumption, green products must still be marketed, packaged, sold, and sold again (Brisman 2009). As regards this commodifying dynamic, perhaps one item is most revealing—an item that my research has turned up time and again, regularly thrown away in trash bins and trash piles: the stylishly reusable shopping bag. As these widely discarded reusable bags suggest, the "greening" of consumer culture seems a self-defeating project, a small green life preserver tossed into a torrent of advertising, planned obsolescence, and waste. Instead, for green criminologists and cultural criminologists alike, subcultures and social movements that promote fundamental ecological alternatives can productively be explored—and with them, emergent issues of crime, policing, and social control.

Everyday ecological resistance and everyday criminalization

My decade of investigating consumer waste has not been undertaken in isolation; it has been part of my ongoing research into, and participation with, the various contemporary subcultures of trash picking, urban scrounging, and as it is called in the U.S., "dumpster diving." Trash picking is pervasive in the U.S.; the title of my book on the subject, *Empire of Scrounge* (Ferrell 2006), was meant to reflect the widespread and varied nature of this subterranean world. Daily, homeless individuals and groups scrounge trash piles and trash containers for discarded clothing, shoes, backpacks, and food; many of them also search for aluminum cans, to be sold for small amounts of cash at urban recycling centers (Botha 2004; Brisman 2010; Pritchett 2009). Others, impoverished but not homeless, drive old pickups trucks or ride rebuilt bicycles around urban and rural areas, searching for copper, brass, and other metals that can be extracted from discarded appliances and machinery, and sold for a bit more cash. Among the working poor, parents mine trash piles and trash containers as repositories of building materials for home repair or school clothes for their children. Freegans and like-minded young punks gather, cook, and eat discarded food in an attempt to withdraw from the harms of consumer capitalism—to "act as a living challenge to waste and over-consumption" (http://freegan. info/what-is-a-freegan/freegan-philosophy/). The group Food Not Bombs likewise mixes social movement activism with on-the-street action, gleaning discarded food so as to cook and serve meals to the homeless across the United States (Butler and McHenry 2000; Clark 2004).

While my participatory research focus has out of necessity been within the U.S., these subcultures and social movements are hardly confined to the United States. In fact, with the globalization of capitalism and the ongoing financial and ecological crises that have accompanied it, subcultures of scrounging and trash picking are flourishing worldwide (see Brisman 2010). As already noted, electronic waste and other consumer trash from the United States and Europe are regularly shipped to Asia and Africa (see Gibbs et al. 2010), where communities of scavengers engage in the dangerous work of reclaiming metals and other materials. In India's major cities, a complex "urban informal economy" revolves around the scavenging and recycling of scrap materials ranging from Pepsi cups to jerrycans (Gill 2010). In Buenos Aires, Argentina, the economic crisis of the past two decades has spawned tens of thousands of *cartoneros*; making at best a meager living from salvaging cardboard and other waste materials, they have nonetheless formed cooperatives and schools, and staged Somos Todos Cartoneros festivals (Ferrell 2006: 15, 170). Outside Rio de Janeiro, Brazil, Jardim Gramacho—one of the world's largest and busiest landfills—hosts a community of catadores, trash pickers who first squatted the landfill during the economic crisis of the 1970s and 1980s and later organized for improved labor and health conditions (Walker, Jardim and Harley 2010). Notably, their subsistence as trash pickers may now be lost to the sheer volume of consumer trash itself; with liquid waste from the towering landfill leaking into the nearby bay, authorities are working to close Jardim Gramacho.

Trash pickers and activists in the United States, then, can be understood as participants in an eclectic, wide-ranging global phenomenon that intertwines alternative economic arrangements, environmental activism, and desperate day-to-day survival. Like their counterparts in China, Brazil and Argentina—and as much so in Viet Nam, Mexico, and Malaysia—they constitute a vast, informal army of everyday environmentalists, unsalaried and uninsured, working the trash heaps of consumer capitalism, salvaging countless tons from the landfills, feeding the hungry and clothing the homeless, and in the process, producing for local governments significant savings in trash disposal and social service costs. For this they are rewarded, increasingly, with criminalization. Across the United States, cities now ban public trash picking, outlaw the possession of the shopping carts utilized by homeless scroungers outside the premises of a business, aggressively enforce ordinances banning accumulations of scrap materials, meticulously regulate the materials that scrap yards can accept, threaten to seize vehicles utilized in illegal scrounging, and deploy police "scavenger patrols" to search for recalcitrant trash pickers (Brisman 2010: 171; Ferrell 2006: 178–83; Ferrell 2011). For its efforts to feed scrounged food to the homeless, city and police officials require that Food Not Bombs obtain permits and then deny their requests for those permits, arrest Food Not Bombs servers en masse, seize Food Not Bombs food supplies, and complain that, if not stopped, Food Not Bombs will continue with the "visible, blatant, and untimely distribution of food." As a result, the group disseminates, along with Tofu Dill Dip and Potato-Pea Curry recipes to serve a hundred people, guidelines on what to do "if the police start taking your food" (Butler and McHenry 2000: 93–103, 110, 114).

City and police officials justify such actions on grounds ranging from identity theft and metal poaching to public health and public safety (Ferrell 2011). As Brisman (2010) argues in his analysis of "the indiscriminate criminalization of environmentally beneficial activities," though, and as I have shown in a series of case studies (Ferrell 2001, 2006), this pervasive criminalization is in fact founded in contemporary political economy. Brisman (2010: 172–73) notes, for example, that municipalities often earn income from city-run recycling programs and garner additional income from fines levied against those who scrounge or recycle outside the framework of such programs. In these cases, illicit scavenging is perceived as threatening not only the rationalized control of city life that is the goal of municipal governance, but city budgets as well. More broadly, everyday informal trash scrounging and do-it-yourself recycling and reuse, along with the intentional consumerist interventions staged by freegans and groups like Food Not Bombs, threaten the dynamics of consumer capitalism. Physically, such activities may well salvage tons of waste from engorged landfills—but from the view of corporations and their political allies, they also deflect potential consumers, allowing them to acquire food and materials without the cost, and corporate profit, of purchase. (This view also underlies the intentional fouling of discarded corporate consumer items, with shoes and clothes often cut or torn upon disposal, and food adulterated with bleach or other pollutants. See Groombridge this volume.) Culturally, the viability of informal waste scrounging threatens to expose the very logic of consumer capitalism itself, revealing that yesterday's items may in fact function as well as tomorrow's, and awakening consumers to the notion that their trash may be made up not of the deteriorated, but of the needlessly discarded (Ferrell 2006).

A distinct, contemporary constellation of economic, cultural, and spatial politics also drives the criminalization of informal environmental reclamation. With the withering of urban industrial production in American and European cities, and the exportation of production to developing countries, these cities increasingly rely on service economies organized around tourism, entertainment, and consumption. Researchers like Markusen and Schrock (2009: 345, 353) promote this sort of "consumption-driven urban development," arguing that "superior local consumption-based offerings help to attract skilled workers, managers, entrepreneurs, and retirees," and emphasizing that "economists and geographers have recently stressed the significance of lifestyle preferences of skilled workers as an important determinant of economic development." Confirming this trajectory, if more critically, radical geographers like David Harvey (2008: 31) conclude that "quality of urban life has become a commodity, as has the city itself, in a world where consumerism, tourism, [and] cultural and knowledge-based industries have become major aspects of the urban political economy." To protect this political economy and its privatized urban "consumption spaces" (Zukin 1997; see also Zukin 2010) from those who might trespass on their intended meanings—to protect, that is, the image-based and consumption-based commodity that is "quality of urban life"—the policing of urban life has in turn come to focus as much on perception as on populations. In the midst of an urban revitalization campaign, for example, an economic official in the U.S. contends that panhandling is a problem precisely because "it's part of an image issue for the city" (Ferrell 2001: 45); an American legal scholar agrees, arguing that "the most serious of the attendant problems of homelessness is its devastating effect on a city's image" (in Mitchell 2003: 201). Or as Aspden (2008: 13) concludes in regard to the recent transformation of a decaying British industrial city into a "corporate city of conspicuous consumption," "There seems to be no place in the new Leeds for those who disturb the rhythms of the consumer-oriented society."

Within this contemporary cultural economy of the city, there is indeed "no place" for peripatetic dumpster divers, for freegans picking food from trash piles, for Food Not Bombs activists gathering homeless folks around them for salvaged meals; such groups must be legally excluded from the spaces of "consumption-driven urban development" so that they will not befoul the appeal of such spaces to the desired sorts of consumers. Noting a new city ordinance banning dumpster diving and other street activities, for example, the *Houston Chronicle* (Turner 2002) explained that "the redevelopment of downtown as a retail, entertainment, and residential center has nurtured an urban spirit less hospitable to the poorest of the poor." Likewise, in a decade as a daily trash picker, I have documented a direct correlation between the aggressiveness of police and private security responses to my presence and the degree to which an area is under consumption-oriented redevelopment—to the point that, in one newly developed retail zone, I discovered that as a dumpster diver I was now on a police list of "known troublemakers." This criminalization of informal recycling and reclamation is further reinforced by contemporary models of risk-based urban policing. Developed and supported by major insurance companies—in the case of programs like Neighborhood Watch in the U.S., even funded by them (O'Malley 2010: 26-27)—these models emphasize a rationalized, actuarial web of crime prevention through systematic surveillance, information collection, and pre-emptive intervention. By this logic, the unregulated and the unpredictable invite criminality and the breakdown of crime control. For conservative criminologists like Wilson and Kelling (1982), homeless trash pickers or panhandlers are in fact defined *only* as signs of social disorder—as metaphorical "broken windows"—to be policed aggressively, lest they dispirit citizens and invite more violent forms of criminality. In this way consumerist urban economies and the risk-based policing that protects them combine to make outlaws of those who would engage day-to-day with the very waste that such economies spawn (Ferrell 2012). The ecological harms of consumer culture double down, ensuring that its waste must not benefit even those willing to wade through it.

These efforts of everyday waste scroungers to glean sustenance for themselves and others, and the legal and political campaigns to criminalize and contain these practices, reveal two useful intersections of cultural and green criminologies. The first builds from cultural criminology's revitalization of the labeling theory tradition in sociological criminology, and with it the notion that power is often most effectively exercised through the imposition of meaning. Cultural criminologists argue that an analysis of this labeling process—this process of assigning meaning and enforcing identity—is more important than ever in a contemporary world shaped by mediated images, marketed identities, and high-profile "wars" on crime (Ferrell 1999; Ferrell, Hayward, and Young 2008; Ferrell and Sanders 1995). From this view, contemporary economies of conspicuous consumption and "consumption-driven urban development" do not sell material goods so much as they sell the lifestyles and status cycles by which such goods are defined, and the experiences of urban "authenticity" (Zukin 2010) and spatial "quality of urban life" through which such goods are acquired. Maintaining these meanings, though, requires a parallel process: the justifiable policing of consumption spaces and experiences so as to protect them for epistemic or experiential intrusion. As a result, homeless trash pickers, freegans, and Food Not Bombs activists are labeled as criminals, and through a process of "cultural criminalization" (Ferrell 1999), advertised as outcasts who would rummage through filth, thieve away consumer identities, and proffer unhealthy food. In the contemporary political economy, the longstanding historical ambiguity of the scrounger identity—part self-reliant innovator, part petty poacher—is resolved in the direction of the poacher and the criminal—and with a vengeance (Ferrell 2006). Corporate greenwashing campaigns, state and corporate recalcitrance in defining ecological harms, and similar core concerns of green criminology would likewise seem amenable to this sort of analysis of labeling and of meanings imposed or ignored; certainly the everyday phenomenon of trash scrounging and its criminalization can be understood in this light.

A careful examination of contemporary trash picking and the cultures that surround it reveals another aspect of labeling as well. Like their global counterparts who have created cooperatives and staged trash-picking festivals, many trash scroungers in the United States, Europe, and elsewhere aim not only to pick valuables from consumer waste, but to reverse the very dynamics by which trash and trash pickers are defined. In this sense, they engage in ecological resistance—resistance defined not simply as disobeying the rules or going outside the mainstream, but resistance undertaken so as to turn the logic of the dominant system back on itself. At a basic level, this involves utilizing the essence of consumer capitalism—the proliferation of consumer goods and their inevitable waste—as a foundation for creating alternative communities, alternative economic arrangements, and alternative forms of survival; as the Industrial Workers of the World (1973 [1908]) famously put it, a formula for "forming the structure of the new society within the shell of the old." Yet this reversal operates at the level of labeling—that is, at the level of meaning and perception—as well. Freegans, as already noted, attempt to live from scrounged food, and so to "act as a living challenge to waste and over-consumption." Food Not Bombs groups certainly undertake the practical work of feeding the hungry from discarded food—but they do so as part of a "decentralized, non-hierarchical movement" designed to publically "create new alternatives and life-affirming structures from the ground up" (Butler and McHenry 2000: xii, 72). Likewise, as part of my own ongoing trash scrounging, I collect and donate truckloads of goods to charities—but I also quite intentionally work with local, national, and international media to craft a disconcerting portrait of a "dumpster diving professor" dedicated to confronting consumer waste (see examples at http://empireofscrounge.blogspot.com/p/media.html). Dumpster-diving his way across America, the anonymous anarcho-punk author of the book *Evasion* (Anonymous 2003: 74) began to question "who the barbarians were, the contemptible. Those operating the machine, enslaving the people, and bleeding the Earth dry. Producing things only to throw them away, digging a hole only to fill it up again. Or those who saw the absurdity of it all, and chose to humbly wait in the shadows of that machine and pick up the crumbs." The larger world of informal waste scrounging often serves to raise that question as well, and so to resist consumer capitalism and its machineries of meaning. After all, if consumer capitalism operates as a cultural enterprise—as a manufacturer of perceptions and identities—then it can perhaps best be confronted on those terms as well.

This discussion of a "decentralized, non-hierarchical" Food Not Bombs movement, of the old Industrial Workers of the World and the new anarchist punks, suggests a second potential intersection of cultural and green criminologies. White (2003, 2008, 2009–2010) and other green criminologists have productively examined legal and regulatory responses to environmental harm, transnational organization and resistance around environmental issues, state repression of environmental protest, and other aspects of green activism. Decentralized, anarchic, do-it-yourself movements that emphasize fluid forms of everyday activism can be more difficult to account for—but as groups like the freegans and Food Not Bombs show, and as cultural criminologists have documented in related contexts (Ferrell 1996, 2001; see also Brisman and South in press), they embody a powerful contemporary model for environmental activism. Building from anarchist traditions of "direct action" and "the propaganda of the deed," they mix practical, on-the-ground activism with the notion that such activism can itself embody and demonstrate the viability of alternative arrangements (Botha 2004: 78–102; see also Brisman and South in press). In this sense, such groups are less interested in protesting for environmental justice or lobbying for environmental regulation than they are in confronting environmental harms directly, and in enacting alternative, environmentally just relationships within the spaces of daily life (Hayward 2012; see also Brisman and South in press). Freegans, Food Not Bombs activists, and urban "guerrilla gardeners" share this orientation; so do groups like Critical Mass and Reclaim the Streets, with their "dis-organized" direct actions against automotive harms to the environment, their innovative forms of playful cultural resistance and redefinition, their disavowal of political and legal authority, and their commitment to "live the way we wish it could be" (in Ferrell 2001: 114; see Carlsson 2002, Carlsson and Manning 2010). Given that Occupy Wall Street and the larger Occupy movement draw on this anarchic, direct action orientation as well (see Brisman 2012), it would seem a propitious time for green criminology to investigate, perhaps even affiliate with, such groups, and so to fulfill the promise of "a green perspective [as] particularly sensitive to cultural politics and the emergence of new social movements concerned with lifestyle, identity and visionary protest" (South 1998: 226).

Coda: lost ecologies large and small

Consumer culture and its wasteful consequences would seem among the defining dynamics of late modernity/late capitalism, and for this reason a primary potential focus for any confluence of cultural and green criminologies. Yet this focus by no means exhausts the possibilities of an interwoven green and cultural criminology. Other important areas of research, some of them already being explored within cultural criminology and elsewhere, would include the sort of reverse greenwashing by which alleged environmental harm is invoked in the criminalization of graffiti, drug use, and other subcultural practices (for example Ferrell 1996); the cultural politics of water and waterfront spatial environments (Kane 2009, this volume); and, most recently, the ecological consequences of changing rural cultures and economies (Tunnell 2011). Beyond this, the overblown fear of crime that is manufactured by media and political institutions would itself seem an ecological issue, promoting as it does the enclosure of the automobile in preference to the perceived vulnerability of walking or bicycling, along with the hyper-consumption of personal and home safety devices (Brisman 2004; Ferrell, Hayward, and Young 2008: 103; Lauer 2005). The aesthetics of manicured lawns and corporate landscaping would seem an appropriate focus for a criminology of ecological commodification; likewise, the prim aesthetics of middle-class professionalism would seem to mitigate against bicycle riding, guerilla garden-ing, trash digging, and other everyday ecological practices, and so might be investigated as a "personal" style with serious ecological implications. The cultural construction of meat, with its seared-in masculinity and conspicuous culinary consumption, certainly intertwines with the vast ecological harms of meat production; on the other side, the subcultural ideologies of animal liberation movements certainly drive them into activism, and into conflict with state and legal authorities all too ready to label their activities as "terrorism" (see Brisman 2008). Most certainly, as groups like Critical Mass and Reclaim the Streets emphasize, the culture of the automobile—the constellation of meanings promulgated by automobile manufacturers, advertisers, city planners, and associated culture industries—is essential to understanding the automobile as ongoing environmental disaster. Within this culture, neighbors' front gardens, and indeed whole neighborhoods, seem naturally to give way to pavement; Middle Eastern oil wars and their ecological consequences seem somehow disconnected from the drive to work; the indebtedness and conspicuous consumption of automotive ownership seems only necessary and normal; and most miraculously, the everyday automotive carnage of dead bicycle messengers, dead pedestrians, dead dogs and cats and squirrels, and dead urban and rural ecologies seems somehow to disappear behind myths of "safe driving" and ecologically friendly automobiles (see for example Bohm et al. 2006; Burns et al. 2005; Carlsson 2002; Ferrell 2001, 2003; Fincham 2006; Furness 2010; Lutz and Lutz Fernandez 2010; Muzzatti 2010).

These issues, and countless others, coalesce into a series of lost ecologies large and small. Ruined rural landscapes, fake plastic trees and gas-powered leaf blowers, middle-class lawns made a deeper shade of green by overdoses of water and fertilizer, sedentary children driven to and from schools three blocks away, professors and other professionals fearful of sweat or rain or dirt, diners digging into double-meat fast food hamburgers, swatches of land cut off from public use by motorway onramps, multiplying "ghost bike" memorials to bicyclists mowed down by speeding autos—all intertwine the cultural and the environmental, and all confirm ecological possibilities lost to us, isolated from us, misplaced from our lives. In all of these we can also see yet another potential cultural criminological contribution to green criminology: the cultural criminological focus on everyday life, and on developing a criminology of the everyday that can discover the momentous in the momentary (Ferrell 2007; Ferrell, Hayward and Young 2008: 85–122; Presdee 2000, 2004). We can, after all, visit vast electronics dumps in China to study consumer culture's environmental consequences—but we can also look into our own dust bins. We can, and should, document the ongoing ecological criminality of the global auto industry—but we can also kneel before a single roadside shrine that commemorates a loved one lost to automotive violence (Ferrell 2003). We can, and should, develop a wide-ranging green criminology of animal abuse—but along the way, we can also usefully take note of the shoes we wear, the food we eat, and the pets we pick for companionship (Beirne 2007). In these small moments and situations, we discover again Mills's (1959: 7) sociological imagination as well—the "capacity to shift from one perspective to another," to discover "the minute points of the intersections of biography and history within society"—and so the sociological seeds of intertwining green and cultural criminologies.

In that light, this chapter ends not with words but with images. Among cultural criminology's more useful innovations has been its emphasis on the visual, not only as an essential criminological subject matter in an increasingly mediated world, but as a mode of criminological documentation and analysis (Hayward and Presdee 2010; Ferrell and Van de Voorde 2010; Redmon 2005; Sabin and Redmon 2009). A visual criminology of this sort seems particularly appropriate for recording and communicating the little lost ecologies of everyday life—lost ecologies like that of a small stream a few miles west of my home. Over the centuries, this stream cut a channel through the open prairie, finding the limestone bedrock a few feet down, as do most natural waterways in this region. Now this little stream has been enveloped by economic development, and by consumer culture in particular. A concrete viaduct today constitutes its headwaters; from there, it flows down a concrete culvert in the middle of a roadway, and then into and around a series of Texas-size shopping centers. Upon arrival at the last of these shopping centers, it is made to disappear beneath a vast parking lot, and by the time it reappears a thousand yards later, as the photos suggest, the stream has not simply been affected by consumer culture. It has been lost to it, and has become it.

Untitled photograph by the author

Untitled photograph by the author

Untitled photograph by the author

References

Anonymous. 2003. *Evasion*. Atlanta: CrimethInc.

Aspden, K. 2008. *The Hounding of David Oluwale*. London: Vintage.

Beirne, P. 2007. "Animal Rights, Animal Abuse, and Green Criminology," in P. Beirne and N. South (eds) *Issues in Green Criminologyy: Confronting Harms Against Environments, Humanity and Other Animals*, pp. 55–83. Cullompton: Willan.

Bohm, S., Jones, C., Land, C. and Paterson, M. (eds) 2006. *Against Automobility*. Malden, MA: Blackwell. Botha, T. 2004. *Mongo: Adventures in Trash*. New York: Bloomsbury.

Brisman, A. 2004. "Double Whammy: Collateral Consequences of Conviction and Imprisonment for Sustainable Communities and the Environment," *William & Mary Environmental Law & Policy Review*, 28 (2): 423–75.

———2008. "Crime-Environmental Relationship and Environmental Justice," *Seattle Journal for Social Justice* 6(2): 727–817.

———2009. "It Takes Green to Be Green: Environmental Elitism, 'Ritual Displays,' and Conspicuous Non-Consumption," *North Dakota Law Review*, 85(2): 329–70.

———2010. "The Indiscriminate Criminalisation of Environmentally Beneficial Activities," in R. White (ed.) *Global Environmental Harm: Criminological Perspectives*, pp. 161–92. Cullompton: Willan.

———2012. "Teaching Occupation: Some Reflection," *The Critical Criminologist* 20(3): 18–22.

Brisman, A. and South, N. in press. "A Green-Cultural Criminology: An Exploratory Outline," *Crime, Media and Culture*.

Burns, R., Ferrell, J., and Orrick, E. 2005. "False Advertising, Suggestive Persuasion, and Automobile Safety: Assessing Advertising Practices in the Automobile Industry," *Southwest Journal of Criminal Justice*, 2 (2): 132–52.

Butler, C.T. and McHenry, K. 2000. *Food Not Bombs*. Tucson, AZ: See Sharp Press.

Carlsson, C. (ed.) 2002. *Critical Mass: Bicycling's Defiant Celebration*. Oakland, CA: AK Press.

Carlsson, C. and Manning, F. 2010. "Nowtopia: Strategic Exodus?" *Antipode*, 42(4): 924–53.

Clark, D. 2004. "The Raw and the Rotten: Punk Cuisine," *Ethnology*, 43(1): 19–31.

Croall, H. 2007. "Food Crime," in P. Beirne and N. South (eds) *Issues in Green Criminologyy: Confronting Harms Against Environments, Humanity and Other Animals*, pp. 206–29. Cullompton: Willan.

Ferrell, J. 1996. *Crimes of Style: Urban Graffiti and the Politics of Criminality*. Boston, MA: Northeastern University Press.

———1999. "Cultural Criminology," *Annual Review of Sociology*, 25: 395–418.

———2001. *Tearing Down the Streets*. New York: Palgrave/McMillan.

———2003. "Speed Kills," *Critical Criminology*, 11: 185–98.

———2006. *Empire of Scrounge*. New York: New York University Press.

———2007. "For a Ruthless Cultural Criticism of Everything Existing," *Crime, Media, Culture*, 3(1): 91–100.

———2011. "Interview with Jeff Ferrell," *MetalTheft.net*, 1(3), December. Available at: http://metaltheft.net/interviews.html

———2012. "Anarchy, Geography and Drift," *Antipode* 44(5): 1687–1704 .

Ferrell, J., Hayward, K. and Young, J. 2008. *Cultural Criminology*: An Invitation. London: Sage.

Ferrell, J. and Sanders, C. (eds) 1995. *Cultural Criminology*. Boston, MA: Northeastern University Press. Ferrell, J. and Van de Voorde, C. 2010. "The Decisive Moment: Documentary Photography and Cultural Criminology," in K. Hayward and M. Presdee (eds) *Framing Crime: Cultural Criminology and the Image*, pp. 36–52. London: Routledge/GlassHouse.

Fincham, B. 2006. "Bicycle Messengers and the Road to Freedom," in S. Bohm et al. (eds) *Against Automobility*, pp. 208–22. Malden, MA: Blackwell.

Furness, Z. 2010. *One Less Car: Bicycling and the Politics of Automobility*. Philadelphia, PA: Temple.

Gibbs, C., McGarrell, E.F., and Mark 2010. "Transnational White-collar Criminal Tasks: Lessons from the Gloabal Trade in Electronic Matter," *Criminology and Public Policy* 9(3): 543–60.

Gill, K. 2010. *Of Poverty and Plastic*. New Delhi: Oxford.

Harvey, D. 2008. "The Right to the City," *New Left Review*, 53: 23–40.

Hayward, K. 2012. "Five Spaces of Cultural Criminology," *British Journal of Criminology*, 52(3): 441–462. Hayward, K. and Presdee, M. (eds) 2010. *Framing Crime: Cultural Criminology and the Image*. London: Routledge/GlassHouse.

Industrial Workers of the World. 1973 [1908]. "Preamble of the Industrial Workers of the World," in *Songs of the Workers*, 34th edn. Chicago, IL: Industrial Workers of the World.

Jenkins, P. 1999. "Fighting Terrorism as if Women Mattered: Anti-Abortion Violence as Unconstructed Terrorism," in Jeff Ferrell and Neil Websdale (eds) *Making Trouble: Cultural Constructions of Crime, Deviance, and Control*, pp. 319–46. New York: Aldine de Gruyter.

Kane, S. 2009. "Stencil Graffiti in Urban Waterscapes of Buenos Aires and Rosario, Argentina," *Crime, Media, Culture*, 5(1): 9–28.

Lauer, J. 2005. "Driven to Extremes: Fear of Crime and the Rise of the Sport Utility Vehicle in the United States," *Crime, Media, Culture* 1(2): 149–168.

Lutz, C. and Lutz Fernandez, A. 2010. *Carjacked*. New York: Palgrave Macmillan.

Markusen, A. and Schrock, G. 2009. "Consumption-Driven Urban Development," *Urban Geography*, 30 (4): 344–67.

Mills, C. W. 1959. *The Sociological Imagination*. London: Oxford University Press.

Mitchell, D. 2003. *The Right to the City*. New York: Guilford.

Muzzatti, S. 2010. "'Drive It Like You Stole It': A Cultural Criminology of Car Commercials," in K. Hayward and M. Presdee (eds) *Framing Crime: Cultural Criminology and the Image*, pp. 138–55. London: Routledge/GlassHouse.

O'Malley, P. 2010. *Crime and Risk*. London: Sage.

Packard, V. 1960. *The Waste Makers*. Harmondsworth: Penguin.

Pellow, D. N. 2004. *Garbage Wars: The Struggle for Environmental Justice in Chicago*. Cambridge, MA: MIT Press. Presdee, M. 2000. *Cultural Criminology and the Carnival of Crime*. London: Routledge.

———2004. "The Story of Crime," in J. Ferrell et al. (eds) *Cultural Criminology Unleashed*, pp. 41–48. London: Routledge/GlassHouse.

Pritchett, L. 2009. *Going Green: True Tales from Gleaners, Scavengers, and Dumpster Divers*. Norman, OK: University of Oklahoma Press

Redmon, D. 2005. *Mardi Gras: Made in China* (documentary film). New York: Carnivalesque Films. Rosenthal, E. 2011. "Used Batteries From U.S. Expose Mexicans to Risk," *The New York Times*, 9 Dec.: A1, A12.

Sabin, A. and Redmon, D. 2009. *Kamp Katrina* (documentary film). New York: Carnivalesque Films. Shuqin, Y. 2010. "The Polluting Behaviour of the Multinational Corporations in China," in R. White (ed.) *Global Environmental Harm: Criminological Perspectives*, pp. 150–58. Cullompton: Willan.

South, N. 1998. "A Green Field for Criminology," *Theoretical Criminology*, 2(2): 211–34.

———2007. "The "Corporate Colonization of Nature": Bio-Prospecting, Bio-Piracy and the Development of Green Criminology," in P. Beirne and N. South (eds) *Issues in Green Criminologyy: Confronting Harms Against Environments, Humanity and Other Animals*, pp. 230–47. Cullompton: Willan.

———2010. "The Ecocidal Tendencies of Late Modernity," in R. White (ed.) *Global Environmental Harm: Criminological Perspectives*, pp. 228–47. Cullompton: Willan.

Takemura, N. 2010. "The Criticality of Global Environmental Crime and the Response of Chaos Criminology," in R. White (ed.) *Global Environmental Harm*, pp. 210–27. Cullompton: Willan.

Tunnell, K. 2011. *Once Upon a Place: The Fading of Community in Rural Kentucky*. Bloomington, IN: Xlibris. Turner, A. 2002. ""Civility' Push, Light Rail Tough on Panhandlers," *Houston Chronicle*, 16 June. Available at: www.HoustonChronicle.com

Varul, M. Zick. 2006. "Waste, Industry and Romantic Leisure: Veblen's Theory of Recognition," *European Journal of Social Theory*, 9(1): 103–17.

Veblen, T. 1953 [1899]. *The Theory of the Leisure Class*. New York: Mentor.

Walker, L., Jardim, J. and Harley, K. (dir.) 2010. Waste Land [*Lixo Extraordinario*] (documentary film). London: Almega.

White, R. 2002. "Environmental Harm and the Political Economy of Consumption," *Social Justice*, 29(1–2): 82–102.

———2003. "Environmental Issues and the Criminological Imagination," *Theoretical Criminology*, 7(4): 483–506.

———2008. *Crimes Against Nature: Environmental Criminology and Ecological Justice*. Cullompton: Willan.

———2009–2010. "Environmental Victims and Resistance to State Crime through Transnational Activism," *Social Justice*, 36(3): 46–60.

Wilson, J. and Kelling, G. 1982. "Broken Windows," *The Atlantic Monthly*, March: 29–38.

Young, J. 2011. *The Criminological Imagination*. Cambridge: Polity.

Zukin, S. 1997. "Cultural Strategies of Economic Development and the Hegemony of Vision," in A. Merrifield and E. Swyngedouw (eds) *The Urbanization of Injustice*, pp. 223–43. New York: New York University Press.

———2010. *Naked City: The Death and Life of Authentic Urban Places*. New York: Oxford University Press.

READING 2

HOW CIVIL SOCIETY CAN HELP
Sweatshop Workers as Globalization's Consequence

BY JEFF BALLINGER

Italy's idyllic region of Tuscany is known as a top-tier tourist destination. Less well known is that it is also one of Europe's frontiers of human trafficking and a case-study in the effects of globalization. The garment and textile factories of Prato figured prominently in Italy's "miracle" economic performance of the 1950s and 1960s, with more than 4,500 small shops producing many of the world's most sought-after brands. Garment production is buoyant there again, but "economia sommersa" (submerged economy) sweatshops account for more than a third of the goods produced, and many of the Chinese workers are working long hours for little or no pay, due to huge debts to trafficking gangs. Now that the new anti-immigration mayor is closing illegal operators, hundreds of workers without legal working papers are in limbo as the Chinese government has refused the Italian government's attempts at repatriation.

Immigrant-bashing media in Italy decry the rise of sweatshops, but NYU's Andrew Ross points out that they had their place in Prato decades ago, when there was a high-wage "core" fed by peripheral sweatshops. Hence, the current situation is not a "Chinese import." This mobile workforce has been a hallmark of globalization, spawning a hugely contentious debate and ugly—if understandable—resentment.

Aside from the worker migration topic, there are other key globalization questions as well. Has globalization turned good companies bad? Has the outsource model forced the buyers to accept the often brutal practices of supplier-factory managers in some of the world's most corrupt and lawless environments? Is the current wage allocation truly fair and efficient? Several myths occlude helpful discussion of these questions and the solutions to their larger underlying issues.

Jeff Ballinger, "How Civil Society Can Help: Sweatshop Workers as Globalization's Consequence," *Harvard International Review,* vol. 33, no. 2, pp. 54-59. Copyright © 2011 by Harvard International Relations Council. Reprinted with permission. Provided by ProQuest LLC. All rights reserved.

There is one myth that has served the most vulnerable industries (electronics, toys, garments, and footwear) well over the last decade: a global brand will meticulously monitor its supply chain because conscientious consumers, informed by the latest technologies, will punish the company at the retail level for any transgression. Rather, according to Jeffrey Swartz, the CEO of Timberland, consumers do not think too much about workers' rights in the supplier factories. "Don't do anything horrible or despicable" and the company will be safe, he

JEFF BALLINGER is Director of Press for Change, a human rights organization with a focus on worker rights in the developing world. He has just finished three years as a Research Associate at the Harvard Kennedy School.

opined in late-2009. His remarks are supported by a striking example: the complete lack of media attention when the toy-maker Mattel scrapped all factory monitoring in 2010.

Another misperception—shared by "free trade" critics and proponents alike—is the race-to-the-bottom discourse, which posits that any improvement in wages or conditions will send factory managers off in search of more vulnerable workers. In 2000, shortly after the anti-WTO protests in Seattle, over 200 economists sent an open letter to college presidents in the United States that chastised them for too easily acceding to the students' demand to clean sweatshop-stained apparel out of university bookstores. The message was simple: they will hurt the very workers that they are trying to help because of this outsourcing imperative to seek lower standards.

In practice, there appears to be much room for wage improvement. Indonesia's "real" wage nearly tripled in the early 1990s, while foreign investment continued to flow. China and Vietnam have pushed up minimum wages several times in the last five years while maintaining double-digit growth rates. The incontrovertible and simplest proof that there is ample room for wage growth may be seen in the cost breakdown for a typical university-logo "hoodie"—the labor cost of the US$38 garment is less than 20 cents, while the university's licensing fee is over two dollars.

One of the most refreshingly honest voices in the global workers-rights field, Dr. Prakash Sethi, has addressed what is perhaps the most pernicious myth: Northern-based "buyers" have an arm's-length relationship with their Korean, Taiwanese, or Chinese suppliers and therefore are not responsible for their well-documented records of contumacy. For years he was the architect of Mattel's efforts to track compliance with supplier "codes of conduct"—pushing outsource factories to observe local laws, prohibit child labor, etc.—and he has done consulting work in this field for several other Fortune 500 firms. He says that the major global players, including the World Bank, the OECD countries, and the International Labor Organization, have failed to apply pressure on low-cost producing countries that do not protect workers' health, safety, or human rights. Boldly, he has also called on corporations to pay restitution to developing-world workers for "years of expropriation" enabled by corrupt, repressive regimes. Particularly poignant is his brusque assertion that "bigotry" was at the root of most companies'

"Has the outsource model forced the buyers to accept the often brutal practices of supplier-factory managers in some of the world's most corrupt and lawless environments?"

refusal even to try to grapple with some of these issues. Lending weight to Sethi's call for restitution is a pair of recent capitulations by Nike in claims against contract factories in Honduras and Malaysia, wherein Nike paid several millions of dollars to harmed workers.

For almost two decades, policy-makers have suffered the deleterious effects of these myths, resulting in inefficient allocations of time and effort. The child labor controversy offers a concise example. Although there were never more than a negligible percentage of 10- to 13-year-olds in factories, hundreds of millions of dollars have been directed at this perceived problem since the early 1990s. A focus on raising adult wages and thereby eliminating the need for the children to help support the family, by contrast, might have resulted in hundreds of thousands of poor families being able to keep those same children in school. What then is the current situation? How has globalization affected the production sector, wages, and working conditions?

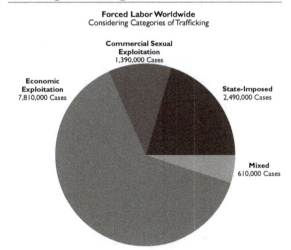

Tracking Trafficking

Forced Labor Worldwide
Considering Categories of Trafficking

Commercial Sexual Exploitation 1,390,000 Cases

Economic Exploitation 7,810,000 Cases

State-Imposed 2,490,000 Cases

Mixed 610,000 Cases

International Labor Organization; 2005

Globalization and Supply-chains

Before globalization, most consumer-product companies were vertically-integrated—design, production, and marketing all occurred in one country. Then, a boom in out-sourcing created the global "supply-chain," an interesting twist to the familiar sweat-shop narrative.

The result may be seen in sub-Saharan Africa, Southeast Asia, and the Middle East. In the last, for example, a reader unfamiliar with the current practices of global garment producers may well ask why Jordanian factories are filled with Asians, when Jordan's unemployment rate lies between 13.4 percent to 30 percent (official/unofficial figures). The answer, of course, is that the supplier factories can pay foreign workers less and being "guests" they are less likely to make trouble.

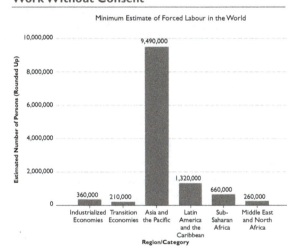

Work Without Consent

Minimum Estimate of Forced Labour in the World

Estimated Number of Persons (Rounded Up)

Industrialized Economies	360,000
Transition Economies	210,000
Asia and the Pacific	9,490,000
Latin America and the Caribbean	1,320,000
Sub-Saharan Africa	660,000
Middle East and North Africa	260,000

Region/Category

International Labor Organization; 2005

311

An observer with more knowledge about global supply chains and garment production after the formation of the World Trade Organization would perhaps point to the remedy in the 2001 US-Jordan Free Trade Agreement, which contains "labor rights" requirements. Unsurprisingly, Jordanian officials aver that all workplaces are inspected and workers, of every nationality, in the 100+ factories are protected. In an altogether too common oversight, the reporters who noted this pledge presented no enforcement statistics to support the claim, and one can only conclude that the agreement's requirements remain empty promises.

New Abuse, Intriguing Opportunity

Sending workers abroad to the newly-rich Gulf countries in the 1970s was perhaps the first meaningful benefit of globalization for states such as Egypt, the Philippines, Bangladesh, Pakistan, and India, since workers' remittances meant billions of dollars. After the outsourcing boom of the 1980s, filling factories with foreign workers became a familiar practice in Taiwan and South Korea, where shoe and apparel brands "nudged" long-time suppliers towards cheaper labor in China and Indonesia. As democratization in the late-1980s began to push up wages in the factories that have churned out millions of pairs of sneakers each month since the mid-1970s, they were soon filled with cheaper immigrant workers from the Philippines, Thailand, and later, Vietnam.

The issue remained below the radar for over a decade, despite Fortune magazine's searing portrayal of factories in Taiwan in 2003, which dubbed it "indentured servitude." With the lack of attention, brands sourcing from the factories suffered no sustained criticism for their contractors' abusive practices, nor for those of labor suppliers or "brokers," who often become prone to corruption on both ends: supply and delivery. Over the last decade, a "perfect storm" has developed: lucrative contract-labor fees (often triple what laws allow); growing demand for workers, coupled with relative impunity for brokers; bigger profits; malleable "host" governments for contract-factories; and finally, complacence on the part of buyers. Most striking about the last is the surprising ease with which Corporate Social Responsibility (CSR) tactics such as simple codes of conduct for supplier factories with cheap (and easily manipulated) "social audits" refuted "sweatshop" allegations.

The Role of Civil Society

There is, however, hope for consumer power: globalization's fallen barriers have made it possible for small civil society organizations to punch above their weight in trans-border solidarity campaigns. One such group is the Committee to Protect Viet Workers (CPVW) which, as the name makes clear, has a narrow focus, with a global reach and membership, as it draws volunteers from Europe, North America, and Australia. One of the clear positives of globalization is the access to news media outlets enabled by hundreds of these new citizen-watchdog nongovernmental organizations, who are joining the more-established legal aid and independent trade union movements.

Being based outside of Vietnam, the CPVW is free to advocate on behalf of several independent union activists now jailed in Vietnam. Although many grievances had come to the fore since foreign investment began to transform the country in the mid-1990s, the powerful 2006-7 wave of wildcat strikes—protests generally spontaneous in nature with ad-hoc leaders preferring anonymity—focused on wages. Inflation had hit double digits in 2006, but Vietnamese workers' wages in exports-factories had been fixed at US$42 per month for over a decade. An assessment of the protests yields some interesting findings: more than 70 percent of the 580 strikes took place at foreign-investment factories, with Nike—the country's largest "buyer" with over 200,000 contract-factory employees—suffering wage-related protests in more than a third of its 35 source factories. These huge shoe and apparel factories are also plagued by extraordinarily high turnover rates, mainly due to forced overtime and pressures to boost production.

The CPVW began observing "destination" countries when Vietnamese authorities dramatically increased the number of workers sent abroad in the period from 2006 to 2008. Workers returning from Malaysia informed CPVW's correspondents about cheating and horrendous living conditions at

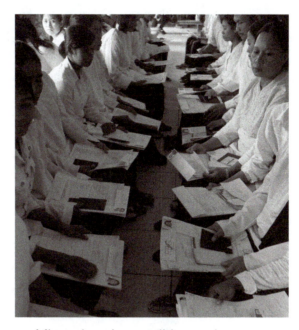

Migrant workers wait to receive passports at an immigration office in Indonesia. In 2010, over 300,000 Indonesians migrated to the Middle East in hopes of finding a job.

a t-shirt factory producing for Nike. The nongovernmental organization then turned the controversy into a minor scandal in Australia, and Nike immediately put the issue on the "fast track" for settlement, which contrasts sharply with the contemporaneous case in Honduras, which dragged on for two years. One possible explanation for the disparate treatment is the media, since the Vietnamese migrants' story was presented as a case of "human trafficking on a massive scale." Nike's contract-workforce in Malaysia numbered around 10,000 at the time; 1,100 foreign workers at the t-shirt factory are receiving about $2,000 each as restitution (paid in installments over nearly three years). The company will not reveal settlement deals at the other workplaces. The investigation itself earned the Best TV award at 2009's Every Human Has Rights ceremony in Paris.

Forcing a Re-examination of CSR?

A CPVW activist recently expressed frustration that Nike has for years had "independent" inspectors inspect its contract factories in Malaysia. How could it be, then, that workers worked under "indentured servitude" conditions which were clear for all to see, but inspections never disclosed this fact? The CPVW merely brought to public view what inspectors should have brought to the fore years ago. Perhaps the answer lay in the circumstance of Nike's "independent" inspectors, which number over 70, in an in-house CSR team of 215. The methodology deployed by most of these "responsibility" operations places great emphasis on the cultivation and maintenance of "stakeholder" relationships—predominantly, civil society organizations in both producer- and consumer-nations. Standard-setting and analysis of supplier-factory performance is certainly a part of their work, but the company's buyers operate with a wholly different set of metrics.

To return to the beginnings of CSR in the mid-1990s would show a very strong link to the sweatshop controversy. In other words, the current proliferation of CSR artifice and funding started with anti-sweatshop activism, as illustrated in the huge jump in mentions of "Corporate Social Responsibility" or "CSR" in major news sources, from 28 articles in the decade 1988-98, to 561 from 1998–2003, to 2,643 between 2003–2008. The means of gathering this data, a simple Lexis-Nexis search, points to another issue. Given that this explosion was driven by worker mistreatment and below-subsistence wages, it would be reasonable to assume that much CSR "action" would be concentrated in this area. As it turns out, the vast majority of CSR press releases deal with environment-related issues and less than 1 percent concern workplace issues.

Just to reiterate, CSR had an incredible growth spurt because of workers' exploitation related to outsourcing, but the industry relies almost exclusively on environmental initiatives to demonstrate some kind of "responsibility" progress. Recently, in recognition of this fact, more CSR officers have simply replaced "responsibility" with "sustainability" in their titles and work-product.

> "If workers are deceived, distracted or dispirited by buyer-driven self-regulation schemes, it
> is possible that the traditional strategies available to workers wishing to form independent
> unions are similarly affected."

Refreshing the Anti-Sweatshop Struggle

The corporate self-regulation "solution" which consisted of codes of conduct for supplier factories and spot-checking by social auditors has been a chimera. Since the early Clinton years, global labor rights received scattershot support; grants would go abroad through the Department of Labor or the State Department's Bureau for Democracy, Labor, and Human Rights. Many of these focused on "capacity-building" for workplace inspectors, but paid little attention to the lack of political will to actually do the enforcement work in any given country. Several millions more are funded more effectively each year through the AFL-CIO, though this has declined precipitously since the 1980s.

Addressing the rule of law as applied to the workplace ought to be a key priority for President Obama's State Department, even given the chance that such a worker-advocacy platform may discomfit countries such as China (a big holder of US Treasury bonds), Turkey (where the Pentagon's needs often drive U.S. policy), and Bangladesh (which has a host of stability concerns), to name a few. For far too long, autocratic regimes have received conflicting advice from American policy makers. The boiler-plate nostrums involving multiparty democracy and clean government made little practical sense when China, pre-reform Indonesia, and Vietnam were experiencing growth rates which were the envy of most poor nations. The off-the-charts venality of these states mocked the World Bank's decade-long focus on fighting corruption. Now is the time and climate to change and strengthen the US signals.

At an appropriate venue—such as a gathering of trade unionists and labor rights activists in Mexico or Thailand—Obama should outline the ways in which workers are disadvantaged in the global economy. Activists across the globe would be thrilled to hear an American president calling into question such neoliberal tenets as the "flexible" workforce and the necessary "reform" (often downward-leveling of worker protections), which together have opened the door to a noxious insecurity of employment. As an exercise in public diplomacy, a clear and forceful statement would bring hope to opposition movements fighting entrenched economic elites allied with autocratic regimes.

Policy and program energies simply need to be redirected. If workers are deceived, distracted, or dispirited by buyer-driven self-regulation schemes, it is possible that the traditional strategies available to workers wishing to form independent unions are similarly affected. Numerous national and international trade union organizations and individual leaders have been drawn into dialogues, partnerships, conferences, and pilot programs with "multi-stakeholder" groups or the corporations directly. Many of these activities lent an undeserved patina of respectability to corporate self-regulation, often under the rubric of CSR. In addition, the long tweaking, critiquing, and field assessing of code-of-conduct "social audits," sometimes undertaken directly by unions and labor rights NGOs, diverted precious resources from the challenging task of devising realistic worker-empowerment strategies.

Further research is desperately needed on the actual labor law enforcement performance in countries where most low-skill assembly takes place. While living in Indonesia twenty years ago, I asked the US Embassy's labor attaché to get labor law enforcement numbers from the Ministry of Manpower in Jakarta. We learned that there were over 700 inspectors who found a total of 12,640 violations that year, but only 60 cases made it to the first adjudicative step; of these, only nine verdicts were reported. Ten years later, the Ministry again provided enforcement statistics: This time 700 inspectors only managed to do 243 factory visits for the entire year. Presumably, government officials—pressured by foreign investors to reduce the amount of bribe-seeking from various departments—restrained inspectors from making factory visits.

It is clear that a new architecture of rights must be erected, beginning with a no-nonsense survey of current practices. Every labor attaché or labor reporting officer at an American embassy should compile the following facts: Has the country signed International Labor Organization Convention 81 (Labor Inspection)? If so, when is the last time a report was sent to Geneva? How many labor inspectors are there? How many factory inspections were done last year? What is the number of violations found? How many prosecutions started? How many back pay awards were made? Our attachés should also map out the bureaucratic chain of command, with names of responsible local officials and an account of who-reports-to-whom—beginning in huge export-processing zones. This is information about dysfunctional governance unavailable to local journalists, legal aid, and worker-assistance organizations. US-based companies importing more than US$50 million worth of goods should have to post these findings on their corporate websites—in both English and the local language—for every country in which they have more than three contract factories.

This data should be folded into a matrix maintained by a nongovernmental organization working under a several-year grant from the State Department's Bureau of Human Rights, Democracy, and Labor. Alongside the raw numbers,

Assessing the Abused

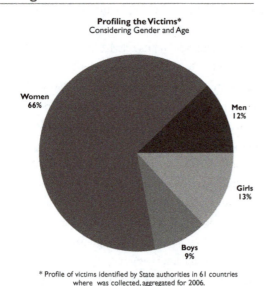

Profiling the Victims*
Considering Gender and Age

Women
66%

Men
12%

Girls
13%

Boys
9%

* Profile of victims identified by State authorities in 61 countries
where was collected, aggregated for 2006.

International Labor Organization; 2005

wiki-style narratives should be included on such issues as freedom for nongovernmental organization operating in the labor sector, labor history, recent strikes, opinions on the adequacy of the minimum wage, academic papers on all these issues, and contact information for unions and activist groups. Such an interactive website would make possible a global dialogue about key issues.

The world's workers need this dialogue both to build resilient movements and to challenge globalized production practices now ruled by top-down declamations, such as those issued in the World Bank's "competitive index," which ranks countries higher for ease of hiring and firing, reduced severance benefits, and other employer-friendly policies, or its recent study which concludes that workers have to sacrifice even more than they have already, in the name of economic growth. These overweening influences—that are keeping the workers' share of a US$38 hoodie frozen at 20 cents—are being challenged by brave activists every day. The Hoover Institution's Larry Diamond sums up the tool-kit succinctly as "struggle, personal risk-taking, mobilization, and sustained imaginative organization." The path to meaningful change may debut some attention-grabbing tactics (perhaps young workers in Vietnam will tweet-up wages using their incredibly cheap mobile phones), but the "struggle" piece of this is age-old.

Leaders in rich countries need to rethink policies that have been foisted upon them by free-market fundamentalists over the past three decades of globalization. Enforcement need not be a cudgel used by politicians pandering to the fearful; lovely Prato should be a model of fair governance over a diverse landscape of small shops, where consumers need not pay more and the bel paese receives tax revenue. It is possible with some of the steps outlined above. Countries wishing to attract foreign investment would feel pressure from rich-nation governments to protect their workers. This modest push may not offset the global business community's antipathy toward regulation, but it may begin to redress the balance.

READING 3

THE PERSONAL IS POLITICAL

SHERRY QUAN LEE

I am sixty-three years old. I wear white tennis shoes, black leather flats, red cowboy boots, and pink high heels. Pairs of recycled Stuart Weitzman, Joan and David, Marc Fisher, Nine West, and Steve Madden shoes line the shelves of my bedroom closet. Each pair calling me to attention. Each pair soliciting happily ever after. Shoes, the sensuous, seductive icons of the twenty-first century.

No man gets to glimpse my menagerie of seduction. No man is allowed in my bedroom, or my writing room—not any more, or at least not today.

My hopes and dreams, yes, I still have them, are no longer an open book, but a little girl's diary locked until someone appears with the only key.

However, today I am reminiscing; I am writing. I am allowing myself to be vulnerable. I am imagining what has been locked away for so many years. Locked away like my Black relatives who could only visit the house on the hill in South Minneapolis at night when the neighbors couldn't distinguish them as anything more than shadows, as secrets climbing the red brick stairs and entering the stucco house, lights off, blinds closed.

I am imagining my Chinese father who, unlike my Black relatives, slithered out the door instead of in, disappearing in the night as if again taking on another identity as he did when he left China, a young boy slipping into a foreign culture, the USA, to earn money to send home to his mother because his father died and he, being the eldest child, was responsible for his family's welfare.

It is not easy to write my story. For years I wrote my story in fragments of not so poetic lines. I spit out anger and revenge, sharp knives cutting through every other line with just enough sass to bear my wounds. I couldn't stop incriminating just about everyone and every institution—schools, churches, places of business, etc., calling out injustices with every harsh word, hoping my poems would birth me, and make sense of who I was and why I wasn't happy.

There are moments I am still not happy. The absence of love debilitating. The need, not only to be loved, but to love someone. The fear of being alone. Being alone. Poverty of the spirit. Poverty.

Maybe it was the chokecherry tree in my childhood back yard that is the metaphor for my writing life. Ripe berries seducing birds to eat, then shit white; droppings scattered like my poems. A professor, reading between my lines, asked if magnolias in my poem "Wintergreen" represented Black men lynched, or if the chokecherry tree in my poem "Chokecherry" signified the tree on Sethe's back (*Color Purple* by Alice Walker). She assumed they were conscious choices. They weren't.

Wintergreen

Minnesota is not compatible
to my growth, it is too cold.

The Ice Age made it clear
Magnolias, you can live
here in SE China, here in Georgia.

My ancestors oppose the heat.

Civil wars and death or just a robin
traveling against the season—
tossed Black/tossed Chinese:

Here I am, a Minnesota mutant.
Snowflake.

Like a magnolia, I am
not white. It is only light
passing through. Mama
cooked tuna noodle casserole
and daddy ate it.

Like a magnolia
—whose sepals never fuse—
my life is disparate
        here a Black
        community,
    there an Asian
    community,
            everywhere, white.

Sherry Quan Lee, *Chinese Blackbird*

Memory resides in the body, in the mind, and appears when I'm not looking. I believe my physical body and the body of my poems unconsciously uncover a history I didn't know.

I believe the personal *IS* political, as many before me have claimed. I believe that a mixed-race child passing for white, growing up in the sixties was more than bell bottom jeans and psychedelic music. That the freedom my peers sought was different from the freedom I ached for. I wanted what they had, the *Ozzie and Harriet* life. They ran from it, I ran toward it. I ran towards love.

READING 4

THE FAMILY HISTORY PROJECT

BY NANCYE E. McCRARY

This project accomplishes multiple outcomes. Historical perspectives are personalized and opportunities for understanding time, continuity, and change are enriched. It also provides a situated context for talking about diversity, especially among cohorts of mostly homogenous teacher candidates. In fact, most of the National Social Studies thematic strands emerge as students complete and present their family histories. This project can foster deeper, and more generative understandings of cultural differences, civic ideals and practices, power and privilege, development and identity.

The expectations for this assignment are understanding: (1) that culture is a system of beliefs, knowledge, institutions, customs/traditions, languages and skills shared by a group of people; (2) history is an account of human activities that is interpretive in nature; and (3) that a variety of tools (e.g., primary and secondary sources) are needed to understand historical events. It is a marvelous tool to make history come alive, especially for children. The project includes the following components: (1) research; (2) collecting, analyzing, and selecting artifacts; (3) using technology as a teaching and learning tool, as well as for presentation; and (4) writing a reflection on the educational opportunities and possible adaptations of this type of project for elementary social studies teaching and learning. I expect them to share the highlights by presenting and discussing the final product with the class. I encourage them to use a variety of media in this presentation, such as still photographs, video clips, original documents, voice-over sound, music and visual art. They may use PowerPoint, Moviemaker, Web site development, or any other program to create the presentation. They can also use a document viewer to project hard copy images. Our classroom is equipped with an online desktop computer, projector, and large screen; and in your own classroom, you may wish to limit or expand these presentation options based on what you have available.

To begin the project, we review questions that can guide their research: What are the cultural origins of your family? Immigrants from what country, when, why? What are your family's most valued family stories? How have family stories evolved over time? Were they altered, exaggerated, or was any critical information left out? What kinds of work have members of your family done? How did your family get to where they are now? What is your place/role in your family? What contributions did members of your family make? Are there any untold or incomplete stories? Who are your family heroes/heroines? What rituals extend over generations in your family? Rituals can be activities centered on holidays, meals, housekeeping, weddings, funerals, births, or anything that seems to be practiced across generations, time, and place.

As they do their research, I ask them to reflect on:

- *Evidence*: How do you "know" this? From where did this information come?
- *Viewpoint*: Whose story is this? Who is speaking and what is their perspective?
- *Cause and Effect*: What led up to the events you describe? What resulted?
- *Importance*: Who cares or why is it important, and to whom? What can be learned?

To complete this project, I ask my students to investigate family history through interviews with family members, searching old and recent photographs and other artifacts that represent their family history, customs, culture, beliefs, values, and contributions. Since some students were adopted, or grew up in multiple families or foster care, they define family as they wish. Further, if they are uncomfortable doing a family history project because their family situation seems unusual or particularly sensitive, I encourage them to be creative in thinking about how they might complete the requirements of this assignment. I reassure them that if their family history includes some disturbing information that makes them uncomfortable, they don't have to share it. I remind them that as a teacher, it will be important to model respect for difference in families, including nontraditional families, families of choice or circumstance, and families with more or less privilege and income.

As they research their own families, I remind them to think carefully about children from very different familial contexts and how you might adapt such a project for diverse learners. I ask them to interview family members, read old letters and investigate the history and geography of their families' origins, going back in time as far as possible and using any sources available. They also read books and articles on important events that relate directly to their families' experiences from a historical perspective. For example, if their ancestors came to the U.S. through Ellis Island, they might include some historical information on the experiences of immigrants arriving at Ellis Island. They might also discuss the ways cultures in their families may have blended over time.

I explain to them that through this project they will combine their own experiences and memories with photographs, documents, and stories told, heard, and remembered by and about family members to create a presentation for the class in some digital/electronic medium. Emphasis will be on the story *they* want to tell about their family that may include time lines, family tree(s), country(s) of origin, conditions of immigration to the United States, recurrent themes, occupations, military service, cultural practices, religious beliefs, etc.

Reflection

Since I teach in Kentucky, it is not uncommon for one student to present a history that includes ancestors owning slaves, while another shows an old photograph of the last slave in her family. Issues related to power, ethnicity, race, class, and gender will emerge in any class doing this project. The discussion that follows about such issues is rich and reflective. This project often affords an opportunity to talk about racially mixed families or the challenges of being the first to attend college. One semester, for example, a student framed her family history as the first time she understood the extent to which her family lived in poverty. The fact that she was the first to complete a secondary education over six generations of self-sufficient farmers had been constructed by her family as abandonment of family values.

A significant outcome of this family history assignment is deeper understanding of issues of power and privilege. Students are often dismayed at their otherwise invisible differences. In Kentucky, for instance, there are striking economic disparities between descendents of coal mine owners and those of miners. There are students who have never traveled beyond their small rural communities who discover global connections in the immigration patterns of their ancestors or similarities and differences in farming or mining families throughout the world.

Perhaps most valuable are the conversations this assignment inspires. Students interview family members, particularly parents, grandparents, great grandparents, aunts, uncles, and distant cousins. Stories emerge, contrasting perspectives become apparent, and students find themselves interacting with the past and the present to make meaning and construct identities. This project thus centers on both the representational and interactional functions of narrative (Wortham, 2001). Students' family histories represent the stories they choose to tell and become a basis for dialogic interaction on a range of social issues. This use of narrative encourages interpretation and imagination in representing human behavior and events as lived experience prompting learners to infer meanings that are not explicit (Bruner, 1990). As a fulcrum for dialogic interaction, the stories they tell and omit about their families create contexts for class discussion on diversity and representation as learners engage in reflective self-narrative. For example, one student included in her family history the fact that her mother is homeless. This disclosure moved the class not only to discuss homelessness, but also prompted discussion of the biases many have towards those living in poverty. The family history project encourages critical thinking, requires the integration of a variety of technologies, and situates the study of history, geography, economics, civics, and anthropological inquiry in contexts that are both personal and meaningful.

The increasing cultural and economic disparity between teacher education students and the children they will teach might contribute to pedagogical approaches that can be characterized as promoting a spectator view of human differences. Without the ability to critically examine one's own perspectives, pre-service teachers may be left to look on changing school environments as spectators, increasingly removed from the students they are preparing to teach and the contexts in which they will work. As spectators, pre-service teachers are unlikely to internalize issues of social justice, civic responsibility, and diversity. In programs where very little diversity exists among teacher candidates themselves, in-class discussions on diversity can become us and them conversations that further separate future educators from the students they will teach. Without teacher education students who represent a range of abilities, cultures, and perspectives, we are often left to talk about diversity in methods courses with little opportunity to interact in meaningful ways with those *others* we view as different from ourselves.

Exploring and sharing one's own family history encourages the kind of dialogue that mediates an understanding of diversity more effectively than *talking about* the differences of others. Both presenting and being audience for the family history presentations are key to the kinds of discussions that can change the way pre-service teachers think and talk about human differences.

As one student said, "This project opened my eyes to a lot of differences that existed among my classmates. As similar as we look on the outside, I have found that we are actually a very diverse group who all have unique histories." Such realizations prompt deeply personal conversations on difference that otherwise might have been more polite than authentic. In this way, the family history assignment provides a unique opportunity for teacher candidates to examine human differences as participants in the diversity of the world in which we live.

References

Bruner, J. (1990). *Acts of meaning*. Cambridge, MA: Harvard University Press.

Wortham, S. (2001). *Narratives in action*. New York: Teachers College Press.

In Other Words . . .

This unit *implies* the very idea of power to the people, in three ways:

- We live in a nation where the Constitution of the United States affords power to the people; in other words, we have the **capacity**.
- We hold the **potential** to exercise power. We are a leading world power, we hold the numbers, the position, and we possess the resources to make a difference.
- We bear the **promise** of responsibility. As a nation of immigrants, as a leader of the "free world," we carry the duty of attentiveness to human rights abuses.

As Americans, I believe that most of us, most of the time, acknowledge and agree in spirit upon these principles. We can point to much evidence that our nation fulfills these leadership roles in many ways. According to a *Time* report (Bremmer 2015), the United States as superpower reigns supreme in five ways: a) economically, our GDP (gross domestic product) remains far above other countries, and the American economy is the bedrock of the global financial system; b) our military power remains unparalleled by far, dominating land, sea, air, and space; c) United States political influence is unrivaled, due to both national strength and also global assistance; d) technological innovation is tops in the United States, with eight of the nine largest tech companies located here; and e) American culture and lifestyle dominate in a collection of markers, including entertainment, quality of life, and philanthropy.

At this point, you may ask, then what's the problem? Why have we just spent eight units and a considerable amount of data documenting and analyzing social issues and obstacles? The answer is clear: because we can do much better (Smith 2013). Because our rankings are declining in education (Desilver 2015, The Hechinger Report 2015), infrastructure (Statista 2016), and health care (Hellmann 2014). Because, on the other hand, we are number one in incarceration rates (by far) (Sentencing Project 2014); lead the world in gun-related violence (by far) (Preidt 2016); and only countries such as China, Iran, and North Korea outrank the United States in executions (the United States is the only G7 country remaining that executes people) (*The Guardian* 2016). How do we find ourselves in the paradoxical position of holding positions of best and worst? I believe three sociological principles can help answer those questions:

- *Growing inequality*—When resources are distributed to an extreme level in inequality, unrest, confusion, and panic prevent collective action. This divisiveness leads to:
- *Polarization, politicization*—When participatory democracy fails to work properly, our two-party system, heavily influenced by big money, results in:
- *Ideological apathy*—People who are either in pain or fear, or both, fail to recognize their own position and power within. Whenever ideas, however unintentional, justify the prevailing distribution of wealth, power, and privilege; hide society's injustices; and thus demand uncritical allegiance to the prevailing social order, we have ideology (Reiman and Leighton 2012).

The Big Idea

Simply put: *United we stand*. Though of ancient origins, the phrase in American use is attributed to founding father John Dickinson and popularized by Patrick Henry in his famous last public speech, in 1799 (Wikipedia 2016). The motto has been touted in many popular culture venues, but social science empirically documents its simple, but profound importance throughout human experience.

So What?

When the whole world is silent, even one voice becomes powerful.—Malala Yousafzai (2013).

United we stand

Works Cited

Bremmer, I. (2015, May 28). "These are the 5 reasons why the U.S. remains the world's only superpower." *Time*. Retrieved October 11, 2016, from http://time.com/3899972/us-superpower-status-military/

Desilver, D. (2015, February 2). "U.S. students improving—slowly—in math and science, but still lagging internationally." Pew Research Center. Retrieved October 11, 2016, from http://www.pewresearch.org/fact-tank/2015/02/02/u-s-students-improving-slowly-in-math-and-science-but-still-lagging-internationally/

The Guardian. (2016). "Death penalty statistics, country by country." Retrieved October 11 2016, from https://www.theguardian.com/news/datablog/2011/mar/29/death-penalty-countries-world

The Hechinger Report. (2016, February 16). "Ranking countries by the worst students." *U.S. News & World Report*. Retrieved October 11, 2016, from http://www.usnews.com/news/articles/2016-02-16/ranking-countries-by-the-worst-student

Helmann, M. (2014, June 17). "U.S. health care ranked worst in the developed world." *Time*. Retrieved October 11, 2016, from http://time.com/2888403/u-s-health-care-ranked-worst-in-the-developed-world/

Preidt, R. (2016, Feburary 3). "How U.S. gun deaths compare to other countries." CBS News. Retrieved October 11, 2016, from http://www.cbsnews.com/news/how-u-s-gun-deaths-compare-to-other-countries/

Reiman, J., and Leighton, P. (2012). *The rich get richer and the poor get prison: Ideology, class, and criminal justice*. 10th ed. New York, NY: Routledge.

The Sentencing Project. (2014). "Trends in U.S. Corrections." Retrieved October 11, 2016, from http://sentencing-project.org/wp-content/uploads/2016/01/Trends-in-US-Corrections.pdf

Smith, J. (2013, Feburary 6). "10 challenges facing the U.S. over the next two decades." Policy.Mic. Retrieved October 11, 2016, from https://mic.com/articles/24967/10-challenges-facing-the-u-s-over-the-next-two-decades#.90V3H1CNQ

Statista. (2016). "Ranking of countries with best infrastructure in 2016." Retrieved October 11, 2016, from https://www.statista.com/statistics/264753/ranking-of-countries-according-to-the-general-quality-of-infrastructure/

Yousafzai, M., and Lamb, C. (2013). *I am Malala: The girl who stood up for education and was shot by the Taliban*. New York, NY: Little, Brown and Company.

Wikipedia. (2016). "United we stand, divided we fall." Retrieved October 11, 2016, from https://en.wikipedia.org/wiki/United_we_stand,_divided_we_fall

Section IV: Social Inequality, Power, and Progress

Beyond the Book: Art Worlds

From the flourish of *The Crucible's* overture, to the spectacular reach of Broadway's *Hamilton*, to the "heaven spot" of graffiti (in dare-devil places), art forms skulk on the margins of revolution, sometimes delivering the knockout punch in moments of social change. Consider, for example, the image of Rosie the Riveter or the clinched fist symbolizing the labor movement of the early twentieth century. The reach of art is unbounded by space and time. Yet, we seldom champion it within the world of science.

Sociology does include subfields referred to as sociology of art and visual sociology, recognizing value in studying social and political implications of crafts of the imagination. Esteemed sociologist Howie Becker developed one such interest; recall that he made extra money in graduate school by playing in piano bars during World War II. He's even written a book called *Art Worlds*, in which he asserts:

> Art works do not result from the activity of a single artist, but from the coordinated work of a network of cooperating specialists: people who make musical instruments or oil paints or theatrical costumes as well as musicians and composers, painters, and actors, playwrights and directors. And they manage to do that successfully because they share some ideas and conventions about how the work should be done (Becker 1982).

Art is not only shared, but is truly a collective project from the ground up; the form may appear to emerge in isolation, but its origin in thought cannot. Every idea emerges in interaction with others, even if an imagined other; art "represent[s] a universal phenomenon of human society in action" (Morris 1958, 310). Art manifests its own power in the world, says Groys (2008), and is "as much a force in the power play of global politics today as it once was in the arena of cold war politics" (MIT Press 2016).

In this Beyond the Book section, I encourage you to probe the art world in whatever way that draws you in. I'm sure you already tramp around it in many ways, though we tend to take its many forms for granted. Pay attention to the source, the ensemble behind it (explicit or imagined), its politics, its power.

Here are just two outstanding examples that recently drew my attention:

Taylor Mac's marathon concert: Veteran critic and reviewer for the *New York Times*, Wesley Morris, recently wrote of performance artist Taylor Mac, who conducted a twenty-four-hour concert in St. Ann's Warehouse in Dumbo, Brooklyn: "Mr. Mac gave me one of the great experiences of my life. I've slept on it, and I'm sure" (Morris 2016). The marathon concert traversed two hundred forty years of American music, from battle hymns to Black spirituals, to work songs, and blues, punk, and rock; it was a virtual workshop of decades of our moral and political past. Morris (2016) reports:

> The "24-Decade" project was, at least in part, about becoming who we Americans want to be, by recognizing who we have been. It's about artist confrontation, reinterpretation and personal transcendence. The scope of the project allows you to consider the centuries of artistic ghosts we live with.

L.A. Street Art Gallery: The second extravaganza is L.A. Street Art Gallery (2016), a site that celebrates "LA's Street Art Culture through pictures, videos, articles, social media, and events." The media site features graffiti, murals, wheat paste, stickers, chalk, yarn … many genres of art that "talk about what's necessary" (L.A. Street Art Gallery 2016) because no one else does. Work is featured by famous artists such as Banksy, El Mac, Retna, Tristan Eaton, D*Face, and Aaron Li-Hill. The blazes of color, the unparalleled scope, the magnificence of vision is exceptional.

I've long been fascinated with street art, which many call graffiti, like it's a bad thing; indeed, it is defined as crime in many areas. Even in Los Angeles, a premier landscape for artistry of all forms, the city enacted a "mural moratorium" in 2003, attempting to regulate displays in many neighborhoods (Reilly 2011). By 2013, the moratorium ended, opening once again the city of angels to all its artists (Saillant 2013).

Living in San Diego, I'm enchanted by what I see here as a cultural and political palette of shockingly diverse talent and passion. It reminds me of inspirational work such as Jeff Ferrell's *Crimes of Style* in which he documents graffiti as that which "marks and illuminates contemporary urban culture, decorating the daily life of the city with varieties of color, meaning, and style" (p. 3). Mark Hamm wrote about Ferrell's stunning work, titling his review "Doing criminology like it matters." Art matters.

As Morris (2016) writes, regarding Taylor Mac's performance, audience is also essential to the performance, teaching us about "the wisdom of staying woke."

Revolucion

Works Cited:

Becker, H. S. (1982). *Art Worlds*. Berkeley, CA: University of California Press. Quote from Howardsbecker.com.

Ferrell, J. (1993). *Crimes of style: Urban graffiti and the politics of criminality*. Boston, MA: Northeastern University Press.

Groys, B. (2008). *Art Power*. Cambridge, MA: MIT Press.

Hamm, M. S. (1993). Review: "Doing criminology like it matters: Review essay on Jeff Ferrell's "Crimes of Style." *Social Justice*, 20, 53–54.

L.A. Street Art Gallery. (2016). "Documenting L.A.'s street art." Retrieved October 14, 2016, from http://www. lastreetart.gallery

MIT Press. (2008). "Art Power." Retrieved October 14, 2016, from https://mitpress.mit.edu/books/art-power

Morris, R. E. (1958). "What is sociology of art?" *The American Catholic Sociological Review*, 19, 310–321.

Morris, W. (2016, October 10). "Review: Taylor Mac's 24-hour concert was one of the great experiences of my life." *The New York Times*. Retrieved October 13, 2016, from http://www.nytimes.com/2016/10/11/theater/review-taylor-macs-24-hour-concert-was-one-of-the-great-experiences-of-my-life.html

Reilly, R. (2011, October 14). "Saber, graffiti artist, fights to lift mural ban in LA." *The Huffington Post*. Retrieved October 14, 2016 from http://www.huffingtonpost.com/2011/10/13/artist-saber-fights-to-li_n_1009758.html

Salliant, C. (2013, August 28). "Council lifts ban on public murals." *Los Angeles Times*. Retrieved October 14, 2016, from http://articles.latimes.com/2013/aug/28/local/la-me-0829-murals-20130829

Section IV: Social Inequality, Power, and Progress

From the Field: Media Matters

"In keeping with Channel 40's policy of bringing you the latest in blood and guts, and in living color ... you are going to see another first: attempted suicide" (Adams 2016).

These were the last words from Christine Chubbuck, a twenty-nine-year-old Florida news anchor, who then proceeded to shoot herself on camera; she fell forward violently and died instantly. It happened on July 15, 1974.

Chubbuck's story is now being chronicled in a movie (*Christine*), released on October 14, 2016 (IMDb 2016). Her suicide was an apparent attempt to protest the ever-growing demand for media sensationalism, a statement that applies even more poignantly to today's media landscape (Adams 2016).

Since Gaye Tuchman's (1978) pioneering work, *Making News*, the construction of knowledge-making through media makers has remained germane, increasing in scope and intensity with the advent of reality-based TV, video games, and social media. The "if it bleeds it leads" theme has evolved from singular news-making to a digital world that now dominates social and political life. Sociologists have plenty to say about this burgeoning field of study.

Below are just a few studies that some colleagues and I have produced. I hope you find them as intriguing as we have!

With scenes of blood and pain: This study looks at a Montana anti-meth campaign, purported to deter teen meth use. At first glance, the anti-meth goal seems worthy. With close examination, however, the authors reveal scare tactics, misleading conclusions, and disturbing images with sexist and racist implications. While the article does not negate actual harm of drug use, it does underscore the perniciousness of the campaign in promulgating myths of meth use (as a white, working-class, rural plague) while remaining silent about misdirected policies such as the so-called War on Drugs. The article analyzes graphic photos in a way that educates readers about the propaganda of images (Linnemann, Hanson, and Williams 2013).

Capote's ghosts: Linnemann again takes on the production of fear-mongering and cultural spectacles, this time starting with the pages of Truman Capote's classic *In Cold Blood*. "Paying close attention to the cultural production of both the present and absent, this paper considers how violence haunts commonplace geographies and the imaginations of everyday actors, through the lens of banal crime reporting and celebrated true crime novels" (Linnemann 2015, 514).

Critiquing *Orange Is the New Black*: Terry critiques the wildly popular Netflix series, *Orange Is the New Black*, based on the true story of Piper Kerman (2011). Terry chronicles many issues concerned with incarcerated women, including victimization, mental health, and gender differences in penal policy and practice; one such passage highlights problematics connected to transgender inmates. This sharp critique takes issue associated with popular characters on the series such as Miss Claudette, Morello, and Crazy Eyes, bringing a combination of validation, reparation, and depth to the portrayal of women in prison (Terry 2016).

Have a quiet, orderly, polite revolution: The authors illustrate how print media sources portray social movements such as the Tea Party and Occupy Wall Street, characterizing them in ways that "consciously or not, support the prevailing status quo—social, economic, and political elites" (p. 1). Using the satirical phrase "Have a quiet orderly, polite revolution," the paper demonstrates how protests are quashed and participants either demonized or alienated, proportional to the degree of threat they pose to the ruling elite (Lynn and Williams 2016).

Trying on gender is the new Black: Through interviews with women prisoners and prototypes from *Orange Is the New Black*, the authors identify two "trying-on-gender" (experimental) strategies for self-empowerment: gender as emphasized femininity and gender as resistance. While both strategies bring connectivity to women in harsh conditions, the greatest promise for change lies in resistance. The authors stress that the highly masculinized prison environment remains a critical battlefield for women and control over their bodies (Williams, Green, and Williams 2017, forthcoming).

Media matters.

Works Cited:

Adams, S. (2016). "What Christine Chubbuck's suicide says about today's media landscape." *Rolling Stone*. Retrieved October 15, 2016, from http://www.rollingstone.com/movies/news/christine-chubbucks-suicide -and-todays-media-landscape-w444635

IMDb. (2016). *Christine*. Retrieved October 15 2016, from http://www.imdb.com/title/tt4666726/

Kerman, P. (2011). *Orange is the new Black*. New York, NY: Spiegel & Grau.

Linnemann, T. (2015). "Capote's ghosts: Violence, media and the spectre of suspicion." *British Journal of Criminology*, 55, 514–533.

Linnemann, T., Hanson, L., and Williams, L. S. (2013). "'With scenes of blood and pain': Crime control and the punitive imagination of The Meth Project." *British Journal of Criminology*, 53, 605–623.

Lynn, T., and Williams, L. S. (2016). " 'Have a quiet, orderly, polite revolution': Framing political protest and protecting the status quo." *Critical Sociology* 2016, 1–19 (advance publication DOI: 10.1177/0896920516666646).

Terry, A. (2016). "Surveying issues that arise in women's prisons: A content critique of Orange Is the New Black." *Sociology Compass*, 1–14.

Tuchman, G. (1978). *Making news: A study in the construction of reality*. New York, NY: Free Press.

Williams, L. S., Green, E. L. W., and Williams, K. R. (2017). "Trying on gender is the new Black: Female to felon." Forthcoming. In S. Jackson and L. Gordy (eds.) *Through the Prison Gate*. New York, NY: Routledge.

Section IV: Social Inequality, Power, and Progress

Reality Check: Streets

Overview

The Streets assignment engages you in a new situation, requires you to observe your surroundings carefully, and asks you to describe both what you felt and what you perceive of other people's reactions to the situation. Your task is to assume an identity of *difference*, and to spend approximately ten to twelve hours totally immersed in that role. You should, as much as possible, take yourself—your new self—to new places and expose your new identity to unfamiliar people, especially to strangers who can assess you within the new role. In short, you will become a street person.

Purpose

To learn through direct experience what it means to be the object of structural disadvantage (social structure).

To understand how social differences influence feelings of belonging and relationships (social interaction).

Preparation

Prepare intellectually. What are the social facts? What groups of people are affected? What causes homelessness? Consequences, both personally and societally? What different perspectives and theories help to analyze and understand homelessness? What other issues are associated with homelessness?

Prepare physically. Plan carefully and know where you will go, what you will do, how you will portray yourself, and arrange your surroundings as a "legitimate" person of the streets.

Prepare mentally. What have you NOT considered? How will you remain faithful to the spirit of the exercise and also keep yourself safe? How will you keep yourself in the mind-set of a person of the streets?

Hints: How would people respond if, for example, you wear a bicycle helmet but have no bicycle? Push a cart of belongings? Find the local homeless shelter; how would you get to work from there? Try to eat at a local soup kitchen. How long can you hang out at the public library or mall before people get nervous? Try to open a bank account without an address.

CAUTION: Under no circumstance are you to place yourself or others in harm's way or in any situation that could jeopardize your safety. Consult instructor for details.

The Report

Abstract and Title Page: The abstract summarizes the ENTIRE report. Include the abstract on your title page. Study journal articles to find good examples of an abstract.

Introduction and Background: Introduce the topic, provide some facts, stats, quotes, or other interesting information about homelessness, and end with a statement of purpose and organizational scheme of your paper.

Methodology: Describe exactly how, where, and when you prepared for and accomplished this project, with special focus on your time in the field. Include a "selfie" portraying your street persona.

Experiential Observations: This section will draw heavily on your field notes and should include salient details, quotes, and other observations that allow the reader to discern what occurred and why it is important to this project.

Sociological Focus: This section asks you to choose ONE issue related to homelessness, providing social facts, expert opinions, analysis from other studies, and/or additional relevant information. Try to relate it—however tenuously—to your own experience. *Be sure to use your sociological imagination and identify at least one big idea.*

Conclusion and Personal Reaction: Here you answer the so-what question. What has this project demonstrated, why is it important, and where do we go from here? Be sure to use critical-thinking strategies. Finally, record your personal reactions to the project. Emphasize the big idea.

Section IV: Social Inequality, Power, and Progress

OLE Resources

Below are a few sources especially helpful in relating to material in this section:

13th documentary. " '13th' documentary shows Black people migrating from slavery to prison." http://www.nola.com/crime/index.ssf/2016/10/13th_amendment_prisons.html. Film available on Netflix.

"Violence against women—it's a men's issue." Jackson, Katz, TED talk. https://www.ted.com/talks/jackson_katz_violence_against_women_it_s_a_men_s_issue?language=en

Tough Guise 2, a short film report on the documentary. The entire film, by Jackson Katz, can be found at http://shop.mediaed.org/tough-guise-2-p45.aspx. Most university libraries carry *Tough Guise 1* and 2.

Killing Us Softly 4, the entire film, by Jean Kilbourne, can be found at http://shop.mediaed.org/killing-us-softly-4-p47.aspx. Most university libraries carry the various editions of the film.

"Play is more than just fun." TED talk by Stuart Brown. https://www.ted.com/playlists/383/the_importance_of_play

"Philosophy in prison." TED talk by Damon Horowitz. https://www.ted.com/playlists/383/the_importance_of_play

The Three. What makes a great story, by filmmaker Ken Burns. https://vimeo.com/channels/redglass/40972394/

Section V:
And Finally ...

So much is at stake in writing a conclusion

We started with so many promises. I enticed you into the world of sociological secrets and invited you to ask *how* we could explore such an odd and remarkable feat, to bare even a few of humankind's mysteries. I encouraged you to ask, not just the *what* and *where* questions, but the most cutting question of all: *Why?* Why should you engage in this book's critical errand of discovering a "revolution of everyday life" (p. 1)? That's a lot of pressure for one collection. And now, it might seem as if we have a lot of unfinished business.

I'm reminded of a quote from Christina Rossetti, a nineteenth-century poet, who wrote, "Can anything be sadder than work left unfinished? Yes, work never begun" (Art Quotes 2016).

Indeed, the word *unfinished* is a paradoxical reference; it may imply unaccomplished, yet we have achieved greatly because we have begun. Composing a sociological imagination is a life journey.

Moving to something a bit more tangible, I encourage my students in class to create their own thirty-second commercial—that is, to have an "elevator pitch" ready for some opportune moment when that person or situation might make all the difference as you pursue your dream. Thus, at the very least, I'll leave you with a few tips for "elevator sociology"—some truisms I hope you've taken away from this collection (the list was inspired by Hirschman, 2013). Any budding sociologist should know:

- Reality is constructed, and it comes with consequences. And no, it's not voodoo; sociology is science.
- The language we use to describe the world matters, so we should watch our words.
- The ideas we hold about the world change the world. What is your idea?
- The market is not free; it is inextricably woven with the political and social world.
- Society cannot be understood by looking at individuals separately. We're all bunched together.
- Studying society is like trying to turn around to see the back of your head. You need a really good mirror.
- Sociology is a lens, peering not into "the thing," but into a representation of the thing.

The substance of this section now turns to three passages: sociology as science, sociology as solutions, and sociology as a personal journey. A concluding passage completes this section. Turning first to sociology as science, this mantra follows closely from the last item in the elevator sociology list: sociology is a lens, peering not into "the thing," but into a representation of the thing. Because we cannot directly and simultaneously observe something as complex as the social world, we must construct a scientific methodology to study it systematically.

Sociology as science

Sociology represents a dialogue between theory and research. The relationship is a complex one, with each part engaged in an ongoing exchange that challenges the other. Theory, as a set of hypothesized statements about how the world works, must be expressed in such a way that its conversation partner, scientific research, may test its propositions. The theory is either supported or not, which, in turn, strengthens the theory or demands modifications. Further, we are confronted not by just one theory, but hundreds, though we have explored but a few here. Similarly, we have observed only examples of scientific methods, each subject to various corollaries. From this continual testing, restating, and retesting, social scientists repeatedly correct, mend, and reorganize an ongoing cycle of knowledge production. Thus, according to the principle of fallible realism, knowledge is corrected, correcting, and correctable (Kuhn 1996).

The ongoing search for accurate and/or improved knowledge is not unique to social science. The so-called "hard sciences" (physics, chemistry, biology, astronomy, et al.) face challenge after challenge. Just recently, yet another "baby" planet was found in our solar system (Cofield 2016). Noted astrophysicist Neil deGrasse Tyson recently stated that our universe might be a computer simulation, "something created for the sheer joy of some being or 'smarter' life form" (Ryder 2016). Although the simulation statement is certainly one of the more extreme possibilities, other commonly accepted facts were once considered quackery. For example, until only a few years ago, astronomers believed that we lived in the only solar system, while so far more than five hundred solar systems have been discovered, with new ones identified every year. Scientists estimate there may be tens of billions of solar systems in our galaxy, perhaps as many as one hundred billion (NASA 2016). No doubt, Galileo would be astonished!

The seeming diversion via astronomy underscores this point: like astronomy, sociology is a science. And while we may be skeptical about the earth-as-simulation hypothesis, we generally accept findings such as the new dwarf planet remarkable, but the logical result of legitimate scientific discovery. Sociology, on the other hand, as a discipline has experienced a more difficult legitimation history, as evidenced by this 2012 title: "Teaching history without the facts? That's just sociology" (Viner 2012). A common refrain is that sociology is "just what you think about things in society" (Sternheimer 2011), or the "study of the painfully obvious" (Allen 2015), even though many experts point out that "common sense" is a myth (Freakonomics 2011).

Yet, sociology has much to offer to individuals and societies alike. All science takes fact as a starting point, and sociology is no different. Durkheim, known as the father of sociology, was the first to assert that social facts are things, and "are to be studied empirically, not philosophically" (Ritzer 1992, 78). Before Durkheim became the first professor of sociology (in France, 1887), the study of human behavior was left to psychics, biologists, and psychologists. With Durkheim's pioneering work, human behavior became the subject of science, not the result of sunspots or inherent traits, not purely biological or psychological, or chemical, and not explained by superstition and other mythical beliefs (Ritzer 1992). Social facts cannot be presupposed from ideas but must be observed, studied, and defined within their environment. As Durkheim (1951) pointed out, even something as extremely personal as sadness becomes a social fact: "Sadness does not inhere in things; it does not reach us from the world and through mere contemplation of the world. It is a product of our own thought. We create it out of whole cloth" (p. 243).

Durkheim defined social facts as things external to the actor, coercive of the actor. These are created from collective forces and do not emanate from the individual. They exist because of social interactions and historical developments over long periods, originating from many forms of social organization (Ritzer 1992). As individuals grow within a society, social facts are learned, conditioned, and generally accepted, but they exist outside the individual. Thus, we are much more than the sum of our parts. Again, citing Tyson, "In science, when human behavior enters the equation, things go nonlinear. That's why physics is easy and sociology is hard" (Tyson 2016).

Sociology as solutions

While sociology as science emphasizes the importance of good scholarship, the flip side of the discipline's mission is to promote social good. In that vein, public sociology has become known as a subfield of the wider discipline, expanding sociological principles beyond academic participation. Public sociology opens a conversation with citizens from all walks of life to deepen understanding of public issues, propose key solutions, and involve civic-minded communities in implementing long-term programs rather than quick fixes (Burawoy 2016). This subsection addresses sociology as solutions.

Sociology, whether in the so-called ivory tower of learning or with boots on the ground, is often about identifying, analyzing, and offering solutions to social problems. Let's take suicide as an example. One of the first social facts that Durkheim (1951 [1897]) studied was suicide, noting that while suicide is a deeply personal act at the individual level, it is also a product of social factors, and not just individual, psychological ones. In his extensive study of suicide rates by country, he found the rate varied by level of integration within a society. Durkheim noted differences between Protestants and Catholics, men and women, soldiers and civilians, and during peacetime versus wartimes (Crossman 2016). The less integrated a person (or group) is in society (resulting in anomie), the more likely that person (or group) is to commit suicide; it's a social fact.

Although Durkheim wrote the book *Suicide* in 1897, patterns regarding suicide as social fact are particularly enduring. Today, the baseline for all suicides in the United States is 13 deaths per 100,000 (Curtin, Warner, and Hedegaard 2016). In comparison, two groups at higher risk for suicide include young American Indians and Alaska Natives (AIAN) (thought to be underestimated at a rate of 34.3 percent for males) (Jiang, Mitran, Minino, and Ni 2015; Santhanam and Crigger 2015); and veterans (at a rate of 32 percent) (Shane and Kime 2016). Although no national measure of rate (adjusted for population) exists for sexual minorities in the United States, most independent studies estimate that between 30 percent and 65 percent of all gay, lesbian, bisexual, and transgender youth have attempted suicide (Bagley and Tremblay 2000; Haas, Rodgers, and Herman 2014). Identifying these staggering social facts and acknowledging a primary cause (alienation) become critical first steps in prevention, resulting in proactive programs such as The Trevor Project (2016), Real Warriors (2016), and Center for Native American Youth (2016).

Sociology's relevance to our world remains both a blessing and a curse. We are never without material! A quick perusal of current news reveals a few public issues; topics, descriptive titles, and short blurbs are provided:

- **Education, gender, and oppression:** "Meet Sultana, the Taliban's worst fear." Afghani young woman, talented and mostly self-educated, seeks acceptance to United States community college; student visa denied by US embassy in Kabul (Kristof 2014).
- **Gun violence, disadvantaged neighborhoods, social control:** "A weekend in Chicago: Where gunfire is a terrifying norm." In three days, 49 shootings, 64 victims, six are dead; all but one were Black or Hispanic (Davey 2016).
- **Gender, stereotyping, inequality:** "Metaphorically speaking, men are expected to be struck by genius, women to nurture it." Study reports gendered metaphors, which result in less credit to women inventors, more to men (Klein 2016).
- **Inequality, homelessness, stereotypes:** "Homeless in America." From the latest report on United States homelessness: On a single night, 564,708 people in the richest nation in the world were homeless; seven million in poor households were doubled up with family and friends. Of the homeless, 37 percent were families, 6.5 percent were unaccompanied teens and children; 8 percent were veterans (this subpopulation has decreased) (Homelessness Research Institute 2016).
- **Poverty and consequences:** "What you may not know about poverty in America." Of the forty-seven million people in the United States who live in poverty, more than 20 percent are children; African Americans have the highest poverty rate; populations experiencing extreme poverty are especially vulnerable to human trafficking (Carter 2016).

Recalling that the essence of the sociological imagination lies at the intersection of biography and history, we can see from this short review that social context is critical. In observing the best practices, we can also see the importance of distinguishing personal troubles from public issues, so that collective approaches, rather than purely individual ones, become a major focus. Throughout this collection, we have emphasized that the personal is political, and the political is personal. Taking care of our youth, our families, our veterans, and other vulnerable populations drives home that theme.

344

Sociology as personal journey

This is the hardest part to write and yet the most rewarding. Here I take inspiration from Randy Pausch's *The Last Lecture* (2008). Professor Pausch was dying of cancer, at age forty-seven, when he delivered his now famous lecture, in which he said to his students (and eventually the world), "If I had only one more day, what would I say?"

For myself, I consider this stage of my life my Third Act—a time of humility, gratitude, and reflection. Here is where I get to say, "If I have only one more page, what would I say to you?"

I would start with the pragmatic. (Interestingly, though, the inspiration comes from Cameron's *The Artist's Way* (2002), recommended to me by my good friend Delores Craig.) A few truisms apply throughout our lives:

- *Do your homework.* Of course. But I don't mean purely in the conventional sense. Put in the hard work to educate yourself about the world.
- *Show up.* Get involved in the world. Decisions are made by those who show up.
- *Tell the truth.* Once you've done your homework and show up, truth telling is easy—if we get Ego out of the way.
- *Let go of the outcome.* The ultimate faith in our ability to make a difference is to let go of the outcome. If I live in truth and let go of the outcome, I will find the perfect destination.

These simple but profound statements represent an element of sociological methodology referred to as reflexivity. Because we study ourselves, we hold two roles: the observer and the observed. That's why it's a lifelong journey. But that doesn't mean we shouldn't get started now, or put ourselves on a timetable. Walt Disney built Disneyland in three hundred sixty-six days. When asked how he accomplished that, he replied, "We used every one of them" (Pausch 2007). We too should use every one of them.

But what can one person do? A great starting place is self-education, becoming aware of legitimate news sources, observing several experts, weighing evidence in the balance, reading a variety of sources about people, places, and purposes, focusing on improving our general social climate, not obsessing about "fixing" one (or one "kind" of) individual.

If you've watched *Lars and the Real Girl* (see Beyond the Book, in Section I), you will remember that Gus (brother of Lars, the painfully shy and socially awkward loner) said to the psychologist: "We got to fix him, Doc. Can you fix him?" In the end—both in the movie and in our own world—the miracle is that Lars's community came together with a collective and empathetic solution: it accepted Lars as himself (Ebert 2007).

United we stand.

Conclusion

Sociology as science provides scaffolding. Sociology as solutions provides grit and makes it matter. Sociology as personal journey gives it soul.

This triad of scholarship describes the mission, and the fate, of sociology. As students of sociology, and of life, we construct our own reality, our own fate. The great scholar C. Wright Mills put it this way:

> Fate is a feature of specific kinds of social structure; the extent to which the mechanics of fate are the mechanics of history-making is itself a historical problem. How large the role of fate may be, in contrast with the role of explicit decision, depends first of all upon the scope and concentration of the means of power that are available at any given time in any given society (Mills 1958, 21).

Our fate, and our power, lies in our collective actions. Like the snowflakes in Unit 2, we are individuals, yes, but imagine the power of a snowball or the thrust of an avalanche. Our power manifests when we are bound together, in sync.

The following poem came to me from an unexpected source; I first heard it on a TV series about a serial killer. With a little more research, I found that it seems to have originated with Fushumongu, a contemporary of Confucious (Bluemist 2011). I want to leave it with you.

> We are none of us alone.
> Even as we exhale it is inhaled by others.
> The light that shines upon me shines upon my neighbor as well.
> In this way everything is connected to everything else.
> In this way I am connected to my friend
> Even as I am connected to my enemy.
> In this way there is no difference between me and my friend.
> In this way there is no difference between me and my enemy.
> We are none of us alone.

Imagine what we can do together. And so we leave with unfinished business.

Works Cited

Allen, S. (2015, March 2). "Private universe theory and the study of the painfully obvious." Professional Wanderlust. Retrieved October 12, 2016, from https://professionalwanderlust.wordpress.com/2015/03/02/private-universe-theory-and-the-study-of-the-painfully-obvious/

Strength in Numbers

Art Quotes. (2016). Christina Rossetti Quotes. Retrieved October 12, 2016, from http://www.art-quotes.com/auth_search.php?authid=3430#.V_7fg6M-IUE

Bagley, C., and Tremblay, P. (2000). "Elevated rates of suicidal behavior in gay, lesbian, and bisexual youth." *Crisis: The Journal of Crisis Intervention and Suicide Prevention,* 2, 111–117.

Bluemist. (2011). "We are none of us alone." Eclipse. Retrieved November 2, 2011, from http://bluemist.tumblr.com/post/58725207/we-are-none-of-us-alone

Burawoy, M. (2016). "Public sociologies." Retrieved October 13, 2016, from http://burawoy.berkeley.edu/PS.Webpage/ps.mainpage.htm

Cameron, J. (2002). *The artist's way: A spiritual path to higher creativity.* 10th ed. New York, NY: Jeremy P. Tarcher/Putnam.

Carter, A. (2016, January 14). "What you may not know about poverty in America." The Salvation Army. Retrieved June 13, 2016, from http://blog.salvationarmyusa.org/nhqblog/news/what-you-may-not-know-about-poverty-in-america

Center for Native American Youth. (2016). Retrieved October 12, 2016, from http://www.cnay.org/ForTribes.html.

Cofield, C. (2016, October 11). "New dwarf planet found in our solar system." Space.com. Retrieved October 12, 2016, from http://www.space.com/34358-new-dwarf-planet-found-2014-uz224.html

Crossman, A. (2016, June 12). "The study of suicide by Emile Durkheim." Retrieved October 13, 2016, from http://sociology.about.com/od/Works/a/Suicide.htm

Curtain, S. C., Warner, M., and Hedegaard, H. (2016). "Increase in suicide in the United States, 1999–2014." Centers for Disease Control and Prevention. National Center for Health Statistics. NCHS Date Brief No. 241, April, 2016. Retrieved October 13, 2016, from http://www.cdc.gov/nchs/products/databriefs/db241.htm

Davey, M. (2016, June 4). "A weekend in Chicago." *The New York Times*. Retrieved August 10, 2016, from http://www.nytimes.com/interactive/2016/06/04/us/chicago-shootings.html

Durkheim, E. (1951). *Suicide: A study in sociology*. Translated by J. A. Spaulding and G. Simpson. Gencoe, IL: Free Press (originally published 1897).

Ebert, R. (2007, October 18). *Lars and the real girl*, review. Retrieved October 13, 2016, from http://www.rogerebert.com/reviews/lars-and-the-real-girl-2007

Freakonomics. (2011). "The myth of common sense: Why the social world is less obvious than it seems." Retrieved October 12, 2016, from http://freakonomics.com/2011/09/29/the-myth-of-common-sense-why-the-social-world-is-less-obvious-than-it-seems/

Haas, A. P., Rodgers, P. L., and Herman, J. L. (2014). "Suicide attempts among transgender and gender non-conforming adults: Findings of the national transgender discrimination survey." American Foundation for Suicide Prevention, The Williams Institute. Retrieved October 13, 2016, from http://williamsinstitute.law.ucla.edu/wp-content/uploads/AFSP-Williams-Suicide-Report-Final.pdf

Hirschman, D. (2013). "A (budding) sociologist's commonplace book: Thoughts on politics, economics, sociology, and such." Retrieved October 12, 2012, from https://asociologist.com/2008/04/03/principles-of-sociology-inspired-by-mankiws-principles-of-economics/

Homelessness Research Institute. (2016). "Homeless in America: An examination of trends in homelessness homeless assistance, and at-risk populations at the national and state levels." National Alliance to End Homelessness. Homelessness Research Institute. Retrieved October 14, 2016, from http://www.endhomelessness.org/library/entry/SOH2016

Jiang, C., Mitran, A., Minino, A., and Ni, H. (2015). "Racial and gender disparities in suicide among young adults aged 18-24: United States, 2009-2013." Centers for Disease Control and Prevention, National Center for Health Statistics. Retrieved October 13, 2016, from http://www.cdc.gov/nchs/data/hestat/suicide/racial_and_gender_2009_2013.pdf

Klein, J. (2016, October 11). "Metaphorically speaking, men are expected to be struck by genius, women to nurture it." *The New York Times*. Retrieved October 11, 2016, from http://www.nytimes.com/2016/10/12/science/women-stem-metaphors.html

Kristof, N. (2016, June 4). "Meet Sultana, the Taliban's worst fear." *The New York Times*. Retrieved September 29, 2016, from http://www.nytimes.com/2016/06/05/opinion/sunday/meet-sultana-the-talibans-worst-fear.html?_r=0

Kuhn, T. S. (1996). *The structure of scientific revolutions*. 3rd ed. Chicago, IL: University of Chicago Press.

Mills, C. W. (1958). *The causes of World War Three.* New York, NY: Simon and Schuster.

NASA.gov. (2016). "How many solar systems are in our galaxy?" Retrieved October 12, 2016, from http://spaceplace. nasa.gov/review/dr-marc-space/solar-systems-in-galaxy.html

Pausch, R. (2007). "Time management." Lecture, University of Virginia, November 27. Retrieved November, 2008, from http://www.cs.virginia.edu/~robins/Randy/TMenglishTranscript.pdf

Pausch, R., and Zaslow, J. (2008). *The last lecture.* New York, NY: Hyperion.

Real Warriors. (2016). http://www.realwarriors.net/family/support/preventsuicide.php

Ritzer, G. (1992). *Contemporary Sociological Theory.* New York, NY: McGraw-Hill.

Ryder, B. (2016, April 22). "Neil deGrasse Tyson drops bombshell, says chance universe is just a computer 'simulation' very high." *Inquisitr.* Retrieved October 12, 2016, from http://www.inquisitr.com/3020964/ neil-degrasse-tyson-universe-simulation-news-intelligent-design/

Santhanam, L., and Crigger, M. (2015, September 30). "Suicide among young American Indians nearly double national rate." PBS. Retrieved October 13, 2016, from http://www.pbs.org/newshour/rundown/ suicide-rate-among-young-american-indians-nearly-double-national-average/

Shane, L. III, and Kime, P. (2016, July 7). "New VA study finds 20 veterans commit suicide each day." Retrieved October 13, 2016, from http://www.militarytimes.com/story/veterans/2016/07/07/va-suicide-20-daily-research/86788332/

Sternheimer, K. (2011). "Sociology vs. the obvious." *Everyday sociology.* Retrieved October 12, 2016, from http:// nortonbooks.typepad.com/everydaysociology/2011/07/sociology-vs-the-obvious.html

The Trevor Project. (2016). Retrieved October 13, 2016, from http://www.thetrevorproject.org/pages/ facts-about-suicide

Tyson, N. D. (2016, February 5). Tweet @nailtyson. Retrieved October 13, 2016, from https://www.facebook.com/ photo.php?fbid=970191546361503&set=a.355758341138163.75018.100001120009014&type=3&theater

Viner, B. (2012). "Teaching history without the facts? That's just sociology." *The Guardian.* Retrieved October 12, 2016, from https://www.theguardian.com/commentisfree/2012/apr/08/teaching-history-without-facts-sociology

CPSIA information can be obtained
at www.ICGtesting.com
Printed in the USA
LVHW061913070720
660013LV00003B/11